# SAT 精解讲义

周 金 编著

南开大学出版社
天 津

**图书在版编目(CIP)数据**

SAT 精解讲义 / 周金编著. —天津:南开大学出版社,
2013.6
ISBN 978-7-310-04219-7

Ⅰ.①S… Ⅱ.①周… Ⅲ.①英语－高等学校－入学考试－美国－题解 Ⅳ.①H319.6

中国版本图书馆 CIP 数据核字(2013)第 136870 号

## 版权所有  侵权必究

南开大学出版社出版发行
出版人:孙克强
地址:天津市南开区卫津路 94 号  邮政编码:300071
营销部电话:(022)23508339  23500755
营销部传真:(022)23508542  邮购部电话:(022)23502200
\*
天津午阳印刷有限公司印刷
全国各地新华书店经销
\*
2013 年 6 月第 1 版  2013 年 6 月第 1 次印刷
285×210 毫米  16 开本  17.5 印张  4 插页  489 千字
定价:35.00 元

如遇图书印装质量问题,请与本社营销部联系调换,电话:(022)23507125

# 前 言

本书读者为准备参加美国高考的高一、高二、高三学生。本书对 SAT 真题的阅读、语法及填空进行了精解，突破了就题论题的应试套路。以阅读为例，本书贯穿如下教学思想：

（1）扫清 SAT 的核心词汇，尤其加深对熟词生义的掌握，熟词生义往往是考生很难逾越的障碍，究其原因是：缺乏身临其境的语境训练和精准的外刊阅读。

（2）学习 SAT 阅读中的地道表达方式，并将真题文章中经典地道的表达方式应用于国内高考或 SAT 考试的作文中。

（3）对于语法欠缺的学生，精读可以彻底攻破高中三年的语法障碍，将"背诵语法"的笨拙学习方法转换为"理解"、"模仿"、"运用"。

（4）学会"同义多词"的重要语言要素，对同样的含义采用多样的方法进行表达是一种很重要的语言能力。

（5）阅读理解能力的提高。该理解是指对文章逻辑关系的领会，对段落之间、句子之间各种关系的理解，这种理解是建立在（1）-（4）的基础之上的。几种能力共同存在，共同消亡，缺一不可。

（6）从文章后面的题目中挖掘语言知识点。

（7）在全面提高阅读能力的基础上，水到渠成地提高 SAT 分数。

本书分为四个部分：

第一部分　对 SAT 阅读与语法中的常用句型进行总结并给出例句；

第二部分　挑选质量较高、难度较大的真题文章进行通篇解析；

第三部分　词汇解析，含题干句式解析；

第四部分　改错。

# 目　录

第一部分　SAT 阅读、语法常用句式总结·····································································1
第二部分　文章精读·······························································································7
　文章 1·············································································································9
　文章 2············································································································13
　文章 3············································································································15
　　文章 3.1······································································································15
　　文章 3.2······································································································21
　文章 4············································································································29
　　文章 4.1······································································································29
　　文章 4.2······································································································30
　文章 5············································································································34
　文章 6············································································································36
　文章 7············································································································39
　　文章 7.1······································································································39
　　文章 7.2······································································································40
　文章 8············································································································43
　文章 9············································································································45
　　文章 9.1······································································································45
　　文章 9.2······································································································46
　文章 10··········································································································50
　文章 11··········································································································52
　文章 12··········································································································54
　文章 13··········································································································67
　文章 14··········································································································68
　文章 15··········································································································70
　文章 16··········································································································72
　　文章 16.1····································································································72
　　文章 16.2····································································································74
　文章 17··········································································································80
　文章 18··········································································································85
　文章 19··········································································································96
　文章 20··········································································································99
　　文章 20.1····································································································99

|   |   |
|---|---|
| 文章 20.2 | 104 |
| 文章 21 | 114 |
|     文章 21.1 | 114 |
|     文章 21.2 | 116 |
| 文章 22 | 121 |
| 文章 23 | 134 |
|     文章 23.1 | 134 |
|     文章 23.2 | 136 |
| 文章 24 | 141 |
|     文章 24.1 | 141 |
|     文章 24.2 | 143 |
| 文章 25 | 148 |
|     文章 25.1 | 148 |
|     文章 25.2 | 152 |
| 文章 26 | 160 |
| 文章 27 | 165 |
| 文章 28 | 168 |
| 文章 29 | 170 |
| 文章 30 | 176 |
|     文章 30.1 | 176 |
|     文章 30.2 | 177 |
| 文章 31 | 179 |
|     文章 31.1 | 179 |
|     文章 31.2 | 181 |
| 文章 32 | 186 |
| 文章 33 | 189 |
| 文章 34 | 191 |
| 文章 35 | 200 |
|     文章 35.1 | 200 |
|     文章 35.2 | 202 |
| 文章 36 | 205 |
|     文章 36.1 | 205 |
|     文章 36.2 | 206 |
| 文章 37 | 208 |
| 文章 38 | 215 |
| 文章 39 | 217 |
| 文章 40 | 219 |
| **第三部分　词汇解析** | 225 |
| **第四部分　改错** | 249 |

# 第一部分

# SAT 阅读、语法常用句式总结

这一部分将总结阅读与语法改错中出现的绝大部分句式。

**句式一**：句子 1. 句子 2.

句子中必须同时含主语及谓语，注意分词、形容词、副词、不定式不能作谓语！

**句式二**：句子 1, 连词 句子 2.

**句式三**：主句, 从句。

注意：主句和从句都含有独立的主语和谓语，两个句子的主语不要求一致。

If it rains today, I will stay at home.

**句式四**：分词短语/形容词短语/不定式/某些介词短语, 主语+谓语。

以上几种形式均要求分词短语、形容词短语、不定式、某些介词短语的逻辑主语与句子主语严格相等，并且逗号前后含有某种逻辑关系。该句式为阅读和改错中的常见句型，影响对文意的理解。

1. 分词短语，主语+谓语。

(1) 分词短语的逻辑主语与句子主语严格相等；

(2) 表示原因、假设、伴随、让步的动词要换为其分词形式；或者可这样理解，当一个句子可改为主句+从句，且从句主语与主句主语一致时，从句中的主语可省略，从句的谓语改为分词；

(3) 若主语与分词呈主动关系，使用现在分词；反之使用过去分词。

例 1. 这款手机比其他手机在可靠性和稳定性方面要优越，因此这款手机很快就流行了起来。

【分析】

(1) 两个句子主语都是"这款手机"，两者有逻辑关系，因此可用"分词短语，主语+谓语"的形式。

(2) 可靠性和稳定性好是原因，如果以"主句+从句"形式改写，稳定性好用 because 引导，因此这一部分用分词取代，主句是"很快就流行"。

Outdoing others in reliability and stability, such cellular phones gained popular appeal instantly.

outdo vt. 句式： A outdo B in C. A 比 B 在 C 方面要好。

本句分词短语表原因状语，others 指代 other phones, 代词尽量放在从句或分词的结构中。Outdoing 的逻辑主语为 such cellular phones。

例 2. 有人告知我下午要开会，我就来了。

【分析】两者呈因果关系：因为有人告诉我要开会，所以我来了。主语不一致，但可用被动使之变为一致；表示原因的能当从句的谓语动词换为相应的分词，所以"告知"作分词。

Informed about the conference in the afternoon, I come.

例 3. 这部动画片是为孩子设计的，但是却意外受到了成年人的青睐。

Intended for children, this cartoon appeals to adults unexpectedly.

sth.（非人）be intended for sb. 某事是为某人设计的

例 4. 尽管流行了很多年，但这个理论近来受到了质疑。

Prevailing for years, such a theory has been challenged recently.

例 5. 她陷入了困境，向我请求经济援助。

Plunging into dilemma, she resorted to me for financial support.

例 6. 这种农药对当地环境有威胁，所以被禁用了。

Posing danger to local environment, the pesticides have been interdicted from adoption.

【句式】主语 pose danger/threat/harm to n.＝主语 endanger/threaten n.

例7. 政府改变了原本对老百姓有利的计划，因此受到了公众的谴责。
Derailing the original plan to facilitate civilians, the Government was denounced intensely.
derail vt. 改变（观点、计划等）。to facilitate civilians 为不定式短语作定语，修饰 plan。facilitate dong sth.为及物动词短语，表示"对某事有利"。

2. 形容词短语，主语+谓语。
例8. 尽管依赖于学校为其输送人才，但该公司独立于这所大学。
Largely dependent of the university for talents, the company is independent of the university.
Largely dependent 为形容词短语作转折状语，逻辑主语为 the company，必须与句子主语一致。

例9. 由于采用了新技术，公司成本大幅降低。
Adopting novel technology, the company witnessed a sharp decline in cost.
adopt vt. 采用。Adopting 的逻辑主语为 the company。a decline in sth.为名词短语，表示"某方面的下滑或数量的降低"。

3. 介词短语（like 和 unlike 表示"像"、"不像"时为介词），主语+谓语。like 和 unlike 的逻辑主语与句子主语一致。
例10. 蔬菜的价格随天气变化而剧烈浮动，而面粉的价格通常保持稳定。
Unlike those of vegetables fluctuating intensely with weather conditions, prices of flour always remain stable.
fluctuating intensely 为现在分词短语作定语，修饰 those，those 指代 prices。复数的指代用 those。

4. 不定式短语，主语+谓语。
不定式短语作状语时，表示目的或结果。
例11. To earn a living, I work hard.
为了生计，我努力工作。
To earn 为不定式，其逻辑主语为 I，必须与句子主语一致。该不定式表目的。

例12. The weather reporter exaggerated severity of the approaching storm, to arouse unnecessary anxiety among audience.
to arouse 为不定式表结果状语，逻辑主语为天气预报员，即天气预报员过度夸大了即将来临的暴风雨的严重程度，结果导致观众不必要的恐慌。
除了不定式以外，还可以用分词短语作结果状语，本句可改为：
The weather reporter exaggerated severity of the approaching storm, arousing unnecessary anxiety among audience.

句式五：主语1+谓语，主语2+分词或形容词等（也称为独立主格）。
该句式须同时满足以下两个条件：
(1) 主语1不等于主语2；
(2) 逗号前后的句子有某种逻辑关系或呈伴随的关系。
与句式四判断谓语和分词的方法相同：表示原因、假设、让步等可以改为相应的从句的部分用分词，主句或真正强调的结果用谓语动词。逗号前后不含连词！

例13. 尽管电磁辐射对人体有害这一观点盛行了很多年，但直到最近并没有科学证据证实这一观点。
[分析] 主语不一致，且有逻辑关系，可用独立主格造句。本句要强调没有科学证据证实这一观点，因此该句为主句。

Not a piece of scientific has been found to substantiate the idea, the position that electromagnetic radiation might compromise health having prevailed for years.

改为主句从句的形式为：

Although the position that electromagnetic radiation might compromise health has prevailed for years, not a piece of scientific has been found to substantiate the idea.

其中 electromagnetic radiation might compromise health 为 position 的同位语从句，position 在这里为名词，意为"观点"。

例 14. He is a celebrated scientist, many of his theories applied to industry.

他是一名著名的科学家，他的很多理论都被应用到了工业。

逗号前后两个分句为伴随关系。本句要强调他是著名科学家，"many of his theories applied to industry"为伴随成分，表明他有多有名。applied 为过去分词，因为理论被应用到工业领域是被动。

apply theories to industry 为动词短语，表示"把理论应用到工业"。

【注】独立主格可用另一种句式来代替：

主语 1+谓语 with+主语 2+分词

例 13 和例 14 可分别改写为以下形式：

Not a piece of scientific has been found to substantiate the idea with such a position that electromagnetic radiation might compromise health having prevailed for years.

He is a celebrated scientist with many of his theories applied to industry.

句式六：名词短语，主语+谓语。

一般来说，句子前面或结尾有名词短语时，该短语往往是主语或宾语等名词的同位语，而名词短语同样可由后置定语修饰，这时，根据文意可判断：不是独立主格！

例 15. An animal surviving hunger and thirst, camel serves as an essential transportation tool in desert.

骆驼能在饥渴环境中生存下来，它是沙漠里一种重要的交通工具。

An animal 为主语 camel 的同位语，单复数必须一致！surviving hunger and thirst 为现在分词短语作定语，修饰 animal。

句式七：

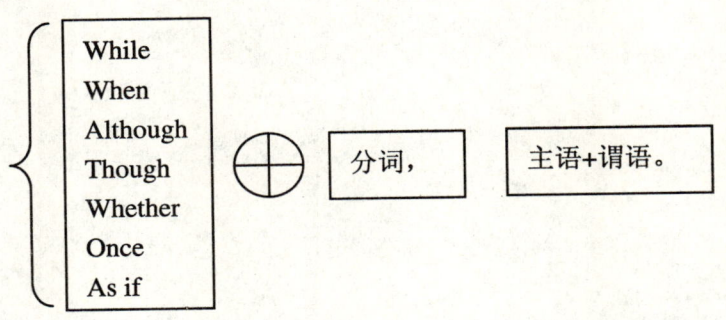

$$\left\{\begin{array}{l}\text{While}\\\text{When}\\\text{Although}\\\text{Though}\\\text{Whether}\\\text{Once}\\\text{As if}\end{array}\right\} + \text{分词,} \quad \text{主语+谓语。}$$

分词的逻辑主语必须与句子主语一致。

例 16. When reaching home, I was exhausted.

到家的时候，我已经精疲力竭了。

reaching 的逻辑主语是 I。

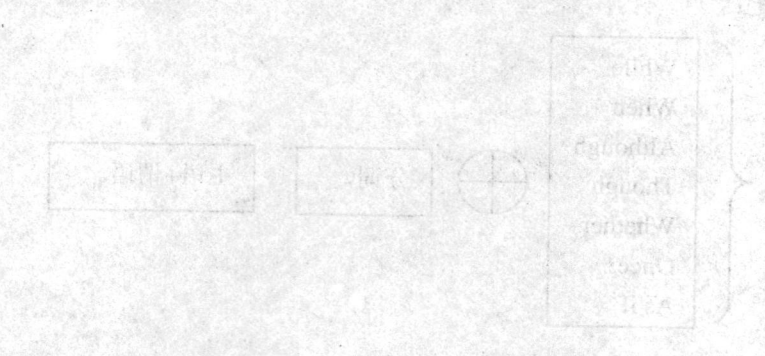

# 第二部分

# 文章精读

第二部分

文章精над

# 文章 1

That nineteenth-century French novelist Honere de Balzac could be financially wise in his fiction while losing all his money in life was an irony duplicated in other matters[1]. For instance, the very women who had been drawn to him by the penetrating intuition of the female heart that he showed in his novels were appalled to discover how insensitive and awkward the real man could be[2]. It seems the true source of creation for Balzac was not sensitivity but imagination[3]. Balzac's fiction originally sprang from an intuition he first discovered as a wretched little school boy locked in a dark closet of his boarding school: life is a prison, and only imagination can open its doors[4].

## 【单词及搭配】

1. financially，副词，经济上地，金融上地。financially wise，副词 financially 修饰形容词 wise，在经济上明智的；a financially risky plan，risky 为形容词，有风险的，在金融上冒险的计划；He is psychologically/financially supportive of us. 他从心理上/经济上支持我们。He is mentally suffered a lot. 他精神上备受折磨。supprotive 为形容词，支持的。be supportive of sb./sth. 支持某人或某事。

2. irony，名词，讽刺。须掌握形容词：ironic，讽刺的。

3. duplicate，文中为及物动词，复制。All the teachers received duplicated notices. 所有老师都接到同样的通知。

4. matter：(1) 这里指"事情"，event，名词（文中意思）；(2) 不及物动词，有重要性。This issue ceased to matter. 这个议题不再重要了。

5. draw，这里作及物动词，吸引。draw attention of sb. 吸引某人注意。be drawn to sb. 被某人吸引。

6. penetrating，形容词，insightful，深刻的，透彻的，有洞察力的。penetrating questions，深刻的问题。还须掌握动词形式：penetrate (1) vt. & vi. 穿过，刺入，渗入；(2) vt. 了解 penetrate (understand) sth. 了解某事；(3) vt. 看穿 penetrate sth. 看穿某事。

7. intuition，名词，直觉。动词为 intuit，及物动词。intuit sth./that+从句，凭直觉知道某事。

8. appalled，形容词，惊讶的。

9. awkward，形容词，笨拙的。

10. spring，动词 (1) vi. spring/originate/issue from sth./doing sth. 源于哪里；(2) vt. 突然提出，spring a surprise attack 发起突袭。

11. wretched，形容词，不幸的，沮丧的。

12. closet，名词，壁橱。

13. boarding school，寄宿学校。

# 【文章精读】

[1] That nineteenth-century French novelist Honere de Balzac could be financially wise in his fiction while losing all his money in life（句子主语） *was*（句子谓语） an irony duplicated in other matters.（定语，修饰 ironoy）

"That nineteenth-century French novelist Honere de Balzac could be financially wise in his fiction while losing all his money in life"为主语从句，由 that 引导，that 没有任何含义，仅起引导作用。比如：That he is clever is known to us all. 我们都知道他很聪明。"That he is clever"为主语从句，that 不能省略，原因是若省略了 that 句子结构很混乱。由 that 引导的主语从句也可用 it 句子代替：It was an irony duplicated in other matters that nineteenth-century French novelist Honere de Balzac could be financially wise in his fiction while losing all his money in life. It is known to us all that he is clever.

"duplicated in other matters"为过去分词短语作后置定语，修饰 irony，一个在其他事件中被复制的讽刺，即其他事情中他也是这样的。

while 在这里为连词，表示"然而"。while 后面可加完整的句子，也可加分词。加分词时，要求分词的逻辑主语必须与句子的主语一致。如本句 losing 的逻辑主语是 Balzac。类似用法有：

主语+谓语 when/until/while/so long as/whether+分词

如：I was all wet when getting home. 我到家时全身都湿了。

## 【分词作定语举一反三】

A meeting intended to solve national disputes will be held. 一个旨在解决国际争端的会议即将召开。intended to solve 为过去分词短语作定语。intend 用法：

(1) intend vt. 打算，旨在
(2) 某人打算做某事：sb. intends to do sth. 主动
(3) 某事（非人）旨在做某事：sth. be intended to do sth. 被动

The meeting was intended to solve national disputes.

The plight confronted by the government aroused public attention. 政府所面临的困境引起了公众关注。confronted by the government 为过去分词短语作定语，修饰 plight（困境，名词）。

主语（人）be confronted with sth. 某人面临 XXX。

Sth. was confronted by sb. 某人面临 XXX。

The book illustrating theory of mobile communications is valuable. 这本阐述移动通信原理的书很有用。illustrating theory 为现在分词短语作定语，修饰 book。因为 book 主动阐述理论，所以用现在分词。

本句意思：19 世纪小说家巴尔扎克在他写小说时在经济上是很明智的，然而在生活中他却失去了全部的财产，在其他事情中也是如此。

## 【重要句型】

That+主语从句 was/is a fact circumstance duplicated in XXX. 这样一种情况在其他情况中同样出现。

例 1. That the experienced staff showed want of enthusiasm of daily work was a phenomenon duplicated as for recent ones owing to economical crisis. 由于经济危机，新老员

工均出现了对工作缺乏热情这一现象。

例 2. That such medicine as XXX might wreak havoc on health of human beings is an idea prevailing for years. 这种称为 XXX 的药物可能损害人体健康这一观点流行了很多年。其中 prevailing 为现在分词短语作定语，修饰 idea。

例 3. We must adapt to climatic changes posed by environment pollution. 我们必须去适应由环境污染所带来的气候变化。其中 posed by 为过去分词短语作定语，修饰 changes，与 duplicated/prevailing 用法相同。

[2] 举例说明巴尔扎克在生活中和小说中截然不同。For instance, the very women who had been drawn to him by the penetrating intuition of the female heart that he showed in his novels were appalled to discover how insensitive and awkward the real man could be. 那些被巴尔扎克在小说中表现出来的对女人的内心敏锐的洞察力所吸引的女人很惊讶地发现巴尔扎克在生活中是一个多么麻木、不敏锐和愚笨的人。who had been drawn to him by the penetrating intuition of the female heart 为定语从句，修饰 women，那些被巴尔扎克在小说中表现出来的对女人的内心的敏锐的洞察力所吸引的女人们。that he showed in his novels 为定语从句，修饰 intuition，在小说中表现出来的洞察力。

very 在这里为形容词，恰恰，表强调。him 指代巴尔扎克。by the penetrating intuition 为介词短语，通过某种方式做什么事情。were 为句子的主语，主语中嵌套了两个定语从句。be appalled to do sth. 很惊讶地做某事。

[3] 推测巴尔扎克小说创作的灵感并非来自敏锐，而是想象力。It seems the true source of creation for Balzac was not sensitivity but imagination. It 引导的主语从句：It seems that+主语从句. not A but B，不是 A，而是 B。the source of sth./the spring of sth.均指某事的来源/源泉，表示源泉的有 source/spring/origination。It seems 表示"看起来"，暗含作者通过对巴尔扎克生活与小说判若两人的行为来推断他写小说的灵感来源，仅仅是作者自己的推断。

[4] he first discovered 为定语从句，修饰 intuition（直觉），这个直觉是他上学时发现的。as 表示"作为"。locked in a dark closet of his boarding school 为过去分词短语作定语，修饰 boy，被锁在学校小黑屋的孩子。its 指代生活的。巴尔扎克的小说最初来源于他孩童时代被关在学校小黑屋时所发现的直觉：生活是一座监狱，只有想象力才能开启它的大门。

【题目解析】

1. The example in lines 4-8（文章第二句） primarily suggests that

(A) Balzac's work was not especially popular among female readers

(B) Balzac could not write convincingly about financial matters

(C) Balzac's insights into character were not evident in his everyday life

(D) people who knew Balzac personally could not respect him as an artist

(E) readers had unreasonable expectations of Balzac the man

【答案】

(A) 选项歪曲了文章意思，巴尔扎克的小说很受女性读者欢迎。见[2]。especially popular，尤其流行，特别受欢迎。注意 popular 与 prevalent 的区别，都表示"流行"，但前者强调受欢迎，后者仅表示流行，不一定流行好的东西。比如名词短语：the campus ills prevalent in campus today 当今校园盛行的校园弊病。prevalent in campus 为形容词短语作定语，修饰 ills（弊端，名词）。

(B) 选项歪曲了文章意思：巴尔扎克写小说时在经济上很明智。

convincingly，副词，令人信服地。do sth. convincingly，做某事让人信服。掌握动词形式：convince (1) vt. convince sb. of sth./doing sth. 使某人确信；(2) convince sb. that+宾语从句；(3) 说服，persuade/convince sb. to do sth. 说服某人做某事。

(C) 见[2]精解：举例的作用是表明巴尔扎克在小说中的敏锐与生活中的他判若两人，原因在[3][4]句进一步解释：他写小说依靠的是想象力而非敏锐。hold a penetrating/superficial insight into sb./sth. 对什么有敏锐的/肤浅的见解。巴尔扎克对日常的人物没有很明显的洞察。everyday life: everyday 为形容词，日常的，相当于 daily。区分 everyday 与 every day: 后者为副词，作状语，前者为形容词，作定语修饰名词。

(D) 作者没有这个意思。

(E) unreasonable，形容词，不理智的，没有道理的。have (an) expectation(s) of sb./sth. 对 XXX 有期望。作者没有这个意思，读者只是发现小说内外的巴尔扎克判若两人，没有表现出来对他有不理性的期待。且文章 for instance 之后举的例子的目的是说明巴尔扎克在小说内外如何不同，这个例子是对[1]的实例证明。

2. The author mentions Balzac's experience as a schoolboy in order to
(A) explain why Balzac was unable to conduct his financial affairs properly
(B) point out a possible source of Balzac's powerful imagination
(C) exonerate the boarding school for Balzac's lackluster performance
(D) foster the impression that Balzac was an unruly student
(E) depict the condition of boarding school life during Balzac's youth

【答案】B

(A) 作者并没有试图解释巴尔扎克为什么丢掉所有钱。这不是文章主旨。conduct，动词，管理。

(B) 这是很精确的答案。a possible source of：一种可能的来源，见[3]精解。作者写孩童时代被关进屋子的目的在于表明巴尔扎克的灵感从何而来。

(C) exonerate A from B，免除……的罪责；宣布……无罪；lackluster performance 不好的表现。因为巴尔扎克表现不好而为寄宿学校开脱。作者没有这个意思。

(D) foster 及物动词

(1) 鼓励；促进

(2) 培养；助长（感情、观念）。foster a sense of unity 培养团结精神。

unruly，形容词，任性的，蛮横的。

让大家有一种印象：巴尔扎克是个任性的学生。作者没有这个意思。

(E) depict，及物动词，描绘。作者没有要描绘学生生活。

# 文章 2

Dr. Jane Wright insisted in later year that her father, surgeon Louis Wright, never pressured her to study medicine; indeed he warned her how hard becoming a doctor would be.[1] His very fame, within and beyond the African American Community, made her training harder in some ways: "His being so good really makes it very difficult,"[2] Wright told an interviewer soon after she graduated from medical school in 1945. "Everyone knows who Papa is." [3]

【单词及搭配】

1. persuade (1) vt. & vi. 说服, 劝告（文中意思）；(2) vt. 使信服
2. fame n. 名声, 名望

【文章精读】

[1]指出 Jane 的父亲从没有劝说她学医，反而警告她学医的艰辛。becoming a doctor 为动名词短语作宾语从句的主语。

[2]—[3] very 为形容词，十足的。父亲十足的名声使得女儿的训练在很多方面非常艰难。父亲太过出色使得训练很困难。it 指代 her training。Papa 指爸爸。His being so good 为动名词短语作主语，修饰动名词用形容词性物主代词。如：Her treating me rudely made me upset. 她粗暴地对待我让我很恼火。

【题目解析】

1. The passage suggests that Jane Wright's medical training was made more difficult because

(A) her father warned her not to study medicine
(B) her father flaunted his success
(C) she did not spend adequate time studying
(D) she shared her father's desire for fame
(E) she was inevitably compared to her father

【答案】E

由[2]-[3]看出父亲的出色使得她的训练很艰难，即人们会将她与父亲作比较。(E) 人们不可避免地将她与父亲进行比较。

(A) 父亲并没有警告她不准学医，而是实情告知学医的艰辛。
(B) flaunt vt. 炫耀, 夸耀。父亲并没有炫耀自己的成功。
(C) 文章没讲她没有足够的时间用来学习。adequate, 形容词，充足的。
(D) 她与父亲都有着对名誉的渴望。文章没有提到父女俩渴望名誉。

2. The passage is primarily concerned with Jane Wright's

(A) views of the medical profession

(B) childhood recollections

(C) perception of her father as a role model

(D) reluctance to collaborate with her father

(E) gratitude for her father's encouragement

【答案】C

本文主要讲父亲身为名医对 Jane 起到的楷模作用，人们总是将她与出色的父亲相比。

(A) 对医药职业的观点。这不是文章主要意图，虽然提到从医的艰辛。

(B) 儿时的记忆。跑题。

(C) 将父亲作为楷模的认知。

(D) 不愿与父亲合作。文章没有这个意思。reluctance to do sth，名词短语，不情愿做某事。

(E) 对父亲鼓励的感激。文中第一句已经交代：父亲并没有劝说她从医，而是告诉她学医的艰辛，因此父亲没有 encouragement。

# 文章 3

## 文章 3.1

In nineteenth-century England, middle-class women were usually assigned domestic roles and faced severely limited professional career options[1]. Of course, one can point to England's monarch, Queen Victoria, as a famous example of a woman at work, and millions of working-class women worked for wages in factories and private homes, and in stores and markets[2]. But aristocrats were often exempt from societal structures that bound the middle class，and working-class women were usually looked down on not being "respectable" for their efforts as workers[3]. As the nineteenth century progressed, it was assumed that a woman engaged in business was a woman without either her own inheritance or a man to support her[4]. Middle-class women already shared with upper-middle-class men the societal stumbling blocks to active pursuit of business, which included the feeling that labor was demeaning and not suitable for those with aspirations to gentility[5]. But unlike a man, whose self-worth rose through his economic exertions, a woman who did likewise risked opprobrium for herself and possibly shame for those around her[6]. Inequality in the working world made it exceedingly difficult for a middle-class woman to support herself on her own[7]. Let alone support dependents.[8] Thus, at a time when occupation was becoming a core element in masculine identity, any position for middle-class women other than in relation to men was considered anomalous[9]. In the 1851 census, the Registrar Geneal introduced a new fifth class of workers, exclusively made up of women[10].

批注 [1]: 关键时间点——19世纪，与后文第五类阶层的时间点息息相关，为考点。

**【单词及搭配】**

1. assign，动词，这里指分配。be assigned sth. 被分配到哪里。
2. domestic，形容词 (1) 家庭的，家事的；(2) 国家的；国内的。domestic policies 国内政策。
3. monarch, 大王。
4. aristocrat, 贵族。
5. exempt, (1) 形容词，被免除的（文中意思）；(2) 及物动词，免除。
6. stricture, 名词, (1) 苛评，指责；(2) 紧束；约束（文中意思）。
7. bound：这里为 bind 的过去式。bind vt. 受……阻碍（或约束）。
8. look down on sb./sth. 轻视某人/某物。
9. progress, vi. 进步。

10. be engaged in sth./engage in sth. 忙于某事/从事某事。

11. inheritance，名词，继承。

12. stumbling block，绊脚石。stumbling 的变形动词形式须掌握：

不及物动词 vi.

(1) 绊脚，绊倒 stumble over/on sth.

(2) 跟跄，蹒跚而行 The tired old man stumbled along.

(3) 结结巴巴地说；踌躇 The boy stumbled through his recitation. 这男孩结结巴巴地背诵。

(4) 步入歧途 stumble into/over. The waiter stumbled several times over our order. 那位侍者好几次弄错了我们点的菜。

(5) 偶然碰见，碰巧发现 stumble on/across/upon

13. engage

(1) vt. 引起（某人的兴趣或注意），吸引，engage one's attention；(2) vt. 雇佣=employ；(3) vt. 允诺，约定；签约保证，engage to do sth.。

(4) vi. 参加，从事；卷入。engage in sth./be engaged in doing sth.。

(5) vi. 紧密结合；有密切关系。engage with sb./sth.。

14. demeaning，形容词，贬低人的，有损人格的。

demean vt. 使降低身份，使卑下。demean sb. by doing sth.。

15. aspiration，名词，志向。

16. gentility，名词，高贵。

17. exertion，名词，(1) 努力；费力。do sth. of one's all exertions 尽全力做某事。

(2)（能力、权力等的）运用；行使。Exertion of authority over others is not always wise. 以权压人并不总是明智的。

18. likewise，副词，(1) 同样；(2) ［用于引出一与前述情况相似或相关的情况］同样。

The banks advise against sending cash. Likewise, sending British cheques may cause problems. 银行建议不要寄送现金。同样，寄往英国的支票也可能会出问题。

(3) in a like manner; similarly 以相似的方式，类似地。

I stuck out my tongue and Frankie did likewise. 我伸出舌头，弗兰克也这样做。

19. opprobrium，名词，训斥，辱骂，耻辱，恶名，侮辱。

20. dependent，名词，靠他人生活的人，受赡养者，侍从；随员，从属物；家眷。

21. masculine，男子的。aspirations to gentility, 追逐显赫地位的志向。

22. anomalous，形容词，不按常规的，反常的；不规则的，例外的。an anomalous situation 异常情况。

23. exclusively，副词，(1) 仅仅；专门地；单独地（文中意思）。be exclusively for sth. 专门用于什么的；exclusively female concerns 只有妇女才关心的事，名词短语。

(2) 专有地。I can exclusively reveal that the plan has been successful. 我可以透露一点的是，计划成功了，这可只有我知道。

**【文章精读】**

[1] 表示某人遇到某事的表达方式：

(1) 主语 face sth. (2) 主语 be confronted with sth.

severely limited：副词 severely 修饰形容词 limited，严格受限的。开篇点题，中产阶级女性往往要从事家庭主妇的角色并且面临着很严格受限的职业选择。

[2]指出特例——确实有一些贵族妇女和工人阶级女性在工作，即她们没有从事家庭主妇的工作。本句是对第一句的特例。point to，指出，指明，point to sth./doing sth., point to sb./sth. as+名词/形容词，指出某人或某事是怎样的。你当然可以指出有一些贵族女性和工人阶级女性在工作。下文将解释这两类女性受到的不同待遇。

[3] 与第二句形成了对比转折。贵族女性工作可免受责难，而平民工人阶级女性这样做却会受到指责。"that bound the middle class"为定语从句，修饰"societal structures"。bound 在此为 bind 的过去式，从下文可以看到，指束缚：贵族可以逃脱对中产阶级构成束缚的社会谴责，这种社会束缚即为"working-class women were usually looked down on not being 'respectable' for their efforts as workers"。respectable 为形容词，受人尊敬的。for 表示原因，as 为"作为"。

for 表示原因用法举例：He was blamed for being late for class.

contempt 名词，轻视，轻蔑，蔑视。show contempt for sb.。

[4] 本句指出 19 世纪人们对无产阶级女性的普遍看法——工作着的女性要么没有继承到遗产，要么身边没有男人养活她们。"without either her own inheritance or a man to support her"为介词短语作定语，修饰 woman，其中又嵌套了不定式作定语，修饰 man。engaged in business 为过去分词短语作定语，修饰 woman，完整短语为：主语+be engaged in sth./doing sth. 某人从事于某事。without either XXX or XXX：介词短语，或者没有这个，或者没有那个。重要句型：It is assumed that+主语从句。assume 在这里有"想当然认为"的含义。注意：assume 本意为"主观臆断"，vt.当文章出现 It is assumed that+从句时，作者对从句中的观点往往是质疑的，即作者认为有人主观臆断地认为某事发生。assume 表"主观臆断"时相当于动词短语 take sth. for granted。

[5] 女性与男性在工作时面临的相同问题，societal stumbling blocks 指"labor was demeaning and not suitable for those with aspirations to gentility"。those with aspirations to gentility 为介词短语作定语，修饰 those。定语不能修饰人称代词，如 they，I，you，him。**这点为改错考点**。

【改错考点剖析】I have to inform **those intending** to be involved in the research of the academic conference this afternoon. 我必须通知打算进行该项研究的人下午的学术会议。其中 intending to be involved 为现在分词短语作定语，修饰 those，即要进行研究的人。those 可改为 researchers，但不能改为 they，them。

本句意思：男性和女性在工作时都遇到相同的阻碍，这种阻碍包括这样一种感受：对追逐高贵地位的人来说，劳动使人身份降低。下一句必定阐述劳动对男女影响的不同之处。

[6] 承接[5]。"whose self-worth rose through his economic exertions"为定语从句，修饰 man。"who did likewise risked opprobrium for herself and possibly shame for those around her"为定语从句，修饰 woman。possibly 为副词，修饰 risk，possibly risk doing sth. 可能冒某种危险。

【句式】Like/Unlike+名词，主语+谓语。当 like/unlike 在这里表示"相似"的意思作介词时，like/unlike 的逻辑主语必须和句子主语一致。这也是改错考点。如本句 unlike 的逻辑主语是"女性"，句子主语也是"女性"。

例：Unlike those of vegetables fluctuating with weather conditions, prices of flour remain constant. 与蔬菜价格不同的是，面粉价格不会随天气情况波动，而是保持稳定。those 指代 prices，为名词复数。Unlike 为介词，其逻辑主语必须与句子主语 prices 一致。

本句省略了 risk，完整语句为 risked opprobrium for herself and possibly risked shame for those around her。这里 for 表示对于谁：冒着为她自己也为她周围的人招致责难和耻辱的危险。those 指代女性周围的人，around her 为介词短语作定语，those 不能换为 they。do sth. likewise，如此这样做。

本句解释男女在工作中的不同结果：男性通过经济上的努力，其自我价值在提升；而这样做的女性却冒着为她自己也为她周围的人招致责难和耻辱的危险。

[7]—[8] 承接[6]，男女工作世界中的不平等使得中产阶级女性很难养活自己，更不用提养活亲属了。表示"非常"的副词：exceedingly, extremely。

[9] 由 thus 引出结论：职业在那个时候（19世纪）成为了男性的特有标识，即只有男性才能工作，只有那些与男性相关的中产阶级女性的地位才被认为是正常的。masculine identity：男人的身份，即工作是男人的专属。other than：除了。in relation to sb./sth.，与某人/某事相关，介词短语，修饰 women，即与男性相关的女性。本句这样改写意思更易懂：

Only the position for middle-class women in relation to men was considered normal.

[10] 引出第五类阶层，注意时间点——1851年，该阶层专由女性构成。exclusively made up of women 为过去分词短语作定语，修饰第五类阶层。exclusively 为副词，修饰分词 made。下文将解释第五类人群的特点。

**第一段总结：19世纪女性若在外面工作会受到社会的责难，由此引出第五类阶层人群——不工作、作为家庭主妇的女性。**

The fifth class comprises large numbers of the population that have no occupation; but it requires no argument to prove that the wife, the mother, the mistress of an English family fills offices and discharges duties of no ordinary importance; or that children are or should be occupied in filial or household duties, and in the task of education, either at home or at school.

批注 [A2]: 定语从句，没有工作，修饰 population

批注 [A3]: 否定句的连接不用 and

【单词及搭配】

1. occupy
(1) vt. 居住；占用
(2) vt. 占据（空间、时间）（文中意思）
(3) 居（某种地位）occupy a dominant position 占据统治地位
(4) vt. 使（大脑、思绪）老想着 be occupied with sth./doing sth.
(5) vt. 使忙碌 occupy oneself doing sth.

【重要句型】

1. It requires no arguement to prove that+主语从句。无需证明 XXX。
2. filial adj. 子女的。filial duties，名词短语，孝道。
3. populate vt. 居住。表示"居住"的用法须掌握以下几个：
主语 populate+地点名词
主语 dwell in/at/on+地点名词
主语 inhabit+地点名词
主语 settle in/at/on+地点名词

主语 live in/at/on+地点名词

人口密集、人口稀疏的表达方式：a place that is densely populated；a densely populated place；a place that is sparsely populated；a sparsely populated place。

本段表明女性在家庭生活中的重要作用，注意这里的第五阶层是被家庭生活束缚、不能参加社会工作的女性。

批注 [T4]: 副词 densely 修饰分词 populated。

批注 [T5]: 副词 sparsely 修饰 populated

## 【文章精读】

but 表转折。虽然第五类人群没有工作，但她们在家庭中起到重要责任。**注意本句难点是 the wife, the mother, the mistress, children 同指女性——女性作为妻子、母亲、主人、女儿起到重要的作用**，尽管她们没有工作。

It requires no argument to prove that the wife, the mother, the mistress of an English family fills offices and discharges duties of no ordinary importance; or that children are or should be occupied in filial or household duties, and in the task of education, either at home or at school.

The wife, the mother, the mistress of an English family 为三个同位语，同指代女性。fill offices，动词短语，从事职责。

本句语法结构为：It requires no argument to prove that+宾语从句 1; or that+宾语从句 2. 宾语从句 2 中的 children 为 mother, wife 的同位语，都在讲女性。

sb. be occupied in sth.，某人从事什么工作。

duties of no ordinary importance，名词短语，非常重要的责任。

批注 [6]: 为 no argument 的并列连词，连接 that the wife, the mistress of an English family fills offices 和 children 直到结尾。即，无须证明作为母亲、妻子的女性有着重要的职责，也无需证明身为女儿的她们完成着尽孝道的职责以及家庭生活的职责和教育的职责，不论她们在家或在学校从事教育活动。

This conception of women had been developing over a long period.[1] For example, in the late seventeenth century, trade tokens used by local shopkeepers and small masters in family businesses carried the initials of the man's and the woman's first names and the couple's surname, but by the late eighteenth century, only the initials of the male proprietor were retained.[2] **This serves to confirm the view of one Victorian man, born in 1790, that whereas his mother had confidently joined in the family auctioneering business, the increased division of the sexes had seen the withdrawal of women from business life.**[3]

## 【单词及搭配】

1. initial (1) adj. 最初的，开始的；(2) n. 首字母（文中意思）
2. retain vt. 保持，保留
3. division 名词，(1) 分歧；争论；(2) 分界，区分 a solid division between A and B：A 与 B 之间的严格区分（文中意思）
4. withdrawal 名词，撤消；撤回

## 【文章精读】

[1] "this concept"指上一段：女性无工作，但在家庭中起重要作用——第五类阶层。本段第一句为关键句，阐述第五类阶层的演进史。

[2] 17 世纪男性和女性的名字的首字母都会在钱币上标识，到了 18 世纪后期，只有男性名字的首字母保留下来。这个例证与 1851 年提出第五类无工作女性人群的历史背景相吻合！

[3] born 为形容词短语作定语，修饰 his mother。that 至结尾为 view 的同位语。whereas 表示"然而"。increased division of the sexes，名词短语，越来越大的性别差异（歧视）。主语（非人）witness/see sth. 某物见证了什么。

【举一反三】因为近期所采用的技术，公司利润太幅上升。The company witnessed/saw a dramatic rise in profits with the recently adopted technology.

the withdrawal of sb. from sth.，名词短语，某人从某事中的退出。

"this"指代[2]，女性在货币上的名字逐渐被取消。

本句给出这种历史趋势下的必然结果——虽然女性满怀信心地从事着事业，但越来越突出的性别歧视使得女性不得不从这些领域中退缩出来（转向家庭，成为第五类阶层）。

Marriage became, more than ever, the only career option offering economic prosperity for women; in business, women appear only as faint shadows behind the scenes.[1] The absence of women in business and financial records makes our knowledge of what middle-class women actually did and how they survived economically quite fragmentary.[2] What we do know is that women's ability to survive economically on their own became increasingly difficult in the course of the nineteenth century.[3]

## 【单词及搭配】

1. division，名词，分界，区分 division of labour 劳动分工
2. survive (1) vi.（尤指在危险、苦难之后）活下来（文中意思）；(2) vt. 幸存 survive the battle
3. filial adj. 子女的；孝顺的
4. unescorted adj. 无人陪同的；无人护送的
5. faint adj.
(1)（景象、气味、声音）微弱的，依稀的
(2)（希望、机会、可能性）微小的；渺茫的
There is a faint chance/probability that +从句：某事发生的概率很小。
(3) 虚弱乏力的
6. fragmentary adj. 碎片的；片断的；不完整的；支离破碎的 fragment n. 碎片；片断

## 【文章精读】

[1] 婚姻成为女性生存的手段。将事业中的女人比做屏幕后微弱的阴影。offering 为现在分词短语作定语，修饰 options。

[2] what middle-class women did and how they survived 为 of 的宾语从句。句子主干为：The absence makes knowledge fragmentary. knowledge 为名词，指对某事的了解。句意为：女性工作和经济记录的缺失使得我们对中产阶级女性究竟如何生存知之甚少。

"survive economically"：靠经济生存，及生存下来。类似用法：support financially 从财政上支持。

[3] what we do know 为名词性从句，is 为句子谓语。increasingly difficult 为形容词短语，increasingly 为副词，副词才能修饰名词和分词。越来越怎样。

in the course of sth.，在某事的进行过程中。

the ability to do sth.，名词短语，做某事的能力，to do sth.为不定式短语作定语，修饰

ability。对比第二句指出：我们所知道的是女性在19世纪的发展历程中，生存越来越艰难。

## 文章 3.2

In the second half of the nineteenth century in England, under the rule of Queen Victoria, because of the long peace and the increasing prosperity, more and more women found themselves able to travel to Europe unescorted.[1] With the increase in travel came an increase in the number of guidebooks, collections of travel hints, and diaries by travelers—many of which were written by or directed to women.[2]

### 【单词及搭配】

1. unescorted adj. 无人陪同的；无人护送的。须掌握动词形式：escort (1) vt. 护送；为……护航 escort sb.；(2) n. 护送者，护卫队；护航舰，护航飞机。
2. guidebook 这里指旅游指南（或手册、要览）。
3. direct vt. (1) 给（某人）指路 direct sb. to somewhere；(2) 针对……发表评论/批评 direct at sth./doing sth. 针对XXX；(3) 使（产品）针对，面向（某人）（文中意思）。The book is directed at the electronic engineers. 这本书是面向电子工程师的。Such a product is designed to be directed at users engaged in business. 这款产品是针对商务人士而设计的。engaged in 为过去分词短语作定语，修饰users，从事某事的人。(4) 命令；指示 direct sb. to do sth./direct sb. that+宾语从句。

### 【文章精读】

[1] 开篇点题，随着时代的和平，女性有了更多的时间外出旅行，且无人护送。unescorted 为过去分词作伴随状语，表明女性独立旅游，没有家人陪同，该单词为考点。

[2] with the increase in travel 为介词短语作状语，伴随着旅游的增加。which 指代旅游日志。

Although nineteenth-century women traveled for a variety of reasons, ranging from a desire to do scientific research to involvement in missionary work, undoubtedly a major incentive was the desire to escape from domestic confinement and the social restrictions imposed on the Victorian female in Britain.[1] As Dorothy Middletone observers, "Travel was an individual gesture of the housebound, mandominated Victorian woman."[2] The "caged birds" of the Victorian parlor found their wings and often took flight in other lands.[3] In a less constrained environment they achieved physical and psychological freedom and some measure of autonomy.[4] In *Celebrated Women Travelers of the Ninteenth Century* (1883), Davenport Adams comments: "Fettered as women are in European countries by restraints, obligations, and responsibilities, which are too often arbitrary and artificial…it is natural enough that when the opportunity offers, they should hail even a temporary emancipation through travel."[5]

## 【单词及搭配】

1. range vi.（在一定幅度或范围内）变动，变化；延伸 range from A to B

2. involvement 名词，卷入；牵连；参与 involvement in sth./doing sth.

3. incentive 名词，刺激，鼓励；动机，诱因 an incentive to do sth.

4. confine
(1) vt. 限制；使局限 confine sth. to sth. (2) 名词，（尤指某个地方限制行动自由的）界限；边界；范围 (3) 名词，（尤指学科或活动领域的）界限；范围

5. impose  (1) vt. 把……强加（于）impose sth. on sth.（文中意思）(2) vt. 实施（限制）(3) vt. 利用（某人）impose on one's kindness

6. housebound adj. 出不了门的；闭门不出的（格外注意这里的 bound 为动词原形 bind 的过去分词，被束缚在家中的），用法与 mandominated 一样。举例：a physics-based subject 以物理为基础的学科。

bind (1) vt. 捆绑，捆扎 (2) vt. 约束 (3) vt. 装订 (4) vt. & vi.（使）结合

7. parlor n. 客厅；起居室

8. autonomy n 自治；独立

9. environment  (1) 可数名词，环境，条件 a good learning environment（文中意思）(2)（计算机）环境，工作平台

10. measure: a particular amount of something 一定量的；a measure of egg white 一定量的蛋清。

11. fetter vt. 限制，束缚，羁绊（人）be fettered by tradition

12. restraint 名词，控制，限制，遏制，抑制

13. emancipate vt. 解放 emancipate sb. from doing sth.

14. hail (1) n. 雹子 (2) n. 一阵 There was a hail of angry words. 愤怒的话语如冰雹似地砸来。(3) vi. 下雹子 (4) v. 致敬；向……欢呼（文中意思）

15. temporary adj. 暂时的，临时的

16. cage (1) n. 笼子 (2) vt. 把……关入牢中

17. obligation n. 义务；责任 obligate vt. 使（在法律或道义上）负有责任或义务 be obligated to do sth.

## 【文章精读】

[1] 指出女性旅行的个人原因。do sth. for a reason that+从句：因某种理由来做某事。"ranging from a desire to do scientific research to involvement in missionary work"为现在分词短语作定语，修饰 reasons，原因涉及做科研到参加传教士工作的欲望。"to do scientific research to involvement in missionary work"为不定式作定语，修饰名词 desire。做某事的欲望：a desire to do sth.。"imposed on the Victorian female in Britain"为过去分词短语作定语，修饰 restrictions。

although 为转折，表明除了科研等因素外，还有更为主要的刺激女性旅行的原因，在 undoubtedly 中提到。

[2] 承接[1]，旅行是维多利亚时代女性的特征。还可以这样表达：The housebound, mandominated Victorian woman was characterized by travel.

[3] 注意本句引号及代词的指代，本句与上一篇文章形成呼应。这往往是出题点。"caged birds" 指代上一篇文章中的 fifth class of women，第五个阶层，即不工作被限制在家庭中的女性。took flight in other lands 可用另外一个单词替代：travel。

[4] 女性在宽松的环境中获得的好处。in a less constrained environment：束缚较少的条件下。constrained 为过去分词作形容词。some measure of autonomy：一定程度上的自主。

[5] "Fettered as … restraints"为 as 引导的倒装让步状语，等价于"Although women in European countries are fettered by …, which … artificial …"。"which"指代"restraints, obligations, and responsibilities"。hail 这里指 welcome。

By the later part of nineteenth century, women travelers began to be singled out as exemplars of the new social and political freedom and prowess of women.[1] Ironically, Mary Kingsley and other women travelers were opposed to extend women's political rights.[2] Thus, when Mary Kingsley returned from West Africa in 1895, she was chagrined to discover that she was being hailed as a "new woman" because of her travels.[3] Despite her often out-spoken distaste for the "new women" agitating for greater freedom, the travel books that she and others had written still suggested, as Paul Fussell has argued, "an implicit celebration of freedom."[4]

## 【单词及搭配】

1. single vt. 挑选，挑出 single out sth.
2. exemplar 榜样；模范；范例；典型
3. prowess 名词，杰出才能，高超本领
4. distaste 名词，不太喜欢；轻微的反感
5. agitate (1) vt. 使不安，使紧张 (2) vi. 鼓动，煽动（文中意思）agitate for sth./doing sth. 鼓动某事
6. implicit adj.
 (1) 含蓄的，不言明的（文中意思）
 (2) 本质相关的，密切相关的；内含的，固有的 sth. implicit in sth. 某物固有的 XXX
 (3) 无条件的；无疑的；绝对的 an implicit faith in sb. 对某人绝对的信任
7. suggest vt. 暗示，委婉地说（文中意思）
The nervousness suggested his sense of guilty. 他的紧张暗示了他的罪恶感。

## 【文章精读】

[1] be singled out as sth./sb. 作为 XXX 被挑选出来。描述 19 世纪后期女性地位的变化。

[2] be opposed to do sth. 反对某事。讽刺的是，其中一位女性旅行者反对将女性的权利拓展到政治领域。rights 指权利。Ironically 承接了上一句：women travelers began to be singled out as exemplars of the new social and political freedom and prowess of women。

[3] Thus 解释了"was chagrined to discover"恼怒的原因。因为反对将女性权利拓展到政治领域，因此当她被欢迎为新女性时，她很苦恼。承接了[2]。be chagrined to do sth. 做某事很苦恼。hail 在这里指 welcome，及物动词，欢迎。

[4] 肯定妇女解放的意义。despite 为介词，后面只能跟随名词或名词性从句！distaste for sth. 对某事的厌恶，为名词性短语。"agitating for greater freedom"为现在分词短语作定语，

修饰 new women。"that she and others had written"为定语从句，修饰 books。suggested 为句子谓语，这里表示"暗示"。as Paul Fussell has argued，由 suggest 可以判断：implicit 为"含蓄的"之意。旅游书籍暗示了一种含蓄的对（女性）解放的庆祝。

> 批注 [A7]：这里表示主张，as sb. did，从句，正如某人所说的那样。

## 【题目解析】

1. For Victorian middle-class women, "self-worth" and "economic exertions" were thought to be

    (A) mutually exclusive
    (B) constantly evolving
    (C) the two keys to success
    (D) essential to finding a husband
    (E) easy to achieve

【答案】A

审题：对女性来讲自我价值和经济上的努力是怎样的？显然，女性越努力，自我价值越卑微。见原文分析。关键词可以看"unlike"。mutually exclusive，形容词短语，相互排斥的。

(B) 不断演进的。constantly 为副词，副词修饰分词 evovling。

(C) 两个通向成功的关键因素。恰恰相反，经济上的努力不能带给女性成功。keys to doing sth.，做某事的关键。

(D) 对找到丈夫很重要，恰恰相反，努力工作的女性会被人看不起。be essential to doing sth.，对某物很有必要。

(E) 容易实现，恰恰相反，第一段提到女性和男性都会遇到工作中的绊脚石。


2. "occupation" most nearly means

    (A) military conquest
    (B) pleasant diversion
    (C) vocation
    (D) settlement
    (E) political repression

【答案】C。这里指职业。

diversion n. (1) 转移，转向 (2) 娱乐，消遣（选项意思）

diverge vi. 分开；偏离；分歧；分道扬镳

repress vt. 抑制，压制；约束


3. The author of passage 1 considers trade tokens as evidence against the prevalence of a fifth class in the 17th century because they

    (A) served as legal currency
    (B) were issued to both middle-class and working-class women
    (C) helped neutralize gender stereotypes of the day
    (D) failed to identify women by their names and positions
    (E) identified men and women as partners in business

【答案】E

issue (1) n. 问题, 议题; 争论点 (2) n. 发行物 (3) n. 放出, 流出; 发出, 发行 (4) vt. 出版, 发行 (5) vt. 发表, 发布

本题难度较大。注意题干含义：作者认为货币是反驳 17 世纪第五类阶层很盛行的证据，理由是什么？evidence against sth., 反驳某物的证据。the prevalence of sth., 某事的盛行，名词短语。

第一段指出第五类阶层这一概念于 1851 年提出。这一概念是不断演进的：17 世纪男女名字平等地印在货币上，直到 18 世纪末期女性的名字才从货币取消，这时才出现了第五类阶层。因此，17 世纪男女在商业上的平等地位证明了当时不可能有第五类阶层。identify men and women as partners, 动词短语，认同女性和男性是合作者。

(A) 主语 serve as+名词=主语 be used as+名词。货币作为合法流通币。这不能作为证据。

(B) issue 这里为 vt, 分发, 分配。货币分配给男性和女性。错误，文中的意思是货币上共同印有男性和女性的名字，而非分发。

(C) gender stereotype, 性别刻板印象, 使得对性别刻板印象中立化。文章没有这个含义。

(D) 没有通过女性的名字和地位来认同女性。错误，文章意思相反，17 世纪认同女性与男性平等的合作人地位。

4. All of the following are referred to in passage 1 as evidence of women's diminished social status in Victorian England except the

(A) disparity between men's and women's career opportunities

(B) shame risked by women who wished to enter commerce

(C) exclusion of women's initials from trade tokens

(D) influence of the queen

(E) absence of financial records documenting women's activity

【答案】D

题干：哪个选项不能证明女性日渐衰败的地位？

(A) 女性和男性工作机会中的差异证明了女性地位的衰败。disparity n. 不同，不等；不一致；悬殊。

(B) risked 为过去分词短语作定语，修饰 shame。愿意从事商业的女性所冒的风险。见文章 1 第一段。该现象体现了女性地位的衰败。

(C) exclusion 名词, 排除。将女性名字首字母从货币中取消体现了女性地位的衰败。

(D) 女王的影响。见第一段第二句，贵族女性可以工作，且不会受到非难。这点不体现女性地位的衰败，只是个例。

(E) 记载女性活动的经济文献的缺失。见文中最后一段。documenting 为现在分词作定语，修饰 records。document 在这里为 vt, 等价于 record, 记载。

5. Which statement about British society, if true, would most directly support the view described in bolds?

(A) 17th century women workers could raise their status by assuming greater responsibilities.

(B) Women worte more novels in the early 19th century than they did in the early 18th century.

(C) Women and girls worked in factories throughout the 19th century.

(D) The practice of married couples jointly running business died out in the early 19th century.

(E) In the 17th century, formal academic institutions were closed to women.

【答案】D

(A) assume 在这里为 vt，承担。

(D) 夫妻共同开办的生意在 19 世纪早期倒闭。见原文分析。正确。

(E) 首先，文中没有直接提到学术机构对女性的排斥，而是商业机构对女性的排斥；其次，时间不对，17 世纪正是女性在商业上与男性平起平坐的时候。

6. "hail" most nearly means

(A) call out to

(B) gesture to

(C) come from

(D) welcome

(E) summon

【解析】D

根据文章意思，hail 显然是"欢迎"的意思。gesture to sb. 向某人做手势。

7. In passage 2, Mary Kingsley's attitude toward women's rights campaigns suggests

(A) a single-minded dedication to equality between the sexes

(B) a way in which dedication to one cause can lead to antagonism toward another

(C) a striking inconsistency between her identity as a British citizen and her identity as a woman

(D) an understanding of the link between women's struggle for freedom and the struggles of other groups

(E) a contradiction between her personal motives and the way her actions are interpreted

【解析】E

文章 2 最后一段指出：Mary 主张女性到国外旅游，但反对将女性的自由拓展到政治领域，她本人反对女权运动；而人们却认为她是"追求更大自由的新女性"。Mary 对此很为恼火。因此，人们对 Mary 行为的解释与 Mary 自身到国外旅游的动机是相悖的。way her actions are interpreted，名词短语，她的行为被人们解释的方法。the way+定语从句，做某事的方法。因此(E)正确。

(A) single-minded adj. 一心一意的；the dedication to sth.，对某事的奉献，即专心致力于性别平等事业。Mary 没有致力于性别平等事业，而是简单地主张女性应该到国外旅游，摆脱家庭工作的束缚，但她反对女性真正的自由，如政治权利。

(B) 对一项事业的投入将导致对另一项事业的对立，cause 在这里为"事业"的意思。文中没有提到两项事业的对立敌意。

(C) 她作为英国公民以及女性两者之间的不一致性。文中没有提到两者的不一致性。

(D) other groups 没有提到。understanding 不正确，人们误解了 Mary 的意图。

8. According to passage 2, 19th century British women were motivated to travel by which of the following?

I. Educational pursuits

II. Humanitarian concerns

III. Entrepreneurial interests

【解析】教育（文中"科研活动"）与人文关注（即女性想要摆脱家庭劳动的束缚）都提到了，没有提到企业利益。interests 这里为"利益"。本题为细节题。所以选择 I 和 II。

9. Which British traveler of the Victorian era would best illustrate the argument made in passage 2?

(A) A middle-class woman who tours Greece and Egypt to examine ancient ruins.

(B) An aristocratic woman who lives in the Asian capital where her father is the British ambassador.

(C) A young woman and her husband, both missionaries, who relocate permanently in a distant country.

(D) A nursemaid who accompanies an aristocratic family to its new home in New York.

(E) A young girl from a poor family who is sent by relatives to make her fortune in Australia.

【解析】本题与第 8 题同出一辙，考查维多利亚时期女性外出旅游的目的。答案为(A)。

女性旅游的目的包括从事科研活动以及进行传道工作，主要是想摆脱家庭的束缚，因此选项中不应有与男性相关的内容，故(B) (C) 排除。(D) 提到贵族家庭，文章 2 中被束缚的女性指文章 1 中的第五类阶层女性，不含贵族。即，陪同贵族家庭迁徙不是维多利亚时期女性旅游的目的。

(E) 为挣钱而出国也不是女性旅游的目的。

10. The "5th class" in passage 1 is most like which group in passage 2?

(A) Women who worked as missionaries

(B) The "caged birds"

(C) The "new woman"

(D) Dorothy Middleton and Mary Kingsley

(E) Davenport Adams and Pal Fussell

【解析】见原文分析，第五类阶层女性指被家庭束缚的女性，即(B)。

11. The information in passage 1 supports which assumption about the women described in passage 2?

(A) They were discouraged from pursuing careers in their native country.

(B) They sought to establish new business in foreign countries.

(C) They traveled with children and other family members.

(D) They were universally admired by British women from every class of society.

(E) They were committed advocates of social reform.

【解析】文章1支持文章2提到的关于女性的哪个观点？assumption 假设，本题为推断题，考查文章2没有直接提出的观点。

(A) native country，名词短语，本国。人们阻止女性在本国追求事业。正确。正是因为这样的束缚，所以女性到国外旅游，原因有她们想从事科研以及传道工作。这些都属于 careers。

(B) 文章2没有提到女性到国外经商。

(C) 文章2指出女性是独立旅游的，摆脱了家庭。

(D) 她们被每个阶层所崇拜。文章1提到女性经营一份事业会被人看不起，所以该项不对。

(E) commit vt. (1) 犯罪；犯错 (2) 承诺；使自己受约束 (3) 托付；交付（文中意思）
advocate (1) vt. 提倡，主张 (2) n. 提倡者，拥护者（选项意思）

选项意思为人们赋予这些女性进行社会变革倡导者的使命。文章2确实有这样的意思——最后一段第三句。人们认为 Mary 等人是社会变革的新女性。但文章1没有这一观点，文章1仅仅讲述女性的职业严格受限，追求事业的女性被人看不起。

句式：sb. be committed+名词，某人被赋予某种责任、义务。

# 文章 4

## 文章 4.1

Farm families are able to achieve efficiency only through a brutal work schedule that few people could tolerate.[1] "The farm family does physically demanding work and highly stressful work at least 14 hours a day (often at least 18 hours a day during harvest season), 7 days a week, 365 days a year, without a scheduled vacation or weekends off," wrote Minnesota politician and farm alumnus Darrell McKigney.[2] "The farmer must endure all of this without any of the benefits that most United States labor unions demand."[3] A dairy farmer, for instance, cannot just take off for a two-week vacation and not milk the cows. "Farmers lose perspective on the other things in life," one psychologist has written. "The farm literally consumes them."[4]

【单词及搭配】

1. brutal adj. 残忍的，野蛮的，残酷的，令人不快的，苛刻的，令人不舒服的
2. schedule
(1) 名词，进度表 (2) 日程安排（表）a busy schedule（文中意思）
(3) vi. 将……列入计划表（或时间表等）(4) vt. 安排；排定 be scheduled to do sth. 计划做某事
3. tolerate (1) vt. 容许，不干预 tolerate dissent 允许分歧 (2) vt. 忍受；容忍，宽恕 tolerate such noise (3) vi. （对药物、毒品或环境状况）有耐力
4. physically adv. 身体上地
5. demanding adj. （任务）难度大的，要求高的 a demanding job
6. stressful adj. 使紧张的，压力重的
stress (1) n. 压力，紧张 (2) n. 强调，重要性 lay stress on sth. 强调某物=emphasize sth. (3) vt. 强调=emphasize
7. endure
(1) vt. 忍耐（痛苦、困难），忍受 (2) vi. 继续存在；持久，持续 endured through time 饱经岁月的洗礼
8. dairy 牛奶房，乳制品场
9. take off 度假
10. perspective n. (1) 透视画法 (2) 景观；远景 (3) 视角；观点（文中意思）
11. literally adv.
(1) 按照字面地，逐字地，确切地

(2) ［表示所指物并非真实，只是为了强调或表达感情］I have received literally thousands of letters. 我收到了好几千封信。（文中意思）

12. consume

(1) vt. 用完，耗尽；消耗（资源）（文中意思）(2) vt. （感情）充满；吸引；使全神贯注 be consumed with guilt 内心充满悔恨

还须掌握同义单词：exhaust vt. (1) 弄空，取出 (2) 用尽，耗尽 (3) 使非常疲倦

## 【文章精读】

[1] 开篇点题：农家只能通过一种残忍的很少有人能够承受的工作来获取效率。"achieve efficiency only through a brutal work schedule"仅仅通过残忍的工作安排来获取效率，即通过不残忍的方式效率很低。"that few people could tolerate"为定语从句，修饰 schedule。本句为文章中心思想。

[2] physically demanding：体力上很累人的。physically 为副词，修饰形容词 demanding，格外注意这种表达方式，historically accurate：从历史角度来讲准确的。scheduled 在这里为过去分词作形容词，被计划好的假期，相当于 a planned vacation。without 到结尾为伴随状语。

[3] 这里用到了引用。all of this 指代上一句"没有假期"。that 到结尾为定语从句，修饰 benefits。

[4] 另一位心理学家的话被引用。引用名人的话是本文特点。them 指代农民，consume them 意思为消耗了农民的精力。

# 文章 4.2

Americans have distanced themselves from the ethics and morals of food production, except where it serves them to think nostalgically about family farms as the source of our better values.[1] Little wonder that a poll taken by *The New York Times* finds a majority of Americans seeing farm life as superior to any other kind of life in this country.[2] As consumers, Americans have enjoyed relatively inexpensive food.[3] What will happen if family farms disappear?[4] What will we do without family farmers to watch over the system for us, to be our dupes, and to create that pleasant situation through their own great discomfort?[5]

## 【单词及搭配】

1. distance

(1) vt. 使远离；使疏远；对……冷淡 (2) vt. 使脱离 distance oneself from sth./sb.（文中意思）

2. serve

(1) vt. 实现；满足=satisfy。实现某种用途/目标：serve a purpose of/that+同位语从句（文中意思）

(2) vi. 有用，起作用 sth. serves as sth.=sth. is used to do sth.

3. nostalgically adv. 思乡地；怀旧地

4. wonder

(1) vt. 想知道，觉得好奇 (2) vt./vi. 感到疑惑；感到惊叹；感到惊奇 wonder at sth./sb.

(3) n. 惊奇；惊讶；惊叹；诧异（文中意思）

5. superior adj.

(1) 较高的；上级的，高质 superior to sth./sb./doing sth.

(2) 高标准的；优质的 superior malt whiskies

(3) （数量或力量）占优势的 superior force 优势兵力（文中意思）

(4) not yielding to sth. 不屈服的；不受影响的

inferior adj. (1) 低等的，下级的 (2) 劣等的，次的

high-ranking adj. 阶级高的，高级官员的，职位高的

6. dupe (1) vt. 欺骗，诈骗，愚弄 (2) n. 受骗者，被愚弄的人（文中意思）

## 【文章精读】

*这篇文章的难度主要来源于对文章首句的理解！*

[1] distance oneself from sth./doing sth.：某人远离什么。"think about sth./sb. as XXX." 将某物考虑为 XXX。it 指代 "food production"。重要句型：主语+ serves sb. to do sth.。serve 在这里表示满足某人怎样做。

"them"指代"Americans"。where 引导宾语从句，作介词 except 的宾语，除了在哪个地方。except 为连词，连接了后面的地点状语从句，意为：而当美国人怀旧地去想家庭农场是我们更好价值的来源。"have distanced themselves from"表明美国人已经偏离了食品生产伦理和道德。这句话与"nostalgically"对应：怀旧地思考农业生产作为他们更好的价值观的来源，即美国人曾经将家庭农场考虑为更好的价值，只有在这一点上，美国人才没有偏离传统的食品生产道德。

等价于下面的表达方式：except in some respect that food production serves them to think nostalgically about family farms as the source of our better values。as the source of our better values 作为我们更好价值的来源。

**[译文]只有当食品生产使美国人怀旧地认为家庭农场是我们更好的价值的来源时，美国人才不会偏离食品生产的伦理和道德标准。**

[2] 省略句，完整句子为：There is little wonder that a poll taken by *The New York Times* finds a majority of Americans seeing farm life as superior to any other kind of life in this country。"wonder"在这里为名词，奇迹，奇怪，奇特。

"taken by *The New York Times*"为过去分词短语作定语，修饰 poll：一份由《时代周刊》做出的调查。take a poll，做一项民意调查。finds 为同位语从句中的谓语。

【重要句型】There is little wonder that+同位语从句。XXX 没什么好奇怪的。"seeing farm life as superior to any other kind of life in this country"为现在分词短语作定语，修饰 Americans：将农场生活视作这个国家中比其他任何一种生活都上等优质的生活。之所以不感到奇怪，原因是："except where it serves them to think nostalgically about family farms as the source of our better values"。

[3] relatively inexpensive food，相对便宜的食品。inexpensive 为形容词，必须用副词来修饰。as 在这里表示"作为"。本句阐述美国人从农业生产中得到的实惠。

[4] would 表示对将来的假设。提出问题：如果没有农业了，我们会怎么样？

31

[5] "without family farmers"为介词短语作状语。"to watch over the system for us","to be our dupes","and to create that pleasant situation through their own great discomfort"为三个并列的不定式作定语，修饰 farmers：为我们看管系统的农民，做我们的傻子的农民，通过他们自己巨大的艰辛为我们创造那样的舒适情形的农民。watch over sth.指"监守","that pleasant situation"指上一句老百姓通过农业得到了便宜的食品，dupes 指"傻子"，这是对美国人偏离了应有的食品生产道德的讽刺：农民付出艰辛的劳动，为我们带来不可或缺的食物，我们却把农民的艰辛视作理所应当。

## 【题目解析】

1. Unlike Passage 2, Passage 1 is primarily concerned with the

(A) ethical implications of food production
(B) harsh working conditions on many farms
(C) need for farmers to form a labor union
(D) plentiful and varied food available in the United States
(E) beliefs of many Americans regarding farm life

【解析】找出第一篇文章与第二篇文章关注点的不同之处。
【答案】B
(A) implication 名词
(1) 含意，暗示 The implication is that +表语从句。题干表示"含义"。(2) 可能的后果
文章1没有提及食品生产的道德含义。
(B) 文章2没提到农场工作环境的艰苦条件，文章1提到了，而且很详细。
harsh adj.
(1) 刺耳的，刺目的，刺鼻的
(2) 残酷的，严厉的 harsh discipline
(3) （现实、事实）残酷的，不愉快的 the harsh realities （文中意思）
(C) 文章1没有提到要组织工会。
(D) 文章1没有提到食物种类的多少。plentiful adj. abundant 大量的，丰产的；丰富的。
varied adj. 各种各样的；各不相同的；形形色色的
available adj. (1) 可利用的；可获得的 sth. is available（选项意思）Is there water available here? 这里有水吗？(2) free 有空（做某事）的
"available in the United States"为定语后置，修饰 food。available 通常后置。
(E) 关于农场生活的观点：文章2提到了美国人对农场生活的误解，文章1只谈了农场环境的艰辛，没有涉及美国人对农场生活的观点。regarding 介词=in respect of; concerning 就……而论，在……方面；关于，至于。
"regarding farm life"为介词短语作后置定语，该用法重要！

2. Both passages serve to discourage the

(A) reliance on polls for accurate information
(B) desire of many farmers to take annual vacations
(C) tendency of Americans to buy inexpensive foods
(D) romanticization of farm life by nonfarmers

(E) rise in price of home-grown produce

【解析】D

discourage (1) vt. 使灰心；使泄气 discourage sb. (2) vt.（通过表示不赞成或创造困难而）阻止 discourage the use of sth. 打消使用什么的想法 (3) vt. 劝阻 discourage sb. from doing sth.

作者不鼓励哪种（观点）？

(A) reliance n. 依靠，依赖 the reliance on sb./sth. 对某人/某物的依赖。两篇文章均未提及为获取准确信息对调查的依赖。

(B) 没有提到。

(C) tend (1) vt. 照料 tend sb. 照顾某人 (2) vi. 往，朝向 (3) vt. 易于；倾向 tendency n. 倾向，趋势 the tendancy of doing sth., 做某事的倾向。

(E) the rise in sth., 名词短语，某方面的上升。

3. The author of Passage 1 would most likely assert which of the following about the "majority" (Passage 2)?

(A) They would be bored by the routine chorers that are performed on a farm.

(B) They have little understanding of the realities of farm life.

(C) They admire the efficiency of the average family farm.

(D) They wish to improve the arduous life of many farmers.

(E) They are impressed by the current research on economical food production.

【解析】B

文章 1 指出农民工作很辛苦，作者 1 认为文章 2 提到的"大多数美国民众"不理解农场生活的艰辛。所以(B) 正确。

(A) 作者在批评美国民众不理解农场生活的艰辛，而非想象如果民众做农活时的态度。所以(A)不是最佳答案。

(C) 文章 2 没有崇拜工作效率之情。

(D) 文章 2 的"大多数人"不理解农民工作的艰辛，并没有希望要农民提高生活质量，相反民众认为农民生活得比从事其他工作的人要好。

(E) 两篇文章均没有提到廉价食品研究。

arduous adj. 艰巨的；艰苦的；费力的；困难的

4. Unlike the author of Passage 2, the author of Passage 1 does which of the following?

(A) Explains a study.

(B) Offers a solution.

(C) Argues a position.

(D) Discusses a phenomenon.

(E) Quotes an authority.

【解析】E

注意题干：文章 2 没提到，文章 1 提到了哪个？

文中引用了权威的讲话。

(C) 争论某个观点，position 指观点。两篇文章都在争辩农场生活很艰辛这一观点。

# 文章 5

The belief that it is harmful to the Black community for authors to explore the humanity of our leaders can have troubling effects.[1] At the least, it promotes the belief that our heroes have to be perfect to be useful.[2] At worst, it censors our full investigation of Black life.[3] If our paintings of that life are stock and cramped, their colors drab and predictable, the representations of our culture are likely to be untrue.[4] They will not capture the breadth and complexity of Black identity.[5]

## 【单词及搭配】

1. censor (1) n.（书刊、电影等的）审查员，审查官；信件检查员 (2) vt. 删剪（书籍、电影等中被认为犯忌、违反道德或政治上危险的内容）（文中意思）
2. stock (1) n. 储备品, 供应物 (2) n.（商店的）现货, 存货 (3) 公债；股份；股票 (4) vt. 储备, 保持……的供应 (5) adj. 通常备有现货的；常备的 (5) adj. 常用的；陈腐的（文中意思）
3. cramp vt. 约束, 限制
4. drab adj. 无生气的, 乏味的, 单调的
5. breadth n. 宽度；宽广的程度, 范围
6. identity n. (1) 身份 (2) 个性, 特性（文中意思） (3) 同一性, 一致性

## 【文章精读】

[1] "that it is harmful to the Black community for authors to explore the humanity of our leaders"为 belief 的同位语；主语 be harmful to A for B to do XXX. B 做某件事对 A 来讲是有害的。B 为 to do sth.的逻辑主语。

【举例】It does harm/is harmful to the plants for farmers to abuse pesticides. 农民滥用杀虫剂对植物是有害的。

本句主语为 belief, 谓语为 can be。

"作家探究我们领袖的人性对黑人社区有害"这一观点可能产生不好的效应。即大部分作者将领袖描绘得非常完美, 而忽略黑人领袖人性的一面, 本文指缺点。

troubling effects, 不好的影响。troubling 为 adj, 令人烦的。

【举例】That the boss had overloaded my schedule troubled me a lot. 老板将我的工作日程安排得过满这件事令我很烦。

overload vt. (1) 使负担太重 overload one's schedule 使某人日程安排过重 (2) 使超载, 使过载

[2]—[3] 指出错误信念的危害, 阻止了我们对黑人生活的全面彻底了解。

至少可以说, 该信念使我们坚信英雄只有非常完美才能有用武之地；该观念最坏的影响是, 它阻碍了我们对黑人生活的全面考察。it 指代[1]中的 belief。to be useful 为结果状

语。不定式可作目的状语和结果状语。

例 1. I work hard to make a living. 我努力工作为的是生存。to make a living 为不定式作目的状语。

例 2. I hurried to the station only to find the train had left. 我匆忙赶到车站，却发现火车已经开走了。to find 为不定式作结果状语，表示结果。

[4] our paintings 指代对黑人生活的描绘。If our paintings of that life are stock and cramped, their colors drab and predictable, the representations of our culture are likely to be untrue. their 指代 paintings'；本句为省略句，原句为：and if their colors are drab and predictable. 如果我们对于生活的描述是陈腐的和被限制的，描述的颜色暗淡且可以推断，则对我们文化的描述可能是不正确的。stock 和 cramped 指对领袖的描述千篇一律，均把领袖描述成完美的。

[5] they 指代对黑人生活的错误描述。本句指出对领导人缺乏人文精神的描述会造成我们不能捕捉黑人身份的复杂性和深度。

## 【题目解析】

1. The passage implies that Black leaders have sometimes been portrayed as being
   (A) overly sentimental
   (B) deeply complex
   (C) above reproach
   (D) without regret
   (E) beyond understanding

【解析】C

文章暗示人们时常将黑人领袖描写成什么样？从原文分析看出，人们忽略了黑人领袖的缺点，认为领袖必须完美。因此选(C)。

above reproach 无可指责；完美；无可厚非；十全十美

reproach (1) v. 责备 (2) n. 批评的话语；带来羞辱的人或事；羞耻，丢脸

beyond reproach 无可指摘；十分完美的，以至于排除了任何受批评的可能性

2. "Paintings" are best understood as a reference to
   (A) realistic sculptures
   (B) historical biographies
   (C) whimsical novels
   (D) political cartoons
   (E) colorful theorems

【解析】从文章分析看出"绘画"指人们对黑人领袖的历史性描述。选(B)。

whimsical adj. 异想天开的，闹着玩的；反复无常的

theorem n.（尤指数学）定理；命题

(A) 具有现实意义的雕塑。首先，雕塑不对。本项为干扰项，取了与"paintings"意思相近的单词 sculptures。但 paintings 在这里是有所指的，不是绘画雕塑，而是 belief, 人们对黑人领袖的看法，而这种看法是片面的。其次，这种看法"censors our full investigation of Black life", "paintings are cramped"，因此 paintings 并非 realistic。

(D) 政治讽刺漫画。不正确。

# 文章 6

The critic Edmund Wilson was not a self-conscious letter writer or one who tried to sustain studied mannerisms.[1] Nor did he resort to artifice or entangle himself in circumlocutions.[2] The young, middle-aged, and old Wilson speaks directly through his letters, which are informal for the most part and which undisguisedly reflect his changing moods.[3] On occasion—in response, perhaps, to the misery of a friend or a public outrage or a personal challenge—he can become eloquent, even passionate, but that is not his prevailing tone.[4]

> 批注 [8]: not self-conscious 和 not sustain studied mannerisms 同义，表明这个人为人处事自然，不做作。

> 批注 [9]: 代词指代人，one 后面可以跟随定语从句。

【单词及搭配】

1. self-conscious adj. 不自然的，忸怩的，害羞的，刻意的

2. studied adj. (1) 有计划的；故意的 a studied smile 硬挤出来的笑容（文中意思） (2) 深思熟虑的；精通的；有知识学问的 a person well studied in geology 在地质方面有丰富知识的人 a studied decision 经精心考虑而作出的决定

3. mannerism n. (1) 习性；言谈举止 (2)（绘画、写作中）过分的独特风格（文中意思）

4. sustain (1) vt. 承受, 支撑 (2) vt. 维持 sustain sb.
On the mere thought of the prospect of losing his job, he felt frightened not capable of sustaining dependants. 一想到他可能会失业，他就很担心不能养活家人。
(3) vt. 长期保持；使继续（文中意思） (4) vt. 经受, 遭受 sustain an injury 受伤

5. resort (1) vi. 求助于或诉诸某事物；采取某手段或方法应急或作为对策 resort to sth.（文中意思） (2) n. 求助，凭借，诉诸 (3) 求助/凭借的对象；采用的办法 (4) 度假胜地 (5) vi. 常去；前往（某处）（常与 to 连用）
in the last resort 最后，在没有其他办法时
In the last resort, we would resort to laws. 在没有任何其他办法的情况下，我们会诉诸法律。

6. artifice n. (1) 诡计；欺骗 (2) 灵巧；巧妙 (3) 虚伪行为（文中意思）

7. entangle vt. 使某人（某物/自己）缠绕, 纠缠于（某物中）；使某人（自己）陷入（困难或复杂的环境中）be entangled in sth. 陷入/卷入某事

8. circumlocution n. 迂回的话语；托词, 推诿的话（文中意思）

9. informal adj. 非正式的

10. for the most part 在极大程度上

11. undisguised adj. 不加掩饰的；坦率的；公开的

12. on occasion 有时，间或

13. outrage (1) n. 义愤, 愤慨（文中意思）(2) n. 暴行 the outrage against sth. 对某物的暴行 (3) vt. 引起……的义愤，激怒

14. passionate adj. (1) 多情的 (2) 表现/充满激情的，激昂的（文中意思）(3) 热切的；

强烈的 be passionate about sth.

## 【文章精读】

[1]-[2] Wilson 不是一个矫揉造作的作家，也不会故意保持矫揉造作的写作风格。one 指代作家，后面跟随定语从句。one 不能换为 she，her 等人称代词。Nor did he 为倒装句，否定词放开头，主谓或系表倒置。

[3] 举例指出 Wilson 在大多数情况下讲话直率。young, middle-aged, and old Wilson 指不同时期的 Wilson——年轻时、中年时、老年时。

[4] 当他时而面对朋友的苦难或公愤或个人的质疑时，他可能变得非常雄辩，甚至慷慨激昂，但这不是他的一贯风格。for the most part 和 on occasion 是相对的。前者指大部分情况下，后者指偶尔。prevailing 为现在分词作形容词，一贯的。in response to sth., 介词短语，回应某事。

## 【题目解析】

1. Based on the information in the passage, Wilson's letters can best be described as

(A) cynical

(B) spontaneous

(C) critical

(D) preachy

(E) witty

【解析】B

从[2]、[3]可看出作者的写作风格很直率。spontaneous adj. (1) 自发的，无意识的 (2) 自然的，天真率直的（选项意思）。

preachy adj. 爱讲道的，爱唠叨的

witty adj. 机智的，言辞巧妙的；情趣横生的

2. The reference to the "young, middle-aged, and old Wilson" serves to suggest the

(A) multifaceted nature of Wilson's literature

(B) maturity Wilson displayed even as a youth

(C) effect aging had on Wilson's temperament

(D) longevity of Wilson's literary career

(E) consistency of Wilson's letter-writing style

【解析】E

很显然，本句指 Wilson 在人生不同年龄阶段的写作风格相近——坦率。[3]与[4]形成了普遍与个例的写作方式的对比。

(A) multifaceted adj. 多方面的；多才多艺的。Wilson 的文学涉及多个层面。文中没有提到这一点。

(B) maturity n. 成熟；成熟期；发育完全。Wilson 在年轻时就表现出来的成熟。文中没有提到这一点，而是讲他写作风格的一致性。display 为 vt，展现。

(C) aging 这里为动名词，变老。年龄增加对 Wilson 性情的影响。aging had on Wilson's temperament 为定语从句，修饰 effect。

aging n. 老化，老龄化，成熟的过程（题干意思）

age v. 使变老

本句换为简单句可表达为：Aging had effect on Wslson's temperament.

【句式】主语 has an effect on sth. 主语对某物有影响。

【名词短语】the effect n1 has on n2  n1对n2的影响力。

(D) Wilson文学事业的长久性。没有这个意思。longevity n. (1) 长寿，长命 (2) n. 长期从事

(E) consistency of sth.，名词短语，某事的一致性。

# 文章 7

## 文章 7.1

Americans should not be taxed to fund the Public Broadcasting Service, and Congress should teminate funding for it.[1] We wouldn't want the federal government to publish a national newspaper.[2] Neither should we have a government television network and a government radio network.[3] If anything should be kept separate from government and politics, it's the news and public-affairs programming that informs Americans about government and its policies.[4] When government brings us the news—with all inevitable bias and spin—the government is putting its thumbs on the scales of democracy.[5] Journalists shold not work for the government.[6] Taxpayers should not be forced to subsidize news and public-affairs programming.[7]

【单词及短语】

1. tax (1) vt. 向……征税（文中意思）(2) vt. 消耗精力；使劳累 sth. taxes sth. 某物使某物劳累。Reading in a poor light taxes the eyes. 在暗淡的光线下看书很累眼睛。(3) n. 税，税额

2. terminate vt. & vi. 结束；使终结

3. policy n. 政策，方针

4. inevitable adj. 不可避免的，必然发生的

5. bias (1) n. 偏见，偏心，偏袒（文中意思）(2) vt. 使倾向于 be biased against sth. 对某物存在偏见

6. spin (1) vt. & vi. 使……旋转 (2) vt. 杜撰 (3) n. 旋转

7. prejudice (1) n. 成见，偏见，歧视 (2) vt. 使有偏见 predudice A against B 使 A 对 B 反感 (2) vt. 不利于，损害

8. scale (1) n. 鱼鳞，鳞片 (2) n. 障眼物 remove scales from the eyes (3) n. 刻度，度数 (4) n. 比例（尺）(5) n. 规模；程度；范围 do sth. on a small scale 小规模做某事 (6) n. 等级；级别 (7) n. 天平，磅秤（文中意思）(8) vt. 刮去……的鳞片

9. subsidize vt. 给……津贴或补贴；资助，补助

【文章精读】

[1] 开篇点题。sb. be taxed to do sth. 某人被征税，税款用于做某事。作者认为美国人不应该被征收税款用于筹建公共广播服务，议会应该停止筹建公共广播服务。it 指代 Public Broadcasting Service。would do sth., 愿意做某事。

[2]—[3] 对照写法：我们不愿意要联邦政府出版国家报纸，同样地，我们也不应让政府参与电视和无线电广播网络。本文主要讨论后者：政府参与电视和无线电广播。Neither 为否定词，否定词在句首，主谓倒装。

[4] 如果某些东西必须从政府和政治中分离出来的话，那么这个东西就是使得美国人了解政府和政策的新闻和公众事务规划。inform sb. of/about sth.，使某人知道某物。it 指代 anything that should be kept separate from government and politics。

[5] 对[4]进行解释：若政府掌控广播服务的话，政府带给公众的是带着不可避免的偏见的新闻，政府在干涉民主的天平。

[6]—[7] 作者得到结论：记者不应为政府工作；纳税人不应被强迫去资助新闻和公众事业项目。

## 文章 7.2

Should the government fund a national public broadcasting system?[1] While many artistically minded people choose to support the appropriation of their tax dollars to PBS, others consider the financial entwining of journalism and the government inappropriate.[2] Some claim that since PBS is no longer the fledgling weakling that it was when it was founded, there is no longer any need for taxpayers to continue to fund it.[3] Arts supporters counter that without government money, PBS will not be able to sustain its financial commitment to the creation of television that deals with nonmainstream, culturally diverse topics and art forms.[4]

批注 [10]: 指代 government

【单词及搭配】

1. entwine vt. 缠绕，盘绕
2. appropriate (1) adj. 适当的，恰当的 (2) vt. 挪用；占用；盗用 (3) vt. 拨出（款项） appropriation n. (1) 拨付，拨发 (2) 占用，挪用
3. inappropriate adj. 不恰当的，不适宜的
4. fledgling (1) n.（刚学会飞的）幼鸟 (2) 名词，无经验的人（文中意思）。还须掌握动词形式：fledge (1) vi.（鸟）长羽毛 (2) vt. 给（箭）装上羽毛 (3) vt. 把（小鸟）养到能够飞翔
5. weakling n. 软弱的人或动物
6. counter (1) n. 柜台，柜台式长桌 (2) n. 计数器 (3) vt. & vi. 对抗，反驳 (4) adv. 反方向地，对立地

【重要句型】A 与 B 相反。
A runs counter to B.
Experiment results are running counter to theoretical analysis.

7. sustain (1) vt. 承受，支撑 (2) vt. 维持 sustain sb. 养活某人 (3) vt. 长期保持；使继续（文中意思）We need money to sustain our company. 我们需要钱来使公司长期保持下去。
(4) vt. 经受，遭受 sustain an injury 受伤
Not able to sustain weight of its seeds, head of the sunflower drooped over against the fence.

8. nonmainstream adj.（思想或行为）非主流的

9. diverse adj. 不同的，多种多样的

10. commitment n. (1) 承诺，许诺，保证 (2) 承担的义务

## 【文章精读】

[1] 开篇提问：政府是否应该为公众广播系统拨款？

[2] artistically minded, 具有艺术意识的, 副词 artistically 修饰过去分词 minded。

the entwining of sth., 某物的缠绕。entwining 在这里为动名词，起名词的作用。the financial entwining of journalism and the government, 新闻业和政府在经济上的相互交织。

指出两种观点：赞成政府拨税款；反对新闻业和政府在经济上有纠缠关系，即反对政府拨款。

be entiwined with sth., 与某物纠缠牵绊。

【重要句型】某物总与某物交织在一起，比如要表达：一个人的成功总是与辛勤的努力交织在一起的、联系在一起的，可以这样讲：

Success of a person is always entwined with prolonged hard work. prolonged, adj. 长期的。

[3] that it was, 定语从句, 修饰 fledgling weakling, 无经验的人或物。此处为过去时，因为是刚刚建立的时候那样的。一些人反对继续为 PBS 投资，因为 PBS 已经成熟起来了。

[4] 某人反对某事：sb. counters sth./宾语从句

that 指代 television。如果没有税收的资助，PBS 将不能负担电视节目创新的经济保证，这些电视节目是非主流内容，涉及文化领域中不同的议题和形式。

## 【题目解析】

1. "We wouldn't…network" makes use of which rhetorical strategy?

(A) Exaggeration

(B) Analogy

(C) Personal anecdote

(D) Historical citation

(E) Figurative language

【解析】B

见文章解析，两句的关系为类比。

anecdote n. 掌故，趣闻，轶事

citation n. (1) 引用, 引证; 引文（选项意思）(2) 表扬, 嘉奖

figurative adj. （用词上）形象的, 比喻的 figurative language 比喻的修辞方式

2. The author of pasage 1 would most likely argue that the "entwining" referred to in passage 2

(A) cannot be justified because it targets certain taxpayers disproportionately

(B) places too much of a burden on the federal government

(C) requires congressional oversight if it is to be done properly

(D) might prove unacceptable to even the most independent minded journalists

(E) interferes with the proper functioning of the American political system
文章1认为新闻业与政府在经济上的纠缠不利于美国政治系统的正常运行。

**【解析】** E

disproportionate adj. 不相称的，不成比例的

(A) it 指代 entwining，target vt. 瞄准某物。对某些纳税人征税太多。文中没讨论纳税多少问题。

(B) place vt. 放置 place sth. on sth.。对政府造成过多负担。没有写对政府造成负担，而是对政治系统的正常运转造成障碍。

(C) oversight n. 疏忽，失察 the oversight on sth.，对某事的失察、忽视

(E) functioning，动名词，美国政治体质的合理运作。function 可以作不及物动词，表示 work。

3. Compared with the tone of passage 2, the tone of passage 1 is more
    (A) balanced
    (B) sincere
    (C) accepting
    (D) emphatic
    (E) ironic

**【解析】** D

emphatic adj. 不容置疑的

4. Which best describes how each passage presents its argument?
    (A) Passage 1 makes a series of points to support a position, while passage 2 presents views that conflict with one another.
    (B) Passage 1 offers multiple examples to illustrate a point, while passage 2 discusses a situation in general terms.
    (C) Passage 1 includes personal anecdotes, while passage 2 relies on factual evidence.
    (D) Passage 1 provides technical explanations, while passage 2 focuses on a familiar hypothesis.
    (E) Passage 1 traces the history of an issue, while passage 2 appeals to common sense to make its points.

**【解析】** A

文章1从若干角度来论证一个观点，文章2并没有给出作者的观点，只是给出其他人的观点，这些人的观点又是不同的，所以选(A)。

position 这里表示观点。conflict with sth.，动词短语，与什么不同。

(B) do sth. in general terms，笼统大致地做了某事。文章2并没有笼统地介绍情况，而是列举出对同一事件的不同人的不同观点。

(E) appeal to sth.，诉诸某事。文章1并没有追溯一个话题的历史，文章2也没有使用常识来指出其观点。实际上，文章2并没有提出作者自己的观点，只是罗列了对同一事件的不同观点而已。

# 文章 8

Through a friend's father, Elizabeth found a job at a publishing company. Her parents were puzzled by this. The daughters of their friends were announcing their engagements in the *Times*, and those who joined the Peace Corps or had gone to graduate school were filed under the heading of "Useful Service," as if they had entered convents or dedicated themselves to the poor. Elizabeth further puzzled her parents by refusing to take a cent of their money, although her mother knew the truth: what you dole out to the young binds them to you. To have Elizabeth owing nothing was disconcerting to say the least.

【单词及搭配】

1. engagement 名词 (1) 订婚 (2) 约定，保证（文中意思）
2. file vt. 把（文件）存档（或归档）
3. dedicate (1) vt. 把（时间、精力、自身）用于，献身 dedicate sth. to doing sth. (2) vt. 把……专用于某课题（或目的）The group of data is dedicated to supporting such an idea that+同位语从句。 (3) vt. 谨以（书或其他艺术品）献给
4. dole out 少量地发放（食物、救济金等）
5. bind
 (1) vt. 紧系，紧拴，固定
 (2) vt. 使亲近，使依恋，使离不开（文中意思） bind sb. to sth./sb.
 (3) vt. 立约保证；明确承诺
6. disconcert vt. 使惊慌失措；使不安
7. to say the least 至少可以说

【题目解析】

1. The narrator mentions the daughters of Elizabeth's parents' friends primarily to
(A) criticize a behavior
(B) praise an activity
(C) explain a reaction
(D) note a transformation
(E) advocate an action

【解析】文章主线：伊丽莎白找到出版社的工作，这令她父母很纳闷。第三句解释了父母为何很不解：伊丽莎白父母的朋友们的女儿与《时代》等杂志社签约，似乎要将自己投身于帮助穷人的事业中。即作者提到父母的朋友是为了解释伊丽莎白的父母为何对女儿去出版社工作感到疑惑，reaction 指代女儿去出版社工作的反应。即 explain a reaction to Elizabeth's engagement with a publishing company。从第三句可以看出出版行业的工作待遇

很差。答案选 C。

2. The passage suggests that Elizabeth's parents found which quality to be "disconcerting" in their daughter?
(A) Magnanimity
(B) Independence
(C) Frugality
(D) Lack of ambition
(E) Unwillingness to take risks

【解析】女儿不接受父母一分钱让父母惶恐不安。即独立。选择 B。

frugal adj. 节俭的，俭省的 lead a remarkably frugal existence 生活非常俭朴
frugality 名词，节约；朴素；节俭

# 文章 9

## 文章 9.1

Ecotourism has been broadly defined as recreational travel that is focused on the natural environment and that seeks to minimize its impact on that environment.[1] However, there is little doubt that increasing numbers of ecotourists also pose a threat to the quality and sustainability of natural ecosystems.[2] Numerous accounts of tourists' "loving nature to death" have been reported, and concern is growing that ecotourism is becoming nothing more than a "green" label that dresses up exploitative and destructive human behavior.[3] Despite widespread advocacy for education as a solution to minimizing ecotoursits' impacts on the natural environment, few tests of the effectiveness of educational programs in controlling tourists' behavior have been conducted.[4]

## 【单词及短语】

1. ecotourism n. 生态旅游
2. recreational adj. 休养的，娱乐的。还须掌握名词：recreation n. 娱乐（方式）；消遣（方式）
3. pose vt. & vi. (1) 摆姿势；以……身份出现 (2) vt. 提出 pose a question (3) vt. 造成（威胁、问题等）；引起；产生=cause; pose a threat to sb./sth. 对某人/某物构成威胁 (4) vt. 伴装；冒充；假扮
4. sustain vt. (1) 承受，支撑 (2) 维持 sustain sb. 维持某人生活 (3) 长期保持；使继续
5. account (1) n. 账，账户 (2) n. 记述，描述，报道（文中意思）the accounts of sth. 对某物的记录或描述 (3) vi. account for sth. 解释，说明 (4) vt. 认为=consider (5) vi.（在数量、比例方面）占；共计达
6. concern n. (1) 忧虑，焦虑，担心（文中意思）(2) vt. 有关于，关系到
7. nothing more than 仅仅
8. label (1) n. 标签，标记 attach label to sth.（文中意思）(2) vt. 贴标签于 (3) vt. 把……列为
9. dress up 打扮，梳理，粉饰
10. exploitative adj. 开发资源的，剥削的
11. advocacy n. 支持，拥护，鼓吹 advocate (1) vt. 提倡，主张 (2) n. 提倡者，拥护者

## 【文章精读】

[1] 对生态旅游的定义：生态旅游被广泛地定义为以自然环境和试图最小化旅游对环境的影响的娱乐性的旅游。that 和 and that 为定语从句，修饰 travel。有两个或两个以上定语从句修饰同一名词时，最后一个定语从句须加 and that 或 or that，前者适用于肯定句，后者用于否定句。

the impact of sth. on sth., 名词短语，某物对某物的影响。

[2] 指出生态旅游对生态系统的潜在危害。人们很少去怀疑越来越多的生态旅游者将对生态系统的可持续性和质量构成威胁。下文必定介绍这种危害。

【重要句型】There is little/no/much doubt/concern that+同位语从句。

[3] 表明人们的担忧：生态旅游只是打着"绿色口号"的标签来装扮具有开采性质和破坏性质的人类活动。这里指出生态旅游可能造成的后果：开采自然资源、破坏自然资源。that 修饰 label，标签。nothing more than，仅仅是，只不过。

[4] 指出解决方法并未得到有效验证。the advocacy for sth. to do/as sth., 倡导某物作为什么。a solution to doing sth., 解决某事的方法。conduct 在这里为及物动词，表示"实施"。

# 文章 9.2

Although a substantial part of tourism is the "sun, surf, and sand" variety, the fastest-growing segment is ecotourism.[1] There is, however, substantial concern about the potential negative impacts of ecotourism on the environment and about the necessity to plan and regulate ecotourism to prevent them.[2] There clearly have been abuses and mismanaged activities.[3] Better planning and regulation are essential.[4] Yet ecotourism brings many people into environments in which they can learn about the locale and learn environmental principles that can heighten their awareness of and commitment to environmental protection in general.[5] Increased emphasis on environmental learning as part of ecotourism could help prevent or reduce ecotoursim's negative impacts.[6]

## 【单词及搭配】

1. substantial adj. (1) 实在的，本质的，重要的 (2) 大体上的，实际上的
a substantial part of 大部分的
还须掌握动词形式：substantiate vt. 用事实支持（某主张、说法等）；证明，证实

2. abuse (1) n. 滥用，妄用，虐待（文中意思）(2) vt. 滥用，妄用

3. mismanage vt. 对……管理不善，对……经营不当

4. locale n. （事件发生的）场所

5. heighten vt. & vi. （使）变高，（使）增大；（使）提高

6. commitment n. (1) 承诺，许诺，保证 (2) 承担的义务（文中意思）the commitment to sth./sb.

commit vt. (1) 犯罪 (2) 承诺；使自己受约束 (3) 托付；交付

7. potential (1) adj. 潜在的，有可能的（文中意思）(2) n. 潜力，潜势，可能性

## 【文章精读】

本文意思：虽然生态旅游存在着监管不力等问题，但其对环境保护有积极作用。

[1] 旅游的大部分含义就是沙滩、阳光、海浪，但发展最迅速的部分是生态旅游。

[2] 指出人类对生态旅游对环境可能造成的威胁的担忧。本句为省略句，完整句式为：concern about impacts and concern about the necessity。to plan and regulate 为不定式作定语，修饰 necessity，做某事的必要性。to prevent them 为不定式作目的状语。them 指代 negative impacts。

[3]—[4] 承认生态旅游过程中存在着滥用和监管不力的活动。因此，更好地计划和监管是必要的。

[5] 指出生态旅游的好处。which 指代 environments，that can heighten 为定语从句，修饰 principles。awareness of sth.，对某事的意识，名词短语；commitment to sth.，对某事的责任。

[6] 作为生态旅游的一部分，不断加强的对环境保护的学习可以帮助阻止或降低生态旅游的负面效应。

## 【题目解析】

1. The authors of both passages would most likely agree that ecotourism

(A) is most popular in sunny coastal environments

(B) may harm the environment it claims to value

(C) may soon be more common than other types of tourism

(D) serves to educate the public about environmental issues

(E) should be tightly regulated in order to minimize its impact

【解析】B

两篇文章作者都认为生态旅游对环境有负面影响。

(B) it 指代生态旅游。

claim (1) vt. 声称，断言（文中意思）

Experts in economics claimed that daily budgets consumed per person for city-dwellers would probably increase dramatically.

claim to do sth. 宣称做某事

(2) vt.（灾难等）使失踪或死亡 The accident claimed hundreds of lives. 这场事故夺走了数百人的生命。

(3) vt. 需要，值得 There are several matters that claim my attention. 有几件事值得我注意。

(4) vt. & vi. 对……提出要求，索取

(5) n. 主张，断言 the claim to do sth. 对某事的主张

value 在这里为及物动词。生态旅游将破坏它宣称所珍视的环境。it claims to value 为定语从句，修饰 environment。本句可拆分为：

(1) Ecotourism may harm the environment.

(2) Ecotourism claims to value the environment.

【举一反三】I will review the project I originally refused to undertake. 我将重新审视我曾

经拒绝接手的工程。

value (1) n. 价值，价格 (2) n. 实用性，有价值，重要性 (3) vt. 估价 (4) vt. 重视，尊重（选项意思）

(A) 两篇文章没有提到。

(C) 第二篇文章首句提出该观点，第一篇没有提及。

(D) 文章 1 对此观点否定，认为不能证明环保方面的教育有效果。

(E) 文章 2 同意此观点。文章 1 没有提及。

2. Unlike passage 2, passage 1 primarily emphasizes ecotourism's

(A) economic consequences

(B) educational value

(C) increasing popularity

(D) uncertain origins

(E) damaging effects

【答案】E

(A) 两篇文章均未涉及。

(B) 两篇文章都提到。但是文章 1 对教育的功能持怀疑态度；文章 2 持肯定态度。

(C) 两篇文章均提及。越来越流行。increasing 为形容词，popularity 为名词。

(D) 不确定的起因。两篇文章均未提及。

(E) 具有毁灭性的效果。damaging 为现在分词作定语，修饰 effects，因为这种效果是主动毁灭的，用现在分词。文章 1 认为生态旅游破坏环境，文章 2 认为虽然生态旅游对环境有负面效应，但可以通过教育来改善这种局面。因此，文章 2 并没有强调生态旅游的破坏性作用，其对生态旅游总体上是积极的、肯定的。

3. The author of passage 2 would most likely characterize the tourists who love "nature to death" as

(A) evidence of the need for further environmental education

(B) proof that ecotourism should be banned within fragile ecosystems

(C) concerned about the impact of their actions

(D) unaware of the regulations governing ecotourism

(E) insincere in their interest in the environment

【答案】A

【解析】characterize vt. (1) 是……的特征，以……为特征 A is characterized with B. A 以 B 为特征。(2) 描述（人或物）的特性，描绘（题干意思）

(A) 文章 2 认为教育可以有效地改善生态旅游对环境的负面影响。

(B) 与文章 2 意思相反。文章 2 肯定生态旅游，认为通过教育可以改善对环境的负面影响。that 至结尾为 proof 的同位语。

ban (1) vt. 取缔，查封（选项意思）(2) n. 禁止，禁令 impose a ban on sb./sth. 对某人/某物实施禁令。

fragile adj. (1) 易碎的，脆的 (2) 虚弱的，脆弱的；经不起折腾的（选项意思）

(C) 没有这个意思。

(D) governing 为现在分词短语作定语，修饰 regulations。

(E) insincere adj. 不诚恳的

4. "conducted" most nearly means

(A) performed

(B) channeled

(C) transmitted

(D) escorted

(E) directed

【答案】A

【解析】做实验，perform the experiment＝conduct the experiment

channel (1) n. 水道，航道 (2) n. 海峡 (3) n. 途径；渠道 (4) vt. 输送，传送

escort (1) n. 护送者，护卫队 (2) vt. 护送；护卫

5. Which statement best characterizes the relationship between the two passages?

(A) Passage 2 provides a historical perspective on a situation that passage 1 portrays as a recent problem.

(B) Passage 2 takes a positive stance on an issue that passage 1 presents somewhat pessimistically.

(C) Passage 2 provides personal experience with a phenomenon passage 1 considers theoretically.

(D) Passage 2 suggests an innovative solution to a puzzle outlined in passage 1.

(E) Passage 2 provides evidence that counters a criticism raised in passage 1.

【解析】B

【解析】文章 1 否定生态旅游，文章 2 承认生态旅游的问题，但对生态旅游的意义予以了肯定。

(A) a historical perspective，历史角度。文章 1 没有从历史角度讨论问题。

(B) that 引导定语从句，修饰 issue。present 这里为动词，展现。文章 2 对文章 1 提出的观点采取了积极的态度，而文章 1 对该议题多少有些悲观。

stance (1) n.（运动员的）始发姿势 (2) n. 看法，立场，观点 the stance on sth.

(D) outlined 为过去分词短语作定语，修饰 puzzle。文章 2 为文章 1 所提到的难题提出了创新性的解决方法。innovative 不恰当，教育的解决方法在文章 1 也提到过，并非创新。

(E) 文章 2 提出了证据，该证据在文章 1 中遭到批评。文章 2 没有提出证据。raised in passage 1 为过去分词短语作定语。

raise (1) vt. 提起；举起；竖起 raise a method/problem/praise/criticism 提出方法/问题/表扬/批评

(2) vt. 增加；提升 raise the output 提高产量，动词短语；raise one's objection 提出反对意见

(3) vt. 集资 rasie money

outline (1) n. 提纲，要点，概要 (2) n. 外形，轮廓，略图 (3) vt. 画[标]出……的轮廓 (4) vt. 概述，列提纲

# 文章 10

At a preconcert interview in 2000 for the performance of one of her works in London, Rhian Samuel was asked about her well-known reluctance to be considered a Welsh composer.[1] Her reply—"I'm not so happy to be called only a Welsh composer because I haven't lived in Wales all my life and have another influences as well.[2] On the other hand, I [have] been a woman all my life!" —brought both laughter and applause from the expectant crowd of concertgoers.[3] In short, Samuel is proud to be considered first a woman composer, one whose connection to the Welsh language and people resurfaces at interludes throughout her musical life.[4]

## 【文章精读】

[1] 有人问起 Rhian Samuel 关于她本人不愿被称为威尔士作曲家的事情。the reluctance to do sth., 对某事的不情愿，名词短语，to do sth.为不定式作定语，修饰 reluctance。下文将解释这种不情愿的原因。

[2]-[3] 破折号后面为原因——她并没有永久性居住在威尔士，并且她的艺术还有其他影响因素。本句解释了不愿被称作威尔士作曲家的第一个原因。第二个原因——她是女性。即她认为女性作曲家的定性比起国籍来更重要。brought 为谓语动词。满怀期待的观众为她的回答送去了笑声和掌声。expectant adj. 期待的，期望的。

[4] 总结，她很自豪首先自己是一位女性作曲家，她与威尔士语言以及人民的联系在她一生的音乐生涯中时隐时现。即，女性艺术家是她最看重的，其次才是她与威尔士的联系，而这种联系不是永久性的，这点与[2]对应——并非终生居住在威尔士。whose 指代 the woman composer's。

resurface (1) vt. 给（路等）铺设新路面 (2) vi. 重新升至表面，重新露面（文中意思）
Serious concerns about the welfare of animals eventually resurfaced. 终于又出现了对动物生存状况的真切关注。
interlude n. (1) （戏剧、电影等的）中间休息，幕间休息 (2) 某事过程中发生的事件或片段  at interludes 时常

文章结构：提出现象，解释原因，总结。本文阐述了一位艺术家对自身的认知。

## 【题目解析】

1. The primary purpose of the passage is to
(A) discuss a composer's musical training
(B) clarify a musician's self-perception
(C) describe an artist's linguistic talents
(D) reveal the preferences of a particular audience

(E) reconcile two antithetical views of a performance

【解析】B

本文主旨为阐述音乐家的自我认知——首先是女性艺术家，其次是与威尔士的联系。

(A) 本文没提到音乐训练。

(B) 阐述了音乐家的自我认识。从[2]-[3]可以看出，本文的主要例证是引用。

(C) 没有提到语言天赋。

(D) particular, adj. 特定的。虽然提到了观众，但这不是文章主旨。

(E) reconcile vt. (1) 使和好；和解 (2) 使一致，使和谐（文中意思）。antithetical adj. 正相反的；对立的。views 指"观点"。使两种对立的观点一致。没有提到演出（performance），也没有使两种不同观点一致。

2. Her "reply" suggests chiefly that Samuel believes which of the following?

(A) Her nationality is not the most important aspect of her identity.

(B) She could not have become a successful composer if she had remained in Wales for her whole life.

(C) One of the obligations of a musician is to relate a humorous anecdote before each performance.

(D) Other people should not refer to themselves as Welsh unless they have always lived in Wales.

(E) Men should acknowledge the importance of their gender as an artistic influence just as women do.

【解析】A

(A) 见文章分析——她认为国籍不是最重要的，她最自豪的是身为女性艺术家。所以(A) 正确。

(B) 她没有这个意思，只是交代自己没有一生都住在威尔士。这是自我陈述。

(C) 文中没有提到。

(D) 她只是针对自己，没有评价别人，因此 other people 不对。refer to sb. as sth., 将某人提及为什么。其他人不应将自己称作威尔士人，除非他们永久住在那里。

(E) 男人应像女性一样认可性别在艺术影响中的重要性。本文没讨论性别影响艺术，而是讲主人公以自己是女性艺术家为豪。

# 文章 11

My daughter, Olivia, and I were going to college. Not together at the same school, thank goodness, just at the same time, but she didn't exactly know about my plans yet. There were a few things that needed work in this arrangement. Any mother who has an eighteen-year-old daughter would completely understand why I didn't mention my decision to go to college to Olivia. *What? I can't believe it. Are you actually copying me? Don't you think you should consider getting your own life?* It wasn't that I planned never to tell her. I just figured I'd wait a bit—until we'd had a little time to miss each other.

【文章精读】

作者和作者的女儿将要在同一时间去不同的学校学习，但女儿还不知她的计划。作出这一计划需要做很多工作。任何一个有 18 岁女儿的母亲都会明白我为何不告诉女儿我要去学校学习的决定。

mention sth. to sb., 向某人提及某事。斜体字是女儿看到作者的决定后的反应：什么？我简直不能相信！你（指作者）是不是在模仿我（指女儿）啊？难道不认为你（指作者）应该有自己的（作者的）生活嘛？"Any mother who has an eighteen-year-old daughter would completely understand why I didn't mention my decision to go to college to Olivia. *What? I can't believe it. Are you actually copying me? Don't you think you should consider getting your own life?*" 即有女儿的母亲都会和作者有同样的做法——不告诉女儿自己的决定。

【题目解析】

1. The narrator's attitude toward her situation is best described as

   (A) perplexed
   (B) prudent
   (C) sentimental
   (D) annoyed
   (E) derisive

【解析】B

从 "It wasn't that I planned never to tell her. I just figured I'd wait a bit—until we'd had a little time to miss each other."看出作者打算在特定时间告诉女儿自己的计划，因此态度是很谨慎的。sentimental 多愁善感的。derisive adj. 嘲笑的，嘲弄的。

2. The narrator uses the questions "*What? I can't believe it. Are you actually copying me? Don't you think you should consider getting your own life?*" primarily to

   (A) voice some pressing concerns

(B) admit to some personal qualms
(C) characterize a likely response
(D) highlight an unpleasant memory
(E) begin a discussion

【解析】C

描述了一种可能的回应，指女儿的回应。见原文解析。characterize vt. (1) 是……的特征，以……为特征 (2) 描述（人或物的）特性，描绘（选项意思）。

# 文章 12

My first commissioned work was to write letters for her.[1] "You write for me, honey?" she would say, holding out a ballpoint she had been given at a grocery store promotion, clicking it like a castanet.[2] My fee was cookies and milk, payable before, during, and after completion of the project.[3]

## 【单词及搭配】

1. commissioned work 受委托的作品

commission (1) n. 授权，委托 the commission for sth. 对某事的委托 (2) 委员会 (3) n. 佣金，回扣 the commission on sth. 因某事所获得的佣金/回扣

He gained a substantial of commission on his contributions to the project. 他因为对工程的贡献获得了可观的佣金。

(4) vt. 委任，委托 commission sb. to do sth. 委托某人做某事

2. promotion n. (1) 提升，晋级 (2) 宣传；推销

promote vt. (1) 提升，提拔 (2) 筹划，发起，创立 promote a match 筹划一场比赛 (3) 推销 promote a commodity (4) 促进；推动；增进

3. click (1) n. 卡嗒声，咔嚓声 (2) vt. 使发出咔哒声（文中意思）(3) vi. 茅塞顿开

4. castanet n.（用硬木或象牙制成的）响板

5. fee n. 费，酬金

6. payable adj. 应付的，可付的

7. completion n. 完成，结束

## 【文章精读】

[1] 我的第一份工作就是为她（有偿）写信。

[2] holding out 为现在分词短语作伴随状语，逻辑主语与 she 一致。祖母问："亲爱的，为我写信好吗？" she had been given 为定语从句，修饰 ballpoint，促销时给她的笔。

She had been given a ballpoint at a store promotion.

[3] 指出写信是有偿的，佣金就是在写信之前、写信过程中或写信结束后给我饼干和牛奶。payable 为形容词作定语，修饰 cookies 和 milk。during 后省略了 completion of the project。project=commissioned work。

I settled down at her kitchen table while she rooted around the drawer where she kept coupons and playing cards and pieces of stationery.[1] The paper was so insubstantial even ballpoint ink seeped through the other side.[2] "That's OK," she would say. "We only need one side."[3]

## 【单词及搭配】

1. root (1) n. 根，根部 (2) n. 根源，根基，根本，基础 the root of sth. 某物的根本 (3) vt.使（某人）站立不动（文中意思）(4) vt. 使（某事物）深深扎根；牢固地树立（某事物） be rooted in sth. 扎根在……

2. coupon n. 礼券，优惠券

3. insubstantial adj. (1) 无实体的，无实质的 (2) 脆弱的（文中意思）

substantial adj. (1) 坚固的；结实的 (2) 大量的，可观的 (3) 重大的，重要的 (4) 实质的，基本的，大体上的

4. seep vi. (1)（液体）渗，渗透 seep away（文中意思）(2) vi. 渗出；漏出 My anger began to seep away. 我的怒火开始消下去了。

5. favour (1) n. 喜爱，宠爱；好感；赞同 (2) n. 善行，恩惠 (3) vt. 喜爱，偏爱 (4) vt. 赞同 (5) vt. 有利于，便于 A favours B. A 对 B 有好处。

## 【文章精读】

[1] 我在厨房写信，她站在抽屉旁。纸太薄了，笔迹透到了另一面。本段描述写信的场景。

[2] 信纸太薄了，圆珠笔的油墨渗到了纸张的另一面。

True. In life she was a gifted gossip, unfurling an extended riff of chatter from a bare motif of rumor.[1] But her writing style displayed a brevity that made Hemingway's prose look like nattering garrulity.[2] She dictated her letters as if she were paying by the word.[3]

## 【单词及搭配】

1. unfurl vt. & vi. 展开，张开，铺开（某物）

2. riff n. 即兴重复段

3. chatter (1) vi. 喋喋不休；唠叨 (2) vi.（牙齿）打战；（机器）震颤 (3) n. 喋喋不休，唠叨（文中意思）

4. motif n. (1)（文艺作品等的）主题, 中心思想；基本模式（文中意思）(2) 基本图案,基本色彩

5. rumor (1) 传闻，风闻；谣言，谣传 (2) 咕哝, 喃喃低语

6. brevity n. (1) 短暂 (2) 简洁

7. prose n. 散文

8. natter vi. 唠叨, 瞎扯

9. garrulous adj. 饶舌的, 多嘴的, 话多的；喜欢讲话的 a garrulous speech. 一个冗长絮叨的讲演 garrulity n. 饶舌

(1) 厌倦了这个冗长讲话，我睡着了。Tired of the garrulous speech, I fell asleep.

(2) 独立主格：The speech garrulous, I fell asleep.

redundant adj. (1) 因人员过剩而被解雇的 (2) 不需要的；多余的

10. gifted adj. 有天赋的，有才华的   gift n. (1) 礼物，赠品 (2) 天赋，天才 have the gift to do sth. 具备某事的天赋

11. gossip (1) n. 流言，闲话 (2) n. 爱拨弄是非的人（文中意思）(3) n. 闲谈，聊天 (4) vi. 传播流言，说长道短

She can spend a whole day gossiping with her neighbours. 她能一整天都跟邻居们说长道短。

12. display (1) n. 陈列，展览 on display 在展览中 (2) vt. 陈列，展览 (3) vt. 显示，显露（文中意思）

He displayed an originality amounting almost to genius. 他显示出近乎天才的创造性。

13. dictate vt. 阐述

## 【文章精读】

[1] unfurling 为现在分词短语作伴随状语，与句子主语 she 一致。unfurl an extended riff of chatter 字面意思为"展开一段被延展的唠叨"；from a bare motif of rumor, bare 表示"仅仅"；她仅仅从一段谣言就能展开一段絮絮叨叨的唠叨。即她很能说。gifted 为形容词，有天赋的。本句表明她很能说。

【举一反三——短语】

He unfurled the research from barely a subtle experiment. 他仅仅从一个微小的实验出发，拓展出了一项科研活动。

【举一反三——分词作伴随状语】

(1) The programme has been initiated at the beginning of this year, enabling teachers to understand the students better. 项目于今年年初启动，该项目可以帮助老师更好地理解学生。

(2) Tuition is much too high, posing a drain on all savings of parents. 学费太贵了，花光了父母的所有积蓄。

(3) The commodity/item has been elaborately conceived, outdoing other items in a variety of aspects. 这款产品经过了精心的设计，在很多方面优于其他产品。

[2] 从写信角度进行转折：写信时却非常简洁。brevity 为名词，that made 为定语从句，修饰 brevity。她的写作风格简洁，这种简洁使得海明威的作品看起来很罗嗦。本句为讽刺的修辞方式，表明作者的祖母写信没有文采，内容枯燥乏味。

[3] by the word 这里不是被动语态，所以 pay 用**主动**！意思是"通过文字来偿付别人"。pay by sth., 通过某种方式付款。

"Dear Sister," she began, followed by a little time-buying cough and throat clearing.[1] "We are all well here." Pause. "And hope you are well too." Longer pause, the steamy broth of inspiration heating up on her side of the table. Then, in a lurch, "Winter is hard so I don't get out much."

## 【单词及搭配】

1. steamy adj. 蒸汽的，充满水汽的
2. broth n. 肉汤，鱼汤，菜汤
3. inspiration n. (1) 灵感（文中意思）(2) 鼓舞人心的人。还须掌握动词形式：inspire vt. (1) 鼓舞 (2) 赋予某人灵感；启迪
4. lurch (1) vi. 蹒跚而行，颠簸着行进 (2) n. 突然倾斜（文中意思）

【文章精读】

　　inspiration 为名词，灵感，她的灵感来了，但是只有一句话：这里的冬天太冷了。本段表明写信人惜字如金，对应上一段的"写信简洁"。the steamy broth of inspiration 为比喻的修辞方法，灵感之汤。

　　This was followed instantly by an unconquerable fit of envy: "Not like you in California."[1] Then she came to a complete halt, perhaps demoralized by this evidence that you can't put much on paper before you betray your secret self, try as you will to keep things civil.[2]

【单词及搭配】

　　1. fit (1) vt. & vi.（使）适合 (2) vt. 安装，配备 (3) adj. 合适的，适宜的 fit+n. 符合条件的某物 (4) n. 突然爆发 a fit of sth. 某事的突然爆发（文中意思）
　　2. demoralize vt. 使士气低落，使意志消沉
　　3. betray vt. (1) 对……不忠，背叛 (2) 泄露，暴露，表明（文中意思）
　　4. civil adj. 公民的，平民的；非军职的，非宗教的；国民间的，民用的，有礼貌的（文中意思）
　　5. unconquerable adj. 不可征服的，克服不了的，压制不了的。还须掌握动词形式：conquer vt. (1) 攻克，征服 (2) 破除，克服 conquer one's dislike for sth. 克服对某事的厌恶
　　6. halt (1) n. 停住，停止，暂停（文中意思）a halt to sth./doing sth. 某事的停止 (2) vt. & vi.（使）停下来

【文章精读】

　　[1] 写信人略带嫉妒：不像你在加州，天气那么好。
　　[2] demoralized 为过去分词短语作伴随状语，逻辑主语为 she。她停顿了一下，似乎因为一个事实而泄气了：一个人在揭示自己的秘密之前，不能在信中透露过多的内容。本句为她惜墨如金找借口。

　　She sat, she brooded, she stared out the window.[1] She was locked in the perverse reticence of composition.[2] She gazed at me, but I understood she did not see me.[3] She was looking for her next thought.[4] "Read what I wrote," she would finally say, having lost not only what she was looking for but what she already had pinned down.[5] I went over the little trail of sentences that led to her dead end.[6]

【单词及搭配】

　　1. brood vt. & vi. (1) 孵蛋 (2) 沉思（文中意思）
　　2. perverse adj. (1) 任性的，固执的（文中意思） (2) 错误的，荒谬的
　　3. reticence n. 不轻易暴露想法或感情；沉默，缄默。须掌握形容词形式：reticent adj. 不轻易暴露思想或感情的；有保留的 be reticent of sth. 对某物不轻易暴露的
　　4. pin down 动词短语 (1) 把……固定住；使动弹不得 (2) 迫使作出决定，采取行动

（文中意思）

【文章精读】

[1]-[2] 她坐着，沉思着，朝窗外凝视。她沉浸在固执的沉默中，构思信的内容。

[3] 作者明白她并没有看自己，而是在构思信件内容。

[4] 她在想下一句信应该写什么。the next thought，下面的想法，即下一句应该写什么。

[5] having lost 为现在分词短语作伴随状语，其逻辑主语为 she。她不仅忘记了她原本在寻找什么，同时也忘记了她已经决定做的事情，所以她只好命我再读一遍信。lost 后面加宾语，其成分必须是名词、动名词或名词性从句。what she was looking for 和 what she already had pinned down 均为名词性从句。what 不能换为 that，因为从句缺宾语。not only…but also…联接两个结构相同的成分，以使句子简洁。

[6] 作者读信，信的内容很简短。dead end 为名词短语，意为"结尾"。

More silence, then a sigh. "Put 'God bless you,'" she said. She reached across to see the lean rectangle of words on the paper. "Now leave some space," she said, "and put 'Love.'" I handed over the paper for her to sign.

【单词及搭配】

1. lean (1) vt. & vi.（使）倾斜，屈身 (2) vt. 倚，靠；依赖 (3) adj. 瘦的；少脂肪的 (4) adj. 贫瘠的；收益差的 lean times 萧条时期（文中意思）(5) adj. 精干的；效率高的 (6) adj. 简洁的；尖锐的；犀利的；直率的

【文章精读】

一阵沉默后，她要求我在结尾写上"上帝保佑你"。本段表明还没有写太多的内容，信就结束了。lean 这里表示"贫瘠的"、"内容不多的"。

She always asked if her signature looked nice.[1] She wrote her one word—Teresa—with a flourish.[2] For her, writing was painting, a visual art, not declarative but sensuous.[3]

【单词及搭配】

1. flourish (1) vi. 茂盛 (2) vi. 兴旺发达 (3) vt. 挥动 (4) n.（为引起注意的）夸张动作 (5) n.（讲话或文章的）华丽辞藻，修饰 (6) n. 艺术字

2. declarative adj. 宣言的，公布的

3. sensuous adj. 刺激感官的；感觉官能的，给感官以快感的 sensuous music 悦耳的音乐

【文章精读】

她总问我她的签名是否漂亮。她用艺术体字来写。对于她来讲，写字就是绘画，是一种视觉艺术，不是用来读的，而是用于给人愉悦视觉感的。not…but：不是……而是……，前后连接两个相似的成分。[3]为第 10 题出处。

She sent her lean documents regularly to her only remaining sister who lived in Los Angeles, a place she had not visited.[1] They had last seen each other as children in their village in Bohemia.[2] But she never mentioned that or anything from that world.[3] There was no taint of reminiscence in her prose.[4]

**【单词及搭配】**

1. reminiscence n. 旧事，回忆
2. taint n. (1) 变质；污染 (2) 玷污，污点 (3) 丑陋或腐败的迹象 (4) vt. 使变质；使污染 (4) vt. 败坏；玷污；损害（某人的）名誉 taint someone's reputation 玷污某人的名誉

**【文章精读】**

[1] 祖母和祖母的妹妹定期通信。
[2] last 为副词，这里指上一次。她们最近一次见面是几十年前小时候。
[3] that world 指祖母儿时生活的世界。
[4] no taint of sth., 没有某物的痕迹。本句表明祖母在信中从不提儿时的事情。

Even at ten I was appalled by the minimalism of these letters. They enraged me. "Is that all you have to say?" I would ask her, a nasty edge to my voice.

> 批注 [16]: 名词，指言语激烈
> 批注 [17]: 第5题出处

**【单词及搭配】**

1. nasty adj. (1) 令人讨厌的 (2) 恶意的；恶毒的 (3) 卑鄙的 (3) 严重的；危险的；造成痛苦的
2. enrage vt. 使暴怒
3. edge (1) n. 边，棱；边缘 (2) n. 刃，刀口 (3) n. 优势；优越条件 hold the edge in sth. 在某方面占有优势 (4) n.（言语等）激烈 an edge to sth. 对某物言语激烈（文中意思）The coverage posed an edge to the event. 新闻报道对该事件言辞激烈。
(5) vt. 使锋利；将（刀）开刃 (6) vt. 给……加上边[(+with)]
The main streets were edged on both sides with grass. 主要街道两边都种上了草。
(7) vt. 使渐进；徐徐地移动；挤掉 She edged her chair nearer to the fireplace. 她把椅子移近壁炉。
(8) vi. 徐徐移动；侧着移动 He edged to the front of the crowd. 他侧身挤到了人群前头。
4. minimalism n. 最低纲领，极保守行动

**【文章精读】**

我为这些信的过于简化感到愤怒。难道这些就是你要说的全部吗？我质问祖母，言辞激烈。

It wasn't long before I began padding the text.[1] Without telling her, I added an anecdote my father had told at dinner the night before, or I conducted this unknown reader through the heavy plot of my brother's attempt to make first string on the St. Thomas hockey team.[2] I allowed myself a descriptive aria on the beauty of Minnesota winters (for the benefit of my

California reader who might need some background material on the subject of ice hockey).[3] A little of this, a little of that—there was always something I could toss into my grandmother's meager soup to thicken it up.[4]

【单词及搭配】

1. pad (1) vt. 给……装衬垫, 加垫子 (2) vi. 步行, 放轻脚步走 (3) n. 垫, 护垫 (4) n. 便笺本, 拍纸簿 (5) vt. 增添（文中意思）

2. meager adj. (1) 瘦的 (2) 粗劣的; 不足的; 贫乏的（文中意思）meager cultural resources 贫乏的文化资源 meager salary 微薄的工资

【文章精读】

[1] 很快, 我在信中增添了内容。pad 在这里为 vt, 意思为 "增添内容"。pad the article, 动词短语, 使文章内容充实。

[2]-[3] "my father had told at dinner the night before" 为定语从句, 修饰 ancedote。add 在这里与 pad 等价: 增添内容。unkonwn reader 指代祖母的妹妹。conduct 这里表示 "指引", 动词。这两句写出作者如何在信中添加内容。这样做的目的是为了祖母的妹妹好, 她可能需要一些冰球方面的背景知识。for the benefit of, 为了……的利益。

[4] it 指代 soup, 比喻祖母的信。即: 我总是可以向祖母的信增添内容, 使其不乏味。I could toss 为定语从句, 修饰 something。meager 为形容词, 意思为 "贫乏的", 即祖母的信内容匮乏。to thicken it up 为不定式作目的状语——在祖母的信中添油加醋, 目的是使信的内容充实起来。

Of course, the protagonist of the hockey tale was not "my mother". He was "my grandson." I departed from my own life without a regret and breezily inhabited my grandmother's. I complained about my tip joint, I bemoaned the rising cost of hamburger, and hinted at the inattention of my son's wife (that is, my own mother, who was next door, oblivious to treachery).

In time, my grandmother gave in to the inevitable. Without ever discussing it, we understood that when she came looking for me, clicking her ballpoint, I was to write the letter, and her job was to keep the cookies coming. I abandoned her skimpy floral stationery which badly cramped my style, and thumped down on the table a stack of rules 81/2 x11.

I took over her life in prose. Somewhere along the line, though, she decided to take full possession of her sign-off. She asked me to show her how to write "love" so she could add it to "Teresa" in her own hand. She practiced the new word many times on scratch paper before she allowed herself to commit it to the bottom of a letter.

But when she finally took the leap, I realized I had forgotten to tell her about the comma. On a single slanting line she had written: Love Teresa. The words didn't look like a closure, but a command.

【单词及搭配】

1. protagonist n. (1)（戏剧的）主角 (2)（故事的）主人公; 现实事件（尤指冲突和争

60

端的）主要参与者，主要人物（文中意思） (3) 领导者；倡导者；拥护者 protagonist of sth. 某事的倡导者

2. hockey n. 曲棍球

3. depart from 动词短语 (1) 离开 (2) 背离，违背

4. hip joint 上弦与斜端杆结点；（锅炉）多斜面联接；髋关节

5. breezy adj. (1) 有微风的，微风吹过的 (2) 活泼的，轻松愉快的

6. inhabit vt. 居住于，栖居于

7. bemoan (1) vt. 为（某人或某事）抱怨，不满于（文中意思） (2) vt. 悲悼；为……恸哭 (3) vi. 悲悼；叹息

8. oblivious adj. 未察觉的；不注意的；忘记的 be oblivious of/to sth. 对某事没有察觉

9. treachery n. 背信弃义，不忠，背叛；欺诈

10. cramp (1) n.（肌肉）痉挛，抽筋 (2) vt. 约束，限制（文中意思）

11. floral adj. (1) 用花做的 (2) 用花装饰的

12. skimpy adj. (1)（衣服）小而暴露的 (2) <贬>（数量或大小）不足的，不够的（文中意思）

13. stationery n. (1) 文具 (2) 信纸（文中意思）

14. scratch (1) vt. & vi. 抓，搔 (2) vt. 刮伤 (3) vt. 勾掉，删掉

**【文章精读】**

I departed from my own life without a regret and breezily inhabited my grandmother's 为比喻，省略了 my grandmoth's life。我毫无悔恨地偏离了自己的生活，快乐地驻扎在了祖母的生活中。即，作者以祖母的身份阐述自己的生活，进行编造。本句表明作者如何编造信件内容。

in time 在文中表示"最终"，相当于 eventually。the inevitable 为名词短语，不可避免的事。ever 表示"曾经"。come doing sth., 过来做某事，looking 和 clicking 并列。I was to write，我即将为她写信，be to do 表示将要做某事，因为这件事发生在作者小时候，因此用过去时。

be off to the race，动词短语，兴奋热情地开始做某事。

I took over her life in prose，我接管了她在信中的生活，即作者写信编造祖母的生活。祖母打算全职于签名。她练习很多遍之后才会在信纸底端写下自己的名字。it 指代 new word。本段指出作者编造信的内容，祖母仅负责签字。

leap (1) vi. 跳，跳跃 (2) vi. 猛然行动，冲 Look before you leap. 三思而后行。(3) vt. 跳过，跃过 (4) n. 跳跃，飞跃（文中意思）(5) n. 激增

slanting adj. 倾斜的；歪斜的

slant (1) vt. & vi.（使）倾斜；歪斜 (2) vt. 有倾向性地编写或报道

The journalist slanted the report so that the mayor was made to appear incompetent. 那位记者做出歪曲报道好让市长显得无能。

(3) n. 斜面，斜线 (4) n. 倾向，偏向，侧重

祖母写信时进行了一个跳跃，她签名时没加逗号，即进行了文字上的跳跃。这样一来，末尾就形成了：你要爱 Teresa。这不是一个信的结尾，而是一个命令。not...but：不是……而是……。正确写法是：Love, Teresa. 爱你的 Teresa。leap 这里作名词，即跳过了逗号。

## 【题目解析】

1. In the opening paragraph, the author characterizes writing letters for her grandmother as a
(A) privilege
(B) favor
(C) business transaction
(D) dreaded responsibility
(E) punishment

【解析】C

characterize sth. as+名词、形容词、分词，把某物描绘成什么样子。

作者将这份写信的工作描述为有偿报酬，所以选(C)。

transaction n. (1) 处理，办理，执行 (2)（一笔）交易（选项意思） (3)（一项）事务

Cooking is an important transaction for most people. 做饭对大多数人来讲都是件重要的事。（作文中表示一件事时不要用 thing，而用 transaction。）还须掌握动词形式：

transact vt. (1) 办理（业务等）(2) v. 交易；谈判

(A) privilege n. 特权，特别待遇；（因财富和社会地位而仅有部分人享有的）权益；特殊荣幸

(B) favor (1) n. 喜爱，赞同 win the favor of sb. 赢得某人的喜爱 (2) n. 偏袒，偏爱 the favor to sb./sth. 对某人的偏袒 (3) n. 善行，恩惠 (4) vt. 喜爱，偏爱 favor sb./sth. 喜爱某人或某物 (5) vt. 赞同 favor the view 赞同某观点 (6) vt. 有利于，便于 = facilitate

Hot climate and plentiful rainfall favor/facilitate the growth of plants. 炎热的气候和充足的雨水有助于植物生长。

(7) vt. 容貌像…… favor sb. 像某人

2. "betray" most nealy menas
(A) tempt
(B) deceive
(C) desert
(D) disappoint
(E) reveal

【答案】E。见原文详解。

tempt vt. 引诱或怂恿（某人）干不正当的事

3. "More silence" emphasizes the grandmother's sense of
(A) anticipation
(B) resignation
(C) despair
(D) satisfaction
(E) resolve

【解析】本句表明了祖母的对现实的默然，是一种对现实的屈从，信写不出来了，就这样吧，结束吧。

resignation n. (1) 辞职 (2) 顺从，听从（文中意思）

He endured great pressure and potential dangers posed by the career he was dedicated to with resignation. 他默默承担着他所从事的事业带给他的巨大压力和潜在的危险。

do sth. with resignation, 默默地做某事。

4. "For her…sensuous" serves primarily to explain why the grandmother

(A) asked her granddaughter to reread her letters

(B) had not felt it necessary to learn to write

(C) was very particular about the style of her stationery

(D) sought approval regarding the appearance of her signature

(E) thought it was important for her granddaughter to write well

【解析】D

approval n. (1) 赞成，同意（文中意思）the approval of sth. 对某事的赞同 (2) 批准，认可 the approval of sth. 对某事的许可

(E) 强干扰项，祖母认为孙女字写得好看很重要，曲解了作者意图。

5. The granddaughter's question in line 50 primarily convey her（出处见右侧批注）

(A) belief that her grandmother's letters did not offer enough details

(B) determination to include everything her grandmother wanted to say

(C) resentment about having to write letters for her grandmother

(D) irritation that her grandmother was avoiding certain painful subjects

(E) sense that her grandmother did not write to her sister often enough

【答案】A

(A) 作者的提问为：难道你要和妹妹讲的话只有这些吗？作者觉得祖母对妹妹讲的话太少了。(A) 正确。信中没有提供足够的信息。

(B) 表明了作者要将祖母要讲的所有话写在信中的决心。主观臆断，太绝对化。作者只是觉得奶奶讲的内容太少，而非要将其讲的全部内容写入信中。

(C) 痛恨为祖母写信。文中没有这个意思。

(D) 为祖母故意回避一些痛苦的话题感到恼怒。文中没有这个意思。

(E) 认为祖母没有经常给妹妹写信。错误。文章前面几段提到祖母每隔一段时间就给妹妹写信。

6. The granddaughter's actions ("It…up") are motivated by her desire to（见原文右侧批注）

(A) have a more interesting life

(B) write a more entertaining letter

(C) make her grandmother happy

(D) encourage her grandmother's sister to visit

(E) develop her own skills as a writer

【解析】her 指代作者。作者的行为受她什么样的欲望所激发？

作者在祖母信中添油加醋的目的是使信不再 meager，详见原文分析，因此(B) 正确。

entertaining，形容词，有趣的。

(A) 作者想要过更有趣的生活。该选项歪曲了作者的意思。

7. The parenthetical reference "(for the benefit of my California reader who might need some background material on the subject of ice hockey)" serves to

(A) explain why the grandmother envied her sister in California

(B) suggest that the child found writing letters for her grandmother to be rewarding

(C) give an example of a subject that the grandmother asked her granddaughter to write about

(D) highlight the granddaughter's desire to have others appreciate her writing skills

(E) emphasize the granddaughter's sense of tailoring her writing to an audience

【解析】parenthetical adj. 插入的。作者插入这些参考是为了强调作者欲迎合看信的祖母的妹妹，故意在信中介绍一些背景知识。(E) 正确。audience 指祖母的妹妹。

tailor (1) n. 裁缝 (2) vt. & vi. 裁制 (3) vt. 调整使适应 tailor sth. to sth. 调整前面的事情使之适应后面的事情（选项意思）

(A)、(B)、(C)、(D)均无中生有。

8. "meager soup" refers to the

(A) emotional ties between family members

(B) grandmother's modest lifestyle

(C) grandmother's limited writing skills

(D) substance of the grandmother's letter

(E) meals served by the grandmother

【解析】贫瘠的汤指代祖母信中的内容。选(D)。substance 指 contents，内容。

(A) 家庭成员之间的情感纽带，文中没有提到。

(B) 祖母朴实的生活方式。文中没提生活方式。

(C) 祖母有限的写作技巧。祖母没有写作，而是作者代写的，更谈不上写作技巧。

(E) served by 为过去分词短语作定语，修饰 meals。祖母提供的饭菜。

9. The granddaughter's attitude ("Of course…treachery) is best described as（见原文右侧批注）

(A) guilty

(B) wary

(C) conscientious

(D) optimistic

(E) self-satisfied

【解析】E

本题考查句子为 I departed from my own life without a regret and breezily inhabited my grandmother's. I complained about my tip joint, I bemoaned the rising cost of hamburger, and hinted at the inattention of my son's wife (that is, my own mother, who was next door, oblivious to treachery).

作者对自己编纂出来的祖母的生活感到很陶醉和满意。

conscientious adj. 认真的，勤奋的

wary adj. 谨慎的；小心翼翼的 be wary of 对某物谨慎

10. The granddaughter used "ruled 81/2 x 11" paper because she

(A) disliked the floral pattern on her grandmother's stationery

(B) began to view the letter writing as an onerous assignment

(C) assumed that she would teach her grandmother how to write

(D) required more space than her grandmother's stationery provided

(E) anticipated having to write multiple letters for her grandmother

【解析】D

(A) 作者没有提到不喜欢这种信纸风格。

(B) onerous adj. 困难的；沉重的；繁重的。view 为 vt, 看作。将写信看作很困难的差事。选项与文中意思违背。

(C) 作者不曾教给祖母如何写作。

(D) 正确，作者需要更多的空间来写信。

(E) 预期到要为祖母写很多封信件。文中没提这一点。

11. The phrase "off to the races" indicated that the author

(A) viewed writing as a game

(B) plunged enthusiastically into her task

(C) rushed to finish the letters as quickly as possible

(D) avoided a direct request

(E) became extremely competitive

【解析】见文章精读，热情地做某事。sb. plunges into sth., 某人投入到某事中。(B) 正确。热情地投入到任务中。作者是热爱写作的。

(A) 将写作视为一种游戏，错误。

(C) 尽快写完信，这是干扰项。该选项有敷衍塞责的含义，作者并没有提到尽快写完信，而是要把信写得生动，没有提到写信速度问题。

(D) 没提到直接询问。

(E) 变得很有竞争力。写信和竞争力无关。

12. "I took ... hand" suggest that the grandmother wanted to learn how to write "Love" because she

(A) wanted to improve her writing skills

(B) realized that her her letters needed an appropriate closing

(C) was impatient with what seemed to be interference from her granddaughter

(D) felt that it was important to contribute more directly to the letters

(E) began to feel closer to her sister as her letters became more personal

【解析】D

祖母觉得自己应该为信件尽一份微薄之力，因此决定亲自签名。

13. The passage is best interpreted as an account of

(A) the formative stage of a writer's development
(B) a long-standing rivalry between two sisters
(C) a common experience of immigrants in the United States
(D) a basic misunderstanding of the purpose of writing letters
(E) a grandmother's aspirations for her granddaughter

【解析】A

本文可能是对什么的记叙？

formative adj.（影响）形成/构成/发展的。(A) 一个作家的成长阶段。作者刚开始为了饼干和牛奶为奶奶写信，随后加入自己想象的内容，并写成不错的信件，这些都可以为本文作者最终成为一名作家做铺垫。

(B) 两个姐妹之间长期的不和。文中没有提到不和。

(E) 祖母对孙女的期待。错误，文中没提到祖母对孙女有何期待。the aspiration of sb., 名词短语，对某人的期待。

## 文章 13

I'm watching Sesame Street with my daughter. Today Grover has transported us to Alaska, where a local lass is suiting up to face the Arctic chill, with the help of her mother, who sews fur pelts together to fashion a coat to repel the subzero temperatures. The child rushes out into the crisp fresh air to meet other children, laughing sweetly. It looks so wholesome, so simple, so uncomplicated. No fancy schools to get into, no apartments to compare. It looked pleasant there, out in the bleak, but weirdly alluring slate of glistening frost punctuated only by playful tykes toting their homemade lunches to school in swinging buckets.

批注 [24]: vt. 面对某事

批注 [25]: 不定式作目的状语,做衣服的目的是驱赶严寒。

批注 [26]: 现在分词短语作伴随状语,逻辑主语与句子主语一致。

批注 [27]: 没有好的学校可以用来比较,这里体现了作者对乡下生活的一点担忧。

批注 [28]: 独立主格。那里看着很有益健康,伴随着某种状态。
tote: vt. 提着某物。weirdly alluring, 副词修饰形容词,闪耀着光芒的石板,石板上结了霜。

### 【单词及搭配】

1. lass n. 小女孩,少女;女朋友
2. chill (1) vt. & vi.(使)变冷,(使)变凉 (2) n. 寒冷,寒气(文中意思)(3) vt. 令失望;使沮丧;使扫兴;使消沉 The news chilled his hopes. 这个消息使他感到失望。
3. fashion (1) n. 方式,样子 (2) n. 流行款式,时尚款式,时装 (3) vt.(尤指用手工)制作;使成形;塑造(~A from/out of B; ~B into A)(文中意思)
4. wholesome adj. 有益健康的
5. uncomplicated adj. 不复杂的,不棘手的
6. fancy (1) vt. 想象,设想 (2) vt. 想要,喜欢 (3) vt. 猜想,以为 (4) n. 设想,空想,幻想 (5) n. 想象力,幻想力 (6) adj. 昂贵的,高档的(文中意思)(7) adj. 别致的,花式的,花哨的
7. bleak adj. (1) 阴冷的;阴郁的,凄凉的(文中意思) (2) 没有希望的,暗淡的
8. weird adj. 怪诞的;神秘而可怕的;超然的
9. alluring adj. 诱惑的,迷人的。还需掌握动词形式:allure vt. & vi. 诱引,吸引
10. slate (1) n. 板岩,石板(文中意思) (2) 石板瓦 (3) 候选人名单,提名名单 (4) vt. 用石板瓦盖
11. glistening adj. 闪耀的,反光的
12. frost (1) vt. & vi.(使)结冰霜 (2) vt. 冻坏 (3) n. 霜(文中意思) (4) 霜冻,严寒天气
13. punctuate (1) vt. & vi.(在文字中)加标点符号,加标点 (2) vt. 不时打断某事物(文中意思)

# 文章 14

What was most likely the original purpose of the human appendix? Experts can only theorize on its use. It may have had the same purpose it has in present-day herbivores, where it harbors colonies of bacteria that help in the digestion of cellulose. Another theory suggests that tonsils and the appendix might manufacture the antibody-producing white blood cells called B lymphocytes; however, B lymphocytes could also be produced by bone marrow. The third theory is that the appendix may "attract" body infections in order to localize the infection in one spot that is not critical to body function.

批注 [29]: 第 2 题题目出处

批注 [30]: 第 1 题题目出处

批注 [31]: 定语从句，修饰 spot。

## 【单词及搭配】

1. appendix n. (1) 附录 (2) 阑尾（文中意思）
2. theorize vt. & vi. 创建理论，建立学说；推理 theorize (on) sth.
3. herbivore n. 食草动物
4. present-day adj. 现在的
5. harbor n. (1) 海港，海湾 (2) 避难所，躲藏处，避风港 (3) vt. & vi. 庇护；藏匿；收养（文中意思）(4) vt. 心怀，怀有
6. colony n. (1) 殖民地 (2)（动植物的）群体，集群（文中意思）
7. digest vt. & vi. (1) 消化 (2) vt. 透彻了解 (3) n. 摘要，文摘，汇编
8. cellulose n. 细胞膜质；纤维素
9. tonsil n. 扁桃体
10. antibody n. 抗体
11. lymphocyte n.（出现在血液、淋巴液中的）淋巴球，淋巴细胞
12. infection n.〈医〉传染，感染 infect (1) vt.（受）传染 (2) vt. 污染 (3) vt. 影响
13. localize vt. 使局部化

The authorities tried to localize the epidemic. 当局试图把流行病限制在局部范围。

Fish populations assume highly localized distributions within each river. 鱼群分布集中在每条河的某些区域。

## 【文章精读】

it has in present-day，定语从句，修饰 purpose。阑尾对现今食草动物的功能和对人类的功能是相同的，即在阑尾内存在着大量细菌，这些细菌用来帮助纤维素的消化。

antibody-producing，形容词，产生抗体的。名词—分词，起到形容词作用，用过去分词或现在分词取决于名词和被修饰名词的关系。

be critical to sth.，对某物来讲是重要的、关键的。

body functioning，动名词短语，身体的正常运转。文章最后一句指出阑尾的另一种作

用：使感染在某个地方固化，不再向其他关乎身体重要机能的地方扩散。

# 【题目解析】

1. The author of the passage uses quotation marks in line 6 in order to indicate that

(A) this theory is the one with which the author most nearly agrees

(B) this theory is less scientifically valid than the other theories in the passage

(C) a common word is being used to describe a unique biological process

(D) a word is being used in a humorous way

(E) a direct quotation from another source is being used

【答案】C

attract 的意思为"吸引"，这里指出阑尾对控制感染发展起到的作用。即，一个普通动词被赋予了独特的意义来描述一种生物过程。

(A) 作者最认同的观点。作者没有表明对哪个观点最认同，只是客观地陈述阑尾的作用。which 指代 the one，即理论。

(B) 作者没有将各个理论进行科学有效性的比较。

(D) 本文与"幽默的基调"无关。

(E) 从其他源文件中的直接引用。没有表明这个说法是从其他文献中引用的。

valid adj. 正当的，有充分根据的，符合逻辑的（选项意思）validate vt. (1) 证实；确证 (2) 使生效；使有法律效力

2. How does the theory described in lines 2-3 primarily differ from the other two theories described in the passage?

(A) It pertains only to plants.

(B) It concerns a physical process that occurs in more than one area of the human body.

(C) It is a theory supported by more experts in the field than are the other two theories.

(D) It is concerned with the prevention of disease.

(E) It makes reference to a process presently occurring in other animals.

【解析】E

考查句子：It may have had the same purpose it has in present-day herbivores, where it harbors colonies of bacteria that help in the digestion of cellulose. 见文章精读。可以看出，该理论在谈及人类阑尾功能时提到了其在其他食草类动物体内的功能。所以(E) 正确。注意：食草动物体内的阑尾功能很发达。make reference to: (1) 谈及 (2) 参考；提到，论及。

occurring in other animals，现在分词短语作定语，修饰 process。presently，目前，currently。副词修饰 occuring 分词，目前发生的某事。

举例：现在发生的事件 presently occurring events

(A) pertain vi. 关于，有关 pertain to sth., 与某物相关

文章没提到该理论仅与植物相关。

(B) 第一种理论并没有提到该生理过程发生于身体内多个部位。

(C) 文中没提到专家最支持哪个理论，只是客观阐述对阑尾功能的几种理论。

(D) 该理论没有提到预防疾病。

# 文章 15

One hazard in historical study is the necessity of dividing the whole into segments, since not everything can be examined simultaneously.[1] Common ways of dividing history are by period, country, topic, artistic or political movement, or theme.[2] Each of these can be justified, but all have their shortcomings.[3] When divisions are made according to country, the interconncections among events occurring in two or more countries may go unnoticed or remain unexplored.[4] Division into time periods may interrupt or obscure ongoing developments, or may give undue emphasis to some event or type of activity (especially war or politics) as crucial in marking the end or beginning of a period or movement.[5]

## 【单词及搭配】

1. undue adj. (1) 过分的；过度的 (2) 不适当的；不正当的（文中意思）(3) 未到（支付）期的

2. hazard vt. (1) 尝试着做/提出 hazard to do sth. (2) vt. 冒风险 (3) n. 危险；公害（文中意思）

3. obscure adj. (1) 不出名的；不重要的 (2) 费解的；模糊不清的 (3) 不易看清的，暗淡的 (4) vt. 使……模糊不清；掩盖（文中意思）

## 【文章精读】

[1] 指出将整个历史划分为若干阶段来研究的危害。hazard 为这里作名词，表示"危害"。since 表示"因为"。因为不能同时研究所有事件，因此研究历史时必须将整个历史划分为若干阶段。这种研究方法是有害的。

[2] 指出划分历史的依据：时间、政治运动、主题等。

[3] 每种划分方法都能被证明是正确的，但每种划分方法都有缺点。justify 这里为 vt，证明某物是正确的。

[4] 解释划分的弊端：当人们依据国家地区来划分历史时，国家之间发生的事件可能就不被人们留意或没有被挖掘了。divisions 这里指代划分。occuring 为现在分词短语作定语，修饰 events。go unnoticed，动词短语，不被人注意。

[5] 指出依据时间划分历史的害处。

## 【题目解析】

1. Which of the following is most analogous to the "hazard" the author sees in the "division" of historical study?

(A) A lawyer accepts cases in too many different areas of legal practice.

(B) A teacher must cope with large class sizes and is unable to give students sufficient individual instruction.

(C) A biologist studies large areas of forest but fails to examine in depth the nesting site of a specific bird species.

(D) An artist produces works in many different media, but does not excel in any one medium.

(E) A doctor diagnoses one ailment but overlooks elements of the patient's overall health.

【解析】E

(A) 律师接收了属于不同立法领域的案件，这与文中提到的划分历史为独立的部分相反，恰恰可以避免这种危害。错误。

(B) 老师不能给予个体学生足够的指导。这与文中划分历史的意思相反。文章提到的危害是忽略整体，而过多地研究历史片段。

(C) 忽略个体，与文意相反。

(D) excel in sth., 动词短语，在某方面出色。与文章无关。

(E) 头痛医头，脚痛医脚，忽略了全局。与文意相同，正确。

2. The author implies which of the following about "war" and "politics" in historical studies?

(A) They make the study of international movements difficult.

(B) They serve primarily as a convenience to the reader.

(C) They are more helpful to use in defining periods than in defining movements.

(D) They are equally important to historians and to readers.

(E) They are commonly used to define historical periods.

【解析】战争和政治均为历史划分的依据，所以(E) 正确。

(A) 文章没提到战争与政治使得对国际运动的研究变得困难。

(B) 以战争与政治来划分历史给读者带来方便。文章没提到这点。convenience 为名词，方便。primarily 为副词，主要地。serve as+n., 作为什么，动词短语。

(C) 文章没提到。

(D) 文章没将这种划分方式的重要性在历史学家和读者之间做比较。

# 文章 16

## 文章 16.1

Even though films now called film noir by critics have been made in Hollywood since 1939, film noir as a genre did not exist until 1946.[1] In that year an exhibition of American movies was held in Paris, and French film critics got their first look at what had been going on in Hollywood since the advent of World War II.[2] Among the films shown were *Laura*; *The Maltese Falcon*; *Murder, My Sweet*; *Double Indemnity*; and *The Woman in the Window*.[3] Those five films shared enough traits that critic Nino Frank gave them a new classification: film noir, or literally, "black film."[4] The traits they shared were both stylistic and thematic.[5] They were dark in both look and mood.[6] Their primary action took place at night on rain-swept city streets, in narrow ash-can alleys, in claustrophobic diners, and in dingy, shadowy hotel rooms with neon signs flashing outside the windows, rooms in which, as hard-boiled author Nelson once put it, "every bed you rent makes you an accessory to somebody else's shady past."[7] The characters in these films were bookies, con men, killers, cigarette girls, crooked cops, down-and-cut boxers, and calculating, scheming, and very deadly women.[8] The well-lit, singing and tap-dancing, happy-ending world of the 1930's had in ten short years become a hostile, orderless place in which alienation, obsession, and paranoia ruled.[9] The universe seemed to conspire to defeat and entrap the inhabitants who wandered blindly through it.[10] They were victims of fate, their own worst enemies who, looking for a score, ended by defeating themselves.

> 批注 [32]: 现在分词短语作定语，修饰 signs。

## 【单词及搭配】

1. film noir 黑色电影
2. genre 〈法〉（文学、艺术等的）类型，体裁，风格
3. advent n. 出现，到来
4. share （1）n.（分享到的或贡献出的）一份 （2）（参与、得到等的）份 （3）vt. & vi. 共有，共用，均摊，参与（文中意思） （4）vt. 分配，均分
5. trait n. 人的个性，显著的特点，特征
6. contemporary adj. （1）当代的 （2）同时代的，同属一个时期的 （3）n. 同代人，同龄人
7. require of 对……要求　I require cooperation of you. 我需要你们的合作。
8. rain-swept 大雨滂沱的
9. hard-boiled adj. （1）（鸡蛋）煮得老的 （2）（指人）不动感情的，冷酷的；久经世故的

（文中意思）

10. accessory (1) n. 附件，配件（文中意思）　(2) 同谋，帮凶，包庇犯　(3) adj. 非主要的；副的

11. alienation n. 离间，疏远

12. paranoia n. 妄想狂，偏执狂

13. conspire vi. (1) 密谋，搞阴谋 conspired to do sth. (2)（事件等）巧合，共同导致 conspire to do sth.

14. entrap vt. 使陷入圈套，使入陷阱 entrap sb. into doing sth. 诱使某人做某事

15. well-lit adj. 采光好的，光线好的

**【文章精读】**

[1] called film noir 为过去分词短语作定语，修饰 films。尽管黑色电影于 1939 年诞生于好莱坞，但黑色电影这种体裁的正式出现起源于 1946 年。即黑色电影刚出现时并没有被人们归为一个新的电影题材。跟随时间状语 since 一般用完成时态。

[2] that year 指代 1946 年，what had been going on 为宾语从句，本句表明黑色电影的内容与二战的历史背景有关。

[3] 指出五部黑色电影名称。shown 为过去分词作定语，修饰 films。

[4] 主语 share characters/traits of sth.，某物共有什么样的特征。这五部电影具有相同的特征，以至评论家赋予这些电影新的分类：黑色电影，或者从字面理解："黑色电影"。

[5]—[8] 指出黑色电影中情节的发生地点，具体解释黑色电影的特征。

[9] in ten years，在十年内，即黑色电影发展的 10 年中，20 世纪 30 年代电影的采光好等风格被黑色电影统治。which 指代 place。alienation, obsession 为黑色电影的特点。

The five films mentioned earlier that were shown at the 1946 exhibition were the ones the French critiqued.[1] These high-budget studio productions most commonly come to the public's mind when the word noir is mentioned because they are cited most often in the spate of contemporary books that have recently been published on the subject.[2] But the noir cycle, although kick-started by the success of those high-budget productions, actually had its roots in the B movie, in particular, in the B crime movie.[3] Film noir was made to order for the B, or low-budget, part of the movie double bill.[4] It was cheaper to produce because it required less lighting and smaller casts and usually entailed story lines that required limited-scale sets—an attractive quality to film studios operating on reduced wartime budgets.[5] Film noir was character-driven, and its story lines, which were unusual and compact, could often be told in the 68 to 80 minutes required of B picture.[6]

**【单词及搭配】**

1. critique (1) n. 评论文章；评论　(2) vt. 写评论；对……发表评论；评判（文中意思）

2. budget (1) n. 预算（文中意思）　(2) vt. & vi. 编制预算，安排开支 budget for sth.

3. spate (1) n. 大量，许多（文中意思）a spate of water 洪水泛滥　(2) n.（河流）暴涨；发洪水　(3) n.（人）口若悬河；滔滔不绝 sb. is in full spate 某人口若悬河

4. kick-start (1) vt. 用脚启动　(2) vt. 促使……开始；使尽快启动（文中意思）

5. entail vt. (1) 使……成为必要, 需要（文中意思）The project entails high budgets. 这个工程预算庞大。(2) 限定继承

6. story line 故事情节

7. compact (1) vt. & vi. 压紧,（使）坚实 (2) adj. 装填紧密的, 整齐填满的

## 【文章精读】

[1] 承接第一段中提到的五部黑色电影。这五部电影为法国人所批判。ones 指代电影。

[2] 只要一提到黑色电影，人们就常常将它与高成本的电影联系起来，因为一提到黑色电影，很多书都会提到高成本的五部电影（从而使人们误认为黑色电影成本都很高）。"These high-budget studio productions"指上文提到的五部开创黑色电影先河的电影，其特点为高成本。

come to the public's mind, 走入公众的意识；they 指代高预算电影产品；on 为介词，表示"关于"，可用 concerning 取代。

[3]—[4] those high-budget productions 指上文中的五部高成本的黑色电影。although kick-started by 为分词短语作让步状语, 分词的逻辑主语必须与句子主语一致：尽管以上五部高成本的电影使得黑色电影获得成功，但是，黑色电影更多的是 B 电影，这类电影成本很低。本句指出[2]中人们认为所有黑色电影均高成本这一观点是错误的，其实大部分黑色电影是低成本的。

[5] that required limited-scale sets 为定语从句，修饰 story lines；an attractive quality to film studios, 名词短语, 指代 limited-scale sets, 为 limited-scale sets 的同位语, to 为介词, 对于。operating on reduced wartime budgets 为现在分词作定语, 修饰 studios。黑色电影之所以造价低是因为它需要较弱的灯光和较小的屏幕，它只需舞台规模有限的故事情节。

[6] which 指代 story lines。

(1) require A of B, 动词短语, 向 B 要求 A；require financial support of the government 向政府要求经济支援

(2) 名词1 required of 名词2, 名词短语, 名词2 所需要的名词1。

60 to 80 minutes are required of the B movie. B 电影需要 60~80 分钟时间。

required of B picture 为过去分词短语作定语, 修饰 60 to 80 minutes。电影 B 所需的时间。

指出黑色电影较情节较紧凑，电影时间较短。

# 文章 16.2

It may be that noir began in a way of photographing that was as economical as it was moody (less light meant less money on decor—an important wartime consideration when studios faced limits on construction material).

## 【单词及搭配】

1. decor n.（房间、舞台等的）布置, 装饰

2. moody adj. (1) 喜怒无常的, 情绪多变的 (2)（无缘无故）不高兴的, 愤怒的

## 【文章精读】

本段为强调句，as economical as it was moody，黑色电影既成本低又情绪多变。括号内解释为何经济合算，consideration 为名词短语，在装饰上投入的钱少，是战争时代电影界在造价上必须考虑的一个问题。本段表明黑色电影的成本受二战的历史背景限制。limits on sth., 名词短语，某方面的限制。face 在这里为 vt，面临。

Where did noir come from?[1] It's an intriguing question and one still not adequately answered, despite the quantity of writing that wallows in that noir mood.[2] Don't rule out the influence of German films from the twenties, if only because there were, by the early forties, so many European refugees (writers, directors, camera operators, designers, actors) working in Hollywood.[3] Don't forget the impact of French films of the late thirties, especially those of Marcel Carne.[4] His *Le Jour Se Leve* was such a success that it was remade in Hollywood in 1947 as *The Long Night*.[5] Finally, don't underestimate the influence Citizen Kane had on anyone whose art and craft was cinematography.[6] The film was a box office flop, but filmmakers were absorbed by it.[7] A landmark in so much, Kane is a turning point in the opening up of a noir sensibility.[8]

> 批注 [33]: 名词短语，某事的失败，文中指票房惨淡。

Equally, don't forget that from the forties onward, Los Angeles was much beset by psychoanalysis, and the growing intellectual interest in guilt, depression, and nightmare. Don't eliminate the impact, the memory, or the mere thought of a war's damage.[9]

> 批注 [34]: 精神分析学

## 【单词及搭配】

1. intrigue (1) vi. 搞阴谋诡计 intrigue against sb. 对某人做坏事 (2) vt. 激起……的好奇心=arouse one's curiosity

   intriguing adj. 非常有趣的；引人入胜的

2. adequate adj. (1) 充分的，足够的 (2) 适当的，胜任的（文中意思）

3. wallow vi. (1) 快活地在泥沼中打滚 (2) 在海浪中颠簸 (3) n. 堕落 (4) wallow in 动词短语，热衷于，沉湎于（尤指不愉快或惹人同情的事）（文中意思）

4. rule out (1) 用直线划掉 (2) 宣布……不可能；排除……的可能性（文中意思）

5. cinematography n. 电影术

6. flop (1) vi.（笨拙地、不由自主地或松弛地）移动或落下 (2)（指书、戏剧等）彻底失败，不成功 (3) n. 失败（文中意思）

7. box office 名词短语，票房

8. beset vt. 困扰；不断围攻

## 【文章精读】

[1] 点明本段主题，探讨黑色电影的起源。

[2] one 指代 question，still not adequately answered 为过去分词短语作定语，修饰 one。adequately 为副词，这里表示"恰当地"，修饰过去分词 answered。despite 为介词，后面跟随名词短语，writing 为动名词，that wallows in that noir mood 为定语从句，修饰 writing。that 作定语从句中的主语，指代 writing，that 不能省略。

SAT 精解讲义

despite+名词短语，主语+谓语。the quantity of sth., 某物的数量，名词短语。wallow in sth.为动词短语，表示很多作品的基调都与黑色电影类似，即阴郁的。

尽管有很多作家执迷于以黑色电影为话题的作品，但黑色电影从哪里起源是一个很有趣的问题，并且至今没有得到恰当的回答。

[3] 指出德国人对黑色电影的影响。rule out 这里为动词短语，相当于 overlook，忽视。如果仅仅因为曾经有很多在好莱坞工作的德国难民的话（这些难民通常为作家、导演、演员等），也不要忽视德国电影对黑色电影的影响。working 为现在分词短语作定语，修饰"难民"。

[4]—[5] 指出法国电影对黑色电影的影响。

[6] 指出 Kane 对从事电影术的人的影响。本句可拆为三个简单句：

(1) Don't underestimate the influence.
(2) Kane had the influence on anyone.
(3) The art and craft of anyone was cinematography.

[7] 尽管 Kane 的电影票房惨淡，但其对黑色电影的开创具有重要意义。

[9] impact, memory, the mere thought of a war's damage 作 eliminate 三个并列的宾语。即 Don't eliminate the impact of a war's damage, the memory of a war's damage, or the mere thought of a war's damage. 不要忽略战争的影响、对战争的记忆的影响，甚至仅仅想到战争的破坏性的影响。

本句指出战争对黑色电影的起源有重要影响。

I want to stress how deeply noir impulses lay in the common imagination—that of the audience as well as the filmmakers.[1] Mildred Pierce, for instance—which appeared in 1945 when many American women were running businesses of their own just to survive while the men were away at war—sighs and seems to say, "It doesn't make any difference, why bother, for there is something malign in human nature or luck that will undermine enterprise and hope."[2] Of course, not every film was so bleak.[3] Look instead at David Selznick's very beautiful and touching *Since You Went Away*, which is all about Claudette Colbert, Jennifer Jones, and Shirley Temple coping in the absence of men. That, too, looks like a film noir. But the mood is entirely that of innocent, ardent, flawless hope, and assurance that when the war ends everything will revert to calm and order.

【文章精读】

本段指出黑色电影带给人们消极与积极的两种情绪。

[1] that 指代 imagination。Noir impulses 指黑色电影带给人们的阴郁、悲观、绝望的感受。作者认为这种感受在大众的想象力中有着深刻作用力。这种想象力不仅包含观众的，也包含电影制作人。即，阴郁的感受同样影响着观众及电影工作者。

[2] just to survive, 不定式作目的状语，为了做什么。

[3] 本句指出黑色电影对情绪的积极一面。

【题目解析】

1. In Passage 1, the author suggests that "films now called film noir by critics"

批注 [35]: 名词，信心

批注 [36]: 这里为名词，镇静

批注 [37]: 指出类似电影中感情色彩积极乐观的一面，that 指代 mood。

批注 [38]: 出处为文章1第一句

(A) were not classified as film noir when first made
(B) were reminiscent of earlier European films
(C) were uplifting in mood and theme
(D) were intended to contrast with films of the 1930's
(E) were disliked by many French film critics

【解析】原文指出，黑色电影最初出现时并未归类为现在的分类。be classified as sth., 归为某一类。故(A) 正确。

(B) reminiscent adj. 提醒的，暗示的；像……的；使人想起……的 be reminiscent of sth. 像什么

(C) uplift vt. 振作；振奋；uplifting adj. 令人振奋的。在主题和心境上令人振奋。本选项意思与原文相反。

(D) 作者并没有将黑色电影与20世纪30年代的电影相比较。

批注 [39]: when+分词，分词的逻辑主语为 films。为 suggest 的宾语从句。从句中嵌套分词时，分词的逻辑主语与从句主语一致。

批注 [40]: 物体（非人）打算做某事，旨在做某事用 sth. be intended to do sth.。

2. It can be inferred that the films listed in lines 9 through 12 were similar in each of the following ways EXCEPT
   (A) visual appearance
   (B) emotional effect
   (C) characters
   (D) theme
   (E) music

【解析】E
黑色电影的相似处为视觉感官、感情效应、人物、主题，但并没提到音乐。本节为细节题。

3. In paragraph 2, the author says that the films discussed in paragraph 1 are NOT typical of their genre in regard to
   (A) setting
   (B) budget
   (C) country of origin
   (D) plot
   (E) lighting

【解析】B
typical of 是……的特点。见文章1分析。

4. The author of Passage 1 uses the quotation in lines 24-26 primarily in order to
   (A) critique a writer
   (B) recount an incident
   (C) evoke a place
   (D) describe a character
   (E) summarize a plot

批注 [41]: 文章1第一段第7句

【解析】C

第 7 句说明黑色电影背景发生的地点。

5. The author of Passage 1 suggests that the "spate of contemporary books" on film noir
(A) discusses only five films
(B) focuses on non-crime films
(C) focuses on relatively costly noir films
(D) is inaccurate in their historical data
(E) is from big-budget publishing companies

【解析】C

costly 为形容词，高成本的。大量书籍只关注高成本的黑色电影，从而给人们带来误解：只要是黑色电影，其成本都会很高。

6. The authors of both passages imply that contemporary writing about film noir
(A) comes mainly from French film critics
(B) has failed to describe the origins of film noir accurately
(C) mischaracterizes the film noir mood
(D) is inferior to earlier writing on film noir
(E) has dramatically improved the understanding of film noir

【解析】B

文章 1 作者认为人们总是将黑色电影的起源归结为五部高成本电影，但忽略了这样一个事实：黑色电影起源于成本较低的 B 电影；文章 2 第二段提到：not adequately answered, 即人们没有正确理解黑色电影的起源。

7. Both passages imply that the development of film noir can be attributed in part to
(A) the presence of European filmmakers in Hollywood
(B) the influential writing of French film critics
(C) economic restraints resulting from World War II
(D) United States filmmakers' dissatisfaction with high-paid actors
(E) the popularity of Citizen Kane

【解析】C

两篇文章均提到黑色电影的发展与战争造成的经济拮据有关。

8. The phrase "wallows in" in line 75 is closest in meaning to
(A) indulges in
(B) conforms to
(C) criticizes
(D) explores
(E) reveals

【解析】A

见原文分析，indulge in 这里表示"过分关注，沉溺于"。

9. The author of Passage 2 mentions *Since You Went Away* in line 116 primarily to

(A) indicate that not all films in the 1940's expressed the same attitude

(B) illustrate the popularity of film noir actors

(C) demonstrate that most film noir dealt with WWII

(D) show that the "absence of men" was a major film noir theme

(E) point out David Selznick's influence in defining film noir

【解析】A

*Since You Went Away* 为黑色电影名，该电影表现了一种对生活积极乐观的态度，与前面提到的黑色电影反应的悲观情绪相对，因此(A) 正确——并非所有电影都是同样的感情基调。

10. The second paragraph of Passage 2 is best described as

(A) a catalog of possible sources of the film noir mood

(B) a description of the mood that characterizes film noir

(C) a refutation of several misconceptions about film noir

(D) an argument for redefining the term "film noir"

(E) a list of the major film noir films

【解析】A

文章2第二段表明影响黑色电影的力量很多，由此指出文中所列举的几种影响力都可能是黑色电影创作的源泉。

11. The quote "It doesn't make…enterprise and hope" is primarily meant to

(A) give an example of dialogue from Mildred Pierce

(B) summarize what critics thought about Mildred Pierce

(C) show how Mildred Pierce differes from other films made in 1945

(D) character the sentiments expressed in Mildred Pierce

(E) demonstrate the influence of Mildred Pierce on *Since You Went Away*

【解析】D

引号中的文字表明该电影表现了阴郁悲观的感情色彩。character 这里为动词，描绘。expressed 为过去分词短语作定语，修饰 sentiments。

12. The word "impulses" is closest in meaning to

(A) incentives

(B) stimulants

(C) fantasies

(D) transformations

(E) feelings

【解析】E

详见文中解析，这里指黑色电影带给人的感受，这种感受有两种不同类型：积极的和消极的。

# 文章 17

Whistling and moaning, a 50-mile-an-hour wind whipped among the telescope domes atop Kitt Peak[1]. A few feet below, turning gray in the dusk, slid a river of clouds that had been rising and dropping all day[2]. High above, comet Hale-Bopp hung like a feathery fishing lure, its tail curving off a bit, as if blown to the side by the punishing wind[3]. One by one, stars winked on in a darkening sky[4]. Nearby, wild horses wandered past. They never glanced skyward at the gossamer swath of Hale-Bopp nor at the wondrous spectacle that is the night sky on a clear night, comet or no.

It felt good to be human.[5]

## 【单词及搭配】

1. whistle vi. 呼啸而行 The wind whistled from south to east.

2. moan (1) vi. 呻吟；呜咽（文中含义） (2) vi. 抱怨；发牢骚

moan about sth.=complain of；主语+moan 的适当形式 that +宾语从句：某人抱怨 XXX。

He is always complaining of/moaning about the bad weather.

bemoan (1) vt. 为（某人或某事）抱怨，不满于 The farmer bemoaned his loss. 农夫抱怨他所受到的损失。

Bemoaning the current situation, he did all he could to improve the plight he had been reduced to. 他不满现状，于是尽其所能改变境遇。

(2) vt. 悲悼；为……恸哭 (3) vt. 哀叹；对……表示惋惜

3. 50-mile-an-hour，作定语，每小时 50 英里的

4. whip 动词

(1) vt. 鞭打，抽；鞭笞，鞭打责罚

(2) vt.（柔韧性的物体、雨、风等）拍打；猛打（文中意思）The wind whipped their faces. 风猛烈地吹打在他们的脸上。

(3) vt. 驱使；促使；激励某人进入（某状态）

The radio host whipped his listeners into a frenzy. 电台节目主持人使听众进入一种狂热状态。

(4) vi. 一下子猛地移动 I whipped round the corner. 我突然转过拐角。

(5) vi. 突然拿出（或移动）

5. atop (1) 介词 on the top of 在……顶上（文中意思）atop sth. 在某物之上

(2) 副词 on the top, be atop of sth.

The air-raid siren is atop of the County Courthouse. 在县政府大楼顶上装着空袭警报器。

6. dusk (1) n. 薄暮 （文中意思）(2) vi. 变暗，变黑

7. slide

(1) vi. 滑行，滑动（文中意思）let sth. slide over sth.

(2) vt. 使滑行，使滑动

(3) vi. 平稳（或快速、悄悄）地走

I quickly slid into a seat at the back of the hall. 我快速地、悄悄地坐到大厅后排座位上。

悄悄移动；悄悄地迅速放置（某物）

She slid the bottle into her pocket. 她悄悄地把瓶子放进口袋。

(4) vi. 逐渐恶化（或退步）slide from A to B

The country faces the prospect of sliding from recession into slump. 该国面临着从衰退陷入萧条的前景。

let sth. slide 放任自流

Papa had let the business slide after Mama's death. 妈妈去世后，爸爸无心经营。

8. feathery adj. 生有羽毛的，柔软如羽毛的

9. lure (1) vt. 引诱，诱惑；诱骗 (2) n. 诱饵；诱惑物；诱惑力，吸引力，魅力

10. curve v.（使）弯曲 Her mouth curved in a smile. 她嘴儿弯弯微笑了。

11. punishing adj. 十分吃力的；使人筋疲力尽的；严厉的 punishing climb 累人的攀登

12. wink

(1) v. 眨眼；眨眼示意（尤用来表示说笑、讳言或作为传情、打招呼的示意）（文中意思）

(2) vi. 假装着没注意（坏事或非法行为）

The authorities winked at their illegal trade. 官方对他们的非法贸易装作不知情。

Winking at the behavior of eavesdropping, the teacher was punished.

(3) 闪烁；明灭

13. wander (1) vi. 漫游，漫步，闲逛（文中意思）(2) vi. 偏移；离开正道，迷路 wander off

His attention had wandered. 他开小差了。

14. glance v. (1) 一瞥（文中意思）(2) 匆匆（或粗略地）阅读，浏览 glance through sth.

15. skyward adv. 朝向天空

16. gossamer. （尤见于秋天的）蛛丝，游丝，脆弱（或精巧）的东西

17. swath n. 收割的刈痕，细长的列

18. wondrous （诗/文）令人惊奇的；奇妙的

19. spectacle n. 壮观；惊人的表演（或展示）；壮观的事件；壮观场面

20．rise/rose/risen (1) vi. 升高, 上升（文中意思） rise in sth., 在某方面增长

**【重要句型】**Sth. rose dramatically/remarkably/steadily. 某物显著/平稳增长。

(2) n. 上升, 升起；增加, 增长 the rise in sth., 名词短语，某方面的增长

(3) n. 兴起；发展 the rise of sth. 某物的兴起

The rise of telecommunications technology facilitates daily contact. 通信技术的兴起方便了日常联系。

(4) vi. 起因；发源 rise from sth.

主语+rise from sth. 主语产生于XXX。

## 【文章精读】

[1] Whistling and moaning, a 50-mile-an-hour wind whipped among the telescope domes atop Kitt Peak.

本句开篇点题，每小时五十英里的风咆哮低吟，鞭笞着 Kitt Peak 上面的天文台。句子主语为 the wind，"Whistling and moaning" 为现在分词短语作状语。分词作状语时，由句子的主语与分词动作的主动被动关系来判断使用现在分词或过去分词。

【举一反三】他取得了杰出的成就，获得了全世界的尊敬。

Gaining brilliant/outstanding/distinguished achievements, he won worldwide respect.

[2] A few feet below, turning gray in the dusk, slid a river of clouds that had been rising and dropping all day. 在天文台下面几英尺处，暮霭变为灰色，滑过一整天都在或上升或下降的云河。

[3] comet Hale-Bopp hung like a feathery fishing lure, its tail curving off a bit, as if blown to the side by the punishing wind. 彗星 Hale-Bopp 像有羽毛的鱼饵一般挂在高高的空中，它的尾巴有些许弯曲，好像被大风刮到了一边去。彗星与它的尾巴不同，逗号后又没有连词，因此使用独立主格。尾巴弯曲为主动的，所以用现在分词 curving。

本句为独立主格。句子的几种形式：

(A) 分词短语，主语+谓语。分词短语的逻辑主语必须与句子主语一致。如果分词表示的动作与主语呈主动关系，用现在分词；反之，用过去分词。详见[1]。

(B) 主语1+谓语1，主语2+分词。这种结构为独立主格。主语1与主语2不同。如果主语2与分词表达的动作呈主动关系，用现在分词；反之，用过去分词。本句结构属于此类。

As if/when/while/once/as soon as/if/whether+从句，主语+谓语。（once 表示"一旦"）

主语与从句中的主语一致时，推荐使用这种形式：

As if/when/while/once/as soon as/if/whether+分词短语，主语+谓语。

【举一反三】Once I was told about the meeting, I will leave.=Once informed of the meeting, I will leave.

blown 为过去分词，尾巴好像被风刮到了一边。blow 和尾巴是被动关系：its tails were blown to the side。

本句等价为：as if its tails were blown to the side.

【考点】独立主格的前后两个成分必然具有**逻辑关系**，表示附带的成分作分词，比如原因、假设等，真正的结果作谓语！详见改错部分分析。

批注 [42]：2009年5月 Section 10 第 10 题，见改错部分分析。

【举一反三】Vehicles of such kind were banned to pass through, the bridge not adequate to sustain the their weight.

Vehicles of such kind were banned to pass through because the bridge was not adequate to sustain the weight of them.

这类车辆被禁止通行，因为桥不能承受车辆的重量。

The fancy tuition posing a drain on his meager salaries, his friend financed him generously.

高昂的学费耗尽了他微薄的工资，因此他的朋友慷慨地资助了他。

The product rapidly gains popular appeal, the staff having designed it elaborately.

由于员工很精心地设计了这款产品，因此该产品迅速流行起来。

The company was on the verge of bankruptcy, its profits declining sharply with severe inflation.

受严重的通胀影响，公司利润大幅下滑，因此公司面临破产。

尽管校长不知道这次事故，但是绝大部分教职员工都知道。

The headmaster not informed of the accident, most of the faculty knew it well.

Although the headmaster was not informed of the accident, most of the faculty knew it well.

尽管吃耳屎致聋这一说法流传了很多年，但是没有证据来证明该说法的科学性。

(1) 独立主格

The parlance that eating cerumen might lead to deafness having prevailed for years, no evidence has been found to substantiate the rationality.

【解析】having prevailed 为分词，可以用从句取代。

(2) 介词短语取代从句部分

Despite/For all/In spite of the chronic parlance that eating cerumen might lead to deafness, no evidence has been found to substantiate its rationality.

(3) 让步状语从句，此种句型最常见。

Although it has been prevalently regarded that eating cerumen might lead to deafness, no evidence has been found to substantiate its rationality.

注意：独立主格中的各种代词尽量置于有分词的句子中。

[4] 星星们在黑暗下来的天空中一个一个地闪耀起来。

[5] 通过上面的对比：动物不懂得欣赏大自然的美，因此本句得到结论：做人真好。It 为形式主语，to be human 为不定式作主语。It felt adj. to do sth., 做某事感觉 XXX。

## 【题目解析】

1. In line 12, the author implied that being "human" indicates

(A) making occasional mistakes

(B) enjoying the company of others

(C) reflecting on past experiences

(D) appreciating nature's beauty

(E) seeking joy through simplicity

【解析】作者暗示，人类怎么样？见文章精读，只有人类才能欣赏大自然的美。

【答案】D

imply (1) vt. 暗示，暗指（题干意思） (2) vt. 必然包含 Drama implies conflict. 戏剧必然包含着冲突。

(A) occasional adj. 偶尔的，不经常的。还须掌握名词和动词：occasion (1) n. 时刻，时候 (2) 机会，时机 take the occasion to do sth. (4) n. 原因，理由 (5) vt. 惹起，引起 occasion sth. 引起某事

(B) company n. 伴随，陪伴 the company of sb., 某人的陪伴

(C) reflect on (1) 仔细考虑 reflect on the matter（题干意思）(2) 有损于 reflect on sth. 有损于某物

past，形容词，过去的。人类可以思考过去的经历，作者没有这个意图。

(D) appreciate (1) vt. 感激，感谢 (2) vt. 欣赏（文中意思）(3) vt. 意识到，体会 (4) vt. & vi.（使）增值，涨价。还需掌握反义词：depreciate (1) vi. 贬值，跌价；减价 depreciate by+ 名词，贬值了多少

(2) vt. 贬低，蔑视，轻视

见文章精读，人类能欣赏大自然的美，而动物不能。故(D)为正确答案。

(E) seek/sought/sought (1) vt. & vi. 寻找；探寻（选项意思）(2) vi. 企图；试图  seek to do sth.

simplicity 为名词，朴素。

2. The rhetorical device primarily featured in this passage is

(A) appeal to emotion
(B) metaphorical language
(C) extended analogy
(D) flashback
(E) irony

批注 [A43]: 修辞方式

批注 [A44]: 策略，手段

批注 [ 45]: 比喻

批注 [A46]: 倒叙

【答案】B

【解析】feature (1) n. 特征，特色 (2) n. 面貌，相貌 (3) vt. 以……为特色 A features B. A 以 B 为特征。(4) vi. feature in (sth.)，在某物中起重要作用

featured in this passage, 过去分词短语作定语，修饰 device, 文中重要的修辞手段是什么？

【重要句型】Sth. is featured in XXX. 某物在 XXX 中起重要作用。

appeal to emotion, 动之以情

鱼饵和云河均为比喻。

# 文章 18

A Kikongo proverb states, "A tree cannot stand without its roots."[1] It seems such obvious wisdom now, a well-worn cliché in our era in which everything truly insightful has already been said[2]. But all clichés derive their endurance from their truth, and my ancestors who coined this adage were sending a clear and powerful message to their descendant: a people cannot flourish without their life-giving foundations in the past[3]. The ties between those who came before and those who live now must be maintained and nurtured if a people is to survive[4]. It's a truth that my grandmother understood when she made a point of directing me to "tell the others" about her[5]. And it's a truth that has been well recognized by successive generations of Black people in America[6]. Another Kikongo proverb reminds us that "one can only steal a sleeping baby: once awake, she will look for her parents."[7] This is a maxim that conveys the seemingly instinctive pull of one's heritage, our inborn curiosity in our origins, the quest we all share for self-identification and self-knowledge.[8]

## 【单词及短语】

1. Kikongo，刚果人
2. well-worn adj. 用旧了的，陈腐的，平凡的
3. cliché n. 陈词滥调 avoid the use of cliche
4. insightful adj. 有见识的，有眼光的；富于洞察力的
还须掌握名词形式：insight n. (1) 洞察力，洞悉，深刻的见解 an insight into sth., 对某事的洞察力 (2) 领悟，顿悟
5. derive 动词 (1) 从……中获得（或取得）derive A from B 从 A 中获得 B（文中意思）(2)＜数＞导出（函数、方程）
6. endurance 名词
(1) 忍耐（力），持久（力）She was close to the limit of her endurance. 她快忍耐不住了。
(2) 耐久性（文中意思）
7. ancestor 祖先；descendant 子孙，后裔，后代。还须掌握各自的动词形式：
descend (1) vt. & vi. 下来，下去 (2) vi. descend from sth./sb. 起源（于），是……的后裔 (3) vi. descend to sth. 把身份降至，沦为
ascend (1) vt. & vi. 上升，攀登 (2) vi. 追溯到 ascend to+时间
8. coin vt. 创造（新词、短语），杜撰 coin sth.
9. adage n. 谚语，格言
10. flourish
(1) vi.（人、动物、其他生物体）繁荣，茂盛 Wild plants flourish on the banks of the lake.

野生植物在湖岸生长茂盛。

(2) 迅速发展；兴旺，成功 The organization has continued to flourish.

重要近义词 boom (1) vi. 激增，猛涨，兴隆 Business is booming. 生意日趋繁荣。Sb. booms as sth. 作为XXX，某人日趋成功。(2) n.（营业等的）激增，（经济等的）繁荣，迅速发展

11. life-giving adj. 赋予生命的；维持生命的；恢复生机的

12. maintain vt.

(1) 维持，保持 maintain close links

(2) 将……维持（在同样水平或速度）maintain agricultural prices 维持农产品价格

(3) 维护，养护，保养（建筑物、机器或道路）maintain the network 维护网络

(4) 扶养，负担 maintain dependants

(5) 坚持；断言；主张=argue 及物动词。Sb. maintained that +宾语从句。

13. make a point of 特意做某事，总是要做某事

14. direct v.

(1) 控制；管理；统治

(2) 针对……发表评论、批评

His criticism was directed at the wastage of water. 他针对水的浪费进行了批评。

(3) 命令；指示（文中意思）direct sb. to do sth.

15. successive，形容词，连续的，接连的；依次的 third successive wins 三连胜

16. maxim 名词，格言，箴言

17. convey

(1) vt. 载送；输送 (2) vt. 表达；传达（思想、感想、感觉等）

18. seemingly 副词，表面上；显得

19. instinctive 形容词

(1) （出于）本能的；无意识的，自发的 an instinctive distaste for sth. 对某物本能的厌恶

(2) 天生的 an instinctive writer 天生的作家

20. heritage 名词 (1) 被继承的（或可被继承的）财产；遗产 (2) 传统，血缘（文中意思）

21. quest, 这里作名词，寻找；追求；探索 quest of/for sth.

22. pull 名词 (1) 拉力；引力；魅力（文中意思）

The moon's pull affects the tides on earth. 月亮的引力影响地球上的潮汐。

(2) 影响力；门路；有利条件

He got the job mainly because his uncle had lots of pull with the president. 他得到这份工作主要因为他叔父与总裁关系很好。

23. inborn 形容词，天生的

24. state (1) n. 状态，状况 (2) n. 国家，政府 (3) vt. 陈述；叙述（文中意思）

25. self-identification 名词，自我认同。还须掌握动词和其他名词形式：

identify (1) vt. 认出，识别

(2) vt. 支持，认同 identify sb. with sb./sth. 前面的人支持后面的人/物 I identify with you. 我认同你。

(3) vt. & vi. 等同于；有关联 identify wealth with happiness 把财富等同于幸福

identity (1) n. 身份 (2) 个性，特性 (3) 同一性，一致性 the identity in sth. 某物的相同之处 the identity in these two ideas 两个观点的相同之处

26. self-knowledge n. 自知之明，自觉。文中指对自身血缘的认知。

27. survive (1) vi. 幸存，活下来（文中意思） (2) vt. 比……活得长，经历……之后还存在 survive the disaster 幸免于灾难

28. share (1) n. 分享到的或贡献出的份 (2) vt. & vi. 共有（文中意思）

## 【文章解析】

[1] 由一句谚语引出本文主旨。state 为及物动词，陈述。"roots"映射人们的"heritage"。树不能离开根生存。树无根不活。

[2] 刚果有一句谚语说，"树无根则不立"。这句话表明了非常显见的智慧，是我们这个时代一个惯用的熟语，这个时代中真正有见地的万事万物都被说尽了。"it"指代[1]中的年代，obvious 指"显而易见的"，in which 至结尾为定语从句，修饰 cliché，"truly insightful"真正有深刻见解的，insightful 为形容词，用副词 truly 来修饰。cliché 本意是"陈词滥调"，这里指"熟语"，即这个谚语流传了很久。作者看似对其呈贬义态度，因为已经被说得泛滥，但下一句表明作者对这句习语是褒奖的。

in which everything truly insightful has already been said in this era, which 指代 era。

[3] 与[2]承接：尽管这句谚语为熟语，但它的持久来自于正确性。解释这句谚语为何会流传这么久。"message"传递的含义为警示性语言。derive their endurance：持久性来自于哪里。"who coined this adage"为定语从句，修饰"祖先"，祖先传递的信息与谚语呼应：一个民族不能离开过去曾经给与他生命的基础而发达繁荣。"life-giving foundations"：赋予生命的根基。注意：foundation 与 give 是主动关系，The foundation gives life. 根基赋予生命。因此，换做形容词时用现在分词。people 指民族。

[4] 一个民族生存下来的必要条件是：联结远古人类与当代人类的纽带的维护与培育。"who came before and those who live now"为定语从句，修饰 those，"is to survive"用不定式表将来，要生存下去。

[5] it 指代[3]中的道理，that 直到结尾为定语从句，修饰 truth。"the others"指现代的人，或后代。

当我的祖母正十分重视教导我（怎样）去"告诉其他人"关于她的事时，她突然明白了这个事情（指[3]中的道理）确实是真实的。

make a point of：把……视为，说成必要的，特别注意，重视

He seemed to make a point of sounding uncultured and dressed the same way. 他好像故意显得没文化并且打扮的也一样。

I always make a point of checking that all lights are shut before leaving. 我离开之前总要检查所有的灯，看是否关好了

[6] it 指代与[5]中的完全相同。这也是一个被在美国的黑人连续的后代很好地认同的事实。

[7] 主语+reminds sb. that+宾语从句：某事/人提醒某人 XXX。once：连词，一旦，引导时间状语从句，后面可加分词、形容词或从句，awake 为形容词，醒的。完整的从句是：once the baby is awake. sleeping：形容词，睡着的。刚果另一句谚语讲：一个人只能偷熟

睡的婴儿，她一旦醒了，就要找父母。

[8] 解释[7]中的另一句谚语：这句谚语传达了看似本能的对自身遗传的吸引力，对自身起源的天生的好奇以及我们人类共同具备的对自我认同和自我认知的寻求。This is a maxim that conveys the seemingly instinctive pull of one's heritage, our inborn curiosity in our origins, the quest we all share for self-identification and self-knowledge. "we all share"作 quest 的定语从句，我们共有的寻求，介词 for 与 quest 连接，quest for XXX，即：self-identification 和 self-knowledge 作 for 的宾语，对自我认同和自我认识的追求，这一追求是我们人类共同的。instinctive 与 inborn 同义，均表示人类对自身历史的好奇是固有的。

**批注 [A47]:** 定语从句，修饰 maxim，传递了看似出于本能的对遗传本身的吸引，以及天生的对人类起源的好奇和寻求。注意：pull，curiosity，quest 三者为并列关系，均作 convey 的宾语。

Black Americans have managed to sustain links with the continent of their origin, against tremendous odds[9]. Through ingenuity and dogged determination, in calculated symbolism and unwitting remembrance, for over 300 years Black Americans have kept various ties to Africa intact[10]. The bond has frayed and stretched, it has become twisted and contorted, but through it all, it has not been broken[11]. And for as long as Black people in America have reached back to Africa to offer and receive reassurance, reaffirmation, fraternity, and strength, Africans have reached to Black people in the Americas, "those who were taken," for the same reasons[12].

## 【单词及短语】

28. origin n. (1) 起点；来源 (2) 出身，血统（文中意思）

29. tremendous adj. (1) 极大的，巨大的（文中意思） (2) 绝妙的，极棒的

30. sustain

(1) vt.（在体力、精神方面）支持，支撑
This thought had sustained him throughout the years. 这个念头支撑他度过了这么多年。

(2) vt. 保持；使持续不断 （文中意思）several years of sustained economic growth 几年的经济持续增长

(3) vt. 支撑 His health will no longer enable him to sustain the heavy burdens of office. 他的健康状况不能再支撑他从事繁重的办公室工作了。

(4) vt. 忍受；经历 sustain severe head injuries 脑部受重伤

(5) vt. 认可；赞成；确认 The allegations of discrimination were sustained. 对歧视的指控被确认。

31. odds n.

(1) 胜败比率（指根据赢或输两种几率得出的各赌家所下赌注大小的比率）at odds of 8-1
It is possible for the race to be won at very long odds. 可能会以很大胜败比率赢得比赛。

(2) 机会，可能性
The odds are that +从句。可能怎么样了。
The odds against this ever happening are high. 这种情况永远不会发生的可能性很大。
不和，相争 at odds with sb. 与某某不和

(3) 区别，差异；差额
It makes no odds whether you give me coffee or tea. 你请我喝咖啡或喝茶都一样。

(4) 不利条件 do sth. against tremendous/overwhelming odds 在极端不利的条件下做了

某事（文中意思）

She succeeded against overwhelming odds. 她在极端不利的条件下获得了成功。

32. ingenuity 名词，机灵；独创性；创造力

33. dogged adj. 坚韧的；坚持不懈的

34. symbolism n. 象征意义

35. calculated 形容词，预先计划的。还须掌握动词形式：calculate (1) vt. & vi. 计算，估计 (2) vt. 打算，旨在

Sth. is calculated to do sth. 某物旨在XXX。=Sth. is intended to do sth.

36. unwitting 形容词，不知晓的，非故意的，无心的

37. remembrance 名词，回想，回忆

38. intact 形容词，完整无缺的

39. bond n. （将人联结在一起的）结合力，纽带

40. fray 不及物动词，磨损

41. stretch vi. （柔软或弹性物）伸展，延伸；延展；被拉长；被拉宽

某个东西在某方面被延展：sth. stretches in n.

42. contorted adj. 扭曲的，弯曲的。还须掌握动词形式：contort vt. & vi. 扭曲，扭弯

distort (1) vt. 歪曲，曲解 (2) vt. 扭曲，使变形 a face distorted with anger 一张因愤怒而变形的脸

43. reassurance n. (1) 清除疑虑；安慰 (2) 保证，消除疑虑的说法（或意见）

44. reaffirmation n. 再断言，再肯定

45. fraternity n. 博爱；友爱 the ideals of liberty, equality, and fraternity 自由、平等、博爱的理想

46. reach to 触/伸及；及于

The railway line will soon reach to our town. 铁路不久就要延伸到我们镇了。

Their works reach to a great height of perfection. 他们的作品到了极完美的境地。

## 【文章解析】

[9] managed to sustain：成功地保持了XXX。tremendous=enormous，形容词，极大的。against heavy odds (=with heavy odds against) 在极端不利的条件下。against tremendous odds 为介词短语作伴随状语。尽管面对极大的挫折，美国黑人成功地与他们起源的大陆保持了联系。

[10] "Through ingenuity and dogged determination, in calculated symbolism and unwitting remembrance"为介词短语作状语，通过足智多谋与顽强的决心，以预先计划好的象征符号以及无意中的记忆，美国黑人已经保持了与完整保留下来的非洲之间的各种纽带长达300多年。ties to Africa：与非洲的纽带。

[11] bond 指 ties, through it all：经历了这一切。"it has become twisted and contorted"中的 it 指代 bond。it has not been broken 中的 it 指代 bond。纽带已经被磨损和拉伸，它已经变得扭曲和变形，尽管经历了这些，这个纽带没有被破坏。

[12] as long as：只要。those who were taken 修饰"美国黑人"，即离开非洲大陆到美国去的那批黑人。同样道理，只要美国黑人到达了非洲来提供和接收安慰、再断言、博爱和力量，那么非洲人就可以触及到被弄走的美国黑人。即纽带的作用对彼此都是一样的。

We have sought to understand each other ever since we were separated so long ago[13]. For centuries, we have gazed at one another across the transatlantic divide like a child seeing itself in the mirror for the first time[14]. And, unable for so long to reach behind the glass and touch the strangely familiar face we saw staring back, we filled in all that we did not know with all that we could imagine[15].

批注 [48]: 动词原形为 seek

批注 [49]: 名词，分水岭

## 【单词及短语】

47. seek (1) vt. & vi. 寻找；探寻 (2) vi. 企图；试图 seek to do sth. (3) vt. 请求，征求；求教

48. gaze vi. 凝视，注视

49. transatlantic adj. 大西洋沿岸国家的；横跨大西洋的

50. divide (1) vt.（使）产生分歧 sth. divides sb. 某人因某事产生分歧 (2) n. 分水岭，分界线（文中意思）

51. strangely adv. 不可思议地

52. imagine vt. 想象，设想

imaginative adj. 富于想象力的；运用想象力的

imaginable adj. 可想象的；想象得到的

imaginary adj. 想象中的，假想的，虚构的

## 【文章解析】

[13] seek to understand 试图理解，we 指美国黑人和非洲大陆上的黑人。自从我们分开那么久以前，我们便试图理解彼此。

[14] 此句表明美国黑人和非洲大陆的黑人在大洋彼岸彼此希望相互了解。"seeing itself in the mirror for the first time"为现在分词短语作定语，修饰 child，一个初次在镜子里看自己的孩子。do sth. for the first time：第一次做某事。gaze at one another: 凝视对方，通常是带有思考的注视。

[15] "unable for so long to reach behind the glass and touch the strangely familiar face we saw staring back"为形容词短语作原因状语，glass 在这里指镜子"mirror"，strangely familiar face 中用副词 strangely 修饰形容词 familiar，令人吃惊的熟悉的脸庞。"we saw staring back"为定语从句，修饰 face，我们看到的正在回望我们的脸，stare back：回望凝视。fill in A with B：用 B 来填充 A。用我们能够想象到的一切来填充我们的一切未知。we did not know 和 we could imagine 为定语从句，修饰 that。

When we finally met, in Africa and America, we were sometimes disappointed[16]. Shadowy imaginings do not usually hold up in the light of real experience[17]. We wondered if we hadn't been mistaken, if the kinship we could feel more than describe was really there, if the roots that had once bound us together had not already withered and died[18]. But time and again we were reminded of what we shared. Africa has left her mark on all of us[19]. And when we have reached out to one another through literature, politics, music, and religion, whenever we've made contact, the world has been forced to take note[20].

批注 [50]: 动词原形为 bind

## 【单词及搭配】

53. wonder v. (1) vi. 想知道，觉得好奇

How many times have I written that, I wonder? 我已经写了多少遍了？我真想知道。

vt. 想知道，不知道

I wonder whether you have thought more about it. 我想知道你是否再考虑过这事。

54. shadowy adj. 多阴影的，模糊的

55. mistake

(1) vt. & vi. 弄错；误解

(2) vt. 认不出 You can't mistake his car in the busiest street; he's painted it red.

你在最繁忙的街上也不会错认他的车，他把它漆成了红色。

56. in the light of doing 鉴于，由于，按照

57. bind vt. (1) 捆绑，捆扎（文中意思） (2) 约束 (3) vt. & vi.（使）结合

58. wither vt. & vi.（使）枯萎，（使）干枯，（使）凋谢

59. share vt.

(1) 与……分享 (2) 共同使用；共同居住；共享

They once shared a flat in Chelsea. 他们曾在切尔西共住一套公寓。

There weren't enough plates so we had to share. 盘子不够，我们得合用了。

(3) 与……共有（观点、品质）（文中意思）

Other countries don't share our reluctance to eat goat meat. 其他国家不像我们一样不愿意吃山羊肉。

60. reach out 伸出 He reached out and took my arm. 他伸出手来扶住我的胳膊。

A tree reaches out its branches towards the light. 树枝向阳光处伸展。

61. contact

(1) n. 接触 (2) n. 传达；联系；遭遇，遇见 lose contact with sb. 与某人失去联系

(3) vt.（尤指为交换信息而）与……接触；与……联系；与……交往

62. take note of 注意，留意

The committee has taken note of objections. 委员会已注意到反对意见。

63. mark (1) n. 痕迹，污点 (2) n. 记号，标记（文中意思）(3) vt. 在……留下痕迹，标出 (4) vt. 表示，指明 A marks B. A 表明了 B。

## 【文章精读】

[16] 承接上一段，彼此相望希望了解对方，真正相见时却有些许失望。下文必定解释失望的原因。

[17] 正面解释原因：对彼此的了解是通过想象力得到的，承接上一段最后一句。虚幻的想象通常不会依照现实中的经历展现出来。shadowy，形容词，虚无的；虚幻的，从"real experience"中可以判断：shadowy 和 real 应该为反义词。美国黑人与非洲大陆黑人对彼此的了解是通过想象得到的，从上一段也可以看出："we filled in all that we did not know with all that we could imagine"。hold up: 动词短语，这里指"展现"。in the light of sth./doing sth.: 鉴于，按照，由于。文中指"按照"。

[18] 上一句表明了现实和想象的偏差，由此，双方开始怀疑，血缘关系是否确实存在？

我们是否被误解了？

【译文】我们想知道：我们是否被误解了？我们能够感觉到的比描述更多的血缘关系是否确实存在？曾经将我们捆绑在一起的根是否没有枯萎和死亡？

wonder: want to know。"if we hadn't been mistaken"为 wondered 的宾语从句，if 表示"是否"。"we could feel more than describe"为定语从句，修饰 kinship，血缘关系。describe 在这里作及物动词，为省略语，省略了"we could feel more than we could describe"。

"that had once bound us together"为定语从句，修饰 roots。

withered adj. 枯萎的；凋谢的；憔悴的。文中 withered 为动词 wither 的过去分词！不是形容词！动词形式要求掌握：wither

(1) vi. 干枯，枯萎；凋零；凋谢

(2) cease to flourish；fall into decay or decline 衰落；萧条；失去活力

Projects would wither away if they did not command local support. 如果得不到当地的支持，项目就会丧失其活力。

(3) vt. cause harm or damage to 损害；毁坏 (4) vt. 使（人）难堪；使窘迫；使羞惭

His clipped tone withered Mary. 他尖刻的语调使玛丽感到难堪。

[19] time and again：无数次，屡次。此句表明美国黑人与非洲黑人的共同根基和烙印，尽管怀疑彼此是否由于想象与现实的不吻合所误解。be reminded of sth. 想起某物。"what we shared"作介词 of 的宾语，"我们共同所有的特征提醒了我们"。"Africa has left her mark on all of us" 即为我们所共同具备的特征。

[20] reached out one another, 动词短语，接触到彼此。make contact, 动词短语，取得联系。

主语+take note+宾语，某人关注什么。

本句表明：当黑人通过文学作品、政治等形式触及到彼此时，只要我们（祖先与后代）之间取得联系，世界就不得不关注我们。本句表现了一种积极的态度。

# 【题目解析】

1. The primary purpose of this passage is to

(A) show the impact Black Americans have had on African societies

(B) discuss African's efforts to embrace American culture

(C) point out the ambivalent feelings one community has for another

(D) emphasize the significance of an ongoing relationship

(E) examine the cultural ties between two nations

【解析】D

考察文章的主旨。文章第一段解释谚语"树无根则不立"的道理，由此引出美国黑人与非洲大陆黑人本是同根生。第二段：美国黑人已经成功地与非洲大陆黑人建立了联系等表明了两方建立持续发展关系的重要意义。ongoing，形容词，持续的，正在进行的，发展的，相当于 sustainable。

(A) show the impact Black Americans have had on African societies。 have an impact on sb.对某人有影响。作者没有强调美国黑人对非洲黑人的影响，从第一段来看：树无根而不立，作者要表达的是根对后代的影响，即非洲大陆黑人对美国黑人的影响，这一点从这一句可以看出：But time and again we were reminded of what we shared, Africa has left her mark

批注 [A51]: 定语从句，修饰 impact，美国黑人对非洲社会的影响。

on all of us.

(B) embrace (1) vt./vi. 拥抱；怀抱 (2) vt. 欣然接受（或支持）（某种信仰、理论、改变）；信奉

(3) vt. 包括，包含 embrace sth. 包含XXX。题干中的意思为"接受，信奉"。非洲欣然接受美国文化。该选项与(A) 犯了一样的错误：非洲文化没有试图接受美国黑人文化，相反作者强调根基对美国黑人的影响。

(C) ambivalent，形容词，有矛盾心态或想法的。文章中唯一体现矛盾心理的是双方对彼此的想象与现实有所出入。但这不等于两个社会对彼此感情的矛盾。作者的意图在于强调美国黑人与非洲黑人在感情上是积极的。

(E) 作者没有审视两个国家的"文化纽带"，而是情感纽带。

2. The "message" (in line 6) is best characterized as
(A) veiled criticism   批注 [A52]: 隐含的批评
(B) cautionary advice
(C) a questionable proposition   批注 [A53]: 值得商榷的观点
(D) a nostalgic recollection   批注 [A54]: 怀旧的回忆
(E) an optimistic prediction

【解析】B

characterize vt. (1) 描述……的特性，形容……的特色 characterize A as B 把 A 描述成 B（题干意思） (2) vt. 成为……的特征，是……的典型 be characterized by sth. 以 XXX 为特征

第一段中的 message 指代 a people cannot flourish without their life-giving foundations in the past，具有警示作用。foundations 相当于 roots。作者告诉我们能否发展取决于与根的连带关系。

(B) cautionary adj.=warning 警告的，告诫的

(A) veiled adj. 掩饰的, 间接表示的

【重要句型】There was a barely veiled +名词 in somewhere. 在XXX隐含/毫不掩饰的XXX。veiled criticism：隐含的批评。该选项为重要干扰项，作者的基调为强调一个民族发展的必要条件：与根的联系。作者并没有批评谁，因此没有隐含的批评。注意警示与批评的含义不同。

(C) 有疑问的主张。很明显错误。该论点毋庸置疑。

questionable adj. 可疑的，成问题的，有疑问的，不确定的（选项意思）

【重要句型】It is questionable that/whether/what/where 或其他主语从句：某事令人怀疑。

proposition 名词，陈述，主张；论点

(D) nostalgic adj. 思乡的；怀旧的。recollection 名词，回忆，记忆；记忆力

固定短语：to the best of one's recollection 据某人回忆

整篇文章作者没有表达自己怀旧的感情。

须掌握 recollection 的动词形式：recollect vt. 回忆，追忆；想起，记起（某事）

(E) 定语运用错误。该 message 包含着对一个民族脱离根基所造成的后果，显然是一种预测，但这种预测不是"乐观的"。

SAT 精解讲义

3. The proverb in lines 15-16 primarily serves to
(A) offer insight into young children's behavior
(B) emphasize the vulnerability of children
(C) show people's inherent interest in their history
(D) demonstrate the complexity of familial relations
(E) warn those who seek to undermine the family

【解析】C

serve (1) vt. 实现；满足=satisfy

【重要句型】Sth. is useful= Sth. serves a useful purpose.
serve the interests of sb. 满足某人的利益
(2) vi. 有用，起作用 Sth. serves as XXX. 某物用于什么。（题干意思）
serve to do sth.=be used to do sth. 用于做什么

primarily 主要，副词。注意题干的意思：谚语的主要目的是什么？

(C) 这段谚语的解释见文章精读中的注释。inherent interest in their history 对人们历史的固有兴趣。与第一段该谚语的解释同义。

(A) 作者没有讨论小孩的行为特点，偏离文中思想。

(B) 强调小孩的弱点。该说法不准确，小孩被偷确实说明了孩子的弱点，但这不是谚语要表达的主要意图。请注意题干的含义：该谚语的主要目的是什么？
vulnerable adj.（身体或情感上）易受攻击的，易受伤害的；脆弱的 vulnerable to sth./doing sth. 易受XXX攻击。She is vulnerable to colds. 她易患感冒。
vulnerability n. 极易受伤害，极为脆弱

(D) 作者没有这个意思。无中生有。

(E) 作者没有这个意思，也没有表明偷小孩的后果，因此更谈不上警告偷孩子的行为。"who seek to undermine the family" 为定语从句，修饰 those。
seek vt. 寻找 seek sth./seek to do sth. 想要做某事（选项意思）
undermine v. 侵蚀（岩层）底基，破坏（建筑、要塞）底基，暗中破坏；逐渐削弱
This could undermine years of hard work. 这会破坏多年的辛勤劳动。

批注 [A55]: 洞察，对某事的洞察：insight into sth., 名词短语

4. In context, "shadowy" primarily serves to suggest something
(A) gloomy
(B) secret
(C) sinister
(D) concealed
(E) unsubstantiated

【解析】E。见文中精读分析。shadowy 必然与 real 反义。unsubstantiated adj. 未经证实的；无事实根据的。须要掌握该单词的变形形式：substantiate vt. 证实，证明。substance n. 物质。

(A) gloomy adj. (1) 黑暗的；光线不好的（尤指看起来压抑或恐怖的）(2) 感到悲伤（或悲观）的 be gloomy about sth. 为某事而悲观 (3) 使悲伤（或消沉）的 a gloomy atmosphere 令人沮丧的气氛

(C) sinister adj. 邪恶的，阴险的；凶兆的

(D) concealed adj. 隐藏的=veiled。须掌握动词形式：conceal
(1) vt. 隐藏；隐蔽；掩藏；掩盖
A line of sand dunes concealed the distant sea. 一排沙丘遮住了远处的海。
句型：A concealed B. A 隐藏了 B。
(2) vi. 隐瞒  conceal from sb. 隐瞒某人

5. In lines 42-50 (we wondered…note), there is a shift in feeling from
(A) fear to courage
(B) anger to forgiveness
(C) uncertainty to despair
(D) regret to determination
(E) doubt to pride

【解析】E。显然本段的感情从对我们之间是否被误解的怀疑转换为骄傲。

6. The author primarily makes use of which of the following to convey his point?
(A) hypothetical scenarios
(B) broad generalization
(C) historical facts
(D) personal anecdotes
(E) scholary analyses

【解析】B

注意题干问法：主要使用了哪种方式表达观点？
point 在这里表示"观点"。作者主要使用了总结的方法来表达观点。
(A) 假设。没有假设出现。
(B) broad adj. (1) 宽的 (2) 清楚的，明显的 (3) 大概的（文中意思） broad generalization，大致的概括。正确，作者提到了美国黑人如何保持与非洲黑人的联系，没有具体历史时间、地点，使用了概括的方式。
(C) 历史事实。作者提到了历史事实，但并不是文章的主要表达方式。
(D) anecdote n. 趣闻，轶事
(E) 学术分析。文中没用到学术分析。

# 文章 19

In 1843 Augusta Ada King published an influential set of notes describing Charles Babbage's concept of an "analytical engine"—the first design for an automatic computer. King's notes, which included her programme for computing a series of figures called Bermoulli numbers, established her importance in computer science[1]. However, her fascinating life and lineage (she was the daughter of the flamboyant poet Lord Byron)—and her role as a female pioneer in her field—have turned her into an icon[2]. She has inspired biographies, plays, novels, and even a feature film[3]. And whereas many women have helped to advance computer science, only King has had a computer language named after her: Ada[4].

批注 [A56]: 耀眼的

## 【单词及搭配】

1. influential adj. 有影响的；有势力的
2. figure
(1) n. 数字 （文中意思）
(2) n. 位数 a three-figure sum of money 一笔3位数的钱
(3) vt. 以为，认为；猜，推断，推测；估计
I figure that wearing a suit makes you look like a bank clerk.
3. lineage n. 直系；祖系，家系
4. icon n. 代表，典型
5. inspire vt.
(1) 激励，激发，鼓舞
(2) 唤起（感情，尤指正面感情）inspire confidence 带来信心
(3) give rise to 引起，导致，使发生（文中意思）
The film was successful enough to inspire a sequel. 电影很成功，足以因此而拍摄续集。
6. whereas 连词，而，却；反之
You treat the matter lightly, whereas I myself was never more serious. 你处理事情很轻率，而我自己却过于认真。
7. advance
(1) vi. 进步 Our knowledge is advancing all the time. 我们的知识在不断地进步。
(2) v. 使（事件）提前发生，加速（事件）进程
I advanced the schedule by several weeks. 我把进度表提前了几周。
(3) vt. 促进（人、事业、计划），帮助发展
(4) put forward 提出（理论、建议）

## 【文章精读】

[1] "describing Charles Babbage's concept of an 'analytical engine'"为现在分词短语作定语，修饰 notes。"called Bermoulli numbers"为过去分词短语作定语，修饰 figures。figure 为"数字"！这点从贝努力数就可以看出来，注意语境。"established her importance in computer science"为现在分词短语作伴随状语。

[2] turn sb. into an icon 将某人变为一个偶像

[3] inspire 在这里指导致什么的产生，她引发了传记、小说，甚至长片的产生。

[4] And whereas many women have helped to advance computer science, only King has had a computer language named after her: Ada. 进一步阐明 King 在计算机领域的杰出之处：尽管很多女性致力于计算机科学的进步，但只有 King 得到了以她的名字命名的计算机语言——Ada。advance 在这里是"促进发展"的意思，及物动词。name A after B：以 B 来命名 A，动词短语。"named after he"为过去分词短语作定语，修饰 language。

## 【题目解析】

1. The passage is primarily concerned with

(A) explaining Augusta Ada King's interest in computer science

(B) providing a character analysis of Augusta Ada King

(C) summarizing how and why Augusta Ada King is celebrated

(D) tracing the development of the modern-day computer

(E) encouraging more women to pursue careers in computer science

【解析】C

be concerned with sth./doing sth. 参与，关于

a conference concerned with global warming crisis，一个关于全球变暖危机的会议，名词短语。concerned with 为过去分词短语作定语，修饰 conference。

文章先提到 Ada 如何成名，再写她为什么这样有名，一方面和她的出身有关，另一方面由于她在计算机领域做出的杰出贡献。celebrated，形容词，著名的。

(D) trace the development of sth. 追溯某物的发展历史，trace 为及物动词，跟踪。本文主旨并非追溯计算机的发展历史。

(E) 作者并没有鼓励其他女性从事计算机科学。

批注 [57]: vt. 追求。
名词形式为：pursuit。be in the pursuit of sth.=pursue sth. 追求某物

2. The author of the passage would most likely disagree with which of the following statements about Augusta Ada King?

(A) Her family history plays no part in the fascination she arouses.

(B) Her contribution to computer science were markedly original.

(C) Interest in her has spread throughout popular culture.

(D) She was well known in the field of computer science after she had completed her work.

(E) Her life was remarkable even apart from her contributions to computer science.

【解析】A。见[2]，她的出身也使她成为人们的偶像。因此，(A) 不对。"she arouses"为定语从句，修饰 fascination：由她引起的人们对她的痴迷。arouse vt. (1) 唤醒=waken sb. up (2) vt. 引起，激发（选项意思）

批注 [58]: 反对

批注 [59]: 介词短语，除什么之外

批注 [60]: 名词短语，在某方面的贡献。contributions to sth./doing

(B) contribution to sth. 为名词短语，对某物的贡献。markedly，显著地，副词。original，这里指"创新的，首创的"。见[1]和[5]。概念是第一次提出，用于计算贝努力数的 Ada 语言也是首创的。

(C) interest 这里指"兴趣"，名词，对她的兴趣已经扩展至多各个流行文化领域。见[3]。艾达本人导致了各种关于自己的文化形式的产生。

(D) 她完成著作后在计算机领域闻名。见[1]和[2]。work 在这里指著作。

【重要句型】Sb. is well known by sth. 某人因什么而闻名。

Sb. is famous for sth. 某人因什么而闻名。

本句的另一种表达方式：Having completed her work, she became well known in the field of computer science.

(E) remarkable adj. 异常的；引人注目的；不寻常的；非凡的；显著的。即使没有她在计算机领域的贡献，她的生活也非常引人注目。符合本文意思，引人注目的焦点一是出身，二是在计算机领域的贡献。须掌握动词形式：

contribute (1) vt. & vi. 捐献，捐助，贡献出 (2) vi. 撰稿，投稿 contribute to sth. 向某个刊物投稿 (3) vi. 起促成作用 Sth. contributes to sth. 某物（前面的）促成了后面的事情。contribute to 为动词短语，后面的事情可好可坏，如：

Sunshine contributes to growth of sunflower.

Chronic malnutrition contributed to his illness.

批注 [61]: to 是介词！后面跟随名词或动名词。

# 文章 20

## 文章 20.1

It hung in Napoleon's bedroom until moving to the Louvre in 1804. It caused traffic jams in New York for seven weeks as 1.6 million people jostled to see it. In Tokyo viewers were allowed ten seconds each[1]. The object of all this attention was the world's most famous portrait, the Mona Lisa.[2]

【单词及搭配】

1. jostle vt.（多指在人群中）推搡，（用肘）推挤，挤撞；vi. 争夺，抢夺；为……而竞争。jostle for attention 目不暇接。jostle to do sth. 争抢着做某事，动词短语。compete for doing sth. / compete to do sth.

There emerge variety of ideas jostling for attention of the general public.

2. cause/invite/inspire/induce/occasion/lead to sth.

Your remarks occasioned his anger.

3. viewer 看客

view n. 意见 opinion/idea/perspective；vt. 看作 view him as a fool=consider sb. as

2. allow

(1) vt. 承认，允许 allow sb. to do sth.

(2) 准许（某人）拥有（某物）She was allowed a higher profile. 允许她有较高的曝光度。（文中意思）

sb. be allowed+时间 to do sth. (each) 每个人只有多长时间做某事。

Competitors were allowed 10 minutes to illustrate/state personal ideas each.

(3) 未能阻止（某事）发生，放任 allow the opportunity to slip away 让这机遇溜走

(4) 为（某物）留出 The house was demolished to allow for road widening. 为拓宽道路而拆了房子。

(5) 考虑到，顾及 Income rose by 11 per cent allowing for inflation. 考虑到通货膨胀，收入增长了 11%。

(6) 承认 He allowed that the penalty appeared too harsh for the crime. 他承认对此犯罪行为来说，惩罚似乎太重了。

3. portray vt. 描绘 portray a character 描绘一个人物 portrait n. 描绘，雕塑，绘画

## 【文章精读】

第一段描述蒙娜丽莎油画的受欢迎。

[1] 每个人只有 10 秒钟时间去看它。each 指每个参观者。traffic jam, 名词短语, 交通堵塞。

[2] The object of all this attention: 关注的对象。本段开篇点题，描绘了蒙娜丽莎画像展出的壮观场面。

Historically, its subject was nobody special, probably the wife of a Florentine merchant named Giocondo[1]. But her portrait set the standard for High Renaissance paintings in many important ways[2]. The use of perspective, which creates the illusion of depth behind Mona Lisa's head, and triangular composition established the importance of geometry in painting[3]. It diverged from the stiff, profile portraits that had been the norm by displaying the subject in a relaxed, natural, three-quarter pose[4].

## 【单词及搭配】

1. historically adv. 从历史角度，在历史上，以历史观点 historically important buildings 有重大历史意义的建筑 a historically inaccurate film 一部与历史有出入的电影

批注 [A62]：用副词修饰形容词

2. set the standard for sth. 为 XXX 制定标准，动词短语

3 perspective n. (1) 透视图法, 远近画法（文中意思）(2) 看法, 观点 (3) 洞察力, 眼力 (4) 远景；展望, 前途

4. illusion (1) 错误的观念；错误的理解 (2) 假象 the illusion of sth. (3) 幻觉, 错觉（文中意思）

5. illusion of depth  立体感效果

6. diverge (1) vi. 分开；岔开 Their ways had diverged at campus. 在大学里他们就分道扬镳了。(2) vi. 向不同方向发展 (3) vi.（意见、理论、方法等）分歧, 相异（文中意思）(4) vi. 偏离；背离, diverge from sth./doing sth.

My idea diverged from his.

7. stiff adj. 僵硬的

8. norm n. 惯例，典范，准则，规范，标准

9. pose

(1) vt. 形成, 构成（问题、危险、困难）pose a threat to sb./sth. 对 XXX 构成威胁

(2) vt. 提出（问题或考虑对象）pose/propose/raise a problem 提出一个问题

(3) vt. 假装, 冒充  pose as sb.

(4) n. 摆造型,（文中意思）

10. (1) establish a theory/subject/law/nation

(2) illustrate the importance of the article

The theory is important.=The theory is of great importance.

## 【文章精读】

第二段首先探讨蒙娜丽莎人物的来源,其次解释蒙娜丽莎油画对后代艺术家的影响。

[1] "Historically"为副词,从历史角度(来看),修饰整个句子,类似的用法还有:Theoretically, a line can extend into infinity. 从理论上来说,直线可以无限地延伸。

"subject"指主题,"nobody special"指不是什么特殊人物,special 为形容词作后置定语。"named Giocondo"为过去分词短语作后置定语,修饰 merchant。

[2] 蒙娜丽莎艺术品的时代意义:为文艺复兴时代的很多方面设立了标准。way 在这里指"方面",aspects。

[3] 承接[2],解释蒙娜丽莎画面的 creation。创造了在蒙娜丽莎头后面的立体感效果的幻影的透视图的运用以及三角形构图的运用建立了画画中几何学的重要性。The use of perspective, which creates the illusion of depth behind Mona Lisa's head, and triangular composition established the importance of geometry in painting. 主语为"The use of perspective, which creates the illusion of depth behind Mona Lisa's head, and triangular composition",其中省略了 the use of triangular composition,"which creates the illusion of depth behind Mona Lisa's head"为定语从句,修饰 perspective。

[4] 主语 it 指代蒙娜丽莎这幅作品。be the norm by doing sth.:以某物为规范。display 在这里指"展现"。蒙娜丽莎这一作品偏离了僵硬的轮廓描绘,这些描绘以在一个轻松的、自然的大半身像展现为规范。"that had been the norm by displaying the subject in a relaxed, natural, three-quarter pose"为定语从句,修饰 portraits。

One of the first easel paintings intended to be framed and hung on a wall, the Mona Lisa fully realized the potential of the new oil medium[1]. Instead of proceeding from outlined figures, as painters did before, Leonardo modeled features through light and shadow[2]. Starting with dark undertones, he built the illusion of three-dimensional features through layers and layers of thin, transparent glazes.[3] This technique rendered the whole, as Leonardo said, "without lines or borders, in the manner of smoke."[4] His colors ranged from light to dark in a continuous gradation of subtle tones, without crisp separating edges[5]. The forms seemed to emerge from, and melt into, shadows[6].

And then there's that famous smile….

批注 [A63]: 架上画
批注 [A64]: 及物动词,在这里指把画放在框子里
批注 [A65]: 油画
批注 [A66]: 画画术语,透明轴

## 【单词及搭配】

1. intend vt. 打算做什么 (1) 人打算做什么 I intend to visit him. 人+intended to do sth. (2) 打算(非人) be intended to do sth. 某个事物旨在做什么。

The graph illustrates the seriousness of global warming.

The graph is intended to illustrate the seriousness of global warming.

The graph intended to illustrate the seriousness of global warming is shown above/below.

The graph was intended to demonstrate the changes in amount of beef and fish consumed per person in a certain country between the year 1979 and 2004.

这幅图片反应了 2000 年到 2010 年之间,中国某省人均上网时间增加的情况。

The graph was intended to illustrate the rise/increase in time duration concerned with/of consumed per person to surf the net in a certain province in China from the year 2000 to 2010.

The graphs was concerned with the rise in time duration consumed per person to surf the net.

Sth. changes/rises/falls dramatically/remarkably/markedly/obviously/sharply/steadily.

Fall to 100. Rise to 100. Increase to 100.

Fall by 30% / fall to 30% of the previous+名词(amount/number…)

The amount of A and B fell to 10 and 20, respectively, leading to/inviting/inducing/causing/bringing about/occasioning environmental crisis.

2. potential

(1) 形容词，潜在的，可能的 (2) 名词，潜力，潜能 (3) 潜在性，可能性 the potential to do sth./for doing sth.

3. proceed from 动词短语 (1) 从……出发/开始

This train is now proceeding from Paris to London. 这次列车从巴黎开往伦敦。

(2) 从……产生；起因于 originate from sth./doing sth.

His mistake proceeded from his ignorance. 他的错误源于他的无知。

4. outlined 形容词，勾勒的

5. feature 名词，这里指"容貌"，与 figure 有同样的意思。注意同样的意思用多个词汇表达。

6. undertone 名词

(1) 低声；小声 They are talking in undertones. 他们在低声说话。

(2) 淡色，浅色；底彩 （文中意思）

(3) 潜在的含义 There is an undertone of regret in what he said. 他的话中带有悔意。

7. transparent

(1) 形容词，透明的 transparent water 清澈的水（文中意思）

(2) 易察觉的，易看出的 transparent attempt to do sth. 明显的某种企图

(3) （思想、情感、动机）易被人所知的 Someone is transparent. 某人易被人看穿。

(4) （机构或其活动）受公众监督的；透明的 transparent management 透明管理

8. render

(1) vt. 给予，提供（服务）

Money serves as a reward for services rendered. 钱用作对所提供的服务的一种报酬。rendered 为过去分词作后置定语，修饰 services。

(2) vt.（供审查、考虑）提交，呈报 render sth.

(3) （诗／文）交出，献出 He will render up his immortal soul. 他将献出他那不灭的灵魂。

(4) vt. 作出（裁决、宣判）render upon sth./sb. 对某人/物做出判决

The jury's finding amounted to the clearest verdict yet rendered upon the scandal. 陪审团的裁决是迄今为止对这丑闻作出的最清楚的结论。"rendered upon the scandal"为过去分词短语作后置定语。

(5) make vt. 使成为；使得 The rains rendered his escape impossible. 下雨使他无法逃跑。

(6) vt. 翻译 The phrase was rendered into English. 这个短语被译成英语。

(7) （艺术上）表现；表演；朗诵；演奏；处理（绘画等的主题）This character was poorly rendered by him. 他把这个角色演得很糟糕。

9. in the manner of 照……的式样；做出……的样子

10. range (1) 名词，幅度；范围 (2) 一系列 a wide range of sth. 广范围的XXX (3) vi. range from A to B 变动，变化

11. gradation （从某色调、音调或颜色向另一种的）微妙变化

12. subtle adj.

(1)（尤指变化或差别）微妙的；细微的；难以描述的；难以分析的（文中意思）

(2)（混合物、效果）精细复杂的；轻描淡写的；隐约的 subtle lighting 隐隐约约的灯光

(3) 灵活迂回的，巧妙的 a subtle approach 巧妙的方法

(4) a subtle mind 敏锐的头脑

13. crisp

(1) 干而脆的

(2)（说话方式）干脆的；干净利落的；简明的 Her answer was crisp.（文中含义）

14. melt into 逐渐消失；逐渐融入

In the rainbow, one color melts into another. 在彩虹中，各种颜色互相交融。

It is difficult to tell where the blue melts into the green. 很难说蓝色是在什么地方变成绿色了。

Night melted into day. 斗转星移，黑夜变成了白天。

**【文章精读】**

第三段解释说明蒙娜丽莎油画的"technique"。

[1] 本段具体解释蒙娜丽莎油画在美术史上的创新性意义。

注意：这句话虽然没有连词 and，但它不是独立主格！所谓独立主格结构，表示分词之前具有自己独立的主语，而这个分词主语不同于主句主语。如：

Weather permitting, we will go fishing. 分词具有自己独立的主语 weather，不同于主句的主语 we。

"One of the first easel paintings intended to be framed and hung on a wall"为同位语结构，因为"One of the first easel paintings"和"the Mona Lisa"指的是同一个对象。"intended to be framed and hung on a wall"为过去分词作定语，修饰同位语"One of the first easel paintings"。陈述句语序为：One of the first easel paintings are intended to be framed and hung on a wall。早期的被有意框裱并挂在墙上的架上画之一。这是一个被动语态。be intended to do sth. 注意何时用被动语态：The plan was intended to protect environment. 该计划的目的是保护环境。

"fully"修饰谓语动词 realized，完全体现了XXX。realize 在这里为及物动词，实现。

**【译文】**作为最早被有意地框裱并挂在墙上的架上画之一，蒙娜丽莎完全体现了新油画表现方式的（艺术）潜力。

potent adj. (1)（药等）效力大的；威力大的

(2) 强有力的；有说服力的

He was once a potent ruler. 他曾经是有权势的统治者。

[2] Instead of proceeding from outlined figures, as painters did before, Leonardo modeled features through light and shadow. instead of doing sth.：代替某物，介词短语作状语。"as

painters did before"为状语从句。Leonardo 没有像以前的画家那样从绘制人物轮廓出发，而是通过光和阴影来绘制人物。

重要句型：Instead of doing sth., 主语+谓语

[3] 本句进一步描述如何用光和阴影来表现层次。start with 与 proceed from 的含义完全相同，从哪里开始。"Starting with dark undertones"为现在分词短语作状语，其逻辑主语与主语相同，为主动，所以用现在分词。

[4] This technique rendered the whole, as Leonardo said, "without lines or borders, in the manner of smoke." 注意：render 在本句指"绘制，表达"。whole 这里作名词，整体。technique 为"技巧"，即绘画的技巧，该技巧以烟雾的样子绘画没有线条或边界的整体。

重要句型：do sth. without / with doing sth.

[5] range from dark to light：从明变到暗，light 和 dark 均为名词。他的颜色以一种连续的微妙的色调变化从明到暗，其中没有干脆的边缘的划分。

[6] 省略句，完整语句为：The forms seemed to emerge from shadows and melt into shadows.

# 文章 20.2

Why is Mona Lisa the best-known painting in the entire world?[1] A small glimpse at even some of its subject's features—her eyes, or perhaps just her hands—brings instant recognition even to those who have no taste of passion for painting[2]. Art historians, poets, and admirers have tried to explain the commanding place that the Mona Lisa has in our cultural life with reference to qualities intrinsic to the work[3]. There is something, they argue, inside the painting that speaks to us all, that unleashes feelings, emotion, and recognition[4]. This idea originated at the beginning of the nineteenth century, though it had precedents.[5] It is still the position of many art critics.[6]

【单词及搭配】

1. feature，文中指"容貌"。同 figure。
2. instant 形容词 (1) 立刻的，立即的（文中意思）(2)（人）立刻（或突然）成为……的 become an instant millionaire 一夜之间成为百万富翁
(3) 立刻成就的，一蹴而就的
We can't promise instant solutions. 我们不能保证马上就能解决。
3. recognition
(1) 认识；识别（文中意思）(2) 承认；确认；认可 (3) 赏识；表彰；报偿
His work was slow to gain recognition. 他的工作尚未得到赏识。
4. commanding 支配的；占优的；权力较大的（文中意思）overwhelming/dominant
5. with reference to 介词短语，参照，关于
6. quality
(1) 质量；品质；优质 quality of a product 产品质量
(2) 优秀，卓越

(3) 特质，特征；才能，功效，素养 leadership qualities 领导才能
7. intrinsic adj. 固有的，内在的，体内的；本质的，基本的，精华的
8. unleash vt. 放开；释放，引发
9. precedent
(1) 名词，先例，前例 precedents for doing sth. 做某事的先例
(2) adj. 在前的，在先的，前面的 a precedent case 一个先例
10. position 名词，观点，立场

## 【文章精读】

第一段解释蒙娜丽莎油画为什么如此有名。第一句点题。

[1] best-known，其中 known 为过去分词，用副词 best 修饰：最被人知道的，即著名的，表示"著名的"单词还须掌握：famous, celebrated, distinguished。

点题，为什么蒙娜丽莎如此有名？

[2] 举例说明蒙娜丽莎的魅力。注意用词：a small glimpse at sth. 无关紧要地撇一眼 a glimpse at sth. 瞥一眼。subject：主题，即蒙娜丽莎本人。feature：这里指"容貌"，从后文对眼睛的概括即可知 feature 在这里不表示"特征"。动词短语 bring sth. to sb./sth. 给某人/物带来 XXX。注意副词 even 的位置。taste of：动词短语/名词短语，文中为名词短语，有某种味道；体验到。"who have no taste of passion for painting"为定语从句，修饰 those。即使无关紧要地撇一眼该人物容貌——她的眼睛，或许仅仅是她的手，甚至都会给那些对画画没有热情体验的人一种即刻的认同。

[3] 本句解释学者总结的蒙娜丽莎吸引人的原因：作品内在的特点。"that the Mona Lisa has in our cultural life"为定语从句，修饰 place。commanding place：支配地位。have a commanding place in sth.：在某方面具有统治地位。艺术历史学家、诗人及崇拜者试图按照作品内在的特征来解释蒙娜丽莎在我们的文化生活中占据的统治性地位。

[4] 注意代词 they 指代"Art historians, poets, and admirers"。argue = consider = maintain = claim，主张。"they argue"为插入语。"that speaks to us all, that unleashes feelings, emotion, and recognition"为定语从句，修饰 something。他们认为画的内部有一些事物在向我们所有人讲话，这些东西宣泄感受、情感与认同。本句对应了[3]中的"qualities intrinsic to the work"。

[5] 本文中出现多个表示"起源于"的短语：originate from, proceed from。尽管先前有人提出过这种观点，但这个观点一般认为首创于 19 世纪初。

[6] position 在这里表示观点，同 opinion, argument。

Art historian Kenneth Clarke, for example, writing in 1973, could not accept that the Mona Lisa was famous for reasons other than its inner qualities[1]. There are millions of people, he explained, who know the name of only one picture—the Mona Lisa[2]. This, he argues, is not simply due to an accident of accumulated publicity[3]. It means that this strange image strikes at the subconscious with a force that is extremely rare in an individual work of art[4].

## 【单词及搭配】

1. other than = apart from = except 除了
He claims not to own anything other than a car. 他声称除了车子他一无所有。

2. due to

(1) due to=caused by=ascribable to 由……导致的，应归功于，应归咎于

Unemployment due to automation will grow steadily. 自动化导致的失业人数将不断增加。

(2) because of；owing to 因为，由于（文中意思）

He had to withdraw due to a knee injury. 他因膝伤不得不退出。

3. accumulate

(1) vt. 聚集；积累 accumulate enough evidence 收集足够的证据

(2) vt.（逐渐）积累 accumulate a huge fortune 积累起一大笔财富

4. publicity 名词，公众的注意，名声 attracted wide publicity：引了公众的广泛注意。

5. subconscious (1) 形容词，下意识的，潜意识的 (2) 名词，下意识（文中意思）

# 【文章精读】

[1] 承接上一段举例说明蒙娜丽莎的出名是由于画本身的艺术品质。主语为"Art historian Kenneth Clarke"，"writing in 1973"为现在分词短语作伴随状语，其逻辑主语与句子的主语一致。"that the Mona Lisa was famous for reasons other than its inner qualities"为宾语从句。be famous for：因XXX而闻名。"other than its inner qualities"为定语，修饰 reasons：除了内在优点的原因。比如美术史学家肯尼斯·克拉克在 1973 年写道：他无法接受蒙娜丽莎不是由于其出色的内在素质而闻名的观点。

[2] 解释蒙娜丽莎由于内在品质而闻名。he explained 为插入语。who know the name of only one picture—the Mona Lisa 为定语从句，修饰 people。他解释道：上百万的人仅仅知道一幅画的名字——蒙娜丽莎。

[3] 主语"this"指代上百万人仅仅知道一幅画的名字——蒙娜丽莎这件事。argue 在这里表示"主张，认为"。这件事情，他认为，并非简单地源自不断积累的公众宣传的偶然性。

[4] 主语 it 指代[3]，strange 这里指"奇妙的，不可思议的"。这意味着这种奇妙的形象下意识地以一种在个人艺术作品中极其罕见的力量去打动人。就是说，这种奇怪的图形具有一种魔力，冲击着人的潜意识，这是任何一件艺术品所罕有的力量。

Clark's conception of art history is now regarded as somewhat old-fashioned[1]. This is not the case with the "postmodern" Paul Barolsky, who in 1994, seeking to explain what it is about the Mona Lisa that "holds us in thrall," pointed to Leonardo's remarkable technique, which creates a sense of texture and depth[2]. The painter, he added, rendered the "inwardness of the sitter, the sense…of her mind or soul."[3] I think one should avoid succumbing to the charm of a myth, to the idea that inside every masterpiece that has remained alive for centuries something imponderable speaks to us.[4] It is of course intensely pleasurable to imagine that, as we face the products of Leonardo, Raphael, and other great artists of bygone ages, armed with nothing but our "innate" sensibility, a mysterious yet almost palpable contact is established[5]. But like most historians, I start with the assumption that the renown of a masterpiece rests on a sequence of events and historical agencies (people, institutions, process) working in a largely unplanned manner for different ends.[6] Such forces have turned the Mona Lisa into the best-known painting in the world.[7] Whether the Mona Lisa "deserves" this position is a judgment I happily leave to the reader.[8]

批注 [A67]：后现代主义。post 表示"在……之后"，如：postgraduate，研究生。

**【单词及搭配】**

1. somewhat adv. 稍微；有点
2. inwardness 内在性质，心性，亲密，灵性
3. sitter 坐着的人（尤指被画像或参加考试的人），文中指蒙娜丽莎
4. succumb vi. 屈服于（压力、诱惑或其他消极力量）submit to sth. 动词短语，屈从
5. imponderable adj. 难以估量（或回答）的，不可估量（或回答）的
ponder vt. & vi. 考虑；深思熟虑
6. intensely adv. 强烈地；极度 an intensely moving film 一部极为感人的电影
7. pleasurable adj. 令人高兴的，使人快乐的，使人满意的；舒适的
8. bygone adj. 过去的，以往的；过时的
9. arm with 动词短语，用……武装；向……提供
10. innate adj. 天生的，生来的，先天的
11. sensibility n. 敏锐；敏感性
12. mysterious adj. 神秘的；不可思议的；难以理解的；无法解释的。文中另外一个单词也表示这个含义：imponderable。
do sth. in mysterious circumstance 神秘地做某事
mysterious about sth. 对某事讳莫如深
13. palpable adj.
(1)（尤指感情、气氛强烈到）能感觉到的，能触摸得到的 a palpable sense of loss 强烈的失败感
(2) 明显的；易察觉的
14. renown 名望，声誉 authors of great renown 声誉卓著的作者
15. rest
(1) vi. 倚，靠，被支撑 rest on sth. 倚靠在哪里
(2) rest sth. on XXX 使……倚在，把……靠在 He rested a hand on her shoulder. 他把手搭在她肩膀上。
(3) rest on=be based on=be grounded in=depend on 倚靠（文中意思）
16. unplanned adj. 意外的；计划外的
17. end 这里作名词，目的；目标 to this end，为此
18. deserve
(1) vt. 应得，应受 deserve to do sth. 应该做某事。We didn't deserve to win, we didn't play well. 我们不应获胜，我们打得不好。
19. thrall n. 奴役；束缚 in one's thrall, in thrall to sb./sth. 受……控制；深受……影响
**【重要句型】** Sth./Sb. is largely in thrall to sth./sb. 某人/某物深受什么的影响控制。

**【文章精读】**

[1] Clark 关于美术历史的概念有些过时，由此引出新的观点。
[2] 指出与第一段不同的后现代派关于蒙娜丽莎如此闻名原因的观点。
句型：This is (not) the case with A. 对于 A（不）是这样的。

## SAT 精解讲义

This is not the case with the "postmodern" Paul Barolsky, who in 1994, seeking to explain what it is about the Mona Lisa that "holds us in thrall," pointed to Leonardo's remarkable technique, which creates a sense of texture and depth.

hold sb. in thrall：动词短语，控制某人

【译文】后现代派 Paul Barolsky 的观点不同，Paul Barolsky 于 1994 年试图解释蒙娜丽莎的什么东西控制了我们时，指出了 Leonardo 的惊人技巧，这个技巧创造了一种质感与深度的感觉。

[3] render 在这里指以艺术的方式表达。"he added"为插入语。he 指 Paul Barolsky。作者（蒙娜丽莎的作者）表现了蒙娜丽莎（坐着被临摹的人）的内在心性与她的内心或灵魂的感觉。这一句讲 technique。

[4] 表明作者自己的观点，之前提到的都是作者之外的艺术家的观点。对之前艺术家理论的质疑。"to the charm of a myth"和"to the idea"接续在 succumbing to 后面，即本句为省略句，省略了：succumbing to the idea …。

I think one should avoid succumbing to the charm of a myth, to the idea that inside every masterpiece that has remained alive for centuries something imponderable speaks to us.

定语从句，修饰 masterpiece。"that inside every…to us"为 idea 的同位语。Something imponderable 是同位语从句的主语，speaks 为同位语从句的谓语。

【译文】我认为一个人应当避免屈从于神话的魅力，避免屈从于这样一种思想：在每一个流传了很多个世纪的杰作内都有一些难以估量的东西在同我们讲话。本句与第一段[4]呼应，批判这种观点。由此引出作者对蒙娜丽莎之所以这样著名的看法。

[5] 这句话进一步阐述作者的观点：因为 innate sensibility 而崇拜蒙娜丽莎作品的观点是不正确的。

It is of course intensely pleasurable to imagine that, as we face the products of Leonardo, Raphael, and other great artists of bygone ages, armed with nothing but our "innate" sensibility, a mysterious yet almost palpable contact is established. "contact"指通过读者的内在的感知与蒙娜丽莎画面建立起的神秘且可以触碰到的联系。作者对此持反对观点。注意句型：it is +adj. to do sth.。

【译文】这样想象当然非常令人愉悦：当我们面对 Leanardo，Raphael 和其他早期艺术家的作品时，仅通过"内在的"感知便能够建立一种神秘且可以触摸到的联系。言外之意，这种想象是错误的。下一句作者会给出正确答案。

[6] "But"表转折：上一句想象的事物与作者观点刚好相反。But like most historians, I start with the assumption that the renown of a masterpiece rests on a sequence of events and historical agencies (people, institutions, process) working in a largely unplanned manner for different ends. 这才是作者认为的蒙娜丽莎如此著名的真正原因。

【译文】但是像大多数历史学家一样，我以这样一个假设来开始，即：一副杰作的名誉是建立在一系列事件和为不同目的以大量无计划的方式来工作的历史机构（人、制度、过程）基础之上的。

[7] turn sth. into sth. 把某物转换为 XXX。forces 在这里指"力量"，即众多以无计划的方式来工作的历史机构的力量。点明这样的力量才是蒙娜丽莎如此闻名的原因。

---

批注 [A68]: 现在分词短语作伴随状语。seek to do sth. 试图做某事 =attempt to do sth.

批注 [A69]: 定语从句，修饰 Barolsky，先行词为 who。

批注 [A70]: 修饰 technique，这里指"技巧"。

批注 [A71]: 宾语从句

批注 [A72]: 极度令人愉悦的

批注 [A73]: 时间状语从句

批注 [A74]: 过去分词短语作伴随状语

批注 [A75]: 以 XXX 开始

批注 [A76]: 现在分词短语作定语，修饰 agencies。

批注 [A77]: 同位语从句，作 assumption 的同位语

[8] 蒙娜丽莎是否值得获得这样一个地位，我高兴地把这个评判权留给读者。Whether the Mona Lisa "deserves" this position is a judgment I happily leave to the reader. place 指代上一句的 the best-known painting in the world。

批注 [A78]: 主语从句

批注 [A79]: 定语从句，修饰 judgment

leave sth. to sb. 把某物留给某人

【题目解析】

1. Both passages call attention to which aspect of the Mona Lisa?

(A) Its subject's mysterious smile

(B) Its subject's identity

(C) Its popular appeal

(D) Its influence on artists

(E) Its deteriorating condition

【答案】C

【解析】两篇文章均提醒人们注意蒙娜丽莎的哪方面？call attention to sth. 提醒人注意某事。

(A) mysterious，神秘的，难以理解的。文章1提到，文章2没提到微笑。

(B) identity n. (1) 身份（选项意思）(2) 个性，特性 (3) 同一性，一致性 the identity in sth.，某物的相同之处。

subject, 主人公，主人公的身份。文章1第二段[1]提到了，蒙娜丽莎的原形为某个商人的妻子。文章2没有交代原形。

(C) 蒙娜丽莎的吸引力。两篇文章都提到。第一篇在第一段对吸引力进行了描述；第二篇开篇点题，探讨蒙娜丽莎如此著名的原因。

appeal n.

(1) dresses with popular appeal 适合大众口味的衣服

(2) the popular appeal for sth. 大众对某事的呼唤

The popular appeal for rise of wages soared. 大众对涨工资的呼唤猛增。

(3) 吸引力 Women's Popular Appeal 最具女性吸引力（选项意思）

(D) the influence on sb., 对某人的影响。文章1第二段和第三段提到了。文章2没提到。

(E) deteriorate vi. 恶化，变坏 deteriorating adj. 逐渐恶化的。蒙娜丽莎逐渐恶化的状况。两篇文章均未提到。

2. The author of passage 2 would most likely regard the phenomena described in passage 1 ("It hung…Mona Lisa") as

(A) circumstances that may themselves have contributed to the renown of the Mona Lisa

(B) occurrences that fundamentally distort the true importance of Mona Lisa

(C) incidents that cause art enthusiasts undue annoyance

(D) events that are not worthy of the consideration of art critics

(E) facts that have proved inconvenient for many art historians

【答案】A

【解析】文章2的作者将如何看待文章1第一段？读懂两篇文章才能做对！

(A) circumstance n. (1) 环境，条件，情况 (2) 境遇，经济状况 (3) 详细情况，细节 (4)

机遇 (5) 事件（文中意思=events）

contribute (1) vt. & vi. 捐献，捐助，贡献出 (2) 撰稿，投稿 (3) vi. 起促成作用 contribute to sth./doing sth.（选项意思）

renown n. 名望；声誉

themselves 指代 circumstances，认为是一系列事件，这些事件本身对蒙娜丽莎的名望起到了促进作用。见文章 2 最后一段[6]。circumstances 相当于第二篇文章最后一段[6]中的 events。作者意思为蒙娜丽莎的名望是一系列历史事件促成的。

that may themselves have contributed to the renown of the Mona Lisa 为定语从句，修饰 circumstances。

B) occurrence n. 事件的发生。fundamentally adv. 基础地；根本地 distort vt. 歪曲，曲解 circumstances=occurrence 事件

认为该事件扭曲了蒙娜丽莎的重要性。与作者意思相反，恰恰是这些没有事先安排的历史事件促成了蒙娜丽莎的名望。

(C) incident n. 发生的事，小插曲 undue adj. 过分的；过度的（选项意思）(2) 不适当的；不正当的

an undue influence on sb./sth. 对某人/某事不良的影响 (3) 未到（支付）期的 an undue debt 未到期的债务

enthusiast n. 热心人，热衷者=devotee

annoyance n. 恼怒；烦恼

认为它是促使艺术热衷者烦恼的事件，曲解作者意图。

(D) worthy adj. 应得某事物的；值得做某事的 worthy of sth./doing sth.

consideration n. (1) 体贴，关心 (2) 考虑；要考虑的事（选项意思）

(E) inconvenient adj. 不方便的，打扰人的，造成麻烦的，让人不舒服的

sth. proves +adj. 某物被证明怎么样

The theory proves wrong. 这个理论被证明是错误的。

(B)、(C)、(D)、(E) 的感情色彩均错了，作者认为类似很多人去看蒙娜丽莎这一偶然事件的叠加促成了她的名望。而这几个选项均为贬义。

3. The observations ("Historically…ways") establish a contrast between a woman's

(A) unremarkable appearance and her portrait's astonishing beauty

(B) humble orgins and her portrait's monetary value

(C) untimely demise and her portrait's immortality

(D) lack of charisma and her portrait's universal allure

(E) ordinary status and her portrait's aesthetic significance

【答案】E

【解析】establish a contrast 建立一种对比

【重要句型】Sth. establishes a contrast between A and B. 某事构成了 A、B 之间的对比。这两句话是对画的普通原形与画本身的历史价值的对比。

(A) unremarkable adj. 寻常的，不值得注意的=ordinary 表示"很普通的"。remarkable adj. 异常的；引人注目的；不寻常的

appearance n. (1) 出现，显露，露面 (2) 外观，外貌，外表（选项意思）

本句没有提到主人公相貌普通。

(B) humble adj. (1) 谦逊的，谦虚的 (2) 低下的，卑微的（选项意思）(3) 简陋的，低劣的 (4) vt. 使谦恭，使卑下

origin n. (1) 起点；来源 (2) 出身，血统（选项意思）monetary adj. 货币的；金融的

(C) untimely adj. (1) 不适时的，不合时宜的 (2) 过早的（选项意思）(3) adv. 过早地；不合时宜地

demise n. (1) 死（选项意思）(2) 终止 immortal adj. 不朽的；流芳百世的

immortalize vt. 使永恒；使不灭；使不朽；使名垂千古

主人公过早的逝世与画像的不朽，作者没有这个意图。

portrait 为名词，画像。

(D) lack (1) vt. 缺乏；缺少 lack sth. 缺少某物 (2) n. 缺乏，不足，没有 charisma n. 魅力 allure n. 诱惑力，魅力

作者没有这个意图。

(E) aesthetic adj. 有关美的，美学的

该对比在阐述主人公的平凡身份和画本身的美学价值。

批注 [ 80]：注意题干中的词性

4. The quotation from Leonardo in lines 24-25 primarily serves to

(A) defend a methodology

(B) characterize an effect

(C) criticize a technique

(D) downplay an accomplishement

(E) acknowledge an influence

【答案】B

【解析】重要句型：Sth. serves to do sth. 某物用于做某事。

(A) defend (1) vt./vi. 保卫 (2) vt./vi. 辩护；辩解（选项意思）

为一种方法辩解、维护。不是这个目的。该段引用旨在说明蒙娜丽莎的画法起到的效果。

(B) characterize vt. (1) 是……的特征，以……为特征 (2) 描述（人或物）的特性，描绘（选项意思）

描绘了一种效果。

(C) technique，技巧。批评一种技巧，恰恰相反，作者在褒扬该技巧。

(D) downplay vt. 减轻……的重要性，贬低，轻视。减轻了该成就的重要性。感情色彩与作者意思相反。

play=act as，充当，起 XXX 的作用

accomplish vt. 完成, 实现, 做成功

(E) acknowledge vt. (1) 承认，供认（选项意思）(2) 鸣谢，感谢

承认某种影响，作者没有这个意图，与 influence 无关。

批注 [ 81]：主动语态

5. Which of Mona Lisa's features would the author of passage 1 most likely add to those mentioned in passage 2, line 32?

(A) Her mouth

(B) Her hair

(C) Her nose

(D) Her chin

(E) Her profile

【答案】A

【解析】文章1的作者很可能在文章2中加入蒙娜丽莎的哪些容貌？见文章2。features 指"容貌"，容貌包含以上所有选项，文章1最后一段提到 the famous smile，故会在文章 2 中加入嘴的描写。

chin n 颏，下巴  profile n. 侧面，侧面像

6. In line 41, "position" most nearly means

(A) rank

(B) role

(C) policy

(D) view

(E) location

【答案】D

【解析】position 指"观点"，详见原文精读。

rank （1）名词，地位；社会阶层 （2）vt. & vi. 占……地位；列为；列入某等级
high-ranking 形容词，高职位的

7. Both the author of Passage 1 and Paul Barolsky (line 53, Passage 2) make which of the following points about the Mona Lisa?

(A) It tends to elicit idiosyncratic responses from viewers.

(B) It is unduly revered by much of the general public.

(C) It has influenced many generations of artists.

(D) It was the first oil painting intended to be framed and hung.

(E) It gives the appearance of having three dimensions.

【答案】E

【解析】make a point of 强调。题干意思：文章1和2均强调了蒙娜丽莎的哪个特点？
详见文章精读：均强调立体效果。

(A) tend （1）vt. 照料 （2）vi. 往，朝向 （3）v. 易于；倾向  tend to do sth.（选项意思）
elicit vt. 引出，探出 idiosyncratic adj. 特殊物质的，特殊的，异质的。试图探出看客的异质反应。

(B) revere vt. 崇敬，尊崇，敬畏。很多公众过度崇拜该作品。作者没有这个意图。

(C) 文章2作者的那句话没有这个意思：影响了几代艺术家。

(D) 第一篇文章是这个意思。但它与第二篇文章无关。

(E) 它给出了三维立体的外形。符合题干。

8. The author of Passage 2 uses quotation marks in line 65 primarily to

(A) label a revolutionary movement

(B) refer to an overused technique in art

批注 [82]: 第三段[2]

批注 [83]: 异质反应

批注 [84]: 过去分词短语作定语，修饰 painting。

批注 [85]: 最后一段[5]

批注 [86]: 革命性的，创新性的=radical

112

(C) emphasize the symbolic meaning of a term

(D) highlight the importance of a finding

(E) imply skepticism about a theory

【答案】E

【解析】见文章精读：作者对该观点持批判态度。引号表示反对、怀疑。

label (1) n. 标签，标记 (2) vt. 把……列为

(B) refer to sth./doing (1) 提及；涉及，谈到，提到；关系到 (2) 暗指（选项意思）(3) 有关，针对 (4)（把……）归因于…… (5) 认为……起源于；认为……与……有关；把……归属于；overuse vt. 过度使用

暗示一书中某种技巧的过度运用。感情色彩错误，作者对立体效果呈褒扬态度。

(C) 强调某种术语中的象征意义。这里不存在术语和象征意义。

(D) highlight vt. 强调，突出，使显著。强调某种发现的重要性。错误，没有提到发现的重要性。

9. Which statement best characterizes the different ways in which the authors of Passage 1 and Passage 2 approach the Mona Lisa?

(A) The first stresses the unique smile in the portrait, while the second focuses on other mysterious qualities of its subject.

(B) The first emphasizes its striking appearance, while the second examines the background of its creator.

(C) The first focuses on its stylistic innovations, while the second seeks to account for its cultural preeminence.

(D) The first speculates about the life of its subject, while the second argues that historical interpretations are irrelevant.

(E) The first alludes to its societal importance, while the second debates its artistic merits.

【答案】C

【解析】题干意思：哪个选项最恰当地描绘了两篇文章作者探讨蒙娜丽莎所采用的不同方法？纵观两篇文章，文章1着重强调画法的独创性，文章2探究作品世界闻名的原因。

(A) 文章1提到了蒙娜丽莎的独特微笑，目的是引出结论：蒙娜丽莎这幅画如此著名，即使不懂欣赏画的读者看到这个微笑都能立即辨认出蒙娜丽莎，之后文章的重点是讨论蒙娜丽莎这幅画使用的艺术技巧。文章2探讨蒙娜丽莎如此有名的原因。 stress (1) n. 压力，紧张 (2) n. 强调，重要性 (3) vt. 强调（选项意思）stress=focus on sth.

unique adj. 独一无二的，仅有的，唯一的

stylistic adj. 风格上的 innovation n. 改革，革新，创新 seek vt. & vi. 寻找；探寻 vi. 企图；试图（选项意思）seek to do sth.

speculate vt. & vi. 思索；猜测，推测 irrelevant adj. 不相干的，不相关的

allude vi. 提及，暗指 allude to sth.（题干意思）merit n. (1) 功勋，功劳；价值（选项意思，价值） (2) 长处，优点

(C) 文章1探讨艺术手段，文章2讨论这幅画如此有名的原因。

(D) 文章1没有对画中的主人公的生活进行遐想，subject 指画中主人公。

批注 [87]: vt. 这里指描绘，depict, portray

批注 [88]: 指代 ways, 方式

批注 [89]: vt. 接近

批注 [90]: 说明，阐述，解释，动词短语

批注 [91]: 名词，杰出

批注 [92]: 说明，阐述，解释，动词短语

# 文章 21

## 文章 21.1

Foraging near the hut that he built himself, cultivating beans whose properties invited speculation, gazing into the depths of Walden Pond, Henry David Thoreau epitomizes a long-standing American worship of nature.[1] Generations of teachers have assigned Thoreau's book *Walden* (1854), which recounts his experiment in living in solitary harmony with nature, as an illustration of the intensity with which nineteenth-century America protested the intrusion into pastoral harmony of forces of industrialization and urbanization.[2] In this sense, *Walden* is revered as a text of regret, a lament for a world passing out of existence.[3]

【单词及搭配】

1. forage vt./vi. 搜寻食物
2. epitomize vt. 代表，象征，体现，浓缩，缩影

The company epitomized the problems faced by British industry. 该公司是英国工业所面临的问题的缩影。

That western cities have been confronted with severe droughts epitomizes water resources crisis prevailing all around the world/faced by worldwide areas.

3. invite vt.（指行为或情况）招致，引起；吸引，诱使，怂恿 invite sth. 招致 XXX，相当于 arouse。
4. speculation n. 沉思，思考，思索，推测（about, on, upon）
5. speculate v. 推测 speculate about/on sth.；speculate that +宾语从句

表示"思考"的其他单词：ponder vt. & vi. 考虑；深思熟虑 dwell on 老是想着，详述

6. gaze v.（尤指因为羡慕、吃惊或思考）盯着看，凝视 gaze at/into sb./sth.
7. long-standing adj. 长存的，长期的
8. recount vt. 叙述，说明
9. solitary adj. 独自完成的；独居的
10. harmony n. 协调，和谐，统一
11. assign vt.
   (1) 分配，分派（工作、职责）
   (2) 指派，委派（某人）（担任某职务、执行某任务或去某机构）

She has been assigned to a new job. 她被派去担任新职务了。

assign sb. to do sth. 指派某人做某事

(3) （为特定目的）指定；拨出，留出 assign money to do sth. 划出钱做某事
(4) attribute sth. to sth.=assign sth. to sth. 把……归属于，把……归因于
12. protest. vt. 抗议，对……提出抗议；反对；申明，声言；断言
13. intrusion n. 侵入，闯入；打扰，侵扰
14. pastoral adj. 畜牧的；用作牧场的
15. urbanization n. 都市化
16. revere vt. 崇敬
17. lament n. 悲伤，悲哀；挽歌，哀乐，哀诗；遗憾，抱怨
18. intensity n.（思想、感情、活动等的）强烈；极度 intensity of feeling 强烈的感情。还须掌握形容词形式：intense adj. 强烈的，剧烈的；极端的 intensive adj. 加强的，集中的，密集的；彻底的。

【文章精读】

[1] Foraging, cultivating, gazing 为三个并列的现在分词短语作伴随状语，逻辑主语为 Henry David Thoreau，必须与句子主语一致。现在分词短语作状语时表示主动语态。"that he built himself" 为定语从句，修饰 hut。"whose properties invited speculation" 为定语从句，修饰 beans。epitomizes 为句子谓语。Henry David Thoreau 为句子主语，他是《瓦尔登湖》一书的作者。hut，名词，小木屋。Walden Lake，瓦尔登湖。

invite speculation 为动词短语，引发思考，相当于 arouse speculation。

Henry David Thoreau 在他自己搭建的小屋子附近寻找食物，培育了豆子，豆子的特性引发其他的思考，凝视瓦尔登湖的深处，他将长期存在的美国人对大自然的崇拜凝缩成了缩影。

句子拆分：
(1) He cultivated beans.
(2) Properties of the beans invited his speculation.

用 whose 修饰 beans，这是因为从句中缺少修饰属性的物主代词：the beans' properties。

[2] Generations of teachers have assigned Thoreau's book *Walden* (1854), which recounts his experiment in living in solitary harmony with nature, as an illustration of the intensity with which nineteenth-century America protested the intrusion into pastoral harmony of forces of industrialization and urbanization. 美国人反对城市化和工业化的势力对传统的田园和谐环境进行入侵。

illustration n.
(1) 说明，图解，图示 (2) 例，实例 an illustration of gravity（文中意思）(3) 插图，图表，图案 magazines full of illustrations 插图多的杂志

与 experiment 对应，illustration 在文中指"例证，说明"。

assign sth. as sth. 把某物指定为 XXX

the intrusion into pastoral harmony of forces of industrialization and urbanization

注意 force（名词）的用法：
1. 力，力量；力气 2. 武力，暴力 3. 势力；威力；有影响的人（或事物）（文中意思）
He was a force behind these social changes. 他是促成这些社会变革的有影响的人物。
4. 影响；支配力；说服力 There is force in what he did. 他的行为有说服力。

批注 [A93]: 定语从句，修饰《瓦尔登湖》

批注 [A94]: which 指代 intensity。

批注 [A95]: 定语从句，修饰 intensity

批注 [A96]: the intrusion into sth. 对某物的侵入

批注 [A97]: 作 intrusion 的定语：intrusion of B into A：B 对 A 的侵入，文章变换了次序。

【译文】世世代代的老师将《瓦尔登湖》指定为 19 世纪美国反抗工业化和城市化的势力入侵田园式和谐的强烈程度的例证。

句子拆分：(1) Teachers have assigned the book as an illustration of intensity.

(2) America protested the intrusion with intensity.= America protested the intrusion intensively.

【举一反三】

(1) 数据反映了价格变动的剧烈程度。

The data manifested the intensity with which prices had been fluctuated.

句子拆分：① The data manifested the intensity. 数据表明了强烈程度。

② Prices fluctuated with intensity. 价格强烈地波动。

(2) 他的反应表明了他等得很焦急。

His reactions manifested the anxiety with which he had been waiting. 其中 which 指代 anxiety。

(3) 她日益虚弱的身体反应了她这些年工作中付出的艰辛。

Her ever increasingly declining health conditions manifest the hardship with which she has been undertaking jobs during recent years.

(4) 这款新生产的手机表明了信息技术的飞速发展。

The recently-yielded cellular phone manifests the rapidity with which information technology has been evolving.

[3] In this sense：从这种意义上讲 revere 的同义动词为：worship，崇拜。be revered as sth. 作为 XXX 被尊敬。

*Walden* is revered as a text of regret, a lament for a world passing out of existence. 动词短语 pass out of existence：不复存在，相当于动词 vanish。passing out of existence 为现在分词短语作定语，修饰 world，一个不复存在的世界的哀歌。

# 文章 21.2

Although Thoreau, in *Walden,* was sometimes ambivalent about the mechanization that he saw around him, at other times he was downright enthusiastic, as in his response to the railroad: "When I hear the iron horse make the hills echo with his snort like thunder, shaking the earth with his feet, and breathing fire and smoke from his nostrils…it seems as if the earth had got a race now worthy to inhabit it."[1] At Walden Pond, civilization and industrialization no longer seemed threatening.[2] Providing a full record of Thoreau's purposeful energy, *Walden* demonstrates that the power unleashed by the machine is not that different from the power required to transform the wilderness into a productive garden.[3]

【单词及搭配】

1. ambivalent adj.（对事或人）有矛盾心态（或想法）的

2. mechanization n. 机械化

3. downright adj. 直率的，直截了当的；生硬的，十足的，完全的，彻头彻尾的 a

downright disgrace 十足的耻辱

adv. 十分，完全地

4. iron horse 火车

5. echo

(1) n. 回声；回响 produce echoes 产生回音

(2) n.（舆论等的）反应；共鸣 aroused echo 引发共鸣

(3) n. 附和者；应声虫 an echo of sb. 某人的附和者

(4) vi. 发出回声，产生回响（文中意思）

(5) vt. 重复（他人的话等）

6. worthy adj. 值得的，应得的；好的，优秀的；适合的，相配的

7. inhabit vt. 居住于；栖息于

8. purposeful adj.

(1) 坚定的；有决心的；果断的（文中意思）(2) 有目的的，有益的，有用的 purposeful activities 有益的活动 (3) intentional 故意的，蓄意的

9. wilderness n. 未开垦之地；荒野；荒无人烟之地；荒凉的地方；（花园中的）杂草丛生处；（城镇中的）荒芜的地方；失宠；下野，不当政

【文章精读】

**本文观点与文章 1 相反**：Thoreau 在《瓦尔登湖》中对工业化、城镇化是认可的。

[1] be ambivalent about sth. 对某事矛盾；at other times：在其他时候，有时

downright enthusiastic 中 downright 为副词，修饰形容词"热情的"。 as：正如。in the response to sb./sth. 对某人/物的回应。"worthy to inhabit it"为形容词短语作定语，修饰 earth。it 指代地球。与上面一段 Thoreau 认为自然受到威胁态度相反。

[2] A seems threatening. A 看起来对其他人/物构成威胁。注意区别：A seems being threatened. A 看起来受到了威胁。

[3] Providing a full record of Thoreau's purposeful energy, *Walden* demonstrates that the power unleashed by the machine is not that different from the power required to transform the wilderness into a productive garden.

transform a into b：将 a 转换为 b。not that：并不是说。

the power required to do sth.：做某事所需的能量，比如：the capacity required to hold enough people 需要容纳足够多人的容量。power 和 require 为被动关系，故用过去分词修饰。

【题目解析】

1. The author of passage 2 and the "teachers" mentioned in passage 1 would probably disagree regarding which of the following about *Walden*?

(A) The extent to which *Walden* presents nature as being threatened

(B) The extent to which *Walden* successfully recounts Thoreau's experiment in solitary living

(C) The extent to which *Walden* has been considered an important work of literature

(D) Whether *Walden* recognizes the spread of industrialization and urbanization

(E) Whether the power of the machine was a topic central to *Walden*

批注 [A98]: 现在分词短语作伴随状语，逻辑主语与句子主语一致，为《瓦尔登湖》这本小说。《瓦尔登湖》展示了 Thoreau 坚定的干劲。

批注 [A99]: 过去分词短语作定语，修饰 power，被机器释放出来的能量。

批注 [A100]: demonstrate 的宾语从句

批注 [A101]: 过去分词短语作定语，修饰 power，将不毛之地转变为多产花园所需的能量。

【解析】注意题干的意思：文章 2 与文章 1 中的"老师"可能在以下哪个关于《瓦尔登湖》的观点上有分歧？

disagree 须掌握以下用法：

(1) vi. 不一致，不符[(+with)] Our answers to the problem disagreed. 我们对这个问题的回答不一致。

(2) vi. 意见不合；有分歧[(+with/on)] We disagreed on which movie to see. 我们对看哪一个电影意见不一致。（题干意思）

(3) vi. 争论，争执[(+on/about)] The two neighbors disagreed bitterly about their boundary line.

(4) vi.（食物、天气等）不适宜，有害[(+with)] Strawberries disagree with me. 我一吃草莓就不舒服。

regarding: 介词，就 XXX 而论

(A) to some extent：某种程度上。do sth. to some extent，在某种程度上做某事。present sb./sth as+adj./分词，将某人或某物展现成某种状态。文章 1 认为《瓦尔登湖》描述了环境受到威胁；文章 2 与该观点相反。该选项正确。

(D) recognize 表示"承认"。两篇文章都表明该书作者认可工业化和城镇化的存在。该选项不正确。

(C) 两篇文章作者均认为《瓦尔登湖》是一部重要的文学著作。

(E) 两篇文章作者均认为机械化的力量是《瓦尔登湖》一书讨论的核心话题。

2. Passage 1 suggests that Thoreau would most likely agree that the "power unleashed by the machine" was

(A) kept in check by comparable forces in nature

(B) largely destructive of nature's tranquility

(C) exaggerated by those who did not seek out nature

(D) necessary to transform nature into something productive

(E) less threatening to one who lived close to nature

【解析】B

(A) keep sth. in check，动词短语，使某物受约束。comparable adj. (1) 类似的，同类的，相当的（选项意思） (2) 可比较的，比得上的。

文章 1 作者认为 Thoreau 可能认为由机器释放出来的能量由于自然界其他同类的力量而受到制约。文章 1 中作者认为：Thoreau 认为机器释放的能量对大自然有破坏力，而没提到这种力量受制约，相反，这种力量对大自然的和谐进行了入侵，即，这种机械化能量没有受到制约。所以(A) 错误。

(B) destructive adj. 具有破坏性的；largely destructive，很大程度上有破坏性，副词修饰形容词；tranquility n. (1) 平静；安静；安宁（选项意思） (2) 平稳；稳定。

很大程度上破坏了自然的宁静，正确。

(C) 错误，文章 1 中作者认为 Thoreau 对机械化完全否定，因此并没有夸大这种破坏力。

(D) 这是文章 2 的观点，文章 1 与此观点完全相反。

(E) threatening 在这里为形容词，具有威胁性的。这种力量对生活地点靠近自然的人来

说，威胁作用小一些。错误。文章 1 认为 Thoreau 对机械化完全否定，机械化的力量已经影响了自然的和谐宁静。who lived close to nature 为定语从句，修饰 one。one 不能换为宾格 him 或 her。人称代词后不能跟随定语从句来修饰。

3. The author of passage 1 would most likely argue that the enthusiasm referred to in passage 2 is

(A) supportive of the idea that *Walden* expresses regret about industrialization

(B) a response that would have resonated with 19th-century Americans

(C) a characteristic of Thoreau's that is often emphasized by teachers

(D) an attitude that derives from Thoerau's experiment in solitary living

(E) atypical of Thoreau's perceived attitude toward mechanization

【解析】E

referred to 为过去分词短语作定语，修饰 enthusiasm，即文章 2 提到的"热情"，定位于文章 2 第一句，Thoreau 对工业化的"热情"。文章 1 的作者可能会怎样评论文章 2 提到的 Thoreau 对工业化表现出的热情？

(A) be supportive of sth., 支持某物。文章 2 并不认为《瓦尔登湖》表达了对工业化的懊悔。因此，该选项错误。

(B) resonate with sth., 动词短语，与什么产生共鸣。文章 1 提到 19 世纪的美国极力反对工业化和城市化，因此该选项错误。

(C) 老师们并没有强调 Thoreau 对工业化的热情，相反，文章 1 中提到的老师们认为 Thoreau 极力排斥工业化。

(D) derive from sth., 动词短语，从哪里得到。错误。这种"热情"与 Thoreau 独处来进行实验的态度截然相反。

(E) atypical adj. 非典型的。这种热情是 Thoreau 对工业化态度的个例，即 Thoreau 对工业化的主导态度是排斥的，文章 2 提到的热情只是一个个例，不能由此得到 Thoreau 支持工业化这一结论。或者说，"热情"只是 Thoreau 的一个非主流观点。该选项正确。

4. The author of passage 1 would probably agree with which of the following statements about the interpretation of *Walden* offered in passage 2?

(A) It exaggerates the destructive power of the machine.

(B) It is overly influenced by the long-standing American worship of nature.

(C) It is not representative of the way *Walden* is often taught in schools.

(D) It overlooks Thoreau's enthusiasm in *Walden* for the railroad.

(E) It is more in accord with the way *Walden* was generally understood in Thoreau's time than it currently.

【解析】C

offered in passage 2 为过去分词短语作定语，修饰 interpretation。

(A) 文章 2 认为机器的能量是有益的，没有破坏性。该选项错误。

(B) 文章 2 与该选项意思刚好相反。文章 1 提到美国人长期以来崇敬自然，因此会反对工业化。

(C) 文章 2 提到的观点并不代表老师教授《瓦尔登湖》一书的方法。正确。即，文章

1认为，文章2提到的观点不会在学校教授。文章1主旨为Thoreau极力反对工业化，老师也按照这一思路去授课。

(D) 文章1的作者并不认为Thoreau对铁路怀有热情，相反，很排斥。

(E) 本句为省略句，句尾省略了than it is generally understood currently，其中it指代*Walden*。in accord with sth., 介词短语，与什么一致。

句意：比起当今该书被大众的理解方式而言，这种解释（文章2）更符合Thoreau那个时代人们对该书的理解方式。但两篇文章都没提到过去观点及现在观点的比较。

# 文章 22

As a scientist, I find that only one vision of the city really gets my hackles up—the notion that a city is somehow "unnatural", a blemish on the face of nature.

## 【单词及搭配】

1. get sb.'s hackles up  使某人发怒
2. notion (1) n. 概念；想法；见解 a notion of/about（文中意思）
I haven't the faintest notion what they mean. 我一点也不知道他们是什么意思。
(2) n. 打算，意图 notion of sth./notion to do sth. 相当于 attempt。
He has no notion of risking his money. 他不打算拿他的钱去冒险。
(3) n. 一时兴起的念头
Eventually I put the map away, but the notion of going to China lingered on. 我终于放下了地图，但是到中国去的念头却挥之不去。
3. somehow  adv. (1) 以某种方式；用某种方法
Somehow I managed to get the job done. 我用某种方法把工作完成了。
(2) 不知什么原因（文中意思）
He looked different somehow. 不知为什么他看起来不一样。
4. blemish  (1) 可数名词，瑕疵，污点（文中意思） a blemish on sth. 对某事的玷污，名词短语 (2) vt. 破坏……的完美外观；玷污

## 【文章精读】

As a scientist, I find that only one vision of the city really gets my hackles up—the notion that a city is somehow "unnatural", a blemish on the face of nature.

开篇点题：大自然"不自然"是大自然的一个污点。破折号表示前后意思一致，由此推断 vision 和 notion 同义。由此看到**根据语境理解单词**的重要性！version 与 notion 在此均表示"看法，观点"。"that a city is somehow unnatural" 为 notion 的同位语从句，即 notion 就等于该同位语从句表达的内容。blemish 指代 a city is somehow "unnatural" 这个观点，为名词短语作定语修饰 notion，用 which is a blemish on the face of nature 替代也可以。

【译文】作为一名科学家，我发现只有一个关于城市的观点令我勃然大怒，即城市不知怎么"不自然"了，这个观点对大自然是一个污点。即作者认为：城市是自然的。下文将驳斥城市与自然对立这一观点。

The argument goes like this: Cities remove human beings from their natural place in the world.[1] They are a manifestation of the urge to conquer nature rather than to live in harmony with it.[2] Therefore, we should abandon both our cities and our technologies and return to an

批注 [A104]: 作 find 的宾语从句

批注 [105]: 作 notion 的同位语从句

批注 [106]: 名词短语，对大自然的玷污，作 a city is somehow "unnatural" 的同位语。这样的句式为**改错考点**。

批注 [107]: drive away from

earlier, happier state of existence, one that presumably would include many fewer human beings than now inhabit our planet.[3]

批注 [108]：第 2 题出处

批注 [A109]: dwell on the planet 替代

## 【单词及搭配】

1. argument n.
(1) 争执，争吵；辩论 argument about/with/over 关于 XXX 的争论
(2) 理由，论据；论点（文中意思） argument for/against sth./doing sth./that+定语从句
(3) 说理；论证 an argument of this theory
2. manifestation n. 显示，表明；证明（尤指理论或抽象概念）
the first obvious manifestations of global warming 全球变暖的明显初始迹象
还须掌握动词形式：manifest vt. 表明。
例句：这幅图片表明了价格波动的剧烈程度。
The graph manifested the intensity with which price fluctuated. / The graph manifested price fluctuated intensely.
3. urge
(1) vt./vi. 力劝，恳求 urge to do sth.
(2) vt. 竭力主张，强烈要求
I urge caution in interpreting these results. 我主张在解释这些结果时要谨慎。
They are urging that more treatment facilities be provided. 他们强烈要求提供更多的治疗设备。
(3) vt. 使加快，使加速 urge sb. to do sth. 催促某人做事
(4) vt. 鼓励，激励 urge sb.
(5) n. 强烈欲望，冲动（文中意思）
4. conquer
vt. 击败，征服；攻占，战胜，破除，克服（问题、弱点）
5. harmony n. (1) 协调，和谐，统一
(2) 和谐，一致；和睦 in perfect harmony 和谐共存
6. abandon
(1) vt. 完全放弃（行动、做法、想法）（文中意思）
(2) vt. discontinue 中止（预定活动）The meeting was abandoned. 会议被迫终止。
(3) vt. 听任（某人、某事物）处于（某种状态）
It was an attempt to persuade businesses not to abandon the area to inner-city deprivation.
试图说服各企业不要放弃此区域而使之沦为内城贫困区。
(4) vt. 放纵于，沉湎于 abandon oneself to doing sth. 放纵某人沉溺于 XXX
7. presumably adv. 据推测；大概，可能
It is presumably that+主语从句。有可能/据推测/大概 XXX。须掌握该词的动词形式：presume
(1) vt. 推测；假设 It is presumed that +主语从句，据推测 XXX。
(2) vt. 认定；想当然
This project demands skills which cannot be presumed and therefore require proper training. 这一工程要求的不是想当然的技术，因此需要足够训练。

Sth. cannot be presumed. 某事不是想当然的。

(3) vt. 放肆，擅做 presume (not) to do sth.

Don't presume to tell me what I will or will not do. You don't know me.

(4) vi. 无理要求，放肆 Forgive me if I have presumed. 若有冒犯，敬请原谅。

(5) vi. 指望……会带来利益，过分寄希望于 presume on sth. 指望某事

8. inhabit，居住，及物动词，与它同义的单词更为重要：

dwell

(1) vi. 居住；生活 dwell in somewhere=inhabit somewhere=live somewhere

(2) vi. 老是想着（尤指不快、不安、不满的事）dwell on sth.

I've got better things to do than dwell on the past. 我有更重要的事情要做，不能老是想着过去。

(3) vi. dwell on/upon=linger on （眼睛、注意力）停留在，凝视

Her eyes dwell on them for a moment. 她的目光在他们身上停留了一会儿。

## 【文章精读】

[1] Something goes like this. 某物是这样的。固定表达。argument 这里指"观点，论据"。城市令人类远离了他们（指人类）在这个世界上的原始生存地方（即自然）。

因为 remove 带有把人类驱逐出自然的意思，或用 drive 替代，句意对"城市"（cities）带有贬义，本段表明城市与大自然是相互对立的。their 指 human being's。注意：这一观点是对第一段城市"不自然"的阐述。作者反对该观点。

[2] 解释本段第一句作者认为错误的观点。注意指代。They 指 cities。to conquer nature 为不定式作定语，修饰 urge（欲望）。it 指代 nature。

习惯表达：an urge to do A rather than to do B：一种做 A 而非 B 的欲望

【译文】他们欲征服自然而非与自然和谐相处的表现。

[3] 由此得到由错误观点得到的极端解决方法，为作者所反对。therefore 表示"因此"，承接上一句的原因，得到结论。

one 为指示代词，指代"the state"，使用 one 可避免重复使用"the state"。state 为可数名词，才可以这样指代。"that presumably would include many fewer human beings than now inhabit our planet"为定语从句，修饰"one"，即修饰 the state。

"now inhabit our planet"为省略句，完整语句为：than human beings now inhabit our planet。前面已有 human beings，在此省略。注意这种表达方式。"now inhabit our planet"为定语从句，inhabit 在这里为及物动词，居住：Human beings inhabit our planet. 人类居住在星球上。

表达替代：include=be inclusive of sth./doing sth.

【译文】因此，我们应该抛弃我们的城市和科学技术并回到原始的更为幸福的存在状态，这一状态很可能包含比现在居住在地球上的少很多的人类。

There is an important hidden assumption behind this attitude, one that needs to be brought out and examined if only because it is so widely held today.[1] This is the assumption that nature, left to itself, will find a state of equilibrium (a "balance of nature") and that the correct role for humanity is to find a way to fit into that balance.[2] If you think this way, you are likely to feel

批注 [A110]: be manifested 代替

批注 [A111]: extensively 可替代地，副词

批注 [A112]: 注意文中表示"人类"的短语的替换！

123

that all of human history since the Industrial (if not the Agricultural) Revolution represents a wrong turning—a blind alley, something like the failed Soviet experiment in central planning.[3] Cities, and particularly the explosive postwar growth of suburbs ("urban sprawl"), are agencies that destroy the balance of nature, and hence are evil presences on the planet.[4]

## 【单词及搭配】

1. bring out

(1) 取出（某物）

(2) 使清楚；使明显（文中意思）bring out=manifest (vt.) 显现出，直接加名词或宾语从句。

(3) 出版，生产 bring out a book

(4) 说出…… bring out a secret 说出一个秘密。bring out=say

2. widely=extensively

3. state of equilibrium 平衡状态

4. humanity=human beings （在文中）

5. fit into （使）适合，（使）合乎……的时间/空间，与……融为一体 fit well into sth.

6. blind adj.

(1) 瞎的，盲的

(2) （行动，尤指试验或实验）未掌握一定信息的，盲目的 a blind tasting of eight wines 品尝八种无任何标签的葡萄酒。

(3) 愚钝的，没有眼力的 (4) 视而不见的 be blind to sth. (5) 无目的的，盲目的

7. explosive adj. 爆炸的 an explosive device 爆炸装置

an politically explosive idea 一个政治上具有争议性的观点

激增的；迅速扩大的（文中意思）the explosive growth of sth. 某物的猛增

8. postwar adj. 战后的

9. explode

(1) （人）爆发；勃然大怒 explode with anger=get one's hackles up 勃然大怒

(2) （强烈的情感、情况）突然出现；迸发；突然演变成为

tension which could explode into violence at any time 随时可能发展成为暴力行动的紧张关系

(3) 猛然开始 A bird exploded into flight. 一只鸟突然飞了起来。

(4) vi. 激增；迅速扩大

The use of computer exploded in the nineties. 电脑的使用在 90 年代剧增。

(5) 证明（信仰、理论）荒谬；戳穿

还需掌握同义词的动词形式：

boom vi. 激增，猛涨，兴隆 Sth. booms. 某事繁荣发展。

soar (1) vi. 高飞，翱翔 (2) vi. 猛增 soar to 猛增到

## 【文章精读】

[1] attitude 指上一段[3]：抛弃科技回到自然状态。

one 与上一段用法完全一致，指代 assumption。that 直到结尾为定语从句，修饰 one,

即 assumption。bring out 指"使清楚",相当于 manifest。"if only because it is so widely held today"为条件状语从句,if 表示如果。hold 这里表示"持有"。比如:hold a view of XXX,持有某种观点。

【重要句型】It is widely held that+主语从句。Sth. is widely held. 某事被广泛接受。过去分词 held 必须用副词修饰,因此使用 widely。

【译文】这种态度背后隐藏着一种假设,如果仅仅因为今天这种假设被广泛接受才这样的话,那么,这个假设需要澄清和检验。

[2] 解释"the hidden assumption"。作者对这种假设是排斥的。

"left to itself"为过去分词短语作条件状语,让它自己来处理的话。完整语句为:

If nature was left to itself, we find XXX. 如果保持自然自己的状态的话,我们将会 XXX。

举例:

Left to himself, he would manage to overcome all difficulties. 让他自己处理的话,他会解决所有难题的。过去分词短语作条件状语。

"is to do sth.":动词不定式表示将要怎么样。

This is the assumption that nature, left to itself, will find a state of equilibrium (a "balance of nature") and that the correct role for humanity is to find a way to fit into that balance.

批注 [A113]: 有两个或两个以上的修饰某物/人的定语从句或同位语并列时,后面一个从句要用 and that 来连接!注意此细节!

【译文】这种假设是:如果让自然保持自己的状态,我们将会找到一种平衡的状态(一种自然的平衡),这种正确的人类的角色将会找到一种与那种平衡融为一体的方式。

[3] 指出持这种观点带来的错误推断。be likely to do sth. =probabably=presumabley。"something like the failed Soviet experiment in central planning"为后置定语,修饰 alley。

a blind alley 死胡同

[4] 继续第三句,持这种错误想法的人会因此而全盘否定城市、战后繁荣。

What bothers me about this point of view is that it implied that human beings, in some deep sense, are not part of nature.[1] "Nature," to many environmental thinkers, is what happens when there are no people around.[2] As soon as we show up and start building towns and cities, "nature" stops and something infinitely less worthwhile starts.[3]

批注 [A114]: 同位语从句,指代 assumption

批注 [A115]: 指代 a state of equilibrium

批注 [116]: 第4题出处

【单词及搭配】

1. infinitely,副词,无限地
2. show up 暴露,露面
3. worthwhile adj. 值得花时间(金钱、精力等)的;有价值的(可作定语)

【重要句型】做某事是值得的。

(1) Something/主语从句 would make a worthwhile contribution to do sth.

(2) It would make a worthwhile contribution to do something.

【文章精读】

[1] 本段解释作者认为第一段和第二段提出的城市不自然以及一些结论的错误之处。

本句包含一个典型的主语从句。句子结构见右侧批注。可用 it 句型代替,但不推荐,太繁琐。

125

**What bothers me about this point of view is that it implied that human beings, in some deep sense, are not part of nature.**

该观点令我恼怒的地方是：这个观点暗示了从某种深度意义上讲，人类不是自然的一部分。point of view=view。imply：vt. 暗示。即从以上观点中可以推断出人类不属于自然的一部分。

[2] 继续阐述第一段观点的错误，nature 加了引号，表明作者认为这样定义自然是错误的！

nature 为主语，is 为谓语，介词短语为状语。

**"Nature," to many environmental thinkers, is what happens when there are no people around.**

【译文】对于很多环境思考者来说，"自然"是四周没有人类时所发生的事情。

[3] 这是一种错误观点。

show up=appear 动词短语。As soon as we show up and start building towns and cities, "nature" stops and something infinitely less worthwhile starts. 当我们出现并且开始建设城镇和城市的时候，"自然"便终止了，一些无限无价值的事情开始了。

It seems to me that we should begin our discussion of cities by recognizing that they aren't unnatural, any more than beaver dams or anthills are unnatural.[1] Beavers, ants, and human beings are all part of the web of life that exists on our planet.[2] As part of their survival strategy, they alter their environments and build shelters.[3] There is nothing "unnatural" about this.[4]

【单词及搭配】

1. web of life 生命网
2. strategy，名词，战略
3. shelter
(1) 名词，遮盖物；躲避处；避难所（文中意思）
(2) 名词，躲避 He hung back in the shelter of a rock. 他缩身躲在岩石后面。
(3) vt. 保护；掩蔽（尤指免受恶劣天气等灾害）shelter sb. from sth. The hut sheltered him from cold weather.

live a sheltered life 过着安逸的生活

(4) vt. 使免交税 Your income must not be sheltered. 你不能不纳税。

【文章精读】

[1] 首次明确提出作者观点：城市是自然的，人等生物是非自然的。

【重要句型】It seems to somebody（宾格） that+主语从句：就某人看来 XXX。

[2] Beavers, ants, and human beings are all part of the web of life that exists on our planet.

[3] 作者认为：包括人类在内的生物将改变他们所处的环境和建立庇护所作为他们的生存策略。As part of their survival strategy, they alter their environments and build shelters.

[4] 再次强调观点：城市是自然的。与前面观点 cities are unnatural 完全相反。这样一来，没有什么所谓的"非自然"。

Nor is there anything unnatural about downtown areas.[1] Yes, in the town the soil has been

---

批注 [A117]: bother=get one's hackles up

批注 [A118]: 主语从句，what 不能用 that 替换，因为 what 有所指代。这个观点使我恼怒的地方是：XXX。

批注 [A119]: 指代 this point of view

批注 [A120]: 表语从句

批注 [A121]: 介词短语，对于大多数环境思考者来说

批注 [A122]: 环境思考者

批注 [A123]: 表语从句，what 不能替换为 that，表示什么的事。周围没有人时所发生的事情。

批注 [A124]: 无限没有价值的

批注 [A125]: 定语从句，修饰 life

批注 [A126]: 指代蚂蚁、人类等生物

almost completely covered by concrete, buildings, and asphalt: often there is no grass or undisturbed soil to be seen anywhere.[2] But this isn't really unnatural.[3] There are plenty of places in nature where there is no soil at all—think of cliffsides in the mountains or along the ocean.[4] From our point of view, the building of Manhattan simply amounted to the exchange of a forest for a cliffside ecosystem.[5]

批注 [A127]：混凝土

批注 [A128]：生态系统

【单词及搭配】

1. downtown=town
2. concrete 文中指"混凝土"。
adj. (1) 具体存在的；实在的；有形的 (2) 具体的；明确的；确定的；确实的 concrete proof 确实的证据
3. undisturbed adj. 未受干扰的；未被扰乱的（文中意思）
4. amount
(1) n. 数量，总额，量 an amount of 多少数量
(2) vi. 总计
(3) amount to sth./doing sth.=be the equivalent of 等同

【文章精读】

[1] 继上一段提出人类不是"非自然的"之后，再次否定闹市区不自然。以 Nor 开头表示并列的否定，句子需要主谓倒装。闹市区也并非"不自然"。当不清楚 downtown 的含义时，第二句给了提示。根据语境来理解单词！

[2] "Yes"承接第一、二段的观点：城市不自然的表象。由此 town 与 downtown 的意思一致，指城镇。"to be seen anywhere"为过去分词短语作后置定语，修饰 soil 和 grass。soil 与 grass 与 see 为被动关系，因此用不定式的过去分词形式修饰。

[3] 但实际上并非"不自然"。看似非自然，但实则自然。下面会解释理由。

[4]、[5]两句解释城市并非不自然。作者认为：城市的建筑仅仅是悬崖上与未开垦的自然生态系统的交换。即，城市是自然的。

Look at the energy source of the downtown ecosystem.[1] There is, of course, sunlight to provide warmth.[2] In addition, there is a large amount of human-made detritus that can serve as food for animals: hamburger buns, apple cores, and partially filled soft drink containers. All of these can and do serve as food sources. Indeed, urban yellow jackets seem to find sugar-rich soft drink cans and excellent source of "nectar" for their honey—just notice them swarming around waste containers during the summer.

批注 [A129]：不定式作定语，修饰 sunlight，提供热量的阳光。

批注 [A130]：岩石

批注 [A131]：用于动物的食物，定语从句，修饰 detritus。serve as food=be used as food

批注 [A132]：小黄蜂

批注 [A133]：复合形容词短语，多糖的

批注 [A134]：花蜜

批注 [A135]：现在分词短语作伴随状语

【单词及搭配】

1. serve
(1) vt. 实现；满足 This computer will serve a useful purpose. 这部电脑有用。
(2) vi. 有用，起作用 This square now serves as a parking spot. serve as sth.（文中意思）
serve to do sth. 用于做某事

## 【文章精读】

[1]、[2] 解释城镇的能量源泉：自然属性部分。

[3] in addition=besides

A glimpse of downtown, in fact, illustrated that the city can be thought of as a natural system on at least three different levels.[1] At the most obvious level, although we don't normally think in these terms, a city is an ecosystem, much as a salt marsh or a forest is.[2] A city operates in pretty much the same way as any other ecosystem, with its own peculiar collection of flora and fauna.[3] This way of looking at cities has recently received the ultimate academic accolade—the creation of a subfield of science, called "urban ecology", devoted to understanding it.[4]

批注 [A136]: 生态系统

批注 [A137]: 盐沼

批注 [138]: 第8题出处

## 【单词及搭配】

1. term 名词

专门名词，名称，术语。a term of abuse 辱骂用语；恶语

特定用语，说话的方式，措辞

a protest in the strongest possible terms 尽可能用最强烈的措辞发出的抗议

条件；条款 do sth. on these terms 依照这些条件作某事

2. normally adv. 通常；正常地；常规地

3. much as

(1) much as=although 引导让步状语从句，尽管。Much as she likes him, she would never consider marrying him.

(2) 和 XXX 一样多，如同 XXX 一样（文中意思）

4. ultimate adj.

(1) 最后的；最终的 ultimate aim 最终目标

(2) 极点的，绝顶的，终极的 the ultimate accolade 至高无上的赞赏

(3) 基本的，根本的；首要的；最初的 the ultimate constituents of anything 万物的基本成分

5. accolade 名词，荣誉；奖励；表彰；赞赏 the ultimate accolade 最高礼遇

6. devote

vt. 将（时间、精力）用于（人、活动、事业）上；尽心竭力于……

devote sth. to doing sth. 花（时间精力等）做某事；devote oneself to doing sth. 某人全身心投入某事

## 【文章精读】

[1] A glimpse of downtown, in fact, illustrated that the city can be thought of as a natural system on at least three different levels.

下面必定解释从哪三种层次来看，城镇属于自然的。本段讲第一层次，其余两段讲第二、三层次。

[2] 注意从本句开始讲解第一层，从 most obvious level"最表层"可以看到。At the most obvious level, although we don't normally think in these terms, a city is an ecosystem, much as a

批注 [A139]: 对城市的一瞥，句子主语

批注 [A140]: 表明，谓语

批注 [A141]: 宾语从句

批注 [A142]: 通常不考虑这些术语，术语在这里指 echosystem

salt marsh or a forest is.

[3] A city operates in pretty much the same way as any other ecosystem, with its own peculiar collection of flora and fauna. "peculiar collection"：独特的汲取方式。with 介词短语表伴随状态，its 指代 city。城市与其他任何一个生态系统一样，都有独特的汲取植物和动物的方式。

[4] "ultimate academic accolade"：至高无上的学术赞誉

这种观点创造了一个新的科学子领域——城市生态学，即以生态系统的观点来研究城市。进一步支持了作者的观点——城市是自然的生态系统。反驳了第一段提出的观点。

At a somewhat deeper level, a natural ecosystem like a forest is a powerful metaphor to aid in understanding how cities work.[1] Both systems grow and evolve, and both require a larger environment to supply them with materials and to act as a receptacle for waste.[2] Both require energy from outside sources to keep them functioning, and both have a life cycle－birth, maturity, and death.

【单词及搭配】

1. metaphor n.
(1) 隐喻 (2) （抽象事物的）代表物；象征物
2. aid
(1) 名词，尤指实际的帮助
(2) 名词，救援 700,000 tons of food aid 70 万吨的食品援助
(3) n. 帮手，帮助者；辅助物，辅助手段
(4) vt./vi. 帮助，协助，支持
3. receptacle 名词，容器，贮藏器；贮藏所
4. function
(1) vi. 工作；运转 Something functions normally. 某物运转正常。（文中意思）
(2) 起……作用；执行……任务 function as sth. 用作 XXX

【文章精读】

[1] 本段讲第二个层次。

"somewhat deeper level"：稍微深一些的层次，somewhat 为副词，修饰形容词 deeper。"to aid in understanding how cities work"为不定式作定语，修饰"代表物"。

[2] "Both systems"指森林生态系统和城市生态系统。"to supply them with materials"与"to act as a receptacle for waste"为并列不定式，与 require 连接。

[3] Both require energy from outside sources to keep them functioning, and both have a life cycle－birth, maturity, and death.

Finally, our cities are like every other natural system in that, at bottom, they operate according to a few well-defined laws of nature.[1] There is, for example, a limit to how high a tree can grow, set by several factors including the kinds of forces that exist between atoms in

批注 [A143]: 就像盐沼和森林一样，都是生态系统。典型的省略句，完整语序为：much as a salt marsh or a forest (as a city) is (an echosytem).

批注 [A144]: 运转，动词，谓语

批注 [A145]: pretty 在这里为副词，相当地，pretty much as 表示"差不多"。

批注 [A146]: 指代森林生态系统和城市生态系统

批注 [A147]: 生命周期

批注 [A148]: 指外界的环境

批注 [A149]: keep sth./sb. doing 使某物保持怎样，functioning 在这里为动名词，意思为"运转"，相当于 working。

wood.[2] There is also a limit to how high a wood (or stone or steel) building can be built—a limit that is influenced by those same interatomic forces.[3]

## 【单词及搭配】

1. at bottom=actually=in fact
2. laws of nature 自然法则，自然定律
3. well-defined 形容词，被定义好的，defined 为过去分词作定语，如：a well-defined concept，一个被定义好的概念。

## 【文章精读】

[1] in that: 因为；介词短语。operate=function=work。

A be like B in that+从句: A 与 B 在某方面是相似的。"they operate according to a few well-defined laws of nature" 中 they 指 cities。我们的城市与自然界其他系统一样，都遵循既定的自然法则来运转。

[2]—[3] 举例说明这种自然法则。a limit to sth./名词性从句/动名词/名词短语，某事的极限。"how a tree can grow"为名词性从句，set by 为过去分词短语作定语，修饰 limit。本句谓语动词为 is，主语为 a limit。including 为现在分词短语作定语，修饰 factors；that exist between atoms in wood 为定语从句，修饰 forces。

本句句式为：There be+名词+定语。

例如，树长到多高有一个限度，这个限度是由很多因素，包括各种各样的存在于木头的原子之间的力限定的。

So let me state this explicitly: A city is a natural system, and we can study it in the same way we study other natural systems and how they got to be the way they are.

批注 [A150]: 清晰地，明确地，副词

批注 [A151]: 指其他生态系统

## 【题目解析】

1. In line 1, "vision" most nearly means

(A) fantasy
(B) illusion
(C) prophecy
(D) conception
(E) apparition

【详解】D

见第一段详解。根据语境判断该单词与 notion 同义。

(A) fantasy 可数名词，幻想，空想
(B) 须掌握 illusion 的动词形式：illude vt. 哄骗，欺骗
(C) prophecy 名词，预言，预告
(D) conception 名词

(1) （计划、想法、作品或产品的）构思，构想，形成，设计
(2) 观点；想法，看法；认识；抽象概念

(3) 理解，想象力

The administration had no conception of women's problems. 行政部门不理解妇女的难处。

须掌握其动词形式：conceive

(1) vt. 想出；构思；设想（计划、主意、作品）

(2) vt. 形成（设想）；认为；想象=imagine/consider

Without society an individual cannot be conceived as having rights. 没有社会就无法设想个人享有权利。

We could not conceive of such things happening to us.=We could hardly imagine such things happening to us. 我们无法想象这种事竟会发生在我们身上。

(3) vt. 怀有（或抱有）（感情）；体验到（感情） conceive a passion/love for sb./sth.对某人/某物怀有激情/爱情

(E) apparition n. 幽灵；（特异景象等的）出现，显形；特异景象

2. The author would most likely describe the "happier state" as a

(A) satisfactory solution

(B) stroke of luck

(C) complicated arrangement

(D) false supposition

(E) bittersweet memory

【解析】D

作者认为这种令人更加愉悦的状态是错误的。

(A) 令人满意的解决方案，错误。

(B) stroke of luck 名词短语，撞大运

(C) supposition n. 猜测，推测，假定

3. According to the author, those who "think this way" view the Industrial Revolution as

(A) an example of an important human achievement

(B) an instance of technology's double-edged potential

(C) an era when cities became successfully self-sufficient

(D) a time when social distinctions became easier to transcend

(E) the beginning of a harmful fiend in human history

【解析】E

见原文分析，这样想的人认为工业革命有害无益。

4. The author would most likely characterize the views of the "thinkers" referred to in line 28 as

(A) carefully resonated

(B) thought-provoking

(C) unintelligible

(D) inconclusive

(E) erroneous

【解析】E

显然，作者认为 thinkers 的观点是错误的。见原文分析。

(B) 引发深思的，形容词，构词方式：名词－分词。如 a man-dominated industry 男人主宰的行业，因为 The industry is dominated by man，所以用过去分词。

5. The author's attitude toward the "downtown ecosystem" is best described as one of

(A) regret

(B) frustration

(C) ambivalence

(D) unconcern

(E) appreciation

【解析】E（赞赏）

6. The three levels discussed serve primarily to

(A) present several arguments in support of a fundamental claim

(B) organize the author's opinions from most to least important

(C) illustrate a process of reasoning from initial assertion to ultimate conclusion

(D) group hypotheses that address two opposing principles

(E) compare alternative theories proposed by the scientific community

【解析】A

7. "peculiar" most nearly means

(A) eccentric

(B) abnormal

(C) rare

(D) distinctive

(E) significant

【解析】D（与众不同的，奇特的）

8. The author's attitude toward the "subfield" is best characterized as one of

(A) approval

(B) curiosity

(C) uncertainty (D) surprise

(E) dismay

【解析】A（赞许）

9. The discussion of the forest ecosystem is best characterized as

(A) a defense

(B) a concession

(C) a comparison

(D) an exception

(E) an allusion

【解析】C

文章提到森林生态系统是为了做比较的。

# 文章 23

## 文章 23.1

Does science fiction serve a useful purpose?[1] I cannot see much justice in the repeated claims that it sugars the pill of a scientific education: most of the science is wrong anyway, and its amount is such that one might as well be reading *Westerns* in the hope of finding out about ranching methods.[2] Science fiction's most important use, I submit, is as a means of dramatizing social inquiry, of providing a fictional mode in which cultural tendencies can be isolated and judged.[3] Many a trend hound would be surprised and perhaps mortified to discover how many of his or her cherished insights are common ground in science fiction.[4]

### 【单词及搭配】

1. science fiction 科幻小说
2. serve a useful purpose/serve no purpose，动词短语，有用/无济于事
3. justice，名词，这里指"公正"，动词为 justify：(1) 证明……是正确的

The person appointed has fully justified our proposal.

被任命的人已经充分证明我们的提案是正确的。

(2) be a good reason for 有理由

The situation was grave enough to justify further investigation.

形势如此严峻，有理由作进一步的调查。

4. sugar the pill 动词短语，或 sweeten the pill，使不容易接受的东西易于接受
5. ranching，经营牧场
6. anyway，副词

(1) 况且，而且，再说，不管怎样

I told you, it's all right, and anyway, it was my fault.

我跟你说过了，这没什么。再说，这是我的过错。

(2) 不论以何种方式，不论从何种角度

You may ask questions anyway you wondered.

7. claim (1) 动词，自称，声称，断言

His supporters claimed victory in the presidential elections.

他的支持者们声称在总统选举中已获胜。

(2) 动词，要求；索取；认领 claim the items 认领这些物件

(3) 可数名词，主张，断言 His claim to own the house is valid. 他主张对此屋的所有权

有效。

  You have no claim on my sympathies. 你无权要求得到我的支持。
  make a claim for damages 要求赔偿损害；a claim upon one's sympathy 要求某人的同情

8. submit (1) 动词，屈服，服从；归顺，投降 submit to somebody/something 屈从；同意忍受；同意对自己进行 submit oneself to sth.

  He submitted himself to a body search. 他屈从让人搜身。

  (2) 使经受，使受到

samples submitted to low pressure while being air-freighted 空运过程中经受低气压的样品

  (3) 提交，呈递

  A report was submitted to the committee.

  (4) 提出说；认为（文中意思，相当于 maintain/argue）

  Somebody submitted that +宾语从句：某人认为XXX。

9. dramatize

  (1) 及物动词，把（小说）改编成剧本；将（事件）用戏剧（或电影）形式表现
dramatize a film from a novel 将小说改编为电影

  (2) 及物动词，戏剧性地表现（或描述），生动地表达
dramatize environmental crisis 生动地表现环境危机

  (3) 及物动词，戏剧化地表达，夸张表达

10. social inquiry，社会调查

11. isolated，形容词，隔离的

12. mortify，及物动词，使感到屈辱；使失面子；使羞愧

13. hound (1) 猎犬 (2) 卑劣的人 (3) 有瘾的人，迷 music hound 音乐迷 trend hound 追逐潮流的人

14. insight，名词，这里指深刻的理解，have an insight into sth. 深刻理解某事

## 【文章精读】

  [1] 开篇提问，科幻小说真的可以带来有用的目的吗？这个需要上下文，因为它这里指大部分科学都是错的，要有上下文才能指出这一点。

  [2] 作者自问自答，"我"并不赞同那些反复陈述的所谓科幻小说美化了科学教育这样的断言；不论怎样，大部分科学都是错误的，错误的程度达到了有人以至于在阅读《西部》杂志时希望找到经营牧场的方法。即科幻小说从这个角度讲，没有带来用处。下一句作者应该会回应那么科幻小说的真正有用的目的是什么。might as well do sth. 做某事也无妨。比如：I might as well go. 我还是去吧。

  that it sugars the pill of a scientific education 为同位语从句，指代 the repeated claims，代词 it 指代 science fiction。

  its amount，它的数量，这里指前面那句话：most of the science is wrong，科学是错误的程度，即科学中错误的数量，这种错误的数量已经多到有人看《西部》杂志时试图寻找经营牧场的方法。即，科幻小说中关于科学的描述在作者看来是错误的。

  such that，如此……以至于

  one 指代读者。

might as well，动词短语，不妨做某事

in the hope of doing sth., 介词短语，希望做某事

我并不认可"科幻小说使得科学教育更有趣"这一被人们重复了多次的论断：科幻小说中描述的大部分科学都是错误的，错误的程度就相当于阅读《西部》杂志的读者一边读书，一边期待在这种杂志中找到经营牧场的方法一样。

[3] 指出科幻小说的真正重要用途，承接上一句。作者认为科幻小说的最重要用途在于使社会调查戏剧化以及提供一个虚构的模式，在这个模式中，文化趋向可以被隔离和评判。即科幻小说可以反映文化潮流。

"I submit"为插入语，可以移到句子外面，不影响句意和句子完整性。注意 submit 的意思为"主张"。as 与前面的名词 use 连接，the important uses as+名词，作为什么重要的用处。which 指代 mode。"我"认为科幻小说最重要的用途为：描绘社会调查、提供一个科幻的模式，在这种模式中人们可以分离出文化潮流并对文化潮流进行评价。

[4] 很多追逐潮流的人会惊讶或羞愧地发现：他们所珍视的洞察中有多少与科幻小说存在共同点。[4]与[3]的关系：科幻小说的重要用途在于提炼出来文化潮流，对社会与文化提供深入的洞察力。

# 文章 23.2

Much of the science in science fiction is hokum: some of it is totally wrong.[1] But beneath all the surface trickery of science fiction, there is a general respect for science and some appreciation of its methodology, which is probably more important than the facts that can be found in a textbook.[2] And because science fiction combines scientific elements with stories involving people and relationships, the genre serves as a link between the culture of the humanities and arts on the one hand, and of science and technology on the other.[3] Younger readers of science fiction, not firmly fixed in either culture, absorb both scientific and humanistic elements from their readings. [4] Thereafter, neither culture can be quite so strange.[5]

## 【单词及搭配】

1. hokum: 名词，废话
2. beneath prep.
(1) 在……之下；向……下面（文中意思）
The sun is now beneath the horizon.
(2) （地位等）低于；劣于
He is beneath his brother intellectually.
(3) 对……不适合（或不值得）
The job is beneath him. 那个工作有失他的身份。
3. involve vt.
(1) 使卷入，连累；牵涉（in/with） That's no concern of mine. I'm not involved. 那与我无关，我未卷入。 involve sb. in sth. 将某人牵扯进什么
(2) 需要，包含，意味着[(+in)] [+v-ing]（文中意思）

His work involves occasional journeys. 他的工作偶尔需要出差旅行。

(3) 使专注，使忙于[(+in)]

He was involved in writing his doctoral dissertation.

4. serve to do sth. 用来，导致  A base station serves to send and receive signals. 基站用来发送和接收信号。This type of gas serves to pollute the environment. 这种气体导致环境污染。serve as sth. 用于什么

5. fixed 形容词

(1) 固定的 fixed phone

(2) 确定的；不变的；不动的

The amount is fixed. 数量确定了。

6. (1) absorb vt. 汲取，理解（知识等）

(2) 全神贯注做某事 be absorbed in doing sth.

7. thereafter adv. 从那以后

He left China in 1994 and we heard no more of him thereafter. 他1994年离开中国后我们再没有他的任何消息。

8. respect for sth. 对某事的崇拜

## 【文章精读】

[1] 表明作者观点：科幻小说中的很多科学是废话，其中的一些是完全错误的。即，科幻小说扭曲了真正的科学。

[2] 承接上一句科幻小说中关于科学的错误之处后，提出科幻小说的益处。但在科幻小说表面花招的下面，科幻小说存在一种普遍的对科学的崇敬以及对它的方法论的某种欣赏，这可能比在教科书中能够找到的事实更为重要。

general，adj. 普遍的。respect for sth., 对某物的崇敬。which 指代 methodology，不能省略，因为它作定语从句的主语。that can be found 为 facts 的定语从句，that 不能省略。but 表转折，尽管在科幻小说下面隐藏着这些伎俩，但人们对科学方法论有着一种普遍的尊敬和欣赏，而这样的方法论可能比教科书中提到的事实更为重要。

[3] 由于科幻小说将科学元素与包含人和各种关系的故事结合了起来，因此这种文学体裁可以作为一个纽带，将人文与艺术的文化同科学与技术的文化连接起来。该句表明科幻小说通过包含人与各种关系的故事将科学与人文学科艺术连接了起来。

involving 为现在分词短语作定语，修饰 stories，即包含人与各种关系的故事，还可以这样讲：inclusive of people and relationships，形容词短语作定语后置，表示包含什么。动词短语 combine A with B，将 A 和 B 结合起来。serve as+名词，作为什么，相当于 be used as a link。between 后面跟随两个名词短语：culture of humanities and arts 和 culture of science and technology。

[4] 本句承接上一句讲人文学科与科学文化融合的实际例子：科幻小说的一些年青读者，他们不是非常坚定于任何一种文化，从而从他们的阅读中同时吸收了科学元素和人文元素。

younger readers 为句子主语，not firmly fixed in either culture 为过去分词短语作定语，修饰 readers。either 指两种文化中的任意一种，即 culture of humanities and arts 和 culture of science and technology。主语+fixed in sth.，某人对某事很专注。

absorb 为谓语。

[5] 承接[4]，自年轻读者汲取了两种文化元素后，不论人文科学还是理工科学对他们来说都不会太奇怪了。neither culture 指 culture of the humanities and arts 和 culture of science and technology。本句肯定了科幻小说的作用。

【题目解析】

1. Both passages express the view that science fiction is

(A) predictably insightful

(B) chillingly realistic

(C) artistically pleasing

(D) socially useful

(E) widely understood

【解析】D

(A) 可以预见的有洞察力的，两段文章均没有提到科幻小说具有预见性。

(B) chillingly adv. 吓人地，惊人地现实，两段文章均没提到。

(C) 在艺术上令人满意的，文章2仅提到科学与人文艺术学科的连接，并没提到在艺术上令人满意。

(D) 有着社会用途。文章1指出科幻小说的科学内容都是错误的，意义在于科幻小说可以使人们看清楚文化的流行潮流。文章2指出科幻小说可以使年轻读者熟悉人文和理工两种文化。这些都是科幻小说的社会意义。

(E) 没提到科幻小说被广泛理解，作者甚至认为科幻小说中的科学是错误的。

注意选项中修饰形容词要用副词！

2. Both passages suggest that science fiction

(A) can motivate people to pursue a scientific education

(B) can provide a bridge between the worlds of art and science

(C) is more appealing to children than it is to adults

(D) intentionally glosses over the difficult challenges that scientists face

(E) does not attempt to reflect scientific reality with rigorous exactness

【解析】E

(A) motivate sb. to do sth. 激励某人做某事 pursue sth. 研究某物，动词短语。名词短语为 in the pursuit of sth. 追求研究某物。文章1: I cannot see much justice in the repeated claims that it sugars the pill of a scientific education. 作者不认为反复宣称科幻小说帮助人们喜爱上科学教育这一论断有任何合理性。由此看到，科幻小说并没有起到激励人来进行科学教育的目的，与选项意思恰恰相反。文章2也没有提到。

(B) 文章2提到了，文章1没有。

(C) 重要句型：主语+be appealing to sb. 某物对某人有吸引力。Maths is appealing to Tom. Tom很喜欢数学。

本句意思不准确，科学对成人与孩子的吸引力并没有进行比较。

(D) intentionally=deliberately，副词，故意地；gloss over sth. 动词短语，掩饰什么。He tried to gloss over his shyness. 两篇文章均没提到科学家所做的工作。

批注 [A152]: 定语从句，科学家所面对的。face及物动词，面对。

批注 [A153]: 严密的准确性

(E) "most of the science is wrong anyway"，科幻小说中大多数科学都是错误的，是对科学事实的严重扭曲，而科幻小说的意义不在于科学教育，而是 dramatizing social inquiry, of providing a fictional mode in which cultural tendencies can be isolated and judged. 文章2说"science in science fiction is hokum"。可见，科幻小说并没有客观、严谨地反映科学事实。

3. The author of Passage 2 would most likely respond to lines 3-6 in passage 1 ("most of …methods") by

(A) claiming that the literary merits of science fiction transcend its scientific fallacies

(B) arguing that science fiction portrays science more accurately than is generally understood

(C) asserting that science fiction, despite its factual inaccuracies, values scientific thought

(D) pointing out that science fiction has increased in popularity despite its factual distortions

(E) suggesting that more people trained as scientists should attempt to write science fiction

【解析】C

题干解释：文章1中作者提到科幻小说的错误，而文章2作者虽然承认这种错误，但对题干中的一句进行了回应，指出科幻小说有它的优点所在。作者通过哪种方式回应的？四个选项中表达"认为/宣称/表述观点"的单词/短语有：主语+claim/argue/assert/point out/suggest that+宾语从句。argue 表示"认为"，不是"吵架"。此外还可以用主语+maintain+宾语从句。He maintains that he once saw Tom. 他坚持宣称曾经见过 Tom。

(A) transcend，及物动词，超越。fallacy，名词，谬误。文章2没有提到科幻小说文学上的优点可以弥补科研上的不准确。transcend 这里指 make up for sth。

(B) 错误，刚好与作者表达的意思相反，科幻小说歪曲了科学，见文章2第一句和文章1第二句详解。

(C) 文章2[2]。尽管[1]表明科幻小说扭曲了科学，其中关于科学的描述是废话甚至是错误的，但是科幻小说中对科学的崇敬以及对科学方法论的欣赏比一本教科书中的科学事实更为重要。这就是科幻小说在意义所在。"asserting that science fiction, despite its factual inaccuracies, values scientific thought"中"factual inaccuracies"指"事实不准确"，名词短语，就是文章2的[1]：科幻小说中的大部分科学是错误的。value 是谓语动词，指"珍惜"，科幻小说珍视科学思想，这就是[2]体现出来的。注意介词短语 despite its factual inaccuracies 的使用：尽管下雨了，他还是去上班了。Although it rained, he went to work as usual. 另一种更简洁的表达：Despite the heavy rain, he went to work.

Despite what we warned of him, he insisted on doing so. 尽管我们警告了他，但他还是坚持这样做。

(D) increase/decrease in popularity 越来越流行/过时。文章2没提到科幻小说的流行度。

(E) suggesting that more people trained as scientists should attempt to write science fiction. 科幻小说对于青年读者来说是一个将人文艺术与科学联系起来的纽带，但作者没有要大家去写科幻小说。

4. The attitude of each author toward the genre of science fiction might best be described as

(A) unabashed admiration

(B) qualified appreciation
(C) open amusement
(D) veiled distaste
(E) utter contempt

【解析】B

作者对科幻小说的态度是认同的，尽管科幻小说存在歪曲科学的缺点，但文章1表明科幻小说的意义在于 cultural tendencies can be isolated and judged，文章2表明科幻小说的意义在于连接人文学科与科学。

(A) unabashed，这里指"不加掩饰的"，彻头彻尾的崇拜。作者不是彻底的崇拜。unabashed=overwhelming

(B) qualified，形容词

(1) 有资格的，适合的，胜任的 be well qualified for sth. 很好地胜任什么

(2) 有限制的；不完全的（选项意思）

The proposals received heavily qualified approval. 那些提案在多种限制条件下获得通过。

作者对科幻小说的崇拜是有一定限制的，既看到科幻小说扭曲科学的事实，又承认科幻小说的优点，即它们都有一定的文化价值。

(C) 取乐，作者没有这个意思。

(D) veiled distaste，一种隐约的厌恶，作者没有表示厌恶科幻小说，只是提出其缺点。veiled，形容词，隐约的，间接的。注意动词形式：veil，及物动词，掩饰。变形：unveil，揭露，动词，同义词还有 reveal。

(E) 完全的蔑视。显然错误，作者均承认了科幻小说对文化艺术的重要意义。短语：hold someone/something in contempt，蔑视某人/物。

140

# 文章 24

## 文章 24.1

In 1929 a teenager named Ridegely Whiteman wrote to the Smithsonian Institution in Washington, D.C., about what he called warheads that he had found near Clovis, New Mexico.[1] These "warheads" were actually spear points, elegantly chipped to sharpness on both edges and finished off with a groove, or fluted, down the center of each side.[2] Eventually, such fluted points turned up in the oldest archaeological excavations elsewhere in North America.[3]

【单词及搭配】

1. elegant adj.
(1) （外观或举止）优雅的；雅致的，讲究的
(2) （科学理论、问题解决方法）简洁的，简练的；巧妙的（文中意思）
The grand unified theory is compact and elegant in mathematical terms. 用数学语言阐述的统一论简洁巧妙。
2. turn up 出现
3. excavation 名词，挖掘
4. elsewhere adv. 在别处

【文章精读】

[1] write to sb. about sth./what/how-从句：关于某事写信给某人。"what"不能用 that 来替代，它表示什么什么的东西，即：他称为子弹的东西。that he had found near Clovis, New Mexico 为定语从句，修饰"子弹"。named Ridegely Whiteman 为过去分词短语作后置定语，修饰 teenager。

[2] "子弹"加引号表明不是子弹，而是一种文物。be finished off, 动词短语，这里指该物体以某种方式被做成，相当于 be completed。

[3] eventually=ultimately, 最终，副词。最终，这一物体在北美的其他地方的最原始的考古发现中出现。

Stone cannot be carbon-dated, but the dating of organic material found with these tools showed that the people who used them were in America no earlier than about 13,500 years ago.[1] The story most archaeologists built on these ancient tools was of a people they nicknamed Clovis, who came into North America via Siberia, moved south through an ice-free corridor, then dispersed, their descendants occupying North and South America within a thousand years.[2] Since their tools were often found with the bones of mammoths and other large creatures, scientists usually described the Clovis people as biggame hunters.[3] As late as 1996 a prominent archaeologist, Frederick Hadleigh West, could state that "Clovis is taken to be the basal, the founding, population for the Americans."[4] But in the past decade such certainty has been dramatically shaken.[5]

## 【单词及搭配】

1. date
   (1) vt. 确定年代 date the paintings to 1460–70 这些画的年代确定在 1460 年至 1470 年之间
   (2) vi. 追溯到，自……起 date back to
2. ice-free adj. 不会冰冻的，不冻的
3. nickname vt. 给……起绰号；以绰号相称
4. corridor（沿着道路、河流或其他交通路线的）地区，地带
5. disperse
   (1) vt. 分散；散布 (2) vi. 疏散；驱散 (3) vi. 使（气体、烟、雾、云）消散
6. mammoth n. 猛犸象属，象科
7. prominent adj.
   (1) 重要的；卓越的，著名的 (2) 显眼的，显著的；突出的 The new housing estates are prominent landmarks. 新住宅群是显著的地标。
8. basal adj. 基底的；基层的
9. dramatic adj.
   戏剧的，有关戏剧的；戏剧表演的；戏剧学的；突然的，显著的，惊人的
   a dramatic increase in recorded crime 犯罪记录的显著增长

## 【文章精读】

[1] carbon-dated，adj. 用碳元素测定年代的。the dating of sth.。 对与这些工具一同被发现的有机物质进行年代测定，人们发现使用这些工具的人们生活在距今不到 13500 年的美国。

[2] most archaeologists built on these ancient tools 为定语从句，修饰 story，build a story on sth. 依据某事编造故事，意为"考古学家依据古代工具所编造的故事"。they 指代考古学家，of a people 之前省略了 story——关于一个民族的故事；they nicknamed Clovis 为定语从句，修饰 people；ice-free，形容词，无冰的；their descendants occupying North and South America within a thousand years 为独立主格部分。

The most straightforward challenge to the old story is the matter of time. The era in which the Clovis people lived is limited by a time barrier that stops about 13,500 years ago: there is geologic evidence that an ice-free corridor between Siberial and North America would not have been open much before them. But in 1997 a blue-ribbon panel of archaeologists visited a site in Chile called Monte Verde and agreed that people had lived there at least 14,500 years ago, about

142

1,000 years before the first sign of Clovis people in North America. Acceptance of the Monte Verde date not only broke the time barrier but also focused new interest on other sites that may have even earlier dates.

**【单词及搭配】**

1. straightforward adj. 简单的；易做的；易懂的
2. challenge 名词 (1) 挑战 (2) 考验 (3) 异议；质疑（文中意思） a challenge to sb./sth./doing sth.
3. ice-free adj. 不会冰冻的，不冻的
4. free adj. 无……的 free from/of 没有……的。a pollution-free city 一个没有污染的城市
5. blue-ribbon adj. 最佳的，顶级的，一流的 blue-ribbon service 一流的服务
6. panel 小组；专题讨论小组；委员会

本文总结：有新的证据表明早在 Clovis 之前美洲已有人类居住，比普遍认同的 13500 年前开始有人类早了 1000 年。

## 文章 24.2

One of the biggest barriers to accepting pre-Clovis sites has been geographic.[1] During the most recent ice age, the New World was pretty much closed to pedestrian traffic: the northwest corridor in Canada would have been covered with ice.[2] Though ancient humans might have masterd prehistoric crampons, mastodons almost certainly did not, and finding food and shelter under those circumstances would have been difficult at best.[3] But the latest idea circulating among archaeologists and anthropologists has people ditching their crampons and spears for skin-covered boats.[4] Maybe the first Americans came not by land but by sea, hugging the ice-age coast.[5]

> 批注 [169]: 注意该时间点：冰川时期，大陆对徒步旅行者来说是封闭的。
>
> 批注 [A170]: 新大陆
>
> 批注 [A171]: 差不多
>
> 批注 [A172]: 步行者
>
> 批注 [A173]: 鞋底钉
>
> 批注 [A174]: 乳齿象
>
> 批注 [175]: adj. 由皮毛覆盖的

**【单词及搭配】**

1. barrier: a barrier to doing sth. (1) 屏障；障碍物（喻） (2) 障碍；隔阂
2. geographic adj. 地理学的；地理的
3. pretty much 几乎，差不多 The experimental result was pretty much to be expected.
4. prehistoric adj. 史前的
5. shelter
(1) n. 避难所 （文中意思）(2) n. in the shelter of sth. 躲藏；躲避；避难；保护；庇护
(3) vt. 保护 pretect sb./sth. from doing The hut sheltered him from the cold wind. 使（某人）免遭（困难、讨厌的事）a sheltered life 安逸的生活
(4) vt. 使免交税
6. circumstance 名词
(1) 情况，条件，形势，环境
(2) 事件，事实（有负面效应事件的发生）

He was found dead but there were no suspicious circumstances. 他被发现已经死亡，但是没有可疑的致死原因。

(3) 经济状况；物质条件 live in reduced circumstances 生活拮据

7. circulate  (1) vi./vt.（使）循环 (2) vi./vt. （使）（在人与人或地点与地点之间）流通（文中意思）

8. ditch   (1) vt./vi. 挖沟于；挖壕于 (2) vt. 摆脱；抛弃，丢弃，放弃（文中意思）

9. skin-covered 形容词，被皮覆盖的，注意这种形式的复合形容词。covered 为过去分词。

10. hug
(1) vt. 拥抱 (2) vt. 和……保持接近，紧挨，紧靠（文中意思）
(3) hug oneself with sth. 因为某事而沾沾自喜
(4) vt. 抱有，持有，坚守（某物，如信念）hug a secret 保守秘密

## 【文章精读】

[1]开篇点题，指出接受史前 Colvis 文明的障碍所在：地理因素。

[2] the most recent=latest，最近的，形容词。本句表明最近的冰川时代，新大陆的交通方式步行被封闭，并解释了原因："covered with ice"。closed to sth./doing sth.。

[3]and 连接了"did not （master XXX，此处为省略）"与"finding food and shelter under those circumstances would have been difficult at best"，主语均为"乳齿象"。人类可以掌握史前钉鞋技术，而大象无法掌握，且在那样的环境下捕食和庇护相当困难（即乐观看来，捕食很难）。"those circumstances"指代上一句的"covered with ice"。circumstances 表示"情况"时通常用复数。difficult at best=difficult seen from the most optimistic aspect，即"很难"。

[4] 指出 2000 年最新观点：与[1]-[3]不同。"but"表示对前面观点的否定。这里往往是作者的本意。"circulating among archaeologists and anthropologists"为现在分词短语作定语，修饰 idea，一个流传于考古学家中间的最新的观点。has 为谓语。ditch sth. for sth. 为某物放弃什么。"ditching their crampons and spears for skin-covered boats"为现在分词短语作定语，修饰 people，那些人们放弃了铁钉鞋，改用皮毛覆盖着的船。由此看出，第一批美国人是通过船只而非步行来到新大陆的。下文会有详细解释。注意替换：latest=most recent。

When the seafaring theory was proposed in the mid-1970's, it sank for lack of evidence but as the time line for New World occupation has changed, the theory seems downright sensible, if not quite provable.[1] The Pacific Rim has vast resources of salmon and sea mammlas, and people need only the simplest of tools to exploit them: nets, weirs, clubs, knives.[2] Whereas ancient landlubbers would have had to reinvent their means of hunting, foraging, and housing as they passed through different terrains, ancient mariners could have had smooth sailing through relatively unchanging coastal environments.[3] And recent geologic studies show that even when glaciers stretched down into North America, there were thawed pockets of coastline in northwest North America where people could take refuge and gather provisions.[4] "Most archaeologists have a continental mind-set," says anthropologist Robson Bonnichsen, "but the peopling of the Americans is likey to be tied very much to the development and spread of maritime adaptation."[5]

批注 [A176]: 太平洋带状地区

批注 [A177]: 大马哈鱼

批注 [A178]: 新水手

批注 [A179]: 老船员

批注 [A180]: 地质研究

批注 [A181]: 冰川

批注 [ 182]: 融化的，形容词

**【单词及搭配】**

1. seafaring   adj. 出海的，航海的 n. 航海

2. sink

(1) vi. 下沉；沉没 (2) vi. 消失；无音信。句型：Sth. sank without trace. 某物消失得无影无踪。

(3) vt. 隐藏，掩盖 sink the differences 消除分歧

(4) （词、情况）完全被理解；被理会

I read the instruction twice before its meaning sank in. 我读了两遍之后才完全理解说明书的意思。

(5) vi. sink to+数量/名词 跌至（价值、数量、质量或强度），逐渐下降，下跌

(6) vi.（心情）压抑

(7) vt. 将（金钱、精力）投入（某事）；投资 sink energy into doing sth. 花精力做某事

3. for lack of   因没有……而，介词短语作状语

Several research institutions were closed down for lack of fund. 由于缺乏资金，好几家研究所被迫关门了。

4. occupation 工作；职业，（被）占领，（被）占领期，（房屋等地方的）居住；使用

5. downright

(1) adj.（贬）十足的，完全的，彻头彻尾的（表强调）(2) adj. 直率的，直截了当的；生硬的 (3) adv. 十分

6. provable adj. 可证明的, 可证实的

7. sensible

(1) adj. 明智的 (2)（物品）实用的，非装饰性的 (3) 能看到的；能觉察到的 sensible of sth. 觉察到某事

8. reinvent

(1) vt. 彻底改造，重新创造（文中意思）(2) vt. 重新开始（全新的工作或生活方式）

9. whereas  连词，而，却；反之

10. stretch

(1) vi. 伸展，延伸；延展；被拉长；被拉宽 Sth. stretched easily.

(2) vi./vt.（使）过分延长，（使）过度延续 stretch to sth.

(3) vi.（资金、资源）足够，够用 The budget won't stretch to equipment costing $1,000.

(4) vt. 大量要求，大量需求

The cost of the court case has stretched their finances to the limit. 那件诉讼案的费用使他们的财务状况紧张到了极限。

(5) 使……最大限度利用（才能、能力）

It's too easy—it doesn't stretch me. 这太容易了，我无需尽全力。

11. thaw

(1) vt./vi.（冰、雪等）融化，融解；（冷冻食品等）解冻；化冻（文中意思）

(2) vi. 变得随和（或缓和）；变得不拘束

She thawed out sufficiently to allow a smile to appear. 她充分放松后，露出了笑容。

(3) vi. 使变得较不拘束；使变得友善（或缓和、随和）

The cast thawed the audience into real pleasure. 演员们使观众摆脱拘束，真正乐起来。

12. refuge 名词，避难；庇护；避难所，收容所
13. provision n.
(1) 供应，提供
(2) （金钱或其他方面的）预备，准备；预先采取的措施
(3) 供应量，供给物
(4) 必需品（如食品、饮料、设备）（文中意思）
14. mind-set n. 思想的形式
15. adaptation 名词 (1) 适应（行为或过程）（文中意思）(2) （根据文学作品）改编成的电影（或电视剧、戏剧）
16. maritime adj. 海的；航海的；（尤指）海事的

## 【文章精读】

[1] 航海理论从不被认可，到随着时间的流逝逐渐被人认为比较有道理，但还没有很好地被证明。下文必定详细讲述这种理论的合理之处。

[2] 该理论的论据：海洋中有众多生物供人类食用。

[3] Whereas ancient landlubbers would have had to reinvent their means of hunting, foraging, and housing as they passed through different terrains, ancient mariners could have had smooth sailing through relatively unchanging coastal environments.

unchanging 的反义词为 different。这里经常为考点，从语境判断单词的含义！本句指出在陆地上行走需要不断发明生存方式，但在海洋行进比较容易，因为沿岸的环境是相对稳定的。

[4] 进一步指出地质研究的结果来证明本段提出的观点。

[5] "Most archaeologists have a continental mind-set," says anthropologist Robson Bonnichsen, "but the peopling of the Americans is likey to be tied very much to the development and spread of maritime adaptation." adaptiation 这里为"适应"。美国人愿意接受通过船只来到新大陆的观点。

[两篇文章的逻辑关系分析]

文章 1 指出可能存在 Colvis 的史前人类文明；文章 2 指出史前文明可能存在，只是人们来到美洲的方式不是步行，而是航海。

## 【题目解析】

1. Both authors agree on which of the following points?
(A) A maritime environment would have presented unique challenges to early Americans.
(B) The first Americans most likely subsisted on mastodons and other big game.
(C) Overland travel to the New World would have been difficult during the most recent ice age.
(D) It may never be definiteively determined when America was initially settled.
(E) The Clovis people were most likey the first Americans.

146

【解析】C

(C) 两篇文章都提到陆地行走来到新大陆在冰川时代是艰难的。

(D) 太绝对，两篇文章没提到决不可能知道美国人最初来到新大陆的时间。

(E) 文章 1 和 2 都认为 Clovis 之前可能还有人来到过美洲。

2. The author of passage 2 would most likely claim that the information presented in the last paragraph of passage 1

(A) validates the notion that the peopling of Americas occurred shortly after the most recent ice age

(B) adds credibility to the theory that the first Americans may have arrived by boat

(C) indicates that overland travel to the New World was not possible

(D) demonstrates that early Americans must have relied on the sea for sustenance

(E) reveals that archaeologists can differ over even the most basic facts

【解析】B

(B) 文章 1 最后一段指出：14500 年前美洲已经有人类到达，但有证据表明 13500 年时才有无冰陆地，即早在 Clovis 到来之前的 1000 年，人类应该是通过其他方式而非陆地到达了美洲，因此对美国人坐船到达美洲这一理论增加了理论支持。add sth. to sth. 对某物增加了某物，动词短语。

(A) 意思反了，文章 2 认为美国人首次来到美洲发生在冰川时代之前。

validate vt. (1) 证实；确证（选项意思）  (2) 使生效；使有法律效力

(C) 太绝对化。文章只提到 challenge（质疑），并没有完全否定最早的美国人徒步来到新大陆的理论。

(D) 与 (C) 错误一样，must have done 太绝对化。

(E) 文中没提到这个意思。

# 文章 25

## 文章 25.1

Reconstructed with the aid of the money and enthusiasm of John D. Rockefeller, Jr., Colonial Williamsburg is not only a brilliant example of an American style in historical monuments; it has become a school for training professionals who will be devotees of popular interpretations of United States history.[1] Meanwhile, academic historians, disturbed by the unorthodoxy and the popular appeal of Williamsburg, have not given it the significance it deserves.[2] Some treat it as simply another example—like Willisam Randolph Hearst's notorious imported castles—of educational "gadget".[3] Or they treat it condescendingly as a harmless but amusing example of American vulgarity—a kind of patriotic Disneyland.[4] But several visits there have persuaded me that it is significant in ways that its promoters did not advertise.[5]

批注 [190]: 威廉姆斯殖民地城堡

批注 [191]: 爱国主义的迪斯尼乐园，人们对城堡的讽刺

【单词及搭配】

1. reconstruct vt. (1) 重建（文中意思）(2) 重现，重整
2. aid (1) vt. 帮助，援助 aid the poor 帮助穷人 (2) n. 帮助，援助，救助 do sth. with the aid of sth./sb. 在某物/人的资助下做某事（文中意思）(3) n. 助手，辅助物，辅助手段
3. professional (1) adj. 职业的，专业的 (2) adj. 内行的，有经验的 professional advice 行家的意见 (3) adj. 有意的，故意的 (4) n. 具有某专业资格的人，专业人士（文中意思）
4. monument n. 纪念碑；遗迹，遗址，名胜古迹
5. devote vt. (1) 把……奉献（给）(2) 专用于 Something was devoted to doing sth. 某物专用于什么。
6. interpretation n. (1) 解释，说明；诠释（文中意思）(2) 表演；演奏
7. deserve vt. 应受，应得，值得 deserve sth./deserve to do sth. 值得做某事
8. appeal (1) n. 呼吁，恳求 the appeal for sth. 对某事的呼吁 (2) n. 感染力，吸引力 Something has appeal to somebody. 某事对某人有吸引力。（文中意思）(3) vi. 呼吁 appeal for something (4) vi. 有吸引力 Something appeals to sb.
9. unorthodoxy 名词，异端 unorthodox adj. 非正统的，非传统的，非正规的
10. notorious adj. 臭名昭著的，声名狼藉的
11. gadget 小配件，新发明，道具；小巧的机械装置；小玩意；小器具；小器械
12. condescending adj. (1) 降低身份的，屈尊的（文中意思）(2) 高傲的；傲慢的 a condescending attitude 傲慢的态度

13. vulgarity 名词 (1) 庸俗，粗俗，粗鄙 (2) 粗野的行为；粗俗的话
14. patriotic adj. 爱国的，有爱国心的
15. advertise vt. (1) 公布，宣传（文中意思） (2) vt. & vi.（给……）做广告宣传
16. promoter n. 承办人，出资人，赞助人
promote vt. (1) 提升，提拔 (2) 筹划，发起，创立 (3) 促进；推动；增进
17. Disneyland n. (1) 迪斯尼乐园 (2) 幻想世界
18. persuade (1) vt. & vi. 说服，劝告 (2) vt. 使信服；使相信（文中意思）
19. whim n. 一时的兴致，突然的念头，突发奇想，异想天开
20. indulge (1) vt. 放纵，容许 (2) vt. 满足 (3) vi. 让自己尽情享受某物（文中意思）

## 【文章精读】

[1] 这个学校已经成为培养乐于从事用通俗方式讲述美国历史的专家的学校。popular interpretations，名词短语，通俗的解释。

Reconstructed with the aid of the money and enthusiasm 为过去分词短语作伴随状语，在某人的资助下被重建，逻辑主语为 it。

reconstruct 为本文核心词汇，重建。

[2] "disturbed by the unorthodoxy and the popular appeal of Williamsburg" 为过去分词短语作伴随状语，由于受到异端和大众流行的困扰，学术历史学家并没有给与城堡赋以应有的重要意义。指出人们对城堡认识的偏颇。"it deserves"为定语从句，修饰 significance。it 指代 Williamsburg。

【重要句型】Sth. deserves the significance of XXX. 某物应该获得 XXX 的重要性。

[3]-[4] 通过两个例子指出人们对 Williamsburg 的不正确的认识。

[5] persuade sb. that+从句，使某人信服什么事。be significant in ways，在某方面很重要。that its promoters did not advertise，定语从句，修饰 ways。advertise, vt., 这里指"宣扬"，相当于 promote。点题：作者通过几次旅行看到了城堡蕴含的并没有被人宣扬过的意义。

[重要用法]在某方面的意义变动/上升/下降：the significance changes/rises/falls in sth.

*段意：* 本段引出作者发现城堡没被人宣扬过的重要意义。

Williamsburg is a strikingly democratic national monument.[1] It presumes an unspecialized and unaristocratic education.[2] Unless one already knows a great deal, one cannot learn much from visiting the Roman Forum or the Athenian Acropolis.[3] The National Gallery in London seems a jungle of canvas and marble to anyone not already instructed in the different arts and periods represented.[4] These places are planned primarily for the connoisseur or the scholar, not for the citizen.[5]

## 【单词及搭配】

1. striking adj. (1) 显著的，突出的（文中意思） (2) 引人注目的；容貌出众的
2. democratic adj. 民主的，有民主精神或作风的
3. presume vt. (1) 以为；假定（文中意思） (2) vi. 冒昧地做某事；错用

I presume to suggest that you should take legal advice. 我冒昧地建议：你应该找律师咨

(3) 自作主张，放肆 Don't presume to tell me what I will or will not do.

4. specialize v. 专门从事，专攻。还须掌握形容词形式：specialized adj. (1) 专门的；专科的 (2) 专业的；专业化的（文中意思）

5. jungle n. (1)（热带）丛林，密林 (2) 乱七八糟的一堆事物

6. connoisseur n. 鉴赏家，鉴定家；行家

7. citizen n. (1) 公民 (2) 平民（文中意思） civil adj. (1) 公民的，平民的 (2) 文明的，有教养的

8. instruct vt. (1) 命令，指示 (2) 教，指导（文中意思） (3) 通知

【文章精读】

本段描述该城堡与其他建筑的不同之处——popularity（大众性）。

[1] 威廉姆斯城堡是一个突出的具有民主特性的建筑物。strikingly 为副词，副词修饰形容词"民主的"。

[2] 进一步指出城堡的特点——非专业化和平民化。

[3] 对比说明其他国家的艺术类博物馆只有当观众通晓艺术专业时才能从中有收获。unless=if not。If one does not yet know a great deal, one cannot learn much from visiting XXX.

[4] 以伦敦博物馆为例，说明其不具有大众性。not already instructed in the different arts and periods represented 为过去分词短语作定语，修饰 anyone，不通晓不同艺术和艺术品做展现的时期的看客。represented 为过去分词作定语，修饰 periods，被艺术品所表现出来的时期：Displays represent periods.

[5] these places 指代类似伦敦博物馆一类的艺术场所，这些场所只适合于鉴赏家和学者，并非为平民所设计。

But because Colonial Williamsburg offers not a segment of the history of a fine art, but a model of an ongoing community, it is intelligible and interesting to nearly everybody.[1] It is a symbol of a culture in which fine arts have become much less important than in other cultures; in which literacy is a higher ideal than literariness.[2] The forbidding ribbon across the antique chair, the "Do Not Touch" sign—these omnipresent features of the European museum have nothing to do with the American restored community.[3] One of the most startling facts to anyone who has toured Europe is that the Willamsburg guides have no set speeches, and are giving visitors their own interpretation of the rigorous course of lectures on colonial life which they are required to attend as part of their training.[4]

【单词及搭配】

1. aristocratic adj. 贵族的；贵族气派的，高贵的

2. presume (1) vt. 以为；假定（文中意思） (2) vi. 冒昧地做某事；错用 presume to do sth.

3. unspecialized adj. 非专业化的

4. jungle n. (1) 丛林，密林 (2) 乱七八糟的一堆事物

5. instruct vt. (1) 命令，指示 (2) 教，指

6. intelligible adj. 可理解的，明白易懂的，清楚的

7. literacy n. 识字，有文化，会读写

8. literariness n. 文学性，文艺性

9. accord (1) n. 一致，符合 (2) vt. 给予，赠予 (3) vi. 符合，一致 accord in/with sth. (3) vt. accord sth. to sb. 给与某人某事

make-believe n. 假装，假扮者 adj. 假装的，虚构的；虚幻的 a make-believe story 虚构的故事

9. rigorous adj. (1) 严格的，严厉的 (2) 枯燥的，枯涩的（文中意思）

## 【文章精读】

[1] 指出威廉姆斯城堡易于被平民接受的原因：它所展现的不是高雅艺术历史的一个片段，而是不断进展的社区的模型。

be intelligible to sb.，对某人易于理解，以下两种表达意思相同：

The book is intelligible to me.

I understand the book well.

[2] It is a symbol of a culture in which fine arts have become much less important than in other cultures; in which literacy is a higher ideal than literariness. It 指代威廉姆斯城堡。which 指代 culture。than 后面省略了 fine arts。威廉姆斯城堡是这样一种文化的标识：在这种文化中，高雅艺术比在其他文化中来得次要。literacy 为名词，能看懂能识字，即通俗性 (popularity)；literariness 为名词，艺术价值。在这种文化中通俗性与艺术性相比是更高的理想。

[3] 指出威廉姆斯城堡与欧洲同类艺术场所的截然不同。A has nothing to do with B. A 这件事与 B 没有关系。forbidding ribbon：forbidding 为现在分词作形容词，表主动含义，禁止人入内的丝带；注意区别：forbidden ribbons，不准被带入内的丝带。

[4] 进一步将欧洲博物馆与威廉姆斯城堡做对比，从游览过欧洲博物馆的游客角度指出令这些游客最惊讶的是：威廉姆斯城堡的导游向游客展示他们自己对于一系列枯燥殖民生活讲座的理解，这些讲座作为导游训练的一部分要求导游参加，而导游并没有固定的解说词。

which 后面的定语从句修饰 lectures。who has toured Europe 为定语从句，修饰 anyone，startling facts，令人吃惊的现实。set speeches：set 为过去分词作形容词，固定的，相当于 fixed。they 指代"导游"。

注意 require 的用法：

Somebody is required to do sth. 某人被要求做某事。

名词短语：sth. required to do sth. 要求做什么的某物。required to do 为过去分词短语作定语，修饰 sth。

【举一反三】The power required to transmit the signal is 1 watt.

A Colonial Williamsburg would be impossible in a country that was not wealthy.[1] It is made for a nation of paved roads and family vacations.[2] Williamsburg—like the American spelling bee and educational television shows—symbolized the American refusal to believe that education need a chore.[3] Business and pleasure ought to be combined.[4] In this sense,

Williamsburg is perfectly suited.[5]

## 【单词及搭配】

1. chore n. (1) 零星工作（尤指家常杂务）(2) 日常事务；例行工作 (3) 令人厌烦的任务；乏味无聊的工作（文中意思）

2. symbolize vt. 象征；作为……的象征 B symbolizes A。B 标识着 A。

3. spelling bee 名词短语，拼字比赛

## 【文章精读】

[1]-[2]：指出威廉姆斯城堡只有在富有的国家才能存在。

[3]-[5]：Williamsburg 为主语。symbolized 为谓语，标志着什么。to believe 为不定式作定语，修饰 refusal，可以取代相应名词性从句，简洁。

比如：他所做的事表明他不愿参加我们的社团。

What he acted manifested that he was reluctant to join our party.

What he acted manifested his reluctance to join our party.

that education need a chore 为 believe 的宾语从句。威廉姆斯城堡表明：美国人不认为教育一定是令人乏味的工作。即事务性工作与快乐应该是如影随形的。perfectly：完美地，副词，威廉姆斯城堡完美地符合美国人的这一观点。

# 文章 25.2

The replacement of reality with selective fantasy is characteristic of that most successful and staggeringly profitable American phenomenon, the reinvention of the environment as themed entertainment.[1] The definition of "place" as a chosen image probably started in a serious way in the late 1920's at Colonial Williamsburg, predating and paving the way for the new world order of Walt Disney Enterprise.[2] Certainly it was in the restoration of Colonial Williamsburg that the studious fudging of facts received its scholarly imprimatur, and that history and place as themed artifact hit the big time.[3] Williamsburg is seen by the connoisseur as a kind of period piece now, its shortsightedness a product of the limitations of the early preservation movement.[4] Within those limitations, a careful construct was created: a place where one could learn a little romanticized history, confuse the real and unreal, and have—then and now—a very nice time.[5] Knowledge, techniques, and standards have become increasingly sophisticated since then.[6] But it is the Williamsburg image and example as originally conceived that continue to be universsally admired and emulated.[7]

批注 [192]: 第 6 题出处

## 【单词及搭配】

1. replacement n. 代替，替换，更换

2. selective adj. (1) 精心选择的 (2) 选择的；不普遍的

3. fantasy n. 想象，幻想

4. stagger (1) vi. 蹒跚 (2) vt. 使……感到震惊[担心] (3) vt. 错开 stagger working hour staggering adj. 难以置信的；令人震惊的；大得惊人的；骇人的；难以想象的

5. profitable adj. 有利可图的；有益的

6. reinvention n. 再创造，重塑

7. themed adj. 有特定主题的

8. predate v. 提早日期，居先

9. studious adj. (1) 好学的，用功的 (2) 仔细的，用心的；故意的

10. fudge vt. 搪塞，篡改

11. imprimatur n. 出版许可，认可

12. artifact n. 人工制品；手工艺品；加工品

13. connoisseur n. 鉴赏家，鉴定家；行家

14. period piece (1) 具有时代特征的作品 (2) 古董（文中意思）

15. shortsightedness n. 近视

16. conceive (1) vt. & vi. 想出，构想，设想（文中意思） (2) vt. 怀孕

17. emulate vt. (1) 与……竞争，努力赶 (2) 计算机程序等仿真；模仿（文中意思）

【文章精读】

[1] The replacement of reality with selective fantasy is characteristic of that most successful and staggeringly profitable American phenomenon, the reinvention of the environment as themed entertainment. 用精选出来的幻想去取代现实是美国最成功同时暴利的美国现象的特征，这一特征就是以娱乐为主题重建现实环境。

短语：the replacement of A with B，用 B 替换 A

[2] 将某个地区定义为选择好的形象以一种严肃的方式起源于 20 世纪 20 年代的殖民地威廉姆斯城堡，而这一定义先于并为迪斯尼乐园的新世界秩序铺平了道路。predating and paving 为现在分词短语作伴随状语。这里的 chosen 指代"被重建的"——replaced, reconstructed。

[3] 威廉姆斯城堡的重建曾经轰动一时并受到了专家学者的认可。

It was+介词短语/名词 that+从句。强调句型。be 动词后使用介词短语或名词要看从句缺什么成分。如果缺状语，用前者；如果缺主语或宾语，用后者。本句 and that 为 that 后引导的第二个从句，两个或多个从句跟随的情况下，最后一个从句前要用连词 and 连接。

The studious fudging of facts received its scholarly imprimatur.

"as themed artifact"为定语，修饰 history and place；hit the big time：红极一时。studious 为形容词，这里为贬义，谨慎的，故意的，小心翼翼的，仔细的，形容对历史的精心篡改，目的是篡改后为娱乐所用。注意后文有一个单词与此单词意思一样。the fudging of sth.：名词短语，对某事的篡改。

[5] 在历史文物保护的局限性下，人们对历史文物进行精心的重建，重建为一个可以使参观者学到罗曼蒂克史的地方，而在这里，人们混淆了真假，并且度过了美好的时光。本句是对重建造成的歪曲历史的全盘否定，含讽刺意味。careful 与 studious 同义。

[6] then 指代从重建威廉姆斯城堡起。从那时起，知识、技巧和标准变得越来越复杂。这是重建带来的作用，使各种知识复杂化。

[7] but 表转折，与威廉姆斯城堡重建后曾红极一时转折。as originally conceived 为分词短语作定语，修饰 image and example；唯有威廉姆斯城堡当初构思时的形象和示例才受到人们继续敬仰和模仿，即重建的城堡仅仅红极一时，已经被人们抛弃。

originally conceived，副词修饰过去分词，最初被构思的，起形容词作用。

最初构思的草稿，originally conceived draft。

It is+名词 that+从句。从句缺主语，完整语序为：

The Williamsburg image and example continue to be universsally admired and emulated.

Restoration is a difficult and unclear procedure at best; unreality is built into the process, which requires a highly subjective kind of cosmetic surgery.[1] At Williamsburg, there was instant amputation with the conceit of a "cutoff date" for the restoration—in this case, 1770—an arbitrary determination of when a place should be frozen in time.[2] After the cutoff date had been chosen, the next step was to "restore it back".[3] That means re-creating a place as someone thinks it was—or would like it to have been—at a chosen moment.[4] This usually means moving or destroying a good deal of subsequent architectural history—exactly the stuff of which real history and art are made.[5] In an act of stunning illogic and innocent hubris, a consortium of preservation architects and historical soothsayers plays God.[6]

> 批注 [193]: 第7题出处

## 【单词及短语】

1. be built into 成为某物的一部分
2. subjective adj.（思想、感情等）主观的
3. cosmetic (1) n. 化妆品 (2) adj. 装点门面的
4. amputation n. 删除
5. conceit n. 高傲，骄傲自大
6. cutoff date=deadline
7. arbitary adj. 专断的，任意的
8. subsequent adj. (1) 随后的，继……之后的 (2) 连续的，接下去的 A is subsequent to B. A 在 B 之后。
9. stuff (1) vt. 以……填进，塞满 (2) n. 材料；东西（文中意思）
10. stunning adj. (1) 漂亮的 (2) 令人惊奇的
11. innocent adj. (1) 清白的 (2) 涉世不深的；天真的，单纯的 (3) 头脑简单的；愚钝的（文中意思）
12. hubris n. 骄傲自大，自恃
13. consortium n. 财团，联营企业
14. cosmetic surgery 整容手术

## 【文章精读】

[1] at best：这里指从最乐观的角度来看＝seen from the most optimistic way/perspective。

be built into sth., 成为某物的一部分。

举例：Difficulties are built into the project. 工程中出现困难是不可避免的。

Sth. (A) built into sth. (B)，成为 B 中必不可少的 A。

"which"指代 unreality。unreality 指"主观想象"，主观想象成为整个重建过程必不可少的一部分，而想象要求有高度主观类似"整容手术"一样的东西。分号之前概括重建的过程是复杂和不清晰的。分号后面解释为什么复杂和不清晰。

Sth. is difficult at best. 从最乐观角度来看，某物难。即，某物相当难。

短语：a kind of sth. 一种类似某物的东西

[2] 本句指出威廉姆斯城堡的野蛮重建。arbitrary 这里指"独断专行的"，与名词 conceit 对应。when a place should be frozen in time 作 of 的宾语从句，即名词性从句。

[3] 截止日期选定之后，接下来就要把城堡"恢复原貌"。打了引号表明不是恢复原貌，而是破坏历史。

[4] "that"指代 restore it back。这就意味着按照某人认为的那样去恢复建筑。as 这里指"正如"。

[5] 本句指出重建城堡造成的危害——破坏一系列历史建筑，而这些建筑恰恰可能是构成真正的历史和艺术的要素。which 指代 stuff。本句拆分：

(1) This usually means moving or destroying a good deal of subsequent architectural history.

(2) The stuff of history are made of real history and art.

[6] innocent 这里为贬义词，愚蠢的。play 相当于 act as 和 serve as，动词短语，充当某种角色。讽刺假借保护历史为名义的历史学家对城堡的肆意破坏。hubris 对应了前文的 arbitary——肆意的拆除。

In the United States, this type of crime against art and history has become an established element of popular culture.[1] It has also given a license to destroy. Approximately 730 buildings were removed at Williamsburg; 81 were renovated and 413 were rebuilt on the original sites. Everything later than the chosen time frame had to disappear. So much for reality. And so much for the messy, instructive, invaluable and irretrievable revelations that are part of the serendipitous record of urban settlements.

批注 [194]: 第 8 题出处

【单词及搭配】

1. renovate vt. 翻新；修复，整修
2. time frame 期限

【文章精读】

[1] the crime against sth., 对某物犯下的罪行。established, 形容词，被建立起来的，比如：an established idea＝a prevalently accepted idear, 被普遍接受的观点。在美国，这种对历史和艺术犯下的罪行已经成为一种人们普遍接受的流行文化。即，公众对破坏历史的行为见怪不怪了。

[2] it 指代 crime。give license to destroy, 允许破坏。

【题目解析】

1. The authors of both passages would most likely agree that Colonial Williamsburg as

(A) achieved popular acceptance in the United States

(B) served as a prototype for European theme parks

(C) benefited from the input of preservation architects

(D) distorted Americans' sense of a collective past

(E) overcome the limitations of historical reconstruction

【解析】A

(A) 两篇文章都指出城堡很受欢迎，第一篇强调通俗性，第二篇强调大家对类似城堡这种破坏历史的行为见怪不怪，即 popular。

(B) 文章1显然不同意该观点，欧洲主题公园的特点是高雅、不通俗，与城堡风格截然相反，因此城堡不可能成为欧洲主题公园的雏形。prototype n. 原型，雏形，蓝本。

主语 serve as+名词=主语起到名词的作用。

(C) 文章2观点相反。城堡破坏历史。benefit from sth., 受益于某物。

(D) 文章1没提到。

(E) Williamsburg is seen by the connoisseur as a kind of period piece now, its shortsightedness a product of the limitations of the early preservation movement. 城堡并没有克服文物保护的局限性。

2. In passage 1, the Roman Forum, the Athenian Acropolis, and the National Gallery are presented as examples of places that

(A) are more interesting to European than to Americans

(B) require expert knowledge to be fully appreciated

(C) educate visitors about different arts and periods

(D) establish aesthetic standards that have been compromised

(E) are interesting to everyone who visits them

【解析】B

(A) 题干提到的欧洲艺术馆需要专业知识才能使游客从中学到东西，所以 interesting to Americans 是错误的。

(B) expert 在这里相当于 specialized，形容词，专业的。appreciate 在这里为 vt.，意思是"欣赏，理解"。这些地方需要游客有专业知识才能理解其内涵。正确。

(C) 这些地方对没有相关知识的游客来说不存在教育意义。

(D) 文章没有提到这些地方建立了被降低的艺术标准。作者对这些地方持否定态度。compromise 这里为 vt.，损害。

(E) 这些地方对没有专业知识的游客来说是毫无意义的。interesting to everyone 错误。

3. The author of passage 1 implies that the "ribbon" and the "sign" have the effect of

(A) helping people understand the cultural significance of objects that are displayed in museums

(B) preventing damage to antiques that have become both fragile and priceless

(C) restricting architects from re-creating places of historic significance

(D) keeping people away from things that represent a link to their culture and history

(E) conveying the misconception that most people once lived amidst such luxury

【解析】D

(A) 错误，这些丝带阻碍了人们对文化历史的了解。

(B) 这是丝带的作用之一，但不是作者要强调的主要负面作用。the damages to sb./sth., 对某物的破坏，名词短语。

(C) restrict sth. from sth.，阻止某物做某事。丝带并没有阻止建筑学家仿造历史文物的作用，而是保护文物不受游客破坏，但造成的后果是使游客不能理解文物所起到的连接文化与历史的桥梁作用。

(D) 欧洲博物馆中的丝带和"禁止触摸"的警示牌使得人们远离了建立文化与历史之间桥梁的文物。即人们不能通过这些文物了解历史和文化。

(E) 文中没有提到这个意思。

4. The author of passage 1 asserts that anyone who has toured Europe would find which of the following most "startling" about Colonial Williamsburg?

(A) The participation by tourists in historic reenactments
(B) The obvious wealth of most of the visitors
(C) The freedom accorded to the tour guides
(D) The concept of a make-believe historic village
(E) The expense of training the tourist guides

【解析】C

(A) 历史再现过程中游客的参与。文中提到最令人惊讶的不是游客的参与。

(B) 文中没提到游客富有，相反，城堡的游客面向普通百姓，具有大众化。

(C) accord (1) n. 一致，符合 come to an accord that+从句：达成XXX的协议。(2) n. （尤指国与国之间的）谅解，协议 (3) vt. 给予，赠予（选项意思） accord sb. sth./accord sth. to sb. 赠与某人某物 (4) vi. 符合，一致 Sth. accord. 某些事物一致。A accords with B.

accorded to the tour guides 为不定式作定语，修饰 freedom。导游被赋予的自由。正确。详见原文分析：城堡的导游没有固定的解说词，这点与欧洲博物馆的导游截然相反。

(D) make-believe adj. 虚假的。文中没提到城堡作为虚假的村庄令欧洲游客惊讶。

(E) 文中没提到导游的培训费用。

5. The approach to education ("Williamsburg…chore") is most similar to which of the following?

(A) A computer game that teaches geography
(B) A museum that displays historic artifacts
(C) A film that provides comic relief
(D) A textbook that examines controversial issues
(E) A scientific experiment that tests a theory

【解析】A

(A) 体现了美国人的教育观念：寓教于乐。

6. The word "studious" serves to emphasize the

(A) hard work that is required to repair historic structures
(B) serious aspects of a place that is designed to provide amusement
(C) ingenuity of those who conceived of Colonial Williamsburg's novel approach
(D) deliberateness with which Colonial Williamsburg was fabricated
(E) academic credentials of the scholars who approve of Colonial Williamsburg

【解析】D

(A) 作者对城堡的重建持反对态度，因此没有 hard work（勤劳）的含义。that 为定语从句中的主语，不能省略，指代 hard work。选项意思为城堡重建所需的艰辛努力。错误。

(B) 一个用于提供娱乐的场所的严肃之处。文章没提到这个意思。

(C) those 后面跟随定语从句，注意 those 不能换成人称代词 they 或 them。构思城堡新方法的人的聪明才智。感情色彩错了，作者对重建持批判态度。

(D) studious 这里为贬义词，指出人们如何精心篡改历史、对城堡进行重建。deliberateness 为名词，选项意思为城堡建造过程中人们的精心。which 指代 deliberateness。

(E) approve (1) vt. & vi. 赞成，同意（选项意思）(2) vt. 批准，通过
文中没提到学术认可的事。

7. "plays" most nearly means
(A) bets on
(B) competes against
(C) acts as
(D) toys with
(E) takes advantage of

【解析】C
见原文分析，play God 指扮演上帝的角色，相当于 serve as 和 act as。
(E) 利用，动词短语。

8. In passage 2, "this type of crime" is
(A) usual because most people treasure architectural history
(B) alarming because it could threaten the livelihood of artists
(C) exploitive because it takes advantage of the good will of others
(D) negligent because historic landmarks must be regularly maintained
(E) ominous because few people seem to be bothered by it

【解析】E
(E) 见原文分析，这种"罪行"美国民众已经司空见惯了。ominous adj. 险恶的。这种罪行指拆除历史文物进行重建，文中 established culture 指民众对这种罪行见怪不怪，作者虽然没有直接表达出 ominous，但整篇文章中作者表达了对肆意破坏历史建筑的担忧，作者认为人们已经习惯了这种罪行，因此这种破坏历史文物的局面是很危险的。

(A) 意思反了，作者认为人们不珍惜历史建筑，所以这种罪行才非常普遍。

(B) livelihood，名词，生计。文中没提到艺术家的生计问题。

(C) 文中没提到利用了他人的好意。

(D) negligent adj. 疏忽的；粗心大意的。这种罪行是粗心大意造成的，因为历史文物必须定期维护。首先，negligent 含义不对，作者反对重建这一行为，与"粗心大意"无关；其次，作者并没提到维护历史建筑。

9. The "brilliant example of an American style" in passage 1 would most likely be discredited by the author of passage 2 on the grounds that

(A) other countries demonstrated a commitment to architectural preservation long before the United States did so

(B) monuments in the United States are striking in appearance but lack true cultural value

(C) nostalgic depictions of history make people yearn for a lifestyle that is no longer possible

(D) attempts to produce a vivid re-creation of the past result in a sanitized version of history

(E) historical restoration is undertaken only when it promises to be profitable

【解析】D

discredit vt. 使不相信，使怀疑；败坏……的名声；拒绝相信，不相信，怀疑 n. 丧失信誉，丧失名誉

do sth. on the ground that+同位语从句：依据某事做某事。

文章 2 的作者会基于哪个原因驳斥文章 1 提到的 "brilliant example of an American style"？

(A) commitment n. (1) 承诺，许诺，保证 (2) 承担的义务 (3) 信奉，献身

demonstrate vt. 展现

文章 2 没提到其他国家（除美国）在历史建筑保护方面作出的贡献。

(B) 文章 2 没提到建筑缺乏文化价值。

(C) yearn vi. 渴望，切盼，向往  yearn for sth.

文章 2 没提到思乡情结。

(D) attemtps 为从句的主语，result in 动词短语，导致某事的发生。sanitize vt. 使清洁，进行消毒。sanitize the history，毁灭历史。重造历史导致将历史洗劫一空，即破坏历史。正确。

(E) 文章 2 质疑文章 1 的原因是重建破坏了历史，并没有讨论重建是否赚钱。

## 文章 26

We should also know that "greed" has little to do with the environmental crisis.[1] The two main causes are population pressures, especially the pressures of large metropolitan populations, and the desire—a highly commendable one—to bring a decent living at the lowest possible cost to the largest possible number of people.[2]

### 【单词及搭配】

1. greed n. 贪婪
2. have little to do with sth. 对……没有影响，与……几乎没有关系
3. environmental crisis 环境危机。类似还有：economic crisis 经济危机，environmental issue 环境议题，environmental awareness 环境意识。crisis 危机
4. at the lowest possible cost 以最可能小的代价。介词必须用 at。
5. metropolitan，大都市
6. commendable, 值得赞扬的，形容词，动词为 commend，表扬，比如：commend sb. for sth. 为某事赞扬某人
7. decent, 体面的 lead a decent living, 过得很体面、很舒服

### 【文章精读】

[1] 作者认为环境危机与人类的贪婪没有关系。主语 has nothing to do with+n., 主语与名词无关。

[2] causes 指引发环境危机的原因：population pressures，desire to to bring a decent living at the lowest possible cost to the largest possible number of people。

to bring 为不定式作定语，修饰 desire。one 指代 desire。bring sth. to sb./sth. 将某事带给某事/某人。

highly commendable one, 用 highly 这个副词修饰 commendable，one 指代 desire。副词修饰形容词。

我们应该知道人们的"贪婪"与环境危机没有什么关系。环境危机的两个主要原因第一是人口压力，尤其是大都市的人口压力；其次是值得赞扬的人们的欲望，它可以以最可能小的成本带给最大多数人体面的生活。这一段谈到了环境危机的起因是什么，作者并没有完全否定人口压力和欲望这两个因素，从 highly commendable one 可以看出这两方面虽然好，但有它的劣势，即它们会对环境产生负面效应。

have nothing to do with sth., 动词短语，与某物无关。

The environmental crisis is the result of success—success in cutting down the mortality of infants (which has given us the population explosion), success in raising farm output sufficiently to prevent mass famine (which has given us contamination by pesticides and chemical fertilizers), success in getting the people out of the tenements of the 19th-century cities and into greenery and privacy of the single-family home in the suburbs (which has given us urban sprawl and traffic jams). The environmental crisis, in other words, is largely the result of doing too much of the right sort of thing.

> 批注 [195]：这个 and 连接的是前面的 out of 和后面的 into

> 批注 [196]：这里必须用副词修饰整个句子，很大程度上地，这句话可以改为：XXX is the result of doing too much of XXX to a large extent.

## 【单词及搭配】

1. mortality，死亡率
2. cut down sth. 动词短语，降低，减少
3. explosion，名词，爆炸（引申意思为"激增"，即"迅速膨胀"）population explosion 人口膨胀
4. output，在这里作名词，意思是"产量"。farm output 农作物产量。
5. sufficient，形容词，充分的。
6. famine，名词，饥饿。starve from famine 遭受饥荒
7. fertilizer，名词，农药。形容词为 fertile，意思是"肥沃的"。
8. contaminate，动词，污染，等同于 pollute。contaminated soil，过去分词作形容词，被污染的土地。contamination，污染物。
9. tenement，名词，租房子
10. suburb，郊区，乡下；反义词为 urban，城市。
11. sprawl，这里是名词，杂乱的蔓延。
12. the right sort of thing，正确的事情，注意表达方式。

## 【文章精读】

环境危机是人类成功的结果——在降低婴儿死亡率方面的成功（该成功使人口激增）；提高农作物产量以阻止饥饿方面的成功（该成功使我们饱受杀虫剂和化学肥料的污染）；使19世纪的城市中的人们从出租的房子中搬移到郊区的暖房和私人的单独家庭的成功（该成功使得城市化蔓延、交通拥挤）。换言之，环境危机从很大程序上是我们刚才提到的这类正确事情做得太多的结果。第二段指出人们取得的这些生活上的成功却对环境造成了负面影响，用排比句列举了这些负面效应。

To overcome the problems that success always creates, one must build on it.[1] But where to start? Cleaning up the environment requires determined, sustained effort with clear targets and deadlines.[2] It requires above all, concentration of effort.[3] Up to now we have tried to do a little bit of everything—and tried to do it in the headlines—when what we ought to do first is draw up a list of priorities.

## 【精读分析】

1. sustained，形容词，在这里指"持续的"；sustainable，可持续的。
2. concentration，名词，全神贯注，concentrate 为动词形式，concentrate on doing sth. 集中精力做什么。
3. when what we ought to do first is draw up a list of priorities 这里，when 修饰前面的

"当我们把这个事情当做头等大事来做的时候"。现在我们还没有把治理环境问题当做重大事情来做,而当我们这样做的时候,应该首先列一个优先级的单子,先做什么,即先治理什么环境问题,再治理什么环境问题。

4. priority,名词,优先级
5. clear,这里作形容词,清晰的,clear target,清晰的目标。
6. draw up sth. 草拟,draw up an overall plan,草拟一个全面的计划。
7. do sth. in the headlines,把做事情放到大标题中,言外之意思就是把什么事情当做头等重要的事情来做。headline,名词,头条新闻。

## 【译文与句子分析】

为克服成功所带来的问题,我们必须采取行动,但是,从哪里开始呢?净化环境需要具备清晰目标和最后期限的坚定的、持之以恒的努力。其中最重要的是全神贯注的努力。截止到现在,我们还没有在某一问题上全神贯注地去解决,也并没有把这件事情当做头等大事来做。我们应该做的是列举其优先级,每次解决一个问题(言外之意,既可以不降低生活质量,又不会引起环境危机问题)。

[1] that success always creates 为定语从句,修饰 problems;it 指代 success。build on sth.,依靠某物。

[2] 注意 with 的用法:带有明确目标和最后期限的努力,with 为介词短语作定语,修饰 efforts。cleaning 为动名词短语作主语,不是现在分词!

## 【题目解析】

1. This passage assumes the desirability of
(A) using atomic energy to conserve fuel
(B) living in comfortable family lifestyles
(C) settling disputes peacefully
(D) combating cancer and heart disease with energetic research
(E) having greater government involvement in people's daily lives

【答案】B

【解答】desirability 是名词,欲望,和 desire 用法一样,但后者可以作动词,表示"有做某事的欲望"。本文考虑了以下人类的哪种欲望?

(A) conserve 保存,动词,用原子能量保存燃料,文中没提到原子能量。

(B) 过舒适的生活,第一段即提到 bring a decent living,正确。

(C) settle,动词,解决,结束,使平静下来,使安定下来。这里指"结束争端"。settle disputse= resolve disputes。

(D) combat 动词,打败,文中没提到 cancer。

(E) 让政府更多地干涉人们的日常生活,文中没提到。involvement,名词,管理,干涉。文中没提到政府的干预是人类的愿望。

2. According to this passage, one early step in any effort to improve the environment would be to

(A) return to the exclusive use of natural fertilizers

(B) put a high tax on profiteering industries

(C) ban the use of automobiles in the cities

(D) study successful efforts in other countries

(E) set up a timetable for corrective actions

【答案】E

选项意思：建立一个日程表来采取矫正性的行动。

【解答】(A) exclude 动词，排除，不包括，形容词为 exclusive，独有的。exclusive use of sth. 专门使用某物。文中没提到。

(B) put a tax on sb./sth.（某种工作行业，industry）对某人或某种行业收税，profiteering，形容词，牟取暴利的，industry 在这里是"行业"的意思，不是"工业"。作者没提到收税。

(C) ban 文中为及物动词，禁止。ban the use of sth.，禁止某物的使用。比如：They threatened to ban the film. 他们威胁要封杀这部电影。还可以作名词，put a ban on sth. 提出禁止某事，比如：We put forward a ban on smoking. 我们提出禁止吸烟。相当于：Smoking is prevented here. 文中没提到。

(D) 学习其他国家经验，文中没提到。

(E) timetable，时间表，可以用 schedule，时间表，日程安排。一个很紧张忙碌的日程安排 a tight/full schedule/timetable。注意 corrective 的含义，不是"正确的"，而是"矫正的"，"正确的"是"correct"。

what we ought to do first is draw up a list of priorities，我们首先应该起草一个单子，单子上有我们做事的优先顺序。本句意思与(E) 相同。

3. The passage indicates that the conditions which led to overcrowded roads also brought about

(A) more attractive living conditions for many people

(B) a healthier younger generation

(C) greater occupational opportunities

(D) the population explosion

(E) greater concentration of population pressures

【解答】overcrowded 形容词，过度拥挤的。bring about，带来，引起，相当于 cause。"success in getting the people out of the tenements of the 19th-century cities and into greenery and privacy of the single-family home in the suburbs (which has given us urban sprawl and traffic jams)"，作者认为城市过度拥挤是人们获得了暖房及属于私人的空间的结果，换言之，虽然城市过度拥挤了，但人们的生活水平改善了。因此，拥挤的城市也带来了人们居住水平的提高。(A) 正确。attractive，形容词，吸引人的。occupational opportunities，就业机会。

4. It could logically be assumed that the author of this passage would support legislation to

(A) ban the use of all pesticides

(B) prevent the use of automobiles in the cities

(C) build additional conventional power plants immediately

(D) organize an agency to coordinate efforts to cope with environmental problems

(E) restrict the press coverage of protests led by environmental groups

【解答】support legislation to do sth. 支持立法来做某事。此题推断作者今后的做法。coordinate 是及物动词，这里是"调节"的意思，调节我们的努力，即齐心协力做某事：coordinate one's efforts to do sth.。显然答案为(D)。

(E) press coverage 新闻报道。protest, 名词，抗议。限制关于由环境组织领导的抗议方面的新闻报道。

总结：本文的意思是，环境问题是由人们的一系列进步所带来的，这些进步改善了人们的生活条件，但也引起了相应的环境问题。人们必须采取措施来纠正这些环境危机。

# 文章 27

Plutarch admired those who could use life for grand purposes and depart from it as grandly, but he would not pass over weaknesses and vices which marred the grandeur[1]. His hero of heroes is Alexander the Great; he admires him above all other men, while his abomination of abominations is bad faith, dishonorable action[2]. Nevertheless he tells with no attempt to extenuate how Alexander promised a safe conduct to brave Persian army if they surrendered[3], and then, "even as they were marching away he fell upon them and put them all to the sword,"[4] "a breach of his word," Plutarch says sadly, "which is a lasting blemish to his achievements."[5] He adds piteously, "but the only one." He hated to tell that story.[6]

## 【单词及搭配】

1. grand, adj. 宏伟的，高高在上的
2. depart from, 离开，出发，depart 为不及物动词，名词为 departure，相当于 leaving。
3. pass over, 忽视，动词短语，相当于 neglect。
4. marred, mar 的过去式。mar 为动词原形，相当于 damage, spoil。
5. grandeur, 名词，宏伟，高尚
6. hero of heroes，最杰出的英雄（英雄中的英雄）；再比如，clever of clevers，绝顶聪明的人，clever 在这里是名词，表示"聪明的人"。 abomination of abominations，罪恶中的罪恶（最大的罪恶）。
7. abomination, 可恶的事情，罪恶
8. faith，名词，诚心
9. dishonorable，形容词，有损名誉的
10. safe conduct, 安全通行权
11. tell, 讲述（并非"告诉"）
12. brave, 形容词，勇敢的
13. fall upon, 攻击
14. surrender, 动词, 投降
15. sword, 名词, 刀, 剑
16. breach, 这里作名词，还可以作动词，意思是"违反"。breach of sth. 对某物的违反（名词用法）
17. blemish, 名词，瑕疵，相当于 flaw。
18. piteously, 副词, 同情地
19. add, 及物动词，在这里指"又说道"。用法为：Someone said: XXX. Then, he added: XXX. 表示他先说了前面的话，后面又进行补充。

## 【文章精读】

[1] Plutarch 尽管很崇拜生命中有着很高尚很宏伟的目的的人，但是，他却不能对这样的一类人所做的有损其生命的宏伟目标的做法忽略不计。这句话为下面 Plutarch 虽然很崇拜亚历山大，却对亚历山大犯下的失言的错误感到痛惜，并不会为之包庇做了铺垫。这句话点明了本文主题。those 后面跟随定语从句，以 who 引导。those 不能换为人称代词 they 或 them，因为人称代词不能用定语来修饰。use life for grand purpose and depart from it grandly 为定语从句，修饰 those（那些人）。for 表示目的，即活着是为了伟大目标的那些人，以及很光辉地离开这个世界的那些人。he 指代 Plutarch。weaknesses and vices 为名词短语，弱点和错误，影射后面亚历山大犯的言而无信屠杀波斯人的错误。which 为定语从句中的主语，不能省略，指代 weaknesses and vices。grandeur 与 grand purpose 同义。

[2] above all other people 是"远远高于其他人之上"的意思，这句话的意思是 Plutarch 对亚历山大的崇拜远远高于对其他任何人的崇敬，他最佩服亚历山大。这句中 his 指"亚历山大的"，很明显，用了"while"表示转折。"while"除了表示"一边……一边……"时间状语的作用，在很多地方都表示转折，这点对看懂全文很重要。崇拜转瞬一转，变为了亚历山大犯下过最大的罪恶——言而无信地杀害了俘虏。

[3] 之所以用到 nevertheless 是想表明：尽管 Plutarch 对亚历山大很崇拜，但 Plutarch 不会因为崇拜他而找借口来为他开脱。Plutarch 这个人还是非常客观和公正的。重要的英语表达方式：do sth. (event A) with (an) (no) attempt to do sth. (event B)，做 A 这件事情的时候带有（没有）做 B 这个事情的意图。比如：I did the experiment without (with no) attempt to find the law of A when law of A was proved to be true. 我做这个实验的时候，并没有想要发现 A 定律，而恰恰就是这个实验证明了定律 A 的正确性。tell 在句子中是"讲述"的意思，他讲述这个故事的过程中并没有试图为亚历山大做辩论/找借口。

[4] march away，部队撤退，动词，意思等于 surrender。强调一篇文章中同样的意思用多种方式表达是一种很重要的语言能力。本句指示代词众多，具体见旁边批注。put sb. all to sword，这是一种比喻的用法，把他们全部放到了刀子上，就是亚历山大杀害了所有已经撤退的波斯军队，造成了他的言而无信和对声誉的损失。照应了文章第一句和第二句。

[5] 这是一个定语从句，修饰了 a breach of his word。breach 这个单词很关键。lasting 不是"最后"的意思，这是一个形容词，意思为"持续的"，相当于 sustained。

[6] He 这里指代 Plutarch。尽管 Plutarch 非常崇拜亚历山大，但无法忽略亚历山大犯下的毁坏一世英名的罪行。作者与 Plutarch 很熟悉，而 Plutarch 恰恰不愿意讲这个故事。

## 【译文】

Plutarch 非常崇拜那些为了高尚辉煌的人生目的而生活并且为了这个目标可以辉煌地离开的人，但是他不能释怀损坏了这样的高尚辉煌的弱点与罪行。Plutarch 最崇拜的人是亚历山大，然而，亚历山大所犯的最严重的罪行是他的不诚信和有损其名誉的行为。然而，Plutarch 在讲述亚历山大故事的时候并没有试图以亚历山大曾经怎样许诺只要波斯军队投降便保证俘虏安全的诺言为借口为他开脱。尽管波斯军队撤离，但亚历山大还是对他们展开了攻击并全部杀害了他们。Plutarch 伤心地说，这是亚历山大的一次食言，这次食言对他取得的成就是一个持续的瑕疵。Plutarch 又同情地说，但这是唯一的一个瑕疵。Plutarch 非常痛恨讲亚历山大的这个故事。

## 【题目解析】

1. Which of the following conclusions is least justified by the passage?

(A) Plutarch considered Alexander basically a great man.

(B) The Persians believed that Alexander was acting in good faith.

(C) The Persians withdrew from the battlefield in orderly array.

(D) The author is familiar with Plutarch's writing.

(E) The author considers Plutarch unfair to Alexander.

【解析】E

(A) 之所以用 basically 这个词，是因为 Plutarch 认为亚历山大基本上算是个伟大的人物，除了他犯下的这个言而无信的罪行。

(B) act in good faith 履行承诺，言而有信。The team acted in good faith to complete the task. 这个团队按照曾经的承诺完成了任务。

(C) withdraw=march away 撤退，orderly array 有顺序的方阵，该选项意思为军队有条不紊依照次序来撤退。

(E) 恰恰相反，作者是很客观地看 Plutarch 评价亚历山大这个人，他认为 Plutarch 是客观的。

2. As used in this passage, the word "extenuate" means

(A) interpret

(B) exaggerate

(C) emphasize

(D) excuse

(E) condemn

【解析】D

(A) interpret 翻译，动词

(B) exaggerate 夸张，动词

(C) emphasize 强调，动词

(D) excuse 找借口，在这里作动词，还有名词的意思

(E) condemn 责备，动词

# 文章 28

It is no longer needful to labor Dickens' power as a portrayer of modern society nor the seriousness of his "criticism of life."[1] But we are still learning to appreciate his supreme attainment as an artist[2]. Richness of poetic imagery, modulations of emotional tone, subtleties of implication, complex unities of structure, intensities of psychological insight, a panoply of achievement, mount up to overwhelming triumph. Though contemporary readers perhaps still feel somewhat queasy about Dickens' sentiment, his comedy and his drama sweep all before them. Even his elaborate and multi-stranded plots are now seen as great symphonic compositions driving forward through theme and variation to the resolving chords on which they close[3].

【精读分析】

1. needful，形容词，需要的

2. labor，这里是动词，labor power as sth. 将劳动力当做 XXX。

3. portray，及物动词，描绘，描述，相当于 depict, demonstrate。portrayer 描绘的人，描绘师，记述者

4. appreciate，感激，欣赏，及物动词 I really appreciate your help.=Thank you very much for your help.

5. supreme，最高的，至高的，形容词 supreme power 最高权利，exert one's supreme efforts 尽某人的最大努力。

6. attainment，名词，成就，相当于 achievement。动词为 attain。attain success in a field of maths 在数学的某个领域取得成绩，attain the goal 达到目的。

7. poetic，形容词，有诗意的。

8. imagery，名词，想象，意向。imagination 名词，想象力。

9. subtlety，名词，细微的差别，细微之处，subtle，形容词，细微的，狡猾的 a subtle person 一个狡猾的人。

10. implication，名词，暗示，动词为 imply。

11. intensity，名词，强烈（程度）；形容词为 intensive, 集中的，密集的，彻底的，加强语气的 intensive reading, intensive agriculture, This word is used as an intensive. 这个单词用于加强语气。

12. insight，名词，洞察力，领悟，相当于 perspective。an acute insight/perspective 敏锐的洞察力。This is a work with an acute insight/perspective. This is an work barren of an acute insight/perspective. 这部作品有/缺乏深刻的洞察力。

13. mount up to (a degree) 积累增加到什么程度，后面加名词或名词性短语。

14. overwhelming，形容词，压倒一切的。动词为 overwhelm。I was intensively

批注 [212]: 名词性短语作主语。richness of sth. 某方面的充足；modulation of sth. 对某事的调和；subtleties of sth. 某事的细致；complex of sth. 某物的结合；谓语为 mount up to。

批注 [213]: 为什么是多层面的？与 the resolving chords 对应！

批注 [214]: 情节

批注 [215]: drive forward through A to B 向前面沿着 A 开向 B，B 这里是 the resolving chords, 名词性短语，将主题和变化向前面开向他们要接近的分解的和弦。

批注 [216]: 分解的和弦，现在分词短语。和弦是由许多不同音程的音符组成的。

168

overwhelmed by his astonishing words. 我被他惊人的话语彻底蒙住了（我被他雷着了）。还有"压制，压迫"的意思，overwhelm by great force 以武力压制对方。

15. triumph，名词，巨大的成功
16. contemporary，形容词/名词，同时代的（人或事）
17. somewhat，有一点，This news somewhat astonished me. 相当于 a little。
18. queasy，形容词，恶心的。queasy transaction，不正常的交易。
19. sentiment，怜悯的感情，柔情，名词
20. drama，名词，戏剧，dramatic，形容词，富有戏剧性的
21. sweep，动词，清除，扫走
22. symphonic composition，交响乐曲
23. elaborate，形容词，精细的，还有动词！详细阐述！作动词时，短语为 elaborate on sth./doing sth. 详细阐述某事，比如：I'd like to elaborate on the importance of this issue. 我将详细阐述这次议题的重要性。

【句子分析】

[1] 我们不必再将狄更斯的劳动成果看做对现代社会的记述，也不必把它（指劳动成果）看作他对生命批判的严肃性。

[2] 然而，我们依然在欣赏着他作为一名艺术家取得的至高无上的成就。

[3] 即便是他精致和多层次的情节也被我们看做沿着主题和变化向前行驶的伟大的交响乐，一直向前行驶到交响乐想要接近的分解开的和弦（之所以要接近和弦，是说他的作品是多层次的，和弦本身就是多种音程的叠加，多层次）。

【题目解析】

1. According to the passage, readers most recently have begun to appreciate Dickens'
(A) feeling for culture
(B) criticisms of life
(C) rhythms
(D) literary references
(E) literary craftsmanship
【答案】E

2. According to the passage, the endings of Dickens' works are most probably characterized by
(A) frequent use of relief
(B) unexpected developments
(C) visually effective symbols
(D) a lack of sense of completion
(E) dramatic power
【答案】E

# 文章 29

Many people who are willing to concede that the railroad must be brought back to life are chiefly thinking of bringing this about on the very terms that have robbed us of a balanced transportation network—that is, by treating speed as the only important factor, forgetting reliability, comfort and safety, and seeking some mechanical dodge for increasing the speed and automation of surface vehicles.

【单词及搭配】

1. concede, vt. 承认
2. bring sth. about 把某物带到身边来，about 相当于 around，不是"左右，大约"。
3. on the very terms 以恰恰这样的条件。very 在其中没有确切含义，仅表示强调。terms 指"条件"。
4. reliability 名词，可靠性，形容词为 reliable，可以依靠的。
5. dodge，伎俩，名词
6. rob sb. of sth. 掠夺了某人的某物，固定搭配

【句子分析】

那些同意将火车带回到我们生活中的人主要考虑以掠夺我们平衡的交通网络为条件来达到此目的，这种掠夺通过以单纯考虑速度为重要因素，而不顾可靠性、舒适性和安全性，并且通过机械的手段来增加机动车辆的速度。

My desk is littered with such technocratic fantasies, hopefully offered as "solutions."[1] They range from old-fashioned monorails and jet-propelled hovercraft (now extinct) to a more scientific mode of propulsion at 2,000 miles an hour, from completely automated highway travel in private cars to automated vehicles a Government department is now toying with for "facilitating" urban traffic.

【单词及搭配】

7. be littered with sth. 被 XXX 混杂着（指被不好的东西所混杂）
8. extinct，灭绝的，形容词
9. propulsion，名词，推动力
10. facilitate，vt. 促进，帮助

批注 [A217]: 定语从句，修饰 terms，以掠夺我们平衡的交通网络为条件。

批注 [A218]: 具体解释怎样破坏我们的交通网络，by treating…是连接着 rob 的。通过单纯考虑提速来掠夺破坏我们平衡的交通系统。

批注 [A219]: 被动分词作定语，修饰"高科技奇迹"。

批注 [A220]: 单轨。mono 是表示"单"的前缀。

批注 [A221]: 定语从句，修饰 automated vehicles，政府正在拿着玩弄的机动车。

批注 [A222]: 目的状语，政府拿着玩的目的是为方便城市交通。

## 【句子分析】

[1] 我的桌子就被一大堆这样的高科技奇迹所包围着，这些高科技奇迹被寄予希望用来提供"解决方案"。

What is the function of transportation[1]? What place does locomotion occupy in the whole spectrum of human needs[2]? Perhaps the first step in developing an adequate transportation policy would be to clear our minds of technocratic cant[3]. Those who believe that transportation is the chief end of life should be put in orbit at a safe lunar distance from the earth[4].

> 批注 [A223]: 主语，主语中又嵌套了 who 引导的定语从句，修饰 those（那些人）。

## 【单词及搭配】

11. transportation，名词，交通运输
12. locomotion，名词，移动，运动，文中指代由交通带来的位置变化。
13. occupy, vt. 占据，占领 be occupied with sth./doing sth.=be busy with 忙于什么事情。名词为 occupant，占有者，相当于 owner。occupant of this house 房屋占有者（房主）。
14. spectrum，名词，在信号处理与通信中指"谱"，比如 power spectrum/frequency spectrum，功率谱/频谱。文中指"范围"，相当于名词 range。
15. adequate，形容词，等于 sufficient。
16. policy，名词，政策，措施
17. clear, 清除, vt. clear sth. 清除 XXX
18. technocratic cant, 技术专家的空话
19. end, 文中为名词，目的
20. lunar，名词，月球的

## 【句子分析】

[1] 作者提问：交通运输的功能究竟是什么？也就是说，上一段提到的仅仅以高速为目标的交通运输观点是作者所反对的，作者在本段和后面将逐渐提出自己的观点。

[2] 那么，在人类的所有需求中，交通运输占了多大范围的地位呢？

[3] 也许，发展通畅无阻的交通政策的第一步是清除我们意识中的技术专家的那一套空话。

[4] 那些认为交通运输是人们生活的主要目标的人们应该被放置到一个轨道中，与地球保持一定的月球安全距离。这是一种讽刺的说法。让这些号称以高速来标榜交通运输的人远离地球。

The prime purpose of passenger transportation is not to increase the amount of physical movement but to increase the possibilities for human association, cooperation, personal intercourse, and choice.[1]

> 批注 [A224]: 首要目的

> 批注 [A225]: 指出交通的确切意义和目标：并非提速，而是要通过交通增加人与人之间的联系。

## 【单词及搭配】

21. amount, 文中为名词，数量，amount of sth. 某物的数量。large/small in amount 在数量上多/少。The equipment they offered are large in amount to satisfy current usage demand. 他们提供的设备可以满足目前的使用要求。还可作不及物动词，amount to +n. 相当于，接

近于。His words amounts to refusal. refusal 这里是名词，也可以用动名词 refusing。他的话等于拒绝。

22．intercourse，名词，交往，have intercourse with sb. 与某人有来往
23．association，名词，交往，联系。动词为 associate。 be associated with sb./sth.

## 【句子分析】

[1] not to do…but to do，不是……而是。amount of physical movement 指物理运动的数量，意思是通过交通让各种交通工具、人都运动起来，作者反对这种观点，认为交通运输的目的是使人与人之间增加联系、合作、私人的交往与机会。这句话点明文章主旨。

A balanced transportation system, accordingly, calls for a balance of resources and facilities and opportunities in every other part of the economy. Neither speed nor mass demand offers a criterion of social efficiency. Hence such limited technocratic proposals as that for high-speed trains between already overcrowded and overextended urban centers would only add to the present lack of functional balance and purposeful organization viewed in terms of human need.[1] Variety of choices, facilities and destinations, not speed alone, is the mark of an organic transportation system[2]. And, incidentally, this is an important factor of safety when any part of the system breaks down[3]. Even confirmed air travelers appreciate the railroad in foul weather.[4]

批注 [A226]: 一个平衡的交通系统，相应地需要经济领域中的其余每个部分的资源、设施与机会的平衡。也就是说单纯的提速不能满足这样的要求，下一句进行了解释。

批注 [A227]: 这里指数量，即物体运动的数量。

批注 [A228]: 增加了，重要短语，详见文中解释。

批注 [A229]: 指出专家们提出的高速铁路带来的危害，详见正文分析。

批注 [A230]: this 指代 "variety of choices, facilities and destinations".

批注 [A231]: 指交通系统

## 【单词及搭配】

24．accordingly adv. 于是，相应地，这里指"相应地"，等于 correspondingly。
25．call for sth./doing sth. 需要做某事。Environmental crisis calls for an urgent solution. 环境问题急待解决。
26．facility 名词，设施；流利。本文指"设施"，可数名词。动词为 facilitate。
27．criterion，名词，标准
28．overcrowded, overextended, 形容词，过于拥挤的，过于延伸的。"over+形容词/名词/动词"的结构往往表示过于怎么样的，比如 overact，夸张，行为过激，动词；overemphasize，动词，过度强调。
29．urban，城市的，urban dwelling，城市居民，rural 乡下的
30．purposeful 形容词，有目的的，意义重大的
31．add to sth./doing sth. 增加了什么，可以指好的也可以指坏的东西。to 是介词，后面必须加名词、动名词或名词性短语从句等。The inflation in almost each field has added to our difficulties. 随处可见的通货膨胀增加了我们的艰辛。
32．view=see from a perspective，从某个角度考虑。这里作及物动词，相当于 consider。
33．in terms of sth./doing sth. 依照某事
34．proposal，名词，提议
35．organic，形容词，有机的，完整的，这是一个褒义词，文中有"健康的"的意思，健康的交通体系。
36．incidentally，附带说一句，副词。还有"偶然"的意思，比如：I met with him incidentally. 我与他不期而遇/我偶然遇到了他。文中指"附带说一下"。
37．break down，垮塌
38．confirmed，形容词，这里指"经常的，习惯的"。动词形式为 confirm：(1) 证实，

confirm sth./that+从句。(2) 坚定，加强，confirm sb. of/in sth. 使某人确信什么。(3) 批准，及物动词，confirm a regulation 批准了某个规范。

39．appreciate，及物动词，这里指"欣赏，感谢"。 I really appreciate your help.=Thank you very much for your help.

**【句子分析】**

[1] 因此，这样的有局限性的在本已过度拥挤和过度扩张的城市中心之间开通高速城铁的提案只会加剧目前从人类需求角度出发来考虑的功能性平衡以及具有重大意义组织的缺失。such limited technocratic proposals as that for high-speed trains between already overcrowded and overextended urban centers 是主语。such proposals as 是一个完整的结构，但根据英语的语言习惯，可能被拆开，这点必须看懂：正如这样的提案。"that for high-speed trains between already overcrowded and overextended urban centers"作定语，修饰 proposals，that 指代"提案"。这不是定语从句，因为没有谓语，而是一个介词短语作了定语，用 A between B 这样的结构作了定语。要习惯这种表达方式。这个句子很简洁，很地道。

would only add 谓语动词，增加什么，present lack of 目前的缺少，present 在这里是形容词，表示"现在的"，可以用 current 代替，目前的。不能用 now！这里需要形容词修饰名词 lack！now 是副词，不能修饰名词！

functional balance and purposeful organization viewed in terms of human need

[2] 表示"仅仅/不仅仅靠某物怎么样"用这样的句型：A alone+谓语+其他补充成分。Not his efforts alone lead to the success of our project. 我们工程的成功靠的不单单是他一个人的努力。alone 在这里是副词，修饰整个句子。

[3]—[4] 当交通系统中的任何一个部分垮掉的时候，这（指交通的多样性、多机会和多交通设施）是系统安全性的一个重要因素。比如，一个经常乘飞机的旅客在天气很糟糕的时候甚至会很欣赏高速铁路。[3]、[4]两句在逻辑上是总说与解释的关系。强调交通的平衡中包含的多样性、多选择性、多设施对整个交通系统的重要作用，而非单单只有速度最重要"regard speed as the only factor"这样错误的观点。

If we took human needs seriously in recasting the whole transportation system, we should begin with the human body and make the fullest use of pedestrian movement, not only for health but for efficiency in moving large crowds over short distances. The current introduction of shopping malls, free from wheeled traffic, is both a far simpler and far better technical solution than the many costly proposals for introducing moving sidewalks or other rigidly automated modes of locomotion. At every stage we should provide for the right type of locomotion, at the right speed, within the right radius, to meet human needs. Neither maximum speed nor maximum traffic nor maximum distance has by itself any human significance.

**【单词及搭配】**

40．recast, vt. 为……重新分配角色

41．pedestrian，形容词，徒步的

42．costly，形容词，昂贵的

批注 [A232]: 过去分词短语后置作定语，修饰"那些组织和功能性的平衡"。

批注 [A233]: 最大程度地使用某物

批注 [A234]: the introduction of sth. 对某物的引进，不是"介绍"的意思！

批注 [A235]: 定语，修饰 introduction of shopping malls。

批注 [A236]: 远比什么好：far+比较级 than XXX

批注 [A237]: 副词，严格地，修饰 aoutomated"机动的"，因为 automated 是形容词，所以必须用副词修饰。

批注 [A238]: 这三者是并列的，作介词 for 的宾语。

批注 [A239]: 目的状语，为的是满足人类要求。

43. sidewalk，名词，人行道
44. free from sth./doing sth. 免于什么 free from punishment 免于惩罚
45. rigidly，副词，严格地
46. significance，名词，意义
47. provide for sth./doing sth. 为什么做好准备

With the over-exploitation of the particular car comes an increased demand for engineering equipment, to roll ever wider carpets of concrete over the bulldozed landscape and to endow the petroleum magnates of some places with fabulous capacities for personal luxury and political corruption[1]. Finally, the purpose of this system, abetted by similar concentration on planes and rockets, is to keep an increasing volume of motorists and tourists in motion, at the highest possible speed, in a sufficiently comatose state not to mind the fact that their distant destination has become the exact counterpart of the very place they have left[2]. The end product everywhere is environmental desolation.

批注 [A240]: 介词短语作状语，放在句首。

批注 [A241]: 在用推土机推掉的风景之上，over 在这里表示"在……上面"。

批注 [A242]: to endow 与 to roll 为并列关系，都作结果状语。

批注 [A243]: 不定式作结果状语。

批注 [A244]: 恰恰是这个地方，very 没有确定的意思，就表示强调。

批注 [A245]: 最终的结局

【单词及搭配】

48. roll, vi. 行驶，roll at a speed of 200 miles/hour
49. ever wider，不断增加的。in the current ever increasingly competitive society：在当今竞争日趋加剧的社会中。
50. concrete，这里作名词，混凝土。
51. bulldoze, vt. 用推土机清除。这里用它的过去分词作形容词，表示被推土机毁掉的用于开车的原本风景地。
52. landscape，名词，风景
53. endow, vt., endow sb. with sth. 赋予某人什么，endow love and care with the sick boy，对这个生病的孩子赋予关爱。
54. fabulous, 形容词，令人难以置信的
55. corruption, 名词，腐败，贪污。动词为 corrupt。corrupt 也可以作形容词。
55. abet，vt. 教唆，煽动，帮助（贬义）
56. concentration，名词，集中
57. comatose，形容词，昏睡的
58. counterpart，名词，复制品
59. desolation，名词，荒芜

【句子分析】

[1] 这是一个以介词短语开头的倒装："With 结构+comes/goes+各种补充成分"。随着 XXX，发生了 XXX。这是固定句型。随着汽车的过度激增，导致了对机械设备要求的增加，它们在被推土机清除掉美丽风景的更宽的混凝土之上行驶（意思是车越来越多，被毁的风景越来越多，需要的地方越来越大，即越来越宽的混凝土路），并对石油权贵赋予令人诧异的涉及个人奢侈品和政治贪污腐败的能力。言外之意：汽车需求增加导致石油商有钱。

[2] Finally, the purpose of this system, abetted by similar concentration on planes and rockets, is to keep an increasing volume of motorists and tourists in motion, at the highest possible speed, in a sufficiently comatose state not to mind the fact that their distant destination

批注 [A246]: 主句的宾语，作 keep 的宾语。

has become the exact counterpart of the very place they have left.

the purpose of this system 为主语；abetted by similar concentration on planes and rockets 为过去分词短语作定语，修饰主语"this system"；is 为谓语。concentration on sth. 名词短语，对某事的关注。人们对铁路系统赋予了与飞机、火箭相同的关注度。

最终，这样一个系统目的是使运动中的开车人和旅客以可能达到的最大速度运动并在人数上不断增加，这些开车人和乘客会处于一种非常不清醒的状态，以至他们没有意识到遥远的目的地刚好变为了他们已经离开的地方。意思是乘客高速行驶，在车上昏昏欲睡，并不知道坐过了目的地。volume 指"数量"。

If this is the best our technological civilization can do to satisfy genuine human needs and nurture man's further development, it's plainly time to close up shop. If indeed we go farther and faster along this route, there is plenty of evidence to show that the shop will close up without our help. Behind our power blackouts, our polluted environments, our transportation breakdowns, our nuclear threats, is a failure of mind. Technocratic anesthesia has put us to sleep. Results that were predictable—and predicted!—three-quarters of a century ago without awakening any response still find us unready to cope with them—or even to admit their existence.

【句子分析】

predictable，可以预测到的；predicted，已经被预测到的。前面讲可以预测到，后面是过去分词作被动语态，已经被预测出来了。without awakening any response：没有激发出任何反应，awaken 是动词，激发。close up shop 比喻按照这样的路线发展下去，即以提速为目标，忽视其他领域的平衡，会导致社会最终走向灭亡。shop 暗指 society。结果可以预测到，并且在 75 年之前已经被预测到了！那时并没有得到任何人对此的反应，而今发现我们依然没有准备好来应付这样的结果，或者说我们甚至承认该结果的存在。作者认为多年前就暴露了这样的结果，直到今天人们对这种结果都无动于衷，确切地讲人们对这种结果的存在甚至是承认的。表明作者对单纯提高速度最终会毁灭整个社会的担忧。

【补充】关于 matter 的用法

1. What's the matter? 怎么了？
2. 名词，事情，This issue aroused a matter of controversy. 这个议题引起了争论。as a matter of fact 事实上
3. 不及物动词，vi. 主语 has ceased to matter. 这个句型非常重要：XXX 事情已经不重要了。cease to do sth. 动词词组，停止做某事；等于 XXX is not important any more. 显然，上面比这句地道得多。matter 在这里表示"要紧"。XXX matters a lot.=XXX is very important.

批注 [A247]: 定语从句，修饰 fact。

批注 [A248]: 不定式的否定形式作定语，修饰"state"。

批注 [A249]: 定语从句，修饰 the very place。

批注 [A250]: 定语从句，修饰 the best。

批注 [A251]: 目的状语，这样做的目的。

批注 [A252]: 副词，很明显地。

批注 [A253]: 名词，昏厥，黑暗。

批注 [A254]: 高科技麻醉

批注 [A255]: 指代 results。

批注 [A256]: 指结果的存在

批注 [A257]: 同位语从句，修饰 results。

批注 [A258]: to even admit 与 unready to cope with 是并列结构。

# 文章 30

## 文章 30.1

Classical physics is the physics of the macroscopic world (our world which we can see, touch and hear). It is very appealing to the purist in that there are no uncertainties in measurement of physical quantities. When we set up an apparatus to measure something, the apparatus does not interfere with the measurement. For example, if we want to figure out how fast something is traveling, we can also find out exactly where it is at the time of measurement of its speed. There is certainty in classical physics, the "exact" physics. Thus when a bridge is built, we know exactly what stress the bridge may withstand. When a car is constructed, we know what specifications the engine must have to have the car do what we want.

【单词及搭配】

1. appealing adj. 有魅力的；动人的；吸引人的 be appealing to sb./sth. 对某人/物有吸引力

appeal (1) n. 呼吁，恳求 the appeal for sth. (2) n. 感染力，吸引力 This kind of music hasn't much appeal for me. 这类音乐对我没有吸引力。 (3) vi. 呼吁 (4) vt. 有吸引力 This job rather appeals to me. 这工作对我有吸引力。 (5) vt. & vi. 上诉

2. macroscopic adj. (1) 肉眼可见的 (2) 宏观的

macro (1) n. 宏（计算机术语）(2) adj. 巨大的，大量使用的

macrobiotic adj. 能促进长寿的；长命的；大型生物群的

3. tangible adj. (1) 明确的，确凿的，实际的 (2) 可触摸的，可触知的，有形的

4. purist n.（在语法、用词等上）力求纯正者，语言纯正癖者

purify vt. 使纯净，使洁净

The air in the room was purified.
房间的空气得到了净化。

5. quantitate v. 测定（估计）的数量，用数量来表示

6. apparatus n. (1) 运动器械，器具，仪器（文中意思） (2) 机构，组织 (3) 器官

7. interfere with (1) 干预，阻挠，妨碍，阻止（文中意思） (2) 擅自使用，摆弄

8. figure (1) n. 数字 (2) n. 图解，图表；装饰性的图案 (3) n. 人或动物的像，画像，肖像 (4) n. 轮廓，人影，身材，体态 (5) n. 算术，计算 (6) vi. 出现，被提及 His name figured among the guests. 宾客名单中有他的名字。 (7) vt. 计算在内 (8) vt. 估计，有可能；认为，料想 I figured that you wouldn't come. 我料想你不会来。He figured himself as a good

candidate. 他认为自己是合适的人选。

9. stress (1) n. 压力，紧张（文中意思） (2) n. 强调，重要性 (3) vt. 强调
10. withstand vt. 经受，承受
11. construction (1) n. 建造，建设；建筑业 (2) n. 建造物，建筑物 (3) n. 解释，意思
12. specification n. 说明书，详细的计划书（文中意思），载明，详述，说明

## 文章 30.2

Modern physics or physics of the sub-microscopic world (the world of electrons, protons and neutrons) is very perplexing since there seems to be an apparent violation of cause and effect.[1] There exists only a probability and not certainty in measurement of important physical quantities because the measurement of device affects the measurement.[2] For example, if we know exactly what position an electron is, we cannot determine its speed.[3] Thus the more we know the value of one physical quantity, the less certain we are of a corresponding physical quantity.[4] To paraphrase Albert Einstein, "the universe does not play dice with nature." Ironically, modern physics really controls and determines the outcome of the physics of the macroscopic physics (since the macroscopic world is really made up of constituents in the sub-microscopic realm). Thus modern physics is the foundation of all physics since it contains the basic and fundamental elements used to create all physics.

【文章精读】

[1] apparent 这里指"明显的"，形容词。另外的意思：貌似真实的，比如：
The apparent truth was actually a lie. 这个貌似的事实实际是谎言。obvious 没有第二个意思。It was an obvious remark. 这段讲话平淡无奇。

[2] violate: 及物动词，违背；侵犯 violate human rights; violate the terms of a company 违反公司条文。文中指现代物理的理论违反了经典物理中的因果关系。

[3] perplex: 及物动词，使复杂化；使混乱。be perplexed by sb./sth.

[4] 原句顺序为：We are less certain of a corresponding physical quantity.

[5] paraphrase v. 改述，意译  outcome  n. 结果

【题目解析】

1. It can be assumed that Albert Einstein believed that

(A) only classical physics existed in nature

(B) there was certainty in all aspects of physics theories

(C) classical physics violates cause and effect

(D) speed and position are not the fundamental characteristics of particles

(E) when a new car is constructed, in order for it to be most efficient a new physics must be employed

【答案】B
爱因斯坦认为上帝不会和人类玩骰子的游戏，骰子游戏存在概率，即爱因斯坦认为物

理量是可确定的，不存在概率问题。

2. Modern physics differs from classical physics chiefly in that
(A) the measurement device does not affect the measurement in classical physics
(B) no quantity in modern physics can be determined
(C) modern physics is not as fundamental as classical physics
(D) classical physics does not deal primarily with measurement
(E) speed is always constant in classical physics

【答案】A

【解析】A differs from B in that+从句：A 和 B 在某方面不同。

# 文章 31

## 文章 31.1

To the world it was half a thousand years younger, the outlines of all things seemed more clearly marked than to us.[1] The contrast between suffering and joy, between adversity and happiness, appeared more striking.[2] All experience had yet to the minds of men the directness and absoluteness of the pleasure and pain of child-life.[3] Every event, every action, was still embodied in expressive and solemn forms, which raised them to the dignity of a ritual.[4]

### 【单词及搭配】

1. outline, 这里作名词, 轮廓。还可以作动词, 表示"概括, 总结"。Outline the case. 概述这个情况。
2. marked, 这里是形容词, 显著的。
3. suffering, 动名词, 遭受苦难
4. adversity, 名词, 灾难, 相当于 misery。disaster 与 misery 的区别：disaster 往往指大的客观灾难, 比如 earthquake disaster; misery 往往表示生活的磨难、苦难, 如 misery of life, 生活的苦难。
5. striking, 形容词, 显著的, 令人震撼的
6. directness, 名词, 直接

### 【文章精读】

[1] clearly marked: 副词修饰形容词, 很清晰。作者指出 1000 年前, 万事万物的轮廓都比现在要清晰得多。本句是文章主题。省略句, 省略了 the outlines of all things to us, 对于现在的我们来说, 早期的万物轮廓比现在我们看到的更加清晰。

[2] 解释[1]: 苦难和快乐、灾难和幸福之间的对比在当时非常明显。contrast 为主语, appeared 为谓语。

[3] experience 这里指"经历", 对于人们的记忆来说, 所有的经历都是绝对直接的欢乐与孩童时的苦难。yet to the minds of men 作状语, 可以把它提到句首便于理解：对于大多数人的记忆来说。to 是介词, 对于某人来说 to sb.。

[4] them 指代 every event and every action。which 指代 forms, 庄严的形式。每一个事件都以很严肃的形式表现出来, 这将这些事件提升到宗教尊严的程度。即万事万物非喜即悲。

Misfortunes and poverty were more afflicting than at present; it was more difficult to guard against them, and to find solace[1]. Illness and health presented a more striking contrast; the cold and darkness of winter were more real evils[2]. Honors and riches were relished with greater avidity and contrasted more vividly with surrounding misery[3]. We, at the present day, can hardly understand the keenness with which a fur coat, a good fire on the hearth, a soft bed, a glass of wine, were formerly enjoyed.[4]

## 【单词及搭配】

1. afflict vt. 使痛苦；afflicting adj. 令人痛苦的
2. guard against sth. 防御某事
3. solace (1) n. 安慰；安慰物（文中意思）(2) vt. 安慰；慰藉
4. relish (1) n. 乐趣 (2) vt. 欣赏，享受（文中意思）
5. avidity n. 欲望

## 【文章精读】

[1] them 指代 misfortunes and poverty。to guard against 与 to find solace 并列，即抵御不幸与贫穷、寻找安慰在当时是很难的。

[2]－[3] 解释第一句话，采用对比的修辞方法。

[4] 今天的我们很难理解曾经人们享受一件大衣、壁炉里的熊熊大火、一张软床和一杯酒时的热切。which 指代 keenness，即：A fur coat was formerly enjoyed with keenness. 该句式在《瓦尔登湖》一文中出现过。formerly 副词，曾经，与 at present 相对。

Then, again, all things in life were of a proud or cruel publicity. Lepers sounded their rattles and went about in processions, beggars exhibited their deformity and their misery in churches. Every order and estate, every rank and profession, was distinguished by its costume. The great lords never moved about without a glorious display of arms and liveries, exciting fear and envy. Executions and other public acts of justice, hawking, marriages and funerals, were all announced by cries and processions, songs and music. The lower wore the colors of his lady; companions the emblem of their brotherhood; parties and servants the badges of their lords. Between town and country, too, the contrast was very marked. A medieval town did not lose itself in extensive suburbs of factories and villas; girded by its walls, it stood forth as a compact whole, bristling with innumerable turrets. However tall and threatening the houses of noblemen or merchants might be, in the aspect of the town, the lofty mass of the churches always remained dominant.

## 【单词及搭配】

1. publicity n. (1) 公众的注意，众所周知（文中意思） (2) 宣传，宣扬
2. deformity n. (1) 畸形（或残缺）的部分（文中意思）(2) 缺陷；丑恶 deformity of the proposal 提案的缺点
3. gird vt. 束缚
4. bristle (1) n. 短而硬的毛发，刷子毛 (2) vi. 被激怒，怒发冲冠；毛发（因惊惧等）直立（文中意思）

The contrast between silence and sound, darkness and light, like that between summer and winter, was more strongly marked than it is in our lives. The modern town hardly knows silence or darkness in their purity, nor the effect of a solitary light or a single distant cry.

All things presenting themselves to the mind in violent contrasts and impressive forms lent a tone of excitement and passion to everyday life and tended to produce that perpetual oscillation between despairs and distracted joy, between cruelty and pious tenderness which characterize life in the Middle Ages.

【单词及搭配】

lend (1) vt. & vi. 把……借给 (2) vt. 增加，增添 lend sth. to sth.
lent a tone to everyday life 为日常生活增添了某种声音

# 文章 31.2

In 1575—over 400 years ago!—the French scholar Louis Le Roy published a learned book in which he voiced despair over the upheavals caused by the social and technological innovations of his time, what we now call the Renaissance.[1] "All is pell-mell, confounded, nothing goes as it should."[2] We, also, feel that our times are out of joint; we even have reason to believe that our descendants will be worse off than we are.[3]

【单词及搭配】

1. voice (1) n. 嗓音，说话声，歌唱声 (2) n.（口头或书面的）意见，发言权，影响 (3) vt. 表示，表达，吐露（文中意思）
2. upheaval n. 突然的巨变；大动荡；大变动
3. learned adj. (1) 有学问的，博学的 (2) 学术上的（文中意思）
4. confound vt. (1) 使惊惶；弄糊涂 (2) 搞乱；混淆（意念等） (3) 击败，挫败 (4) 证明……有错

【文章精读】

法国学者 Roy 反对文艺复兴运动，他认为文艺复兴运动中的各种创新运动是混乱的。由此引出作者的观点：我们的时代是混乱的，我们的后代可能比我们现在生活得更差。

[1] which 指代 a learned book，voice 这里为及物动词，表达。caused by 为过去分词短语作定语，修饰 upheavals；despair over sth./sb. 为名词短语，对某事或某人很绝望；what we now call the Renaissance 为名词性从句，作 upheavals 的同位语。本句指出法国学者 Roy 对由技术变革带来的巨变（即文艺复兴）很绝望。of his time 表示"他所生活的时代"。

[2] pell-mell，形容词，凌乱的。nothing goes in the way as it should be 为省略句，没有一件事情按照它应该遵循的路线来进行。

[3] out of joint 为介词短语，混乱地。be worse off 为动词短语，更不愉快。times 在这里指"时代"。

The earth will soon be overcrowded and its resources exhausted. Pollution will ruin the environment, upset the climate, damage human health. The gap in living standards between the rich and the poor will widen and lead the angry, hungry people of the world to acts of desperation including the use of nuclear weapons as blackmail. Such are the inevitable consequences of population and technological growth if present trends continue. But what a big if this is!

The future is never a projection of the past. Animals probably have no chance to escape from the tyranny of biological evolution, but human beings are blessed with the freedom of social evolution. For us, trend is not destiny. The escape from existing trends is now facilitated by the fact that societies anticipate future dangers and take preventive steps against expected upheavals.

**【文章精读】**

人类采取措施预防混乱的变革带来的灾难，不会重蹈历史覆辙。

Despite the widespread belief that the world has become too complex for comprehension by the human brain, modern societies have often responded effectively to critical situations.

长句分析：

(1) 尽管人们普遍认为世界的复杂性已经令人类的大脑很难理解了，但现代社会常常有效地回应一些关键情形。

(2) critical situations 指下面章节的内容。

(3) "that the world has become too complex for comprehension by the human brain"为同位语从句，修饰 belief。

(4) despite 为介词，结构为：despite+名词/动名词/名词性从句，比如：Despite being ill during my interview, I still love Rome. 本句 "the widespread belief" 为名词短语，后面用同位语从句修饰。

The decrease in birth rates, the partial banning of pesticides, the rethinking of technologies for the production and use of energy are but a few examples illustrating a sudden reversal of trends caused not by political upsets or scientific breakthroughs, but by public awareness of consequences.

**【文章精读】**

(1) 出生率的下降、对杀虫剂的部分禁用、对生产中的科学技术的反思以及对能源的使用仅仅是一些例证，这些例证阐述了由公众对后果的意识而非由政治不满或科技突破所引发的潮流的突然反转。

(2) "caused not by political upsets or scientific breakthroughs, but by public awareness of consequences"为过去分词短语作后置定语，其中嵌套了短语 not..., but...。

(3) 本段为人们意识到可能引发的后果而采取的对策。回应了上一段 "modern societies have often responded effectively to critical situations"。

Even more striking are the situations in which social attitudes concerning future difficulties undergo rapid changes before the problems have come to pass—witness the heated controversies

批注 [A285]: 动词，加宽

批注 [A286]: lead sb. to sth. 导致某人做某事

批注 [A287]: 敲诈，威胁，名词

批注 [A288]: 未来不是过去的投影

批注 [A289]: 幸运地享有

批注 [A290]: vt. 促进

批注 [A291]: 预计，expect

批注 [A292]: 预防性的

批注 [A293]: 介词，respond to sth./doing sth.

批注 [A294]: 反义词"死亡率"：mortality

批注 [A295]: 杀虫剂

批注 [A296]: 反思，动名词

批注 [A297]: 形容词，反转的

批注 [A298]: 显著的

about the ethics of behavior control and of genetic engineering even though there is as yet no proof that effective methods can be developed to manipulate behavior and genes on a population scale.

【文章精读】

(1) 更显著的是这样一些情况：公众对于未来困难的态度在问题发生之前经历快速变化，这一变化目睹了行为控制伦理学与基因工程伦理学之间激烈的争论，尽管目前没有证据表明人们可以采取有效方法对一定规模的人口控制其行为和基因。

(2) sth. concerning (about) +n. 关于什么的，a survey concerning the unemployment rate 一份关于失业率的调查；come to pass：发生；manipulate，及物动词，控制。

(3) Even more striking are the situations in which social attitudes concerning future difficulties undergo rapid changes before the problems have come to pass—witness the heated controversies about the ethics of behavior control and of genetic engineering even though there is as yet no proof that effective methods can be developed to manipulate behavior and genes on a population scale.

One of the characteristics of our times is thus the rapidity with which steps can be taken to change the orientation of certain trends and even to reverse them. Such changes usually emerge from grassroot movements rather than from official directives.

批注 [A299]: 主句谓语动词。这是一个倒装句，正常语序是：The situations（附加从句）are even more striking.

批注 [A300]: which 指代 situations，在这种情况中

批注 [A301]: 定语从句

批注 [302]: 指代 rapidity，迅速，名词

批注 [303]: 指代 certain trends，即由于科技进步带来的混乱局面。

【题目解析】

1. In Passage 1, all of the following are stated or implied about towns in the Middle Ages except

(A) towns had no suburbs
(B) towns were always quite noisy
(C) towns served as places of defense
(D) towns always had large churches
(E) merchants lived in the towns

【答案】B

2. The author's main purpose in Passage 1 is to
(A) describe the miseries of the period
(B) show how life was centered on the town
(C) emphasize the uncontrolled and violent course of life at the time
(D) point out how the upper classes mistreated the lower classes
(E) indicate how religious people were in those days

【答案】C

3. According to Passage 1, people at that time, as compared with people today, were
(A) worse off
(B) better off

(C) less intelligent

(D) more subdued

(E) more sensitive to certain events

【答案】E

4. In the first paragraph of Passage 2, the mood expressed is one of

(A) blatant despair

(B) guarded optimism

(C) poignant nostalgia

(D) muted pessimism

(E) unbridled idealism

【答案】A

5. According to Passage 2, if present trends continue, which one of the following situations will not occur?

(A) New sources of energy from vast coal deposits will be substituted for the soon-to-be-exhausted resources of oil and natural gas.

(B) The rich will become richer and the poor will become poorer.

(C) An overpopulated earth will be unable to sustain its inhabitants.

(D) Nuclear weapons will play a more prominent role in dealings among peoples.

(E) The ravages of pollution will render the earth and its atmosphere a menace to mankind.

【答案】A

6. Which of the following is the best illustration of the meaning of "trend is not destiny" in line 65?

(A) Urban agglomerations are in a state of crisis.

(B) Human beings are blessed with the freedom of social evolution.

(C) The world has become too complex for comprehension by the human brain.

(D) Critical processes can overshoot and cause catastrophes.

(E) The earth will soon be overcrowded and its resources exhausted.

【答案】B

7. According to Passage 2, evidences of the insight of the public into the dangers that surround us can be found in all of the following except

(A) an increase in the military budget by the president

(B) a declining birth rate

(C) picketing against expansion of nuclear plants

(D) opposition to the use of pesticides

(E) public meetings to complain about dumping chemicals

【答案】A

批注 [A304]: 明显的绝望

批注 [A305]: 有所保留的乐观

批注 [A306]: 伤心的怀旧

批注 [A307]: 沉默的悲观

批注 [A308]: 彻底的理想主义

批注 [A309]: 这里为名词，破坏

批注 [A310]: 使，make

批注 [A311]: threat

批注 [A312]: 作者意思：社会的进步使人类反潮流而行，从而抑制这些威胁。

批注 [A313]: 都市聚焦

批注 [A314]: vt. 夸张

批注 [A315]: 公众对危险的洞察力

8. The author's attitude in Passage 2 is one of
(A) willing resignation
(B) definite optimism
(C) thinly veiled cynicism
(D) carefree abandon
(E) angry impatience

【答案】B

9. If there is a continuity in history, which of the following situations in Passage 1 is thought to lead to violence in the future of Passage 2?
(A) the overcrowding of the population
(B) the executions in public
(C) the contrast between the social classes
(D) the contrast between illness and health
(E) the contrast between religion and politics

【答案】C

10. One can conclude from reading both passages that the difference between the people in Passage 1 and the people in Passage 2 is that
(A) the people in Passage 2 act on their awareness in contrast to the people in Passage 1
(B) the people in Passage 2 are more intense and colorful than the people in Passage 1
(C) there was no controversy between sociology and science in the society in Passage 2 in contrast to the society mentioned in Passage 1
(D) the people in Passage 1 are far more religious
(E) sociological changes were faster and more abrupt with the people of Passage 1

【答案】A

11. From a reading of both passages, one may conclude that
(A) people in both passages are equally subservient to authority
(B) the future is a mirror to the past
(C) the topic of biological evolution is of great importance to the scientists of both periods
(D) the evolution of science has created great differences in the social classes
(E) the people in Passage 1 are more involved in everyday living, whereas the people in Passage 2 are usually seeking change

【答案】E

批注 [316]: 该观点被文章2否定

# 文章 32

The Rosetta Stone![1] What a providential find that was.[2] And what a remarkable set of circumstances it took for people to be able to read Egyptian hieroglyphics after a hiatus of some 1,400 years.[3] It even took a military campaign.[4] In 1798, Napoleon Bonaparte's army attacked British-held Egypt, seeking to cut off England from the riches of the Middle East.[5] Rebuilding a fortress, a French soldier uncovered a block of basalt inscribed with writing in three distinct scripts: Greek, demotic script (an everyday cursive form of Egyptian), and Egyptian hieroglyphs.[6] At that moment, modern Egyptology began.[7]

【单词精解】

1. providential adj. 凑巧的；幸运的
2. remarkable adj. 异常的；引人注目的；不寻常的（文中意思）
3. hieroglyphic n. 象形文字，象形文字写成的文章
4. hiatus n. 裂隙；缺漏；脱漏；间断
5. circumstance n. (1) 环境，条件，情况 (2) 境遇，经济状况 (3) 事件；事实 (4) unforeseen events out of one's control 机遇（文中意思）a victim of circumstances 命运的牺牲品。
6. hold vt. 在这里表示 occupy，占有，占领。British-held：形容词复合词，被英国占领的。类似用法：a mathematics-based subject，一个以数学为基础的学科；a man-dominated industry，男人为主宰的行业。
7. seek (1) vt. 寻找；探寻 (2) vi. 企图；试图 seek to do sth.（文中意思） (3) vt. seek one's advice 征求某人的建议
8. attack (1) vt. & vi. 攻击，进攻；抨击（文中意思，进攻 vt.）(2) n. 攻击，袭击 (3) n. （疾病）侵袭, 发作 heart attack 心脏病发作
9. riches (1) 财富=wealth (2) 宝贵的自然资源（valuable natural resources）（文中意思）
10. fortress n. 堡垒，要塞
11. rebuild vt. (1) 重建，重新组装（文中意思）(2) 再形成某事物；恢复 rebuild one's courage/hope
12. uncover (1) vt. 揭开……的盖子 (2) vt. 揭露，发现（文中意思）=unveil=reveal
13. basalt n. 玄武岩，黑陶器（似玄武岩的制品）
14. inscribe vt. 写；刻
15. distinct adj.
(1) 截然不同的，完全分开的 （文中意思）
(2) 清晰的，明白的，明显的 a distinct improvement in doing sth. 在某方面有明显的进步

16. script n. (1) 剧本，脚本，讲稿 (2) 笔迹 (3) 文字（文中意思）
17. demotic adj. (1) 民众的 （文中意思）(2) 口语的，通俗的
18. cursive (1) adj.（指字迹）草书的 (2) n. 草书（文中意思）
19. hieroglyph n. 象形字（如古埃及等所用的）
20. Egyptology n. 埃及古物学
21. everyday adj. 每天的，日常的

## 【文章精读】

[1]-[2] The Rosetta Stone: 罗塞塔石碑。开篇点题，讲述罗塞塔石碑。that 指代罗塞塔石碑。罗塞塔石碑！多么幸运的发现啊！"providential"的原因在[3]中进行了讲述。

[3] "took"在这里指"花费"，"circumstances"与"providential"对应，指"机遇，机缘"。a set of sth 一套XXX。remarkable 在此指"不同寻常的"。"it"指代罗塞塔石碑。

[句型] "What a remarkable set of circumstances"作 took 的宾语，字面意思：罗塞塔石碑的发现花费了人们大量的机遇，即：人们重复进行了大量小概率事件的探索，最终发现了石碑。发现石碑是一件很巧合的事件，本句的 take 与下一句同义，指"耗费"，等价于 consume。

[4] it 指代石碑。该石碑甚至耗费了一场军事运动。took 的含义与上一句相同：一场军事运动引发了石碑的发现。

The company expects to resume production of the vehicle again after a two-month hiatus. 公司希望在两个月的中断之后能重新开始车辆的生产。主语+谓语 after a period of hiatus. 某人/物多久后做某事。

[5] Napoleon Bonaparte's army attacked British-held Egypt, "seeking to cut off England from the riches of the Middle East"为现在分词短语作状语，修饰 attack，为了阻断英国获取中东的宝贵自然资源，拿破仑的军队攻打英国占领的埃及。

[6] Rebuilding a fortress, a French soldier uncovered a block of basalt inscribed with writing in three distinct scripts: Greek, demotic script (an everyday cursive form of Egyptian), and Egyptian hieroglyphs. 本句交代这场战争中偶然发现了该石碑的经过。

**批注 [317]**：现在分词短语作伴随状语

**批注 [318]**：过去分词短语作定语，修饰 basalt。

[7] 承接[6]，石碑的重大意义：创立了现在埃及考古学。

## 【题目解析】

1. The primary purpose of lines 1-5 is to
(A) describe the physical attributes of an artifact
(B) underscore the difficulty of translating ancient texts
(C) indicate a new direction for linguistic research
(D) qualify an excessively sweeping generalization
(E) emphasize the unusual background of a discovery

【答案】E

【解析】attribute vt. 认为……是；归因于……
He attributes his success to working hard.
underscore vt. 强调

2. The author's tone in writing of the discovery of the Rosetta Stone can best be characterized as

(A) ironic

(B) enthusiastic

(C) condescending

(D) nostalgic

(E) objective

【答案】C

题干意思：作者在描写石碑的发现这件事时的口吻是什么？

condescending adj. 1.降低身份的,屈尊的 2.表现出优越感的；居高临下的 a condescending attitude（题干意思）

# 文章 33

*A Portrait of the Artist as a Young Man* recounts the tale of Stephen Dedalus, a sensitive young Dubliner. As a child, he suffers because of his classmates' cruelty, his Jesuit teachers' authoritarianism, and his country's political turmoil. Growing older, Stephen becomes increasingly isolated from his friends, his church, and his country, viewing them all as heartless and hypocritical. Intent on becoming a writer, he eventually concludes he must serve all ties—family, friends, church, and country—to achieve fulfillment as an artist.[1] The hero must leave Ireland, leave the Church, to set off alone "to forge in the sanity of his soul the uncreated conscience of his race."[2]

批注 [319]: 指代 his friends, his church, and his country。

批注 [320]: 指出他必须离开爱尔兰的原因

【单词精解】

1. portrait n. (1) 肖像，画像 (2) 生动的描写（文中意思）
【重要句型】主语 gave a portrait of sth./sb./an idea+同位语从句。
2. recount vt. 详细叙述某事；讲述某事
3. sensitive adj. (1) 易受伤害的，易损坏的；易受影响的；敏感的 (2) 易生气的；感情容易冲动的 (3) 有细腻感情的；同情理解的 (4) （指仪器等）灵敏的 (5) 需要小心处理（以免引起麻烦或冒犯）的，敏感的，微妙的
4. suffer (1) vi. 受痛苦；受损害（文中意思） (2) vt. 忍受，容忍=bear (3) vt. 容许，允许 suffer sb. to do sth. 允许某人做某事
5. cruelty n. 残忍，残酷
6. turmoil n. 混乱
7. heartless adj. 无情的；狠心的 heartless cruelty 无情的残暴行为
8. intent (1) n. 意图，意向，目的 (2) adj. 专心的，专注的 be intent on sth./doing sth. 专注地做某事 (3) adj. 意愿坚决的，一心想……的（文中意思）be intent on doing sth. 一心想做某事。须掌握其动词形式：intend vt. 打算 This article was intended to discuss an issue of environmental protection.
9. conclude vt. & vi. 结束 vt. 得出结论；断定（文中意思）=draw (vt.)
10. serve (1) vt. 为……服务；为……服役（文中意思） (2) vt. 供应 serve with sth. (3) vt. 任（职）；服（刑）；当（学徒）(4) vt. 适合（特定用途或目的）；对……有用；供……使用 serve to do sth.=be used to do sth. (5) vt. 发（球）(6) vt. 对待
11. fulfillment n. (1) 完成，履行；实现 (2) 满足（感），成就（感） (3) 实施过程
12. tie n. (1) 关系；联系（文中意思）ties with sb./sth. 与某人/物的关系 (2) 束缚
13. set off (1) 出发，动身 （文中意思）(2) 开始；引起 If uncontrolled, the shortage would set off a new rise in food prices. 如果不加控制，这种短缺会引起食品价格再次上涨。(3) 点燃，爆炸

14. forge (1) vt. 锻造（文中意思） (2) vt. 伪造，仿造 forge money 伪造钱币 (3) vi. 突然向前

15. sanity n. (1) 神志正常；心智健康 (2) 明智，稳健，理智

16. uncreated adj. 自存的，未创造的，尚未产生的

17. conscience n. 良心，良知

18. authoritarianism 名词，权力主义，独裁主义

## 【文章精读】

[1] Intent on becoming a writer, he eventually concludes he must serve all ties—family, friends, church, and country—to achieve fulfillment as an artist.

打算成为一个作家，他最终得到结论：他必须权衡好家庭、朋友、教堂和国家之间的关系。conclude 这里为及物动词，后面为宾语从句，可以用 draws 来取代。serve all ties：权衡各方面关系，ties 在这里指"关系"。"to achieve fulfillment as an artist"为不定式短语作目的状语。 "Intent on"为形容词短语作伴随状语，等价于 Intending to become a writer.

【重要句型】主语+be intent on doing sth.=主语+intended to do sth. 某人打算做某事。

[2] to forge in the sanity of his soul the uncreated conscience of his race

目的状语，表明英雄离开爱尔兰的目的。in the sanity of his soul 为介词状语，forge 为"铸造"，宾语为"the uncreated conscience of his race"。在他灵魂清醒的状态下，铸造他的民族尚未创立的良知。

## 【题目解析】

The hero must leave Ireland, leave the church, to set off alone to forge in the sanity of his soul the uncreated conscience of his race. "Forge" most nearly means

(A) counterfeit
(B) fashion
(C) duplicate
(D) alter
(E) melt

【解析】B

forge 在这里指"铸造"，铸造民族尚未创立的良知。

counterfeit (1) n. 仿制品，伪造物 (2) vt. & vi. 仿制，造假

fashion (1) n. 方式，样子 (2) n. 流行款式，时尚款式，时装 (3) vt. 制作；使成形 fashion A from B 用 B 制作 A（选项意思）

# 文章 34

When the child was about ten years old, he invited his sister, Mrs. Penniman, to come and stay with him. His sister Lavinia had married a poor clergyman, of a sickly constitution and a flowery style of eloquence, and then, at the age of thirty-three, had been left a widow—without children, without fortune—with nothing but the memory of Mr. Penniman's flowers of speech, a certain vague aroma of which hovered about her own conversation.[1] Nevertheless, he had offered her a home under his own roof, which Lavinia accepted with the alacrity of a woman who had spent the ten years of her married life in the town of Poughkeepise.[2] The Doctor had not proposed to Mrs. Penniman to come and live with him indefinitely; he had suggested that she should make an asylum of his house while she looked about for unfurnished lodgings.[3] It is uncertain whether Mrs. Penniman ever instituted a search for unfurnished lodgings, but it is beyond dispute that she never found them.[4] She settled herself with her brother and never went away, and when Catherine was twenty years old, her Aunt Lavinia was still one of the most striking features of her immediate entourage.[5] Mrs. Penniman's own account of the matter was that she had remained to take charge of her niece's education.[6] She had given this account, at least, to everyone but the Doctor, who never asked for explanations which he could entertain himself any day with inventing.[7] Mrs. Penniman, moreover, though she had a good deal of a certain sort of artificial assurance, shrunk, for indefinable reasons, from presenting herself to her brother as a fountain of instruction.[8] She had not a high sense of humor, but she had enough to prevent her from making this mistake; and her brother, on his side, had enough to excuse her, in her situation, for laying him under contribution during a considerable part of lifetime.[9] He therefore assented tacitly to the proposition which Mrs. Penniman had tacitly laid down, that it was of importance that the poor motherless girl should have a brilliant woman near her.[10] His assent could only be tacit, for he had never been dazzled by his sister's intellectual luster.[11] Save when he fell in love with Catherine Harrington, he had never been dazzled, indeed, by any feminine characteristics whatever; and though he was to a certain extent what is called a ladies' doctor, his private opinion of the more complicated sex was not exalted.[12] He nevertheless, at the end of six months, accepted his sister's permanent presence as an accomplished fact, and as Catherine grew older, perceived that there were in effect good reasons why she should have a companion of her own imperfect sex.[13] He was extremely polite to Lavinia, scrupulously, formally polite; and she had never seen him in anger but once in her life, when he lost his temper in a theological discussion with her late husband.[14] With her he never discussed theology, nor, indeed, discussed anything; he contented himself with making known, very distinctly in the form of a lucid ultimatum, his wishes with regard to Catherine.[15]

批注 [321]: doctor

批注 [322]: 女主人公，医生的妹妹

批注 [323]: doctor

批注 [324]: 指代 this mistake

## 【单词及搭配】

1. clergyman n. 牧师，教士

2. sickly adj. 有病的；多病的；不健康的

3. constitution n. (1) 宪法，法规，章程 (2) 体格（文中意思）(3) 构成方式，构造 (4) 制定，设立，组成，任命

4. eloquence n. 口才；雄辩

5. flowers of speech 华丽辞藻

6. vague adj. 模糊的

7. hover (1) vi. 盘旋（文中意思）(2) vi. 犹豫，摇摆不定

8. alacrity n. (1) 敏捷，活泼，轻快 (2) 欣然，乐意（文中意思） do sth. with alacrity=do sth. readily

9. propose vt. & vi. 提议；建议 propose to do sth. /propose doing sth.

10. indefinitely adv. 无限期地

11. asylum n. 避难所；庇护

12. unfurnished adj. 无装备的，无家具的

furnish vt. (1) 陈设，布置 (2) 提供

That shop furnishes everything that is needed for camping.

这家店铺供应野营所需的一切。

The old man furnished the guerrillas information.

老人给游击队提供情报。

No one in the class could furnish the right answer to the question.

班上没有一个人能给出问题的正确答案。

13. lodging n. 出租的房间，寄宿宿舍；暂住；寄宿；借宿

14. institute (1) vt. 建立，制定；开始，着手（文中意思）(2) n. 协会，学会；学院，研究院

15. beyond dispute 毫无疑问

【重要句型】It is undoubted that+主语从句=There is no doubt that+主语从句=It is beyond dispute that+主语从句：某事是毫无疑问的。

16. settle (1) vt./vi. 安排；安放；安家，定居（文中意思）(2) vt. 解决；决定；调停 settle the matter 解决问题 (3) vt. 支付，结算

17. striking adj. (1) 显著的，突出的 (2) 引人注目的；容貌出众的

18. feature (1) 名词，特征，特色 (2) 面貌，相貌，容貌（文中意思，常用复数）(3) 特写，专题节目 (4) vt. 以……为特征 A feature B. A 是 B 的特征。B is characterized with A. (5) vt. 特写；（书刊）特载；（电影）由……主演；以……为号召物 The magazine is featuring his articles. 这份杂志正在特载他的文章。(6) vt. 看来像，与……容貌相似 (7) vi. 起重要作用；作为主要角色，主演 A is featured in B.

19. immediate adj. (1) 立即的，即刻的；紧迫的 (2) 目前的，当前的 long interests 长远利益 immediate interests 眼前利益 (3) direct 直接的 (4) 最接近的（文中意思）

20. entourage n. 随从，随行人员

21. account (1) n. 账，账户 (2) n. 记述，描述，报道（文中意思）(3) vi. 解释；说明

account for sth. (4) vt. 认为

22. entertain (1) vt./vi. 款待, 招待 (2) vt. 使欢乐, 使娱乐 (3) vt. 抱有, 考虑 entertain a firm belief in sth. 对某事有坚定信心

23. artificial adj. (1) 人造的, 人工的, 假的 (2) 虚假的, 不真挚的, 矫揉造作的 (3) 人为的

24. assurance n. (1) 保证, 担保, 确信 (2) 把握, 信心（文中意思）

25. shrink vt. & vi. 收缩；退缩 shrink from sth./doing/名词性从句：从某事中退缩

26. indefinable adj. 难下定义的, 难确切表达的

27. fountain 名词 (1) 喷水；喷泉 (2) 来源, 根源, 源泉（文中意思）fountain of sth. 某事的来源

28. present vt. 出现；出席；显示（文中意思）

29. excuse vt. 原谅, 宽恕

30. lay vt. 放置

31. assent (1) n. 同意 (2) vi. 同意（文中意思）assent to sth./doing sth./名词性从句

32. tacit adj. 缄默的, 不说话的

33. considerable adj. 相当大（或多）的

34. brilliant adj. (1) 明亮的 brilliant big eyes (2) 才华横溢的；英明的；出色的（文中意思）

35. dazzle (1) vt. 使目眩 be dazzled by sth./sb. (2) vt. 使惊异不已 dazzle sb. with sth. 用什么使人赞叹惊讶。

36. luster (1) n. 光泽；光辉；光彩 Sth. has a adj. luster. 某物有什么样的光泽。(2) 荣耀, 荣光（文中意思）add luster to sb./sth. 为某人/物增光 (3) vt. 使有光泽；使有光彩；给……增光 luster sth./sb. (4) vi. 有光泽, 发光

37. exalt (1) vt. 赞扬；歌颂 (2) vt. 提升, 提拔（文中意思）

38. accomplished adj. (1) 完成了的；实现了的；竣工的（文中意思）(2) 聪明的；有才艺的

39. perceive vt. 感觉, 察觉, 理解

40. companion n. (1) 同伴, 伙伴（文中意思）(2) 成双成对的物品之一

41. scrupulous adj. 严格认真的, 一丝不苟的

42. lucid adj. 表达清楚的, 明白易懂的

43. ultimatum n. 最后通牒

44. distinct adj. (1) 截然不同的, 完全分开的 (2) 清晰的, 明白的, 明显的（文中意思）

45. formally adv. (1) 正式地；正规地 (2) 拘泥形式地；形式上（文中意思）
Everyone was formally lined up to meet the king. 大家拘谨地列好队迎接国王。

46. content (1) n. 所容纳之物, 所含之物 (2) n.（书等的）内容, 目录 (3) n. 容量, 含量 No other food has so high an iron content. 没有别的食物有这么高的含铁量。(4) adj. 满足的, 满意的 (5) n. 满足, 满意 (6) vt. 使满足, 使满意（文中意思）

【文章精读】

[1] of a sickly constitution：介词短语作定语，修饰 clergyman：一个病歪歪的牧师。a sick man=a man of sickly constitution；an important issue=an issue of great importance。sickly 在这

里作形容词。of a sickly constitution and a flowery style of eloquence。"a flowery style of eloquence"为并列的介词短语作定语，修饰"牧师"。be left sb./sth.：某人处于某种状态。Sb. was left a widow. 某人成为了寡妇。"without children, without fortune—with nothing but the memory of Mr. Penniman's flowers of speech, a certain vague aroma of which hovered about her own conversation"，介词短语作状语，修饰 left，成为寡妇，没有孩子，没有财产，什么都没有，只有他丈夫的舌绽莲花，以至连她自己的话语中也多少掺杂了一种淡淡的香气。which 指代 a certain vague aroma，an aroma of sth.，某种物质的气味。

【重要句型】主语+谓语 without A, but with B（名词/动名词/名词性从句）.
I set out with nothing, but what he said lingered around me.
a+名词 of sth.=a 名词 of which+定语从句。
hover about sth. 在某物周围盘旋

[2] He had offered her a home under his own roof, which Lavinia accepted with the alacrity of a woman who had spent the ten years of her married life in the town of Poughkeepise. 弟弟为她提供了一个可以安身的房子，她欣然接受了这一切，她曾经在某个城镇度过了十年婚姻生活。accept sth./sb. with alacrity=do sth. readily：欣然接受什么。

[3] looked about for sth.：四处寻找某物。while：这里指"当……的时候"。

[4] "whether Mrs. Penniman ever instituted a search for unfurnished lodgings"为主语从句，whether：是否；ever：adv, 到底 ever=on earth。institute sth.=engage in sth.：着手做某事。It is beyond dispute that+主语从句：某事是毫无疑问的。Penniman 太太到底有没有在找房子不确定，但有一点可以肯定：她从来没找到房子。

他开始着手回复客户的投诉。He instituted a reply to complaints of consumers.

[5] settle oneself with sb., 与谁住在一起，相当于 live with sb.。

[6] remain to do sth., 留下来做某事。与上一句 Penniman 太太与弟弟住在一起对应。matter 指代 Penniman 太太与弟弟住在一起的事实。account：说明，名词。Penniman 太太对这件事的解释是：她要留下来负责侄女的教育。

[7] "who never asked for explanations…inventing"为定语从句，修饰 doctor。give sth. to A but B：把某物给了 A，而没给 B。"which he could entertain himself any day with inventing"为定语从句，修饰 explanations。any day，任何一天。with inventing，状语，修饰 entertain。which 指代 explanations。entertain 表示"考虑"。

[8] assurance：文中指自信（self-confidence）。shrunk 为谓语，shrink for reasons from doing sth., 因为某种原因而从某事中退缩。present sb./sth. to sb./sth. as+名词：把某人（物）作为什么展现给某人（物）。尽管 Penniman 太太有相当多虚伪的自信，但因为一些不可名状的原因，回避在她弟弟面前展现自己为一个教育指导者。

[9] She had not a high sense of humor, but she had enough to prevent her from making this mistake; and her brother, on his side, had enough to excuse her, in her situation, for laying him under contribution during a considerable part of lifetime. excuse sb. for sth./doing sth.：原谅某人做了某事。lay sb. under+名词：使某人处于某种状态下，lay sb. under dilemma，使某人身处困境。contribution：这里指"付出"。她的弟弟有足够的幽默感来原谅她在相当长一段时间内让自己付出了很多。

[10] "which Mrs. Penniman had tacitly laid down"，定语从句，修饰 proposition。"that it was of importance that the poor motherless girl should have a brilliant woman near her"为

proposition 的同位语从句。assent to the proposition，认可这个建议，tacitly，默许地，这个单词表明医生没有明确表示赞成姐姐永久性居住，因为他认为姐姐并不明智，所以对姐姐提出的"失去母爱的孩子需要她"的建议持默许态度。下一句解释 tacitly 的原因。

[11] for 表示原因，可以用 in that+从句取代。"intellectual luster"为讽刺——高智商的光环。言外之意：姐姐并不聪明。

【重要句型】主语+谓语 in that+从句。因为某事，主语做了某事。

[12] save=except for，介词，except when=save when，某个时候除外。"by any feminine characteristics whatever（无论什么样的女性特征）与 dazzled 连接；be dazzled by sth.，被某事弄得神魂颠倒。本句表明他没有被姐姐弄得神魂颠倒。

除了与 Catherine Harrington 坠入爱河时，事实上他从来都没有被任何女性特征弄得神魂颠倒；虽然一定程度上他被叫做女士的医生，但他关于更复杂的性的个人意见并没有被激发。

[13] He nevertheless, at the end of six months, accepted his sister's permanent presence as an accomplished fact, and as Catherine grew older, perceived that there were in effect good reasons why she should have a companion of her own imperfect sex.

批注 [U334]: 既成事实，as 这里指"随着"。

[14] He was extremely polite to Lavinia, scrupulously, formally polite; and she had never seen him in anger but once in her life, when he lost his temper in a theological discussion with her late husband.

He 指 Doctor。本句指出 Doctor 从未和 Lavinia 发过脾气，对 Lavinia 很客气。

[15] 他从来不和她谈论神学，事实上，什么都不谈论。他满足于以一种清晰明了、不容商榷的方式让人们知道他对女儿的期望。

正常语序：He contented himself with making his wishes with regard to Catherine known, very distinctly, in the form of a lucid ultimatum. "with regard to Catherine"，介词短语作定语，修饰 wishes，"very distinctly, in the form of a lucid ultimatum"修饰 make，以清晰明了、不容商榷的方式来使期望被人们知道。"make wishes known"的另外一种表达：make wishes well informed of。下文阐述如何清晰地表达对女儿的期望。

Once, when the girl was about twelve year old, he had said to her—

"Try and make a clever woman of her, Lavinia; I should like her to be a clever woman."[1]

Mrs. Penniman, at this, looked thoughtful a moment. "My dear Austin," she then inquired, "do you think it is better to be clever than to be good?"[2]

From this assertion Mrs. Penniman saw no reason to dissent; she possibly reflected that her own great use in the world was owing to her aptitude for many things.[3]

【单词及搭配】

1. reflect (1) v. 反射 (2) vt. 考虑（文中意思）(3) vt. 表达；反映 (4) 给……带来，博得；蒙受（名誉或耻辱等）His behaviour reflects dishonour on his parents. 他的行为有损于他父母的声誉。(5) vt. 招致；证明（某人）以某种方式行动

2. thoughtful adj. (1) 沉思的，思考的 a thoughtful look on one's face 沉思的表情（可作定语）（文中意思）(2) 体贴的，关心的 be thoughtful/considerate for/to sb. 对某人体贴

3. inquire vt. & vi. 打听，询问

4. dissent (1) n. 意见的分歧 (2) vi. 不同意,持异议 dissented from sth. 对某事有不同意见(文中意思)

5. owing to 因为 Owing to the rain, the match was canceled. 因为下雨,比赛取消了。
owe (1) vt. 欠……债;应当给予 owe sb.+钱 (2) vt. 应把……归功于 owe sth. to sth. 把某事归功于某事 (3) vt. 感激=appreciate sb. owe much to sb. 某人非常感谢某人

6. aptitude n. 才能,资质,天资 aptitude for sth./doing sth.(文中意思)

7. assert vt. 声称,断言

## 【文章精读】

[1] Try and make a clever woman of her, Lavinia; I should like her to be a clever woman. 医生对女儿的殷切期望,希望女儿聪明,clever 与后文的某个单词意思对应。注意语境,理解"聪明"的含义。make a clever woman of sb. 使某人做一个聪明的女人,即让她的女儿做一个聪明的女人,言外之意,医生认为自己女儿不够聪明,没有达到他的要求。

[2] Mrs. Penniman, at this, looked thoughtful a moment. "My dear Austin," she then inquired, "do you think it is better to be clever than to be good?"

at this=hearing this,介词短语作状语,相当于 when she heard this,或 when hearing this,或 on hearing this。this 指代医生说的让女儿变聪明一些这句话。

[3] From this assertion Mrs. Penniman saw no reason to dissent; she possibly reflected that her own great use in the world was owing to her aptitude for many things.

see no reason to dissent=assent,to dissent 为不定式作定语,修饰 reason。Penniman 太太完全同意医生要求女儿变得聪明的观点。且她很可能在思考自己由于在很多方面具备的才华对世界的巨大作用。表明 Penniman 太太过度自信,为讽刺,本句与"Mrs. Penniman, moreover, though she had a good deal of a certain sort of artificial assurance"对应。

"Of course I wish Catherine to be good," the Doctor said next day; "but she won't be any the less virtuous for not being a fool.[1] I am not afraid of her being wicked; she will never have the salt of malice in her character.[2] She is 'as good as good bread,' as the French say; but six years hence I don't want to have to compare her to good bread-and-butter."[3]

## 【单词及搭配】

1. any the less 更少一点
2. virtuous adj. 品德高的,有美德的;善良的;正直的;自命清高的
3. wicked adj. (1) 邪恶的,恶劣的;缺德的(文中的) (2) 淘气的,顽皮的
4. character n. 品质,特性,特色特征,好的品质;人物,角色
5. malice n. 恶意,蓄意害人
She did it out of malice. 她出于恶意做了这件事。
6. salt n. (1) 增添趣味的事物(文中意思) add salt to sth. 使某事增加趣味 (2) vt. 使更有趣 salt sth.
7. hence (1) adv. 从此时起,从此处(文中意思)
The sports meet will be held three days hence. 运动会在三天后举行。
(2) 因此,所以

## 【文章精读】

[1] "Of course I wish Catherine to be good," the Doctor said next day; "but she won't be any the less virtuous for not being a fool."

【译文】"当然，我希望女儿好，"医生转天说："但是如果她聪明一些的话，也不会有丝毫不好。"即：聪明一些还是照样好，与其都是那么好，何妨不更加聪明一些呢？医生希望女儿更聪明一些。

virtuous 在这里与 good 同意，由语境理解。for 表示"因为"。字面意思：因为不是傻子，所以她不会比以前不好。引申意思见译文解释。

[2] She is 'as good as good bread,' as the French say; but six years hence I don't want to have to compare her to good bread-and-butter.

compare to：把什么比作什么。字面意思：她像优质的面包一样优质，正如法国人所讲；但是从现在起六年后我不希望把她比作好的面包和黄油。

引申意思：希望女儿不仅好，而且要不乏味，幽默。

"Are you afraid she will be insipid? My dear brother, it is I who supply the butter; so you need not fear!" said Mrs. Penniman, who had taken in hand the child's "accomplishments," overlooking her at the piano, where Catherine displayed a certain talent, and going with her to the dancing-class, where it must be confessed that she made but a modest figure.

## 【单词及搭配】

1. insipid adj. 枯燥的，无生气的；乏味的。须掌握名词形式：insipidity。
2. accomplishment n. (1) 完成，实现 (2) 技能，（社交上的）才艺（文中意思）(3) 成就；完成的工作
3. overlook (1) vt. 忽视 (2) vt. 原谅 overlook one's fault (3) vt. 监督，管理（文中意思）(4) vt. 俯视
4. confess v. 承认，供认。三个表示"承认"的单词辨析：acknowledge 是一般的用语，大多数都用它。concede 一般指不情愿的"承认"，通常用在比赛或失败的时候；confess 一般用于向警方坦白（错误、罪行等），有"招供，招认"的意思，还有就是承认自己尴尬的事。
5. modest adj. (1) 谦虚的 (2) 适中的，中庸的（文中意思）
6. figure (1) 名词，数字 (2) 名词，图解 (3) 名词，肖像 (4) 名词，轮廓，人影，身材，体态，风姿（文中意思）(5) 名词，计算 (6) vi. 出现，被提及 Sth. / sb figured+介词短语，某物/人在某地出现。(7) vt. 计算在内 figure sth. (8) vt. 估计=estimate
7. display (1) n. 陈列，展览 (2) n. 陈列的货物、艺术品等（可数名词）(3) vt. 显示，显露（文中意思）
8. fear (1) n. 害怕，恐惧 (2) n. 可能性=probability=chance=odds the fear of sth. 某物发生的可能性 (3) vt. 畏惧（文中意思）fear to do sth./fear that+宾语从句

> 批注 [335]：指出医生的担心：担心女儿无趣乏味。
>
> 批注 [336]：对应 salt，Penniman 太太在高估自己的才能。

## 【文章精读】

"Are you afraid she will be insipid? My dear brother, it is I who supply the butter; so you need not fear!" said Mrs. Penniman, who had taken in hand the child's "accomplishments," overlooking her at the piano, where Catherine displayed a certain talent, and going with her to the dancing-class, where it must be confessed that she made but a modest figure.

【题目解析】

1. The word "constitution" means
(A) establishment
(B) charter
(C) ambience
(D) physique
(E) wit

【解析】D

(A) establishment (1) n. 建立 (2) 企业，机构 a well/badly run establishment (3) 当权派，当局（大写首字母）

(B) charter (1) n. 许可证 (2) n. 纲领，宪章，宣言 (3) n. 包租 a hotel for charter 可以包租的旅馆 (4) vt. 发给……许可证 charter sth. 颁发 XXX 许可证

(C) ambience n. 环境，气氛。须掌握形容词形式：ambient adj. 周围的，包围着的

(D) physique n. 体格

(E) wit n. (1) 风趣 (2) 心智

2. From the description of how Mrs. Penniman came to live in her brother's home (lines 1-14), we may infer all of the following EXCEPT that
(A) she readily became dependent on her brother
(B) she was married at the age of 23
(C) she was physically delicate and in ill health
(D) she had not found living in Poughkeepise particularly gratifying
(E) she occasionally echoed an ornate manner of speech

【解析】C

(A) do sth. readily 欣然做某事 dependent on sb. 依靠某人，形容词短语。见第一段[2]分析。

(B) 33 岁守寡，那时已经在小镇度过了十年的婚姻生活。33-10=23 岁结婚。

(C) physically delicate：身体虚弱的。adv.+adj.通常表示从某方面来讲怎样的。This book is historically inaccurate. 这本书从历史角度讲不准确。注意副词才能修饰形容词。

delicate adj. (1) 娇弱的，纤细的；易碎的，脆弱的 (2) 微妙的，有技巧的，得当的

(D) gratify vt. 使高兴；使满意 find sth./sb. gratifying：认为某人/事令人愉快。Penniman 太太欣然接受弟弟邀请她居住下来，说明她对乡下的生活没有太多留恋。

(E) 见第一段[1]分析。ornate adj. 装饰华丽的 be ornate with sth. 以什么来装饰。

3. The word "asylum" means
(A) institution
(B) sanitarium

198

(C) refuge

(D) sanction

(E) shambles

【解析】C

sanction n. (1) 批准，认可 (2) 约束力 sanction against sth. (3) vt. 批准；认可

shambles n. 混乱；杂乱 My room is a shambles. 我房间里乱七八糟。

毁坏（景象）；废墟 The earthquake reduced the city to a shambles.

4. In the passage the Doctor is portrayed most specifically as

(A) benevolent and retiring

(B) casual and easy-going

(C) sadly ineffectual

(D) civil but imperious

(E) habitually irate

【解析】D

benevolent adj. 好心肠的；与人为善的

retiring adj. (1) 即将退休的 (2) 过隐居生活的，孤僻的；害羞的

ineffectual adj. 不起作用的 He won't be able to deal with the situation; he's too ineffectual. 他无法应付局面，他太无能了

选项中的意思是"无能的"。

imperious adj. 专横的，飞扬跋扈的

habitual adj. 习惯的，惯常的

(B) 随和的，平易近人的。文章没表现他平易近人。这点从他从不许诺姐姐永久住下来可以看出。

5. It can be inferred that the Doctor views children primarily as

(A) a source of joy and comfort in old age

(B) innocent suffers for the sins of their fathers

(C) clay to be molded into an acceptable image

(D) the chief objective of the married state

(E) their parents' sole chance for immortality

【答案】C

# 文章 35

## 文章 35.1

Being funny has no place in the workplace and can easily wreak havoc on an otherwise blossoming career.[1] Of course, laughter is necessary in life.[2] But if you crack jokes and make snide remarks at work, you will eventually not be taken seriously by others.[3] You will be seen as someone who wastes time that could better be spent discussing a project or an issue.[4] Additionally, many corporate-minded individuals do not have the time to analyze comments with hidden meanings—they will take what you say as absolute and as an accurate representation of your professionalism in the workplace.[5]

【单词及搭配】

1. workplace 车间，工作场所

2. wreak

(1) vt. 大量造成（破坏、伤害）wreak havoc on sb./sth. 对某人/物造成破坏

(2) vt. 施行（报复）wreak revenge on sb.

【重要句型】Sth. wreaks havoc on sth.=Sth. damages sth. 某物破坏了某物。

3. otherwise adv. 不是那样；另外情况下

I would that it were otherwise. 我宁愿事情不是那样的。

otherwise：in an another aspect

blossoming：开花的，蓬勃发展的。直译：从另外一个方面来看蓬勃发展的事业。暗含的意思是：如果不是这样一种破坏的产生，还算得上一项蓬勃发展的事业。

a blossoming career 形容事业飞黄腾达，a rapidly progressing career，中译为"事业（美丽）如花" = 事业兴旺，无缺点的职业 = a spotless career, a career without any setbacks

【重要句型】

(1) Failure of the experiment cast a shadow on the otherwise highly-anticipated project. 试验的失败给这个人们高度期待的工程带来了一层阴影。

(2) The scandal cast a shadow on his otherwise blossoming career. 这件丑闻给他的（兴旺）事业投上了一层阴影。

4. blossom vi. 成熟，繁荣，发展

boom vi. (1) 激增, 猛涨, 兴隆 Sth. is booming. 某物猛增/某项工作日趋繁荣。

Sth. is booming as+名词。作为XXX，某物/某人日益成功。

【重要句型】The conference is booming as a counterbalance to deficiency in natural resources. 作为抗衡自然资源短缺的方法，该会议日趋成功。

(2) n.（营业等的）激增，（经济等的）繁荣，迅速发展

soar (1) vi. 高飞，翱翔 (2) vi. 猛增 soar to +数量：猛增到 XXX (3) vi. 高耸，屹立

5. crack (1) vi./vt.（使）开裂；（使）破裂 (2) vi. He cracked into a smile. 他咧嘴而笑。

(3) vi. 大笑

6. corporate-minded：有团队意识的，复合形容词

7. snide adj. 讽刺的，挖苦的；嘲弄的；贬低的；低劣的；卑鄙的；假的，伪造的

8. professionalism n. 职业特征，职业行为，专业技巧；专业人员的特质

9. issue (1) n. 问题，议题，争论点 (2) n. 发行物 (3) n. 放出，流出 (4) n. 发出，发行 (5) vt. 出版，发行 (6) vt. 发表，发布 issue a call 发出号召 (7) vt. 分配，发给 issue loans 分配贷款 (8) vi. 冒出，流出；传出 Sounds issued from +名词，某地传出什么声音。 (9)（由……）产生（常与 from 连用）；导致，造成（常与 in 连用）issue from=originate from; issue in sth.=lead to sth. (10) n. 结果

【重要句型】carry a plan/scheme to a successful issue：成功地完成方案/计划；该短语等价于 complete/carry out the plan successfully。

10. additional adj. 增加的，额外的，另外的 additionally adv. 加之，又 besides adv. 而且，还有

## 【文章精读】

[1] wreak vt. damage sth. 他们消极的回应对我们的计划造成了破坏。

Their negative reactions wreaked havoc on our plans.

easily=readily, do sth. readily 很容易地做成某事

主语+谓语 XXX otherwise+adj. 名词.

(1) His pride/arrogance wreaked havoc on his otherwise reputational achievements. 他的傲慢对他原本很有威望的事业构成了破坏。

(2) Failure in experiments cast a shadow on the otherwise highly-anticipated project. 实验的失败对人们高度期待的工程投下了一层阴影。

(3) Drought has worsen the otherwise gradually-improving environment. 干旱使原本逐渐改善的环境变得恶化。

National economics boom in domestic trade. 国家经济在对内贸易方面很繁荣。

comment 指代 jokes 或 snide remarks。

本句开门见山指出作者观点：幽默会毁坏一项蓬勃发展的事业。即作者对在工作中幽默持否定态度。

[3] 指出在工作中开玩笑带来的后果。

take sth. seriously：严肃地对待某物。别人不会严肃地对待开玩笑的人，take 在这里指"对待"。

[4] who wastes time 为定语从句，修饰 someone；that could better be spent discussing a project or an issue 为定语从句，修饰 time。本句为从句套从句。

你会被视为浪费时间的人，而这些时间可以更好地用于讨论问题。

[5] additionally=besides；comments 在这里指"snide remarks"，comments with hidden meanings：具有隐含含义的语言（玩笑）。

take sth. as sth.：把某物视作什么。"what you say"为名词性从句作 take 的宾语；what 不能替换为 that，因为该从句缺少宾语成分：you say what。从句中不缺少成分时可以用 that 引导，缺少成分时不能用 that 引导。举例：

(1) What he said surprised me. 他说的话使我吃惊。

(2) That he said rude remarks surprised me. 他说粗话这件事使我吃惊。

## 文章 35.2

Are we now compelled, as a culture, to be comical, no matter the setting or the endeavor?[1] And if so, what on earth gave rise to this troubling idea?[2] One possible culprit may be corporate America, where being funny is now seen as a valuable asset.[3] Fortune 500 companies actually dole out big fees to comedy consultants who offer humor seminars and improvisational workshops—all in the name of improved productivity.[4] But how exactly are funnier employees better for business?[5] According to Tim Washer, a former improvisional performer who is now a communications executive at a large corporation, humor helps foster team building and, of course, "thinking outside the box."[6]

批注 [A343]: 表明作者否定该观点

批注 [344]: 研讨会

批注 [345]: 讨论会，与 seminar 同义。另外一个意思为"车间"。

批注 [346]: do sth. in the name of sth./doing 以什么样的名义做什么

### 【单词及搭配】

1. compel (1) vt. 强迫 compel sb. to do sth.（文中意思）(2) vt. 引起，导致 compel attention 引人注目 Sth. compels attention of the public.

2. setting n. (1) 环境（文中意思）(2)（某事、戏剧、小说等的）背景

3. culprit n. (1) 罪犯，犯人；导致过错的人 (2) 导致问题的原因，产生不良后果的事物（文中意思）

Low-level ozone pollution is the real culprit. 低层臭氧污染是真正的根源。

【重要句型】Sth. is the real culprit of sth. 某物（前面）是某物（后面）的罪魁祸首（根源）。

Absorption of too much salt poses a culprit on heart diseases. 盐分的大量摄入是心脏病的诱因。

4．dole out 少量地发放（食物、救济金等）

5. improvisational adj. 即兴的

6. foster (1) vt. 培养，促进 (2) vt. & vi. 收养，养育

7. asset n. (1) 有价值的人或物；优点，长处（文中意思）(2) 资产，财产

### 【文章精读】

[1] 作者提出疑问：我们是否被强制的具有幽默感？不论某人所处的环境如何或正在努力做什么。as a culture：幽默已经成为一种文化。

Deficiency in water compels attention of publicity. 缺水问题引发全社会的关注。

[2] give rise to sth./doing=lead to sth. 导致某事。"this troubling idea"指"to be comic wherever poosible"。由此可见，作者对时刻保持幽默这个观点持反对态度。下文必然分析这种观点形成的原因。

[3] 指出导致该观点的诱因：corporate America。where 修饰 in America。culprit 指某事的罪魁祸首。导致这个观点的原因是具有团队意识的美国，在美国幽默被视为一种宝贵的优点。

[4] 举例说明美国人如何努力培养员工的幽默感。do sth. in the name of sth.：在某物的名义下做某事。

[5] 作者对[4]中的做法提出质疑。具有幽默感的人在业务上具有多大优势呢？

本句另一种表达方式：How exactly do funnier employees outdo in business?

do sth. better than sth.=outdo sb./sth. in XXX 在某方面比某人做得好

[6] 幽默的意义：跳出框架思考问题。

## 【题目解析】

1. "But if … workplace" serve primarily to

(A) provide a creative solution to an ongoing problem

(B) mock a particular way of behaving

(C) outline the consequences of particular actions

(D) suggest a more tolerant approach

(E) criticize a common practice

【答案】C

【详解】(A) ongoing adj. 继续进行的；不断前进/发展中的 ongoing national tensions：持续的国际局势的紧张。ongoing work：正在做的工作

【重要句型】Sth. is ongoing.

第四代移动通信是一个尚在发展中的技术。4G is an ongoing technology.

(B) mock (1) vt. 嘲笑，讥笑；嘲弄（题干意思） (2) vt. 使显得徒劳，使显得可笑 Arguments and friction mock our pretence at peace. 争吵和摩擦使我们想佯装平安无事变得徒劳可笑。

【重要句型】Sth. mocks sth. 某物使某物变得徒劳。

(C) 指出开玩笑在工作中造成的恶劣后果。

outline (1) n. 提纲，要点，概要 (2) n. 外形，轮廓，略图 (3) vt. 画/标出……的轮廓 (4) vt. 概述，列提纲 outline sth.

(D) tolerant adj. (1) 容忍的，宽容的 (2) 能耐的，耐（受）性的

(E) practice 惯常做法，惯例；习俗

2. In passage 2, the author's attitude toward the value of comedy consultants is best described as

(A) fascination

(B) approval

(C) ambivalence

(D) skepticism

(E) hostility

【答案】D

fascination n. 着迷，入迷

approval n. 批准，同意，认可

ambivalence n. 矛盾情绪；矛盾心理

3. Tim Washer would most likely respond to the author of passage 1 by

(A) auging that humorous employees can help to create a more productive work environment

(B) suggesting that corporate executives spend more time analyzing humorous comments

(C) agreeing that humor can harm the careers of ambitious corporate employees

(D) challenging the assertion that laughter is necessary in life

(E) disagreeing that humor occurs regularly in the workplace

【答案】A

题干：Tim Washer 会如何回应文章 1 的作者？

(A) 很显然，Tim 认为幽默使工作有效率。从文章[2] improved productivity 可看出。

(B) Tim 没有这个意图。

(C) 与文意相反。

(D) 与文意相反。challenge sb./sth. 动词短语，质疑某人/某物。

(E) Tim 认为工作中应有幽默感以提高生产效率。本句意思与文意相反。

4. Both authors would agree with which of the following statements?

(A) Workplace culture has gradually changed over time.

(B) Consultants can help employees learn how to succeed professionally.

(C) Humorous employees are usually popular.

(D) Humor is not appropriate at all situations.

(E) Humor is not valued by corporate executives.

【答案】D

(A) 工作文化在逐渐改变，文章 2 第一句表达了这个含义：现在我们被强迫去幽默，言外之意，曾经不这样。可文章 1 没提到这个问题。

(B) succeed professionally：在事业方面获得成功。类似用法：The book is incredible historically. 这本书从历史角度上不可信。

作者 1 没提到此观点；作者 2 提到了"顾问以提高工作效率为名义培养员工的幽默感"，但作者 2 对此现象持怀疑态度。

(C) 文章 1 作者意图与此相反。

(D) 正确。作者 2 对幽默怀疑态度，他认为幽默并非何时何地都适用。

(E) 与文章 1 意思相同，与文章 2 意思相反。

# 文章 36

## 文章 36.1

American writers Henry Adams (1838-1918) and Samuel Clemens (1835-1910) gradually approached, during their careers, a mood of total despair.[1] Personal tragedies have been set forth to explain this development: the deaths of loved ones, the humiliation of family bankruptcies.[2] These certainly are contributory causes, but the writings of Adams and Clemens reveal that the despair is in a slow process of incubation from their earliest work, and that it is finally hatched by the growing political discords, moral conflicts, and economic problems of their age.[3] It is not despair of personal bereavement but of country—and ultimately of humanity—that manifests itself in their works.[4]

### 【单词及搭配】

1. approach
(1) vt./vi. 接近，靠近
(2) vt. 接近，临近（未来时刻、未来事件）
He was approaching retirement. 他快退休了。
(3) 数量（或质量）上接近（某一数字、某种水平、某个标准）
(4) 名词，处理事情的方法 an approach to sth./doing sth.
(5) 名词，接近，相似，近似 do sth. with approach to accuracy 某事做得丝毫不差

2. mood
(1) 名词，心境；心情，情绪；精神状态 (2)（艺术作品）基调，色调；气氛（文中意思）

3. set forth
(1) 起程，出发 (2) 提出 propose （文中意思）set forth sth. (3) 展示，陈列

4. humiliation n. 丢脸；羞辱；耻辱；蒙羞

5. bankruptcy 名词，破产，掌握其他形式：
bankrupt adj. go bankrupt 破产
彻底缺乏（某种好品质或价值）的 adv.+ bankrupt：某方面缺失的，比如：morally bankrupt 无道德价值。
vt. 使（人、机构）破产 bankrupt sth.：使……破产

6. contributory adj.
(1) 起促成作用的，有助于……的 a contributory cause of sth. 导致某物的原因

(2)（养老金、保险金制度）捐助的 contributory benefits 抚恤金

7. slow process 慢过程

8. incubation 名词，孵化；培养；潜伏；酝酿

9. hatch vt. 策划

10. discord

(1) 名词，不和，争论 (2) 名词，不一致，不协调 (3) vi.（事物）不同；不协调 discord with sth.

11. conflict

(1) 名词，（尤指持久的）意见不一；争论 (2) vi. 相左；冲突，抵触

12. bereave v.（死亡）使丧失亲友

13. despair

(1) 名词，绝望；无望。In despair, 主句。绝望中，XXX。In despair 作状语。

(2) vt. despair of 对某事绝望

## 【文章精读】

[1] during their careers 为介词短语作时间状语，approached 为谓语，及物动词，表示"接近"，a mood of total despair: 一种完全绝望的基调，mood 在这里指艺术作品基调。

[2] set forth 文中指"提出"，可以用 posed 过去分词代替。本句解释两人作品基调悲哀的原因。

[重要句型] 主语+be posed to do sth. 某事被提出来用来做什么。of their age 指代他们的生存年代。

[3] 解释作品基调悲观的根本原因！失去亲人只是连带因素。contributory causes：连带原因。 a slow process of incubation：一个缓慢的培养酝酿过程。it is finally hatched by the growing political discords, moral conflicts, and economic problems of their age.

[4] 那并不是对失去亲人的绝望，而是对国家，最终对人类的绝望，这在小说中进行了说明。itself 指代 despair of country and humanity。but, 而是，not...but，不是……而是。

## 文章 36.2

The bankruptcy of Samuel Clemens, the death of his daughter, and the chronic illness of his wife are agonizing as personal history. Our interest, however, is in the works that came out of these disasters. Literary critics are usually unable to say how an author's experience is transformed into art. In Clements' writings from 1895 onward, however, we can watch while he repeatedly tries and fails to make something of these experiences that were so vitally important to him—and finally we can see him fuse and transform them into a culminating work of art, the book (published posthumously) that we know as *The Mysterious Stranger*.

## 【单词及搭配】

1. chronic adj.

(1)（疾病）长期的；经常复发的；慢性的。急性的：acute (2)（问题）长期难以根除

的，顽固的

2. agonize vt. 感到极其痛苦，受折磨 agonize over the problem

3. onward adv. (1) 向前 (2) 从……以后

4. vital

(1) adj. 必不可少的；必要的 be of vital importance 极其重要

(2) adj. 维持生命所必需的 the vital resources

5. fuse vt. 合并，使融为一体

6. culminating adj. 到绝顶的，终极的，最后的。须掌握动词形式：culminate

(1) vi./vt. 到达顶点

句型：Sth. culminated sth. 某物将某物推向顶峰。This conference culminated the 3G technology.

7. posthumous adj. 死后的，身后的；死后出版的

# 文章 37

In self-consciously writing for a white, northern, middle-class audience, Harrite Jacobs did not differentiate herself from the most celebrated male authors of slave narratives.[1] Frederick Douglass, for example, firmly identified himself with the triumph of manliness and individualism that slavery suppressed.[2] In so doing, he explicitly called upon his northern readers to recognize that the sufferings and inequities to which he had been subjected by the very condition of enslavement directly contravened their deepest principles of individualism.[3] Harriet Jacobs faced a more difficult task.[4] For her, a woman, to claim that enslavement violated the principles of individualism would be to risk having her story dismissed.[5] A few northern white women were beginning to work out the analogy between slavery and the oppression of women, but their view had not won general sympathy.[6] Inequalities between women and men still appeared to many northerners, even those who opposed slavery, as manifestations of natural differences.[7] Northern women who sought improvement in their own condition clung to the discourses of true womanhood and domesticity to make their case.[8] Northern gender conventions differed from southern ones, but they, too, dictated that a woman should address the public modestly and deferentially, if at all.[9] A poignant account of the violation of a woman's virtue stood a much better chance of appealing to northern sensibilities than a pronouncement for woman's individual rights, if only because such an account reaffirmed woman's essentially domestic nature.[10] Perhaps Jocobs would have written differently had she been able to write for an audience of slave women, but few slave women could read, and she could not, in any case, have reached them.[11] Her only hope for a hearing lay in reaching the same people who avidly read Harriet Beecher Stowe.[12] Jacobs left no doubt about her intended readers: "O, you happy free women, contrast your New Year's day with that of the poor bond women!"[13]

## 【单词及搭配】

1. self-conscious adj. 不自然的，忸怩的，害羞的

2. differentiate vt. & vi. 区分，区别，辨别 differentiate A from B。同义单词：discriminate (1) vt. & vi. 分别，辨别，区分（文中意思）(2) vi. 歧视，有差别地对待 discriminate against sb. 歧视某人。

distinguish (1) vt. & vi. 辨别，区别（文中意思）(2) vt. 显扬自己，使自己扬名 Sth. distinguished sb. 某事使某人有名。

distinguished adj. 卓越的；著名的；受人尊敬的

3. narrative n. 记叙文；故事

4. identify (1) vt. 认出，识别 (2) vt. & vi. 使支持；使参与，使关系密切（常与with 连

用）

　　identify with （1）认为……等同于。我们不能将无线通信和移动通信混为一谈。We shouldn't identify wireless communications with mobile communications.（文中意思）
　　（2）觉得与……有联系
People will identify with cellular phones at the mention of mobile communications.
　　（3）同情（某人）；和……有同感
　5. triumph (1) n. 胜利, 成功（文中意思） (2) vi. 获胜, 得胜；克服 triumphant adj. (1) 胜利的, 成功的 (2)（因胜利而）喜气洋洋的, 欢欣鼓舞的
　6. slavery n. 奴隶身份, 奴隶制度
　7. manliness n. 刚毅
　8. suppress (1) vt. 压制；镇压 (2) vt. 禁止发表, 查禁；隐瞒 (3) vt. 抑制（感情等），忍住（文中意思） (4) vt. 阻止……的生长（或发展）相当于 hinder。
　9. explicit adj. (1) 详述的, 明确的, 明晰的 (2) 直言的, 毫不隐瞒的, 露骨的（文中意思）outspoken adj.（同义词）直言的；坦率的。如: What he did was an explicit slight on me. 他所做的事是对我的公然蔑视。
　10. call upon 号召, 要求 call upon sb. to do sth.
　12. recognize (1) vt. 认出 (2) vt. 承认……有效/属实；认可
The medicine is widely/prevalently recognized to be efficient in relieving pains of patients. 人们公认, 这种药对减轻病人痛苦是有效果的。
　　（3）vt. 承认/认清（某事物）；认识到（文中意思）
　11. subject (1) adj. 须服从……的；受……支配的 be subject to sth./doing (2) vt. 使服从, 征服, 制伏（文中意思）
　12. enslave vt. 使成为奴隶；奴役
　13. contravene vt. 取消, 违反。需要掌握名词形式：contravention n. 违犯, 违背；抵触
　14. dismiss (1) vt. 解雇, 撤职；开除 (2) vt. 使退去；解散 (3) vt. 自心中摒除, 不再考虑或谈论 dismiss sth. as sth. 将某物视为什么不予考虑 dismiss sb./sth. as+adj. 将某物视为什么而拒绝（文中意思）
　15. risk (1) n. 危险（性）, 风险 (2) vt. 冒险；冒……险（文中意思）risk doing
　16. analogy n. 类似, 相似
　17. oppress vt. (1) 使烦恼 (2) 压迫, 压制（文中意思）
　18. manifest (1) vt. 清楚表示；显露 (2) adj. 明白的, 明显的
　19. seek (1) vt. & vi. 寻找；探寻 (2) vi. 企图；试图 seek to do sth.（文中意思）
　20. cling (1) vi. 附着于 (2) vi. 坚持 cling to sth. 坚持做某事
　21. discourse (1) n. 论文；演说；讲道（文中意思） (2) vi. 讲述, 著述 discourse on sth.
　22. womanhood n. 女子成年期；女子特征, 女子气质
　23. domesticity n. 家庭生活
　24. formulate (1) vt. 构想出, 规划（题干意思） (2) vt. 确切地阐述 formulate one's idea 确切地阐述某人的观点
　24. differ (1) vi. 不同, 有异 (2) vi. 持异议 differ about sth. 对某物持不同观点
　25. dictate vt. 指示；指定；指令
　26. deferential adj. 恭敬的。还需掌握动词形式：defer (1) vt. 拖延, 延缓, 推迟 defer

sth. for+时间 将某事推迟多久 (2) vi. 服从某人的意愿,遵从 defer to sth.

27. poignant adj. 伤心至极的；辛酸的，痛切的；令人心碎的，深深打动人的；强烈的，深刻的

28. virtue 名词，美德

29. appeal (1) n. 呼吁, 恳求 the appeal for sth. 名词短语,恳求什么 (2) 名词,感染力,吸引力 Sth. has appeal for sb. 某物对某人有吸引力。(3) vi. 呼吁 appeal for sth. 呼吁某物 (4) vi. 有吸引力 Sth. appeals to sb. 某物对某人有吸引力。

还须掌握形容词：appealing adj. 有魅力的；动人的；吸引人的 sth. appealing to sb. 吸引某人的某物。

Sth. appeals to sb.=Sth is appealing to sb.

30. sensibility n. (1) 感觉 sensibility to sth. (2) 敏感，善感 sensibitlity to sth. (3) 感情（文中意思）

31. pronounce vt. 宣布；宣称

32. account (1) n. 账，账户 (2) n. 记述，描述，报道（文中意思）an exhaustive account of sth. 对某物的详尽说明 (3) vi. 解释；说明 account for sth. 说明某事 account to sb. for sth. 向某人说明某事 (4) vt.认为 accont sb. as sth. 认为某人怎样 account it+adj. to do sth.认为某事怎样 (5) vi. account for+百分比，占多少百分比 (6) vi. 为……负责；导致，引起 His carelessness acconted for the accident. 他的粗心大意导致了事故的发生。

33. address vt. 向……讲话

34. reaffirm vt. 重申；再确认

affirm vt. & vi. 断言；证实 affirm to sth. 证明什么 affirm that+宾语从句

35. violate (1) vt. 违反，违背 violate the regulation 违反法规 (2) vt. 侵犯,妨碍（文中意思）violate one's sleep 妨碍某人睡眠。a sleep-violated driver：睡眠被妨碍的司机,即没睡好觉的司机。

36. principles of individualism 人权

## 【文章精读】

[1] Harriet Jacobs 并没有将她和最著名的奴隶故事男性作者区分开来,即 Harriet Jacobs 认为自己和最著名的男性作家地位同等。

differentiate A from B：将 A 和 B 区别对待

[2] slavery suppressed: 定语从句,修饰 triumph。例如，佛雷德瑞克·道格拉斯坚定地将自己标榜为刚毅和个人主义的胜利，而这些恰恰是被奴隶制所压迫的。

[3] call upon sb. to do sth.：号召某人做某事。which 指代 sufferings and inequities（苦难和不平等）。

主语为 he,谓语是 called,"that the sufferings and inequities to which he had been subjected by the very condition of enslavement directly contravened their deepest principles of individualism"为宾语从句，作 recognize 的宾语。contravned 为宾语从句的谓语。他直白地号召读者认识到由奴役环境的控制对他的苦难和不平等直接抹杀了个人主义的原则。

从语境分析,self-conscious 与 explict 成反义词。女性作家在写奴隶故事时是"害羞的"，而男性作家写同类故事是"直白的"。以此对比男女在关于奴隶泯灭人性问题上的"inequality"。

[4] 指出女性作者面临的困难。

Somebody faced sth.=Somebody be confronted with sth. 某人面临什么。

[5] "To claim that enslavement violated the principles of individualism"为不定式作主语，"that enslavement violated the principles of individualism"为 claim 的宾语从句，would be 为谓语。指出女性作家面临的艰难，如果女性作家宣称奴役会阻碍人权的话，那么她的作品就会被人抛弃。

[6] 指出一小部分白人女性面对女性以及奴役压制人性的现象进行思考，而现实情况是：这些女性的观点不能得到普遍的认可。

[7] 指出北方人的流行观点：男性和女性间的不平等即使在那些反对奴隶化的人看来，仅仅解释为自然的差异。即他们不认同奴化抹杀了女性人权这一观点。

Sth. appears to sb. as+形容词：某物在某人看来是 XXX 的。

The idea appeared to us as original. 我们认为这一观点是新颖的。

"who opposed slavery"为定语从句，修饰 those。

[8] 大部分北方女性通过寻求家庭主妇一类的读物来寻求自身境遇的提升。这是大部分北方女性的观点。

"who sought improvement in their own condition"为定语从句，修饰 women；clung 为谓语。

[9] they 指代 southern conventions（南方习俗）。北方和南方对性别传统虽存在差异，但南方的性别传统同样认为女性在公众面前应表现得温婉恭敬。

[10] 一篇令人伤心的阐述阻碍女性优点的文章比起宣扬女性人权的文章对北方人的情感来讲更具吸引力，如果仅仅因为这样的阐述能够再次确认女性的家庭属性。

such an account 指代阐述阻碍女性优点的文章。

[11] 虚拟语气倒装形式。如果 Harriet Jacobs 能接触到女性奴隶的话，她写的内容可能会与现在不同。但是现实是：她接触不到那些女性奴隶，而且那些女性奴隶不识字。

[12] lie in sth.：在于什么。动词短语。指出 Harriet Jacobs 的唯一希望——希望接触到那些迫不及待地读她作品的读者。

[13] leave sth. about sb.：为某人留下什么。Harriet Jacobs 并没有为她的预期读者留下什么疑问，即很直白地在书中表达这样的情感：你们这些幸福的自由女性，将你们在纽约的生活与那些可怜的被束缚的妇女做个对比吧！bond 在这里为过去分词作形容词，被束缚的。

Jacobs shaped her presentation of herself to conform, at least in part, to the expectations of her intended readers.[1] Like Douglass, who invoked the rhetoric of male individualism to encourage identification with his narrative, she had to make her reader take the oppression of slave women personally, to see it as a threat to their own sense of themselves as women.[2] To touch their hearts, she had to address them in their own idiom, tell her story in a way with which they could identify.[3] For her readers to accept her as a woman, she had to present herself as a woman like them.[4] She exposed slavery as a violation of the norms of womanhood and portrayed slave women as essentially like their northern White sisters in their goals and sensibilities.[5] Slavery, in this portrayal, constituted a crime against woman's essential nature—her yearning for virtue, domesticity, and motherhood.[6] Jacobs followed Douglass in accepting the norms of society as absolutes—the articulations of innate human nature—which

批注 [355]: 指代 intended readers

were directly contradicted by slavery.[7]

## 【单词及搭配】

1. shape vt. 表达出 to shape a statement 发表声明
2. presentation n. (1) 提供，显示 the presentation of sth. 出示某物 (2) 外观 the presentation of sth. 某物的外观 (3) 报告
3. conform vi. 遵守，符合 conform to sth. 遵守某物 (2) vi. 顺应, 一致
   Sth. conforms with sth. 某物与某物相互一致。
4. intend vt. 意欲, 打算
5. invoke vt. 援引, 援用；行使（权利等）
6. rhetoric n. 雄辩言辞, 虚夸的言辞
7. identification n. (1) 鉴定, 验明, 认出 (2) 身份证明 (3) 认同 the identification with sth. 对某物的认同
8. personal adj. 个人的；私人的
9. threat n. 可能造成威胁的人（事、想法）a threat to sb./sth. 对某人/某物构成的威胁
10. sense n. 意义，意思
11. encourage vt. 促进, 助长, 激发
12. norm n. 标准, 规范
13. yearn vi. 渴望, 切盼, 向往 yearn for sth. 渴望某物
14. constitute vt. (1) 构成, 组成（文中意思）(2) 建立, 制定 (3) 选定, 任命
15. articulate (1) adj. 表达能力强的 (2) vt. & vi. 清楚地表达（文中意思）
16. contradict (1) vt. & vi. 反驳, 否认……的真实性 (2) vt. 与……发生矛盾
17. innate adj. 天生的, 固有的

## 【文章精读】

[1] 本段解释 Jacobs 如何通过塑造作品来触及到相应的读者。to conform 为不定式作目的状语，shape 为谓语，即"塑造"，或用 render 来取代。presentation 为名词，展现。presentation of herself 为名词短语，对她自身的展现。intended 为过去分词作形容词，目标的，预期的。

Jacobs 依照预期读者的期待来在作品中展现自己。

[2] 解释 Jacobs 接触读者的具体做法。正如 Douglass 引入了男性个人主义的修辞方式来使他的作品得到认同，Jacobs 必须使读者站在个人角度看待奴隶制对女性的压迫，从而将奴隶制看作对女性自身意义的威胁。take something personally: 站在个人角度看待某物。"it"指代 oppression。

[3] their 指 intended readers'。address vt. 陈述。they 指代 readers。Jacobs 为了使其作品触及到读者的内心，依照读者的语言习惯来陈述观点，以一种读者能够认同的方式去叙述故事。which 指代 the way。indentify with sth.: 认同某物。句子拆分:
(1) Jacobs told her story in a way.
(2) Readers could identify with the way.

[4] for 表示目的, 为了。for sb. to do sth.: 为了某人能够做某事, 介词短语作状语。present 为 vt., 向某人展现。them 指代上一句的女性读者。为了让读者以一名女性来接受自己，

Jacobs 必须向读者展现自己是和读者一样的女性。

[5] expsose 这里表示"揭露，揭示"，及物动词，与 display 同义。portray sb. as+名词，将某人描述得如同……一样；like 在这里为介词，相似，相当于 resembling，like in sth./resembling in sth.：在某方面相似。

[6] 指出奴隶制对女性根本特质的犯罪。yearning 为动名词，作 essential nature 的同位语，动名词由形容词性物主代词 her 修饰！奴隶制度违背了女性的人权，即女性渴望的美德、家庭生活以及做母亲的权利。

[7] absolutes，文中为名词，绝对真理，可数名词。

## 【题目解析】

1. The primary purpose of the passage is to

   (A) probe the emotional world of a famous author

   (B) present a comprehensive history of a particular period

   (C) denounce the injustice of slavery

   (D) explore the narrative choices of a writer

   (E) argue in favor of a particular style of writing

【解析】D

(A) probe (1) n. 探索，调查 the probe into sth. 对某事的探究 (2) vt. 盘问；追问；探究 探究作者的感情世界，本文没提到感情经历。

(B) comprehensive adj. (1) 广泛的，综合的（选项意思）(2) 领悟的；有理解力的，能充分理解的
展现某一时期的历史，文中没有提到历史。

(C) 文章提到奴隶制的不公正，但这不是文章的主旨。

(D) 探寻作家叙事的选择，即作者的文章为谁而写、写些什么。文章第二段第一句提到作家迎合 intended readers，即 narrative choices。文章第一段"Perhaps Jocobs would have written differently had she been able to write for an audience of slave women"，Jocobs 想为女性奴隶写书。这是本文的主线，正确。

(E) in favor of 赞成……；支持……；有利于…… argue in favor of sth.：支持某事
选项意思为赞成某一种写作风格，文章没提到写作风格。

2. Frederick Douglass' rhetorical strategy as described in sentences [2] and [3] might best be summarized as

   (A) identification with a concept followed by partial rejection

   (B) recognition of a group's wrongdoing followed by explicit steps to correct it

   (C) elaboration on an unfamiliar argument followed by unusual qualifications

   (D) evocation of a revered concept followed by a specific reference to its undermining

   (E) analysis of a particular event followed by a subjective plea

【解析】D

(D) evocation n. 唤起。revered adj. 被人尊敬的。followed by 为过去分词短语作定语，修饰 concept，由某事跟随的。reference 这里为名词，提到。its 指代 a revered concept。先唤起一个被人们敬仰的概念——manliness and individualism，这是[2]提到的；再讲这种人

性被奴隶制所压迫，即 undermined，这是[3]提到的。concept 指文中的 manliness and individualism。undermining 为动名词，由物主代词 its 修饰。

(A) 部分的否定，关于人权的概念没有被道格拉斯否定。

(B) wrongdoing n. 坏事，对一系列坏事的识别，紧接着阐述了如何纠正这些坏事。错误。

(C) unfamiliar 不对，文章也没提到 qualifications（资质）。

(E) 道格拉斯没提主观请求。plea 的感情色彩也不对。道格拉斯对奴隶制是批判的，谈不上"请求"。

3. "work out" most nearly means

(A) exercise

(B) conciliate

(C) struggle for

(D) formulate

(E) solve

【解析】D

见第一段[6]。

(A) exercise vt. 执行

(B) conciliate (1) vt. 使（某人）息怒或友好；安抚，劝慰 (2) vt. & vi.（使）意见一致；调节

conciliator n. 安抚者，劝慰者

formulate vt. (1) 构想出，规划（选项意思） (2) 确切地阐述

work out 在文中指构思出一种想法。

# 文章 38

She set out from Poughkeepsie early this morning—a six-hour ride, but as they headed north, the snowstorm started, and the traffic slowed to a crawl. She kept checking her watch. There was time to spare. Her afternoon class visit was scheduled for four. The presentation itself wouldn't take place until evening.

【单词及短语】

1. head vi. 朝……行进  head for somewhere 朝哪里走

2. slow (1) adj. 迟钝的；不灵巧的 (2) adj.（生意等）清淡的 (3) adv. 慢慢地 (4) vt. & vi. 放缓  The policy slowed the inflation to a crawl. 政策放缓了通胀的速度。（文中意思）

3. crawl (1) vi. 爬，爬行；徐缓而行 (2) n. 缓慢的爬行（文中意思）

4. spare (1) vt. 节省，节约，舍不得  spare doing sth. 舍不得做某事 (2) vt. 抽出，让给，分出  spare time to do sth. 抽时间做某事（文中意思） (3) vt. 省去，免除  spare sb./sth. from doing sth. 使某人/某物免受什么 The doctor tried to spare him from pain. 还须掌握同义动词：

relieve vt. 缓解，消除，减少

The doctors did their best to relieve the patient. 医生们尽力减轻病人的痛苦。
We were relieved to hear that she was out of danger. 听说她脱险了，我们的心才放下来。
alleviate vt. 减轻，缓解，缓和  alleviate pain 减轻疼痛

(4) vt. 饶恕，赦免，不伤害 (5) adj. 多余的；备用的  spare parts 备用零件

5. schedule (1) vt. 排定，安排（文中意思） (2) n. 时间表，日程安排表

【文章精读】

[1] head north: 向北前进。指出道路的难走。

[2]－[5] 她不断地看手表，to spare 为不定式作定语，修饰 time。随后说明下午的采访安排在四点，报告本身直到晚上才会开始。表明她不断看手表的原因——要按时参加下午的采访。

The talk she has prepared is one she will be delivering countless times this year, the centennial of her mother's birth. It is academic, and uninspiring, and she knows it. Other scholars can talk about Salome's poetry and her pedagogy, but she, Camila, the only daughter, is supposed to shed a different light on the woman.

【单词及短语】

1. deliver (1) vt. & vi. 递送，交付 (2) vt. 发言（文中意思）deliver a speech (3) vt. 发动，

提出 deliver an attack。还须掌握名词形式：delivery n. (1) 投递 (2) 讲话方式，演讲风格

2. centennial n. 一百周年（纪念）

3. uninspiring adj. 引不起兴趣的；无鼓舞作用的；无指望的

4. shed light on sth. 为……提供线索，对……透露情况，使……清楚地显出

5. pedagogy n. 教育学，教学法

## 【文章精读】

[1] she has prepared 为定语从句，修饰 talk。she will be delivering countless times this year 为定语从句，修饰 one。one 指代 the talk。will be doing 为将来进行时，表示将来的某一段时间内一直持续在做的事情。

I will be doing research on CDMA in the future five years. 在未来五年，我将持续进行 CDMA 的研究。

[2] 第一个 it 指代 the talk，第二个 it 指代"It is academic, and uninspiring"这件事。

[3] she 是 Salome 唯一的女儿。由于她是 Salome 唯一的女儿，因此她在做报告时，可以谈到对 Salome 独到的个人见解，而那些学者只能谈论 Salome 的诗歌和教育方法。

## 【题目解析】

1. The character's actions ("She…watch") primarily convey her

(A) fear of traveling in the storms

(B) annoyance at having to make the trip

(C) concern about arriving on schedule

(D) eagerness to interact with her collegues

(E) excitement about delivering her speech

【解析】C。本句表明她担心不会准时到达目的地。

do sth. on schedule 准时做某事

2. The "light" referred to would most likely include

(A) bibliographic information

(B) direct literary citations

(C) historical analyses

(D) personal insights

(E) scholarly critiques

【解析】D

light 在这里指"个人看法，个人见地"。

## 文章 39

Summer 1995. School children collecting frogs from a pond in Minnesota discover one frog after another with deformities.[1] The story immediately seizes the attention of national media.[2] Is this an isolated occurrence or a widespread trend?[3] What is causing these deformities?[4]

**【单词及搭配】**

1. frog n. 蛙
2. deformity n. (1) 畸形状态 (2) 缺陷 deformities of style 文体上的瑕疵
还须掌握动词形式：deform vt. 使变形，使残废；丑化

**【文章精读】**

"collecting frogs from a pond" 为现在分词短语作定语，修饰 children。本段指出孩子们发现了畸形青蛙。然后提出问题，是什么导致了畸变的发生？是偶然独立事件还是普遍现象？

Malformations have since been reported in more than 60 species of amphibians in 46 states. Surprising number of deformed amphibians have also been found in Asia, Eruope, and Australia. Investigators have blamed the deformities on amphibians' increased exposure to ultraviolet radiation, the chemical contamination of water, even a parasite epidemic.[2] Every time another report appears, the media tout the new position, thus providing a misleading view. Most likely, all of these factors have been working in tandem.[4]

**【单词及搭配】**

1. amphibian (1) n. 两栖动物（文中意思）(2) n. 具有双重性格的人 (3) adj. 水陆两用的
2. exposure n. (1) 暴露，显露 the exposure to sth.（文章意思）(2) 揭发，揭露
3. ultraviolet adj.（光）紫外的
4. contaminate vt. 把……弄脏，污染
5. parasite n. (1) 寄生物（文章意思）(2) 靠他人为生的人
6. epidemic n. 流行病
7. malformation n. 难看，畸形

**【文章精读】**

[2] blame n1 on n2：动词短语，将 n1 归咎于 n2。注意名词短语并列的用法：increased exposure to ultraviolet radiation, the chemical contamination of water, even a parasite epidemic。

这种表达多次在改错中出现。连词 and 联接结构相同的成分显得句子整齐。thus 后可以接分词，分词的逻辑主语必须与句子主语一致。

She felt sick, thus deciding to stay at home. 她生病了，于是决定留在家里。

[4] these factors 指代过量的紫外线辐射、水的化学污染、寄生虫流行病。work in tandem: 以串联的方式工作，即畸形的发生是众多因素共同构成的结果，缺一不可。而媒体在每次报告后都会提出一个新的观点。其实不然，青蛙的畸变是多种因素共同作用的结果。由此看到作者对媒体是批判的。

## 【题目解析】

1. The opening paragraph primarily serves to

(A) highlight a phenomenon by dramatizing it

(B) advocate a particular course of action

(C) illustrate how a story can cause general panic

(D) compare a local situation to a national one

(E) demonstrate children's inherent interest in science

【解析】dramatize 动词，戏剧化，使夸张化。本段使用 dramatize 的用法体现在：一个接一个地，one after anther；提出问题，而不给出解释。这些都属于戏剧化的描述。目的是通过戏剧化的描述来强调一种现象——大量青蛙出现畸变。(A) 正确。

(B) 本段没有倡导一种特殊的行为，只是提出青蛙畸变的这种现象，进而讨论引发该现象的原因。

(C) panic，名词，惊慌。该现象并未引发惊慌。

(D) one 指代 situation。本段并未将当地局势与国际局势相比较。相反，第二段进行了这样的比较。

(E) 本文与孩子的兴趣无关。

2. The author's attitude toward the "media" might best be described as

(A) respectful

(B) indifferent

(C) ambivalent

(D) resentful

(E) critical

【解析】E

见文章分析，作者对媒体呈批判态度。

# 文章 40

We cannot fully appreciate some Native American objects we consider art without also appreaciating the contexts in which they are produced.[1] When our understanding of art is heavily focused on objects, we tend to look in the wrong place for art.[2] We find only the leavings or by-products of a creative process.[3]

【单词及搭配】

1. context n. 背景，环境（文中意思）；上下文，语境
2. tend (1) vt. 照料，照顾，伺候 (2) vi. 往，朝向 (3) vt. 易于；倾向 tend to do sth.（文中意思）
tendency n. 倾向，趋势 have the tendency to do sth. 有做某事的趋势
Prices continue to show an upward tendency. 物价呈继续上涨的趋势。
3. leavings n. 剩余，残渣
4. native adj. 出生地的，故乡的，本国的

【文章精读】

[1] which 指代 contexts。they 指代 Native American objects（本土美国对象）。如果不理解美国本土艺术产生的背景，我们就不能理解这种艺术。

do sth. in the context of: 在某种背景下做某事，context 在文中指"背景"。"they"指代本土美国对象。

本句可拆分为以下两个句子：

(1) We cannot fully appreciate some Native American objects we consider art without also appreaciating the context.

(2) Some Native American objects are produced in the context.

[2] 解释什么时候会犯错：注意力全部放在 objects（物质本身）时，我们会在错误的地方寻找艺术，即寻求艺术的方式是错误的。look in the wrong place for sth.: 在错误的地方寻找某物。

[3] 指出这样做的结果：找到的仅仅是具有创造性过程的残渣或副产品，即没有理解该创造性过程的实质。这里引申的意思是：本土美国物质是一种创造性过程，而非单纯的艺术。只有理解了这一点，才能理解本土美国物质。下文必定阐述这种本土美国物质的具体实例。

The concerns I have are deepened as I begin to compare how we, as outsiders, view sandpaintings with how the Navajo view them, even just from a physical perspective.[1] Let me list several points of comparison.[2] We have only representations of sandpaintings drawn or painted on paper or canvas, which we enjoy as objects of art.[3] The Navajo strictly forbid making representations of sandpaintings, and they are never kept as aesthetic objects.[4] Even the use of figures from sandpaintings in the sand-glue craft has not met with the approval of most Navajo traditionalists.[5] Sandpaintings must be destroyed by sundown on the day they are made.[6] They are not aesthetic objects; they are instruments of a ritual process.[7] The sandpainting rite is a rite of re-creation in which a person in need of healing is symbolically remade in a way corresponding to his or her ailment.[8] This person sits at the center of the very large painting and identifies with the images depicted, experiencing the complexity and the diversity, the dynamics and the tension, represented in the surrounding painting.[9] The illness is overcome when the person realized that these tensions and oppositions can ben balanced in a unity that signifies good health and beauty.[10]

## 【单词及搭配】

1. representation n. 表现……的事物，图画，雕塑
2. ailment n. 疾病（尤指慢性病），不适
3. identify with  (1) 认为……等同于 (2) 觉得与……有联系 (3) 和……有同感（文中意思）
4. signify vt. 表示……的意思，意味着
5. heal (1) vt. & vi.（使）愈合，治愈，（使）恢复健康（文中意思） (2) vt. 调停，消除
6. diversity n. (1) 多样化（文中意思）(2) 分歧
   diverge (1) vi. 分开；偏离；分歧；分道扬镳 (2) n. 分开；偏离；分歧；分道扬镳

## 【文章精读】

[1] 具体解释作者的担心，首先从身体角度来解释。主语为 concerns，"I have"为定语从句，修饰 concerns：我所有的担心。"are deepened"为谓语动词。as 表示"当……的时候"。how we…为 compare 的宾语从句，比较的内容是：我们如何看待沙画，Navajo 人如何看待沙画。言外之意，我们普通人与 Navajo 人看待沙画的方式截然不同，这点引起了作者的担忧，担心我们普通人并没有理解沙画的实质。

view sth./sb. from a perspective: 从某种角度来看待某人/某事。physical 有多个含义，从下文可以看到，在这里指"身体上的"。注意从语境中理解单词。deepen 这里为及物动词，加深。

The concerns are deepened as+从句。当某事发生的时候，某种担忧被加深。

[2] 举例说明不同点。

[3] drawn or painted 为过去分词作定语，修饰 representations of sandpaintings。

[4] they 指代 representations of sandpaintings。

[6]-[7] 举例说明这种沙画必须在制作的当天被毁掉，因为它不是一件艺术品，而是一个严肃的宗教仪式。

[8] The sandpainting rite is a rite of re-creation in which a person in need of healing is symbolically remade in a way corresponding to his or her ailment. 沙画的作用是以一种与身体不适相对应的方法对人进行重塑。进一步表明沙画的本质并非艺术品。

which 指代 rite，in need of healing 为介词短语作定语，修饰 person。corresponding to

[9] 本句表明沙画的作用方式。identifiy with 文中指"与……有共鸣",depicted 为分词作定语,修饰 images。experiencing 为现在分词短语作伴随状语。represented 为过去分词作定语,修饰 complexity 等几个名词。主语分词作伴随状语时其逻辑主语必须与句子主语一致。某个人坐在画的中间,并且与画中的形象产生共鸣,同时经历着周围的绘画中的复杂性、多样性、动态以及紧张。

[10] 疾病在某种条件下会被治好。这是沙画达到的最终目的。

In terms of visual perspective, we traditionally view sandpainting from a position as if we were directly above and at such a distance that the whole painting is immediately graspable, with each side equidistant from our eyes.[1] This view is completely impossible for the Navajo.[2] I got a laugh when I asked some Navajo if anyone ever climbed on the roof of a hogan to look at a sandpainting through the smoke hole.[3] When a painting 6 feet in diameter, or even larger, is constructed on the floor of a hogan only 20 feet in diameter, the perspective from the periphery is always at an acute angle to the surface.[4] A sandpainting cannot be easily seen as a whole.[5] The most important point of view is that of the person for whom the painting is made, and this person sees the painting from the inside out because he or she sits in the middle of it.[6] These differences are basic and cannot be dismissed.[7] The traditional Navajo view is inseparable from the significance that sandpainting has for the Navajo.[8]

## 【单词及搭配】

1. graspable adj. 能理解的,可以懂的 grasp vt. (1) 抓住,抓紧 (2) 理解,领会
2. hogan n. 泥盖木屋
3. dismiss vt. (1) 解雇;撤职;开除 (2) 不再考虑或谈论(文中意思)

## 【文章精读】

[1]-[2] 本段从视觉角度论证我们普通人与 Navajo 人看待沙画的不同点。

[3] 作者问这个问题时 Navajo 人发笑是因为这个问题很荒唐。

[4] 解释为何发笑,沙画不可能作为一个整体被观看,由它的几何特点决定。

[6] point of view 有两个意思: (1) 观点; (2) 视角(文中意思!),与 visual perspective 同义。that 指代 point of view, it 指代 painting。最重要的视角是为之作画的那个人,因为这个人坐在画的中间来看作品。言外之意,别人的视角都不重要,重要的是为他作画的那个人的视角。

该句可拆分为:

(1) The most important point of view is the point of view of the person.

(2) The painting is made by the person.

含有介词短语的定语从句:

主语+谓语+其他成分+被修饰名词+介词+先行词+定语从句

[7] 视觉角度方面的差异不能忽视。

[8] sandpainting has for the Navajo 为定语从句,修饰 significance。

传统的 Navajo 人关于沙画的观点与沙画对 Navajo 人的重要意义是不可分的。

I think we can say that for the Navajo the sandpainting is not the intended product of the creative process in which it is constructed.[1] The product is a healthy human being or the re-creation of a well-ordered world.[2] The sandpainting is but an instrument for the creative act, and perhaps it is the wisdom of the Navajo that it be destroyed in its use so that the obvious aesthetic value of the instrument does not supplant the human and cosmic concern.[3] The confinement of our attention to the reproduction of sandpaintings is somewhat analogous to hanging paint-covered artists' palettes on the wall to admire, not acknowledging that these pigment covered boards are not paintings but the means to create them.[4] There is a certain aesthetic value in artists' palettes, I suppose, but surely most would think of this action as foolishly missing the point.[5]

## 【单词及搭配】

1. intended adj. 有意的，故意的
2. supplant vt. 把……排挤掉，取代
3. palette n. 调色板

## 【文章精读】

[1] which 指代 process。it 指代沙画。给出作者的观点：对 Navajo 人来说，沙画并非是一种创造性进程的产物，在该进程中，人们创造了沙画。下文必然指出沙画究竟是什么。

[2] 指出沙画的内涵：沙画的产物是一个健康的人或秩序良好的重新塑造的世界。

[3] 沙画用过之后必须被毁掉的原因：不能因其明显的艺术价值而淡化了对人类和宇宙的关注。从本句可看出：沙画具有明显的艺术价值。

[4] the confinement of A to B：将 A 限制在 B 的范围内。A、B 均为名词或动名词。to admire 为不定式作目的状语——悬挂起来颜色鲜艳的艺术家的调色品，目的是用于欣赏调色板。not acknowledging 为现在分词短语作伴随状语。them 指代 paintings。调色板暗指沙画。means 为"方法"——创作艺术的方法。即，我们不应将创造艺术的方法当作艺术品来欣赏。

[5] 指出[4]中的错误导致的结果——忽略重点。

## 【题目解析】

1. According to Navajo tradition, the most significant perspective on a sandpainting is that of the

(A) group that requests the sandpainting's creation
(B) persons represented by the sandpainting figures
(C) Navajo leader conducting the sandpainting rite
(D) artists who conceive and design the sandpainting
(E) person for whom the sandpainting is made

【答案】E
【解析】见原文解析。对沙画最重要的视角是什么视角？that 指代 perspective。

2. "deepened" means

(A) darkened

(B) heightened

(C) immersed

(D) made distant

(E) made obscure

【答案】B

【解析】deepen 这里为及物动词，加深，强调。

3. What would happen if Navajo practices regarding sandpaintings were strictly observed?

(A) Only the Navajo would be permitted to exhibit sandpaintings as works of art.

(B) All sandpaintings would be destroyed before the rite of re-creation.

(C) The sandpaintings could be viewed only during the sandpainting rite.

(D) The sand-glue craft would be the only art form in which figures from sandpaintings could appear.

(E) The Navajo would be able to focus exclusively on the sandpaintings' images of unity.

【答案】C

(A) 见原文：沙画不能当作艺术作品被展示。

4. The information in the passage suggests that museum's exhibition of reproduced Navajo sandpaintings would

(A) undermine the effectiveness of sandpaintings in the healing process

(B) help to safeguard the traditions and treasures of Navajo civilization

(C) devalue the representations of sandpainting figures in the sand-glue craft

(D) discourage non-Navajo people from preserving actual sandpaintings

(E) perpetuate the importance of a painting's form rather than its function

【答案】E

沙画的展览将导致什么？沙画的展览突出了其艺术性，却忽略了沙画的实际作用。

5. Why did the Navajo listeners laugh?

(A) It would be dangerous for a person to climb onto the roof of a hogan.

(B) The view from the periphery is more amusing than the view from the center of the paintings.

(C) Only the person in need of healing should act in the way suggested by the author.

(D) Critical details in the sandpainints would be imperceptible from such a distance.

(D) A bird's eye perspective is irrelevant to the intended function of the paintings.

【答案】E

6. The phrase "obvious aesthetic value" suggests that

(A) despite an attempt to separate sandpaintings from the realm of art, the author recognizes their artistic qualities

(B) imposing artistic rules on sandpaintings diminishes their symbolic value

(C) the Navajo believe the sandpaintings' artistic qualities to be as important as their function

(D) the author discourages artistic elitism, yet acknowledges the esteemed reputation that sandpainters enjoy within the Navajo community

(E) aesthetic value should be associated with objects of natural beauty as well as with things created by humans

【答案】A

(A) recognize 指"认可"，及物动词。

7. The author's discussion of artists' palettes emrhasizes the
(A) array of colors in the creation of sandpainting
(B) insight required to appreciate technically unique art
(C) growing legitimacy of sandpainting reproductions
(D) value of sandpaintings as a means rather than an end
(E) benefit of combining several compoments to produce a single painting

【答案】D

# 第三部分

# 词汇解析

## 第三部分

## 固定资产

1. Unsuccessful in her first campaigns, Barbara Jordan _____, eventually becoming the first Black woman elected to the Texas State Senate.

(A) persisted

(B) gloated

(C) retired

(D) despaired

(E) hesitated

【解析】A

campaign n. 竞选活动。本句为典型的形容词短语 Unsuccessful in her first campagins 作让步状语，形容词短语的逻辑主语与句子主语一致。becoming 为现在分词短语作结果状语，其逻辑主语必须与句子主语一致。

【举一反三】Completely aware of potential hazards posed by decline in profits, the leader took immediate measures. "aware of potential hazards"为形容词短语作原因状语，逻辑主语为 leader。posed by 为过去分词短语作定语，修饰 hazards，由利润下跌带来的潜在危机。

本句可改写为：Although Barbara Jordan was unsuccessful in her first campaigns, she persisted, and eventually became the first Black woman elected to the Texas State Senate.

其中 elected to…为过去分词短语作定语，修饰 woman：被选为德州议员的女性，相当于 the woman who was elected to the Texas State Senate。

persist vt. & vi. 坚持，固执

gloat vi. 幸灾乐祸地看/想，贪婪地看/想 gloat over sth./sb.

retire (1) vt. & vi. 退职；退役；（使）退休 (2) vi. 退下；撤退

2. Some scientists speculate that children who wash frequently are more likely to become asthmatic than those who wash infrequently: that _____, not the lack of it, is the problem.

(A) pollution

(B) negligence

(C) nutrition

(D) misbehavior

(E) cleanliness

【解析】E

asthmatic (1) adj. 气喘的；患气喘的；发出呼哧声的（文中意思） (2) n. 气喘患者；哮喘患者

the lack of it 为名词短语作主语，某事的缺少，it 指代"cleanliness"。

一些科学家认为经常洗手的孩子比不经常洗手的孩子更容易患哮喘病：过度干净，而非不干净是问题所在。

3. Newspaper advertisers feel their messages are more believable and _____ when they are printed next to news report, hence advertising charges are higher for such _____.

(A) dominant…investigation

(B) irrelevant…proximity

(C) precise…delivery

(D) persuasive…positioning

(E) vague…thoroughness

【解析】D

they 指代 their messages。believable 的同义词为 persuasive，令人信服的。such 后面加名词，因此 positioning 为动名词，安排位置。句意为：报纸广告人认为如果他们的消息挨着新闻报道的话，那么消息会更令人信服，因此这样的位置安排需要的广告费用较高。

persuasive adj. 能说服的；善于游说的。还需掌握其动词形式：persuade (1) vt. & vi. 说服，劝告 (2) vt. 使信服

同义词记忆：compelling adj. (1) 引人入胜的；扣人心弦的 (2) 非常强烈的；不可抗拒的 (3) 令人信服的，有说服力的

position 可以作 vt，安排位置，定位。

proximity n. 接近，附近 in proximity to sth. 靠近某物

4. Despite accusations to the contrary, it is unlikely that he intended to _____ the articles, since he cited them in his bibliography.

(A) analyze

(B) illuminate

(C) plagiarize

(D) acknowledge

(E) contradict

【解析】C

accusations to the contrary，名词短语，不利的指控。尽管存在不利的指控，但他好像并非要剽窃文章，因为他已经在参考文献中列出了这些文章。引用文章即不算剽窃。

句式：Despite+名词、动名词、名词性从句，主语+谓语。

Somebody intended to do sth.，某人主动打算做某事。them 指代 articles。

plagiarize vt. 剽窃，抄袭

contradict (1) vt. & vi. 反驳，否认……的真实性 (2) vt. 与……发生矛盾，与……抵触

illuminate (1) vt. 使明亮；照亮 (2) vt. 装饰 (3) vt. 说明，阐明

5. Ralph Ellison learned the hard way about the _____ of a written manuscript: he suffered the _____ of the only draft of a work in progress in a household fire.

(A) magnitude…isolation

(B) fragility…preservation

(C) illegibility…eradication

(D) vulnerability…destruction

(E) proliferation…division

【解析】D

vulnerable adj. 易受伤的，脆弱的，敏感的 vulnerable to sth. 对某事很敏感

vulnerability n. 弱点，易损性

draft (1) n. 草稿，草案，草图（题干意思）(2) vt. 起草，画草图，草拟

in progress 进行中 a work in progress 进展中的作品

Ralph Ellison 体会到了手稿的脆弱：他曾经历一份还未完成的手稿在一场家庭火灾中毁于一旦。

magnitude n. 巨大；重要性

illegible adj. 难辨认的；字迹模糊的

eradicate vt. 摧毁 eradication n. 摧毁, 根除 eradicator n. 根除者；褪色灵

proliferate vi. (1) 激增；(迅速) 繁殖；增生 (2) 扩散

division n. (1) 分开；分配 (2) 部门 (3) 界限 (4) 分歧, 分裂 division over sth. 关于某事的分歧。还需掌握动词形式：

divide (1) vt. & vi. 分, 划分 (2) vt.& vi. 分离, 隔开 (3) vt.（使）产生分歧（核心用法）(4) n. 分水岭, 分界线

6. The new human resources director is both _____ and _____ about being able to improve employment opportunities for women at the executive level: she has great resolve but harbor no illusions.

(A) practical…deceptive

(B) cynical…irrational

(C) excited…approachable

(D) uncooperative…naïve

(E) determined…realistic

【解析】E

executive level，领导层。great resolve 对应形容词形式为"有决心的"，harbor no illusions，动词短语，不抱不切实际的幻想，即很现实。所以选择(E)。

resolve (1) vt. & vi. 决定；决心 (2) vt.（指委员会或集会）表决 (3) vt. 解决（问题、疑问等）resolve the problems (4) vt. 分解, 解析（某物）(5) n. 决定；决心（选项意思）

approachable adj. (1) 可亲近的 (2) 可接近的。还需掌握：approach (1) vt. & vi. 接近, 走近, 靠近 (2) vt. 接洽, 交涉；着手处理 approach sth. 着手处理某事 (3) n. 靠近, 接近, 临近 (4) n. 通路, 入口, 途径 the approach to sth.

7. Years of neglect had left the inside of the building in _____ condition: workstations were filthy and furnishings were dilapidated.

(A) a squalid

(B) a volatile

(C) an undaunted

(D) a rudimentary

(E) a cataclysmic

【解析】A

Years of neglect 为名词短语作主语，长久的疏忽。left 在这里为动词，使什么处于什么状态。

主语 leave sth.+adj./分词/介词短语/名词：主语使某物处于某种状态。

dilapidate v.（使）荒废,（使部分）毁坏, 浪费 dilapidated 为过去分词作定语, 被荒废的。

filthy adj. 肮脏的；污秽的
furnishing n. 陈设
squalid adj.（尤指因被忽视而）污秽的, 不洁的, 邋遢的
volatile adj. (1) 易变的, 反复无常的, 易激动的 (2)（液体或油）易挥发的
undaunted adj. 顽强的；不惧怕的；无畏的
cataclysmic adj. 洪水的, 大变动的

8. *The Wild Parrot of Telegraph Hill* is only _____ about birds; despite its title, the documentary actually examines human relationships.

(A) ostensibly
(B) distinctively
(C) intelligibly
(D) saliently
(E) incontrovertibly

【解析】A

its 指代 documentary's。尽管这部纪录片的题目是关于野生鹦鹉的, 但是这部纪录片实际在审视人类的关系。这部纪录片只是表面讨论鸟类。

ostensible adj.（指理由等）假装的, 表面的
distinctive adj. 有特色的, 与众不同的 the role distinctive to the book 这本书特有的作用
intelligible adj. 可理解的, 明白易懂的, 清楚的 The book is intelligible to me. 我能够看懂这本书的意思。Sth. is intelligible to sb. 某人懂什么。
salient (1) adj. 显著的, 重要的, 主要的 (2) adj.（指角）凸出的
controvertible adj. 可争论的, 有辩论余地的, 可辩论的
incontrovertible adj. 无可辩驳的, 不容置疑的
controvert vt. 争论, 反驳

9. Because the majority of the evening cable TV programs available dealt with violence and sex, the parents decided that the programs were ____ for the children to watch.

(A) exclusive
(B) acceptable
(C) instructive
(D) inappropriate
(E) unnecessary

【解析】D

因为大多数可观看的电视节目都与暴力和性有关, 所以父母们认为这些节目对孩子来说是不适合的。decide 在这里表示 consider, 认为。violence 名词, 暴力。deal with (1) 处理事情, deal with difficulties, 解决困难 (2) has something to do with A (noun) 与什么事情有关, 本句是后一种意思。

exclusive 形容词 (1) 独断的, 专有的 exclusive use for him 专为他所用; (2) 排除的, be exclusive of sb./sth. All of us will attend the meeting, exclusive of him. 除他以外我们都去

230

开会。The expense is 200 yuan, exclusive of rent. 不包括租金的费用是200元。

（3）sole, 独一无二的，an exclusive interview with the princess 对公主的独家采访

instructive 形容词，有教育意义的。

10. The novel *Uncle Tom's Cabin*, which effectively ____ the unfairness toward black people, was a major influence in ____ the anti-slavery movement.

(A) portrayed…strengthening

(B) attacked…pacifying

(C) glamorized…launching

(D) viewed…appraising

(E) exposed…condemning

【解析】A

小说《汤姆叔叔的小屋》有效地描绘了黑人受到的不平等状况，这本小说对加强反奴隶运动起到了很重要的影响作用。protray, vt. 描绘。 strengthen, vt. 加强，巩固。pacify, vt. 安抚，直接加名词作宾语。glamorize, vt. 美化，迷惑。launch, vt./vi. 发起 launch a movement。view, vt. 看做，view sb./sth. as。appraise, vt. 评价，估量。

expose, vt. (1) 使暴露于…… expose children to violence and sex on TV

(2) reveal, 揭露 The conspiracy was exposed/revealed to all. 阴谋被揭穿。

(3) 使看得到 Cleaning exposes the grain of wood.

condemn vt.

(1) 责难，责备，谴责 We condemn his foolish behavior. 我们谴责他的愚蠢行为。

(2) 宣告……有罪，判……刑

The judge condemned the thief to one year of hard labor. 法官判这个贼服一年苦役。

(3) 迫使……处于（不幸的状态）condemn sb. to

Paralysis of the lower limbs condemned him to a wheelchair. 下肢瘫痪使他只好坐轮椅。

11. Aleksandr Solzhenitysyn's ____ proved keenest when he accurately predicted that his books would someday appear in his native Russia.

(A) foresight

(B) nostalgia

(C) folly

(D) despair

(E) artistry

【详解】A

(1) keen adj.

热心的，热切的，渴望的；热情的 a keen desire to do sth. 一种做某事强烈的欲望

（活动）激烈的；（感情）强烈的 keen competition 激烈的竞争

对……有兴趣的；被……吸引的 be keen on sth.

锋利的；敏锐的，尖锐的，（感觉）灵敏的，敏锐的（题干意思）

(2) foresight 名词，预见；先见之明。hold a foresight to do sth.

(3) nostalgia 名词，怀旧；（尤指对某段快乐时光或某地的）思念，怀念

(4) folly 可数名词，愚笨，愚蠢

(5) artistry 名词，艺术创造技巧（或才能）

与 prove 相关的重要单词：justify vt. 证明……有理；为……辩护。另需掌握 prove 的名词和形容词形式：proof (1) n. 证明，论证；证据，证物 (2) n. 校样，样张 the proofs of the book (3) adj. 防……的；抗……的 water-proof 防水的。掌握其反义词：vulnerable adj. 易受伤的，脆弱的，敏感的 be vulnerable to sth. 易受 XXX 干扰

【举例】This area is vulnerable to droughts for years. 该地区连年干旱。

长期受电磁辐射的人易患癌症。The person exposed to prolonged electronic radiation is vulnerable to cancer.

substantiate vt.

用事实支持（某主张、说法等）；证明，证实

Do you have any proof to substantiate your alibi?

你有证据表明你当时不在犯罪现场吗？

12. The simple and direct images in Dorothea Lange's photographs provide ___ reflection of a bygone social milieu.

(A) an intricate

(B) a candid

(C) an ostentatious

(D) a fictional

(E) a convoluted

【详解】B

(1) bygone adj. 过去的，以往的；过时的

(2) milieu 周围环境；出身背景

(3) intricate adj. 错综复杂的，盘根错节的；复杂精细的

(4) candid adj. (1) 诚实的，正直的，坦率的（题干意思）(2) （某人的照片）偷拍的；随意拍摄的

(5) ostentatious adj. 炫耀的，卖弄的；讲究排场的，惹人注目的

(6) convoluted adj.（尤指论点、情节或句子）极其复杂的；难以理解的；（错综复杂地）折叠的；扭曲的；盘绕的

reflect (1) vt. & vi. 反射（光、热、声或影像）(2) vt. 考虑 (3) vt. 表达；反映

calculate (1) vt. & vi. 计算，估计 (2) vt. 打算，旨在

The advertisement is calculated to arouse public appeal for such an item. 该广告旨在引发人们对该商品的喜爱。

The public appeal for tax reduction is becoming increasingly intense. 公众呼吁降低税收的呼声越来越强烈。

13. Kate's impulsive nature and sudden whims led her friends to label her ___.

(A) capricious

(B) bombastic

(C) loquacious

(D) dispassionate

(E) decorous

【详解】A

(1) impulsive adj. 冲动的，没有事先考虑的

(2) whim n. 突然产生的念头；一闪而过的念头；异想天开的念头；怪念头 do sth. on a whim=do sth. on an impulse 由于一时冲动做了某事

lead (1) vt. 促使，让 主语+lead somebody to a conclusion that+同位语从句：某事使人得到一个什么结论。主语 lead somebody to do sth. 某事促使某人怎样。

(2) vi. 导致（特定事件）lead to sth./doing sth.

label vt. 给……贴标签；把……归类，把……列为（题干意思）

people who were labelled as "mentally handicapped" 被归类为"智力残疾"的人

capricious adj（心情、行为）突然且莫名改变的；任性的（题干意思）

随心所欲的；变化莫测的 a capricious climate 多变的气候

bombastic adj. 夸大的

loquacious adj. talkative 健谈的，多话的

dispassionate adj. 不动感情的；理性的；公正的 do sth. in a calm, dispassionate way 此单词须掌握变形形式：

passionate adj. 热情的；感情强烈的 be passionate about sth.=like sth. very much

易动情的，情绪激昂的

decorous adj. 得体的；有礼貌的，庄重的

14. Neurosurgeon Alexa Candy maintained that choosing a career was a visceral decision rather than ___ judgement; that is, it was not so much rational as ___.

(A) an emotional…intellectual

(B) a chance….random

(C) an intuitive…impulsive

(D) a deliberate…instinctive

(E) an intentional…logical

【详解】D

(1) visceral adj.（与）内脏（有关）的 the visceral nervous system 内脏神经系统。出自内心情感深处的 visceral fear of sth. 内心对某物的恐惧（题干意思）

(2) rather than 要……而不……，与其……倒不如……

(3) not so much A as B 与其说 A 不如说 B

(4) deliberate adj. 有意的，故意的

深思熟虑的，非一时冲动的（题干意思）a deliberate decision 深思熟虑的决定 an impulsive decision 一个一时冲动的决定

小心谨慎的 a deliberate worker

由题目的意思可知：两个选项意思相反。

(5) instinctive adj.（出于）本能的；无意识的，自发的 an instinctive distaste for conflict 对冲突本能的厌恶

(6) maintain vt. (1) 维持，保持（某种状态或形势），将……维持（在同样水平或速度）

Agricultural prices will have to be maintained. 必须维持农产品价格。
Immediate measures have to be taken to maintain/stabilize the intensely fluctuating prices.
(2) 维护，养护，保养（建筑物、机器或道路）
扶养，负担 maintain a child 扶养一个孩子
坚持；断言；主张（题干意思）assert/argue/state

15. Creative business stratagems frequently become ___ as a result of ___, their versatility and adaptability destroyed by their transformation into rigid policies.

(A) streamlined…infighting
(B) mitigated…jingoism
(C) ossified…bureaucratization
(D) politicized…innovation
(E) venerable…legislation

批注 [359]: 独立主格通常用表示结果的部分作动词！

批注 [360]: 独立主格中通常使用分词表示原因、假设等附加成分，相当于大家熟悉的状语从句。

批注 [A361]: 沙文主义

【详解】C
题干为独立主格典型形式，前后两个主语不一致！其中一个句子用分词的形式，不存在谓语。their 指代"creative business stratagems"（创造性的商业战略）。destroyed 为过去分词。

译文：创造性的商业策划通常由于官僚主义的作用变得僵化，它们的灵活性及适应性由于其向严酷的政策的转型而被毁掉了。

逻辑关系：本句主句为逗号前面的内容：商业策划变得僵化；逗号后面为主语+分词的结构，逗号后面的内容是逗号之前句子的伴随成分。本句强调的是商业策划变得僵化这件事。their 指代 stratagems。在独立主格中和分词作状语时，代词尽量放在含有分词的结构中。

本句另一种表达：Creative business stratagems frequently become ossified as a result of bureaucratization with their versatility and adaptability destroyed by their transformation into rigid policies.

后一个分句没有谓语，主语也与第一个分句不同，为独立主格。

(1) ossify 停滞；僵化 ossified political institutions 僵化的政治制度。题干中与 rigid 意思相同。
(2) bureaucratization 名词，官僚化
(3) versatile adj. 多功能的；多才多艺的 a versatile sewing machine 多功能缝纫机
He was versatile enough to play on either wing.
(4) adaptability n. 适应性，顺应性，可用性；灵活性
the adaptability of sb. to do sth. 某人做某事的适应力
infighting n. 内讧，内部纠纷，勾心斗角
mitigate vt. 减轻，缓和 mitigate the effect of something 减轻某事的影响
venerable adj.（因年岁、品格、有某种关联等）值得尊重的，受敬佩的
streamline vt. (1) 把……做成流线型 (2) 简化使效率更高 streamline methods 简化方法

16. Known for her ___, Miranda eagerly welcomes anyone into her home.
(A) cowardice

(B) prudence
(C) hospitality
(D) aloofness
(E) loyalty

【详解】C

Known for her hospitality 为过去分词短语作状语，完整句子为：

As Miranda was known for her hospitality, she eagerly welcomes anyone into her home. 可用分词取代原来的从句，变为 Known for her hospitality。分词放置句首或句尾时，分词的逻辑主语必须与句子主语一致，否则就要另换形式。

Sb./Sth. is known for sth. 某人/某物因什么而闻名。

cowardice n. 懦弱  prudence n. (1) 智慧；远见 (2) 谨慎  prudent adj. 审慎的；有先见之明的；判断力强的  hospitality n. 殷勤, 好客  loyalty n. 忠诚, 忠心

aloof adj. 冷淡的, 疏远的, 淡漠的

17. Not surprisingly, supporters of the governor's plan to set aside land for a forest preserve were disappointed when a court decision ___ the plan.

(A) applauded
(B) derailed
(C) acknowledged
(D) permitted
(E) anticipated

【答案】B

【解析】to set aside land for a forest preserve 为不定式作定语，修饰 plan。were 为谓语。

【举一反三】一本阐述无线通信原理的书（名词短语）a book to demonstrate the theories of wireless communication

set aside (1) 把……放置一旁, 不理会 (2) 取消, 驳回 (3) 留出（题干意思）

preserve (1) vt. 保护 (2) vt. maintain 维持 (3) n. 保护区

applaud vt. 称赞, 赞许

derail (1) vt. & vi. 出轨 (2) vt. 使某物偏离原计划 derail the plan

acknowledge (1) vt. 承认, 供认 (2) vt. 鸣谢, 感谢

anticipate (1) vt. 先于……行动 anticipate sb. 先于某人 (2) vt. 预感, 期望

18. Because playing a musical instrument increases brain activity, it is sometimes used as a ___ to promote learning in children.

(A) condition
(B) highlight
(C) stimulus
(D) dictum
(E) respite

【答案】C

condition (1) vt. 制约, 限制  Ability and effort condition success. 才干和努力是成功的

条件。

(2) vt. 作为……的条件；规定；决定；约束 My expenditure is conditioned by my income. 我的支出取决于我的收入。

(3) vt. 置于适当情况，使处于正常状态 You need to condition yourself if you are to play in the football match on Saturday. 如果你要参加星期六的足球比赛，就需要把你自己调整到最佳状态。

(4) n. 条件；情况；环境

highlight (1) vt. 强调，突出 (2) n. 最精彩的部分，最重要的事情

stimulus n. 刺激物；激励物；促进因素 a stimulus to sth.

stimulate vt. 刺激；激励

dictum n. 宣言，声明，名言，格言

respite n. 休息（时间），暂时的缓解或轻松

19. The ambassador argues that, in diplomacy, there is a subtle but important difference between a country's showing a willingness to ___ and a too-obvious readiness to make ___.

(A) negotiate…concessions
(B) antagonize…friends
(C) surrender…enemies
(D) dominate…inquiries
(E) equivocate…denunciations

【答案】A

【解析】that 直至结尾为宾语从句。but 表示"然而"，转折。showing 为动名词，修饰动名词用物主代词或形容词，动名词的用法与名词完全一样。

批注 [362]: 认为
批注 [363]: 空白处两个单词为同义词
批注 [364]: 动名词的修饰：用形容词或物主代词！与普通名词完全一样。
批注 [365]: 不定式作定语

【举一反三】I couldn't bear his rudeness.= I couldn't bear his being rude.

大使认为，在外交上，一个国家愿意谈判与太过明显地作出妥协的意愿之间有细微但非常重要的差别。

ambassador n. 大使，使节

diplomacy n. 外交，外交手腕，外交术

subtle adj. 微妙的；难以捉摸的；细微的

readiness n. (1) 准备就绪 be in readiness 准备就绪 (2) 愿意，乐意 the readiness to do sth. 名词短语，愿意做某事

negotiate vt. & vi. 谈判；协商；议定

concession n. 承认，允许；妥协，让步。还须掌握动词形式：concede (1) vt. & vi. 承认 (2) vt. 出让，容许

antagonize vt. 使成为敌人；引起……敌对/对抗

surrender (1) vt. & vi. 投降 (2) vt. 放弃；抛弃 surrender a dream (3) n. 投降，放弃

dominate (1) vt. & vi. 控制，支配，统治 (2) vi. 在……中占首要地位

inquire vt. & vi. 打听，询问

equivocate vi. 使用模棱两可的话隐瞒真相

denunciation n. 公开的谴责，指责；告发 denunciation of sb./sth.。还须掌握动词形式：denounce vt. 公开指责

20. The dancer's performing style was ___ and ___ with each move taken from another aritist, and poorly executed at that.

(A) rousing…memorable

(B) pedestrian…evolving

(C) chaotic…unprecedented

(D) derivative…inept

(E) spontaneous…graceless

【答案】D

主语为 style，谓语为 was。with XXX 为介词短语表伴随，结构为：with sth.+分词/形容词，其中 move 表示"动作"，这里为名词，taken from another aritist 为过去分词短语作定语，修饰 move，每一个动作都是从其他舞蹈演员那里拿来的（模仿来的）。executed 和 taken 并列分词短语作定语，修饰 move。

陈述句语序为：Each move was taken from another artist, and each move was poorly executed at that. at that 在这里表示"而且"。

名词短语 each move poorly executed and taken from others 中，副词 poorly 修饰过去分词 executed，相当于 badly。

句意：这个舞蹈演员的表演风格是抄袭他人的，是笨拙的，她的每个动作都是模仿别人的，而且表演得非常糟糕。

**with 介词短语用法举一反三：** *The rencently-taken measures are efficient with a range of facts demonstrating the benefits brought to the company.*

rousing adj. 充满活力的；激励的；激动人心的。还须掌握动词形式：rouse (1) vt. & vi. 醒来；唤醒=wake (2) vt. 使……活跃起来  rouse sb. to indignation 引起愤怒

arouse (1) vt. 唤醒 (2) vt. 引起，激发  arouse sb. to do sth.

execute (1) vt. 处决 (2) vt. 执行，实现；使生效（文中意思）

memorable adj. 值得纪念的，值得记忆的

evolve vt. & vi. 演变；进化

chaotic adj. 混沌的；一片混乱的；一团糟的

pedestrian adj. 平淡无奇的

unprecedented adj. 前所未有的，无前例的。还须掌握动词形式：

precede vt. & vi. 在……之前，先于 the days that preceded 前几天

derivative (1) n. 派生物，引出物 (2) adj. 模仿他人的；衍生的；派生的

inept adj. (1) 无能的，不称职的，笨拙的 (2) 不恰当的，荒谬的

spontaneous adj. 自发的，无意识的，自然的，天真率直的

graceless adj. 不雅的；粗野的；难看的

批注 [366]：注意 at that 的用法！

批注 [367]：现在分词短语作定语，修饰 facts。

21. Lewis Latimer's inexpensive method of producing carbon filaments _____ the nascent electric industry by making electric lamps commercially _____.

(A) cheapened…affordable

(B) transformed…viable

(C) revolutionized…prohibitive

(D) provoked…improbable

(E) stimulated…inaccessible

【答案】B

【解析】filament n. 灯丝

nascent adj. 初期的；初生的，新生的 the nascent republic 新生的共和国

cheapen vt. 减价

afford (1) vt. 买得起，担负得起 (2) vt. 提供，给予 The plant affords medicine. 该植物可以作为药材。

affordable adj. 付得起的，不太昂贵的

transform vt. & vi. 改变

viable adj. 切实可行的；可实施的 adv.+viable==从某种角度讲可实施的。theoretically viable 理论上可实施的。

prohibitive adj. (1) 禁止使用或购买的，禁止性的 (2)（指价格等）高得买不起的

provoke vt. 激起；惹怒

improbable adj. 不大可能是真实的，不大可能的

access (1) n. 通道，入口 (2) n. 接近/取得……的方法（权利等）(3) v. 进入，到达

accessible adj. (1) 容易取得的，容易获得的 (2) 可理解的，易懂的

intelligible adj. 可理解的 Sth. is intelligible to sb.

stimulate vt. 刺激；激励 stimulate sb. to do sth. 激励/刺激某人做某事

22. After winning the award, Phillip adopted a haughty pose, treating even his best friends in a _____ manner.

(A) cryptic
(B) judicious
(C) jubilant
(D) supercilious
(E) pugnacious

【答案】D

【解析】treating 为分词短语作伴随状语，其逻辑主语与句子主语一致！

adopt (1) vt. 收养 (2) vt. 采用，采纳，采取 (3) vt. 正式接受，通过 adopt the new way of life 接受新的生活方式

haughty adj. 傲慢的，目中无人的

pose (1) vt. & vi. （使）摆姿势 (2) vt. 提出 pose a proposal (3) vt. 构成，造成 pose a threat to sb. 对某人构成威胁

manner n. (1) 方式，方法 (2) 态度（题干意思）

cryptic adj. 秘密的，隐秘的 decode a cryptic message 译解神秘信息

judicious adj. 明智的；明断的

jubilant adj. 兴高采烈的，喜气洋洋的

supercilious adj. 高傲的；傲慢的

pugnacious adj. 好战的；好斗的；好挑衅的

23. The general was so widely suspected of _____ during the war that his name

批注 [368]: 副词修饰形容词

eventually became synonymous with disloyalty.

(A) belligerence

(B) indigence

(C) perfidy

(D) aspersion

(E) tenacity

【答案】C

【解析】It is generally/prevalently regarded that+主语从句。人们普遍认为……

general (1) adj. 普遍的，全面的；总体的 (2) n. 将军

suspect vt. 猜疑（是），怀疑（是），觉得（是）suspect sb. of sth./doing

synonymous adj. 同义的，类义的

disloyalty n. 不忠实，不信，不义，背信弃义

belligerence n. 交战，好战，斗争性

indigence n. 贫乏，穷困

perfidy n. 背信弃义

aspersion n. 诽谤，中伤

tenacity n. 固执；坚持，顽强，不屈不挠

24. The prose of Richard Wright's autobiographical *Black Boy* (1945) is _____, free of stylistic tricks or evasiveness.

(A) imprecise

(B) straightforward

(C) deficient

(D) obtrusive

(E) elliptical

【解析】B

straightforward adj. (1)（人或其态度）正直的，坦率的；老实的 (2) 简单的；易懂的（题干意思）

deficient adj. (1) 有缺点的，有缺陷的 (2) 缺乏的，不足的 deficient in sth. 在某方面不足

obtrusive adj. (1)（难看得）刺眼的 (2) 冒失的，莽撞的，强加于人的

obtrude vt. 强行向前；强行；强迫 obtrude sth. on sb. 将某物强加在某人身上

elliptical adj. (1) 椭圆的，像椭圆形的 (2)（指语言）难懂的，晦涩的 (3) 省略的

evasive adj. 逃避的；推托的

25. Once the principal ___ that the fire alarm had been set off by accident, she apologized to the suspected students and announced that they had been ___.

(A) realized…exonerated

(B) denied…reprimanded

(C) perceived…enlightened

(D) understood…apprehended

(E) confirmed…obligated

【答案】A

【解析】principal (1) adj. 最重要的；主要的 (2) n. 负责人，校长（题干意思）(3) n. 资本，本金

fire alarm n. 火警

set off (1) 出发，动身 (2)（使）开始；引起 (3) 点燃，爆炸

exonerate vt. 使免罪，免除 exonerate sb. from blame 免除某人的罪责

deny vt. (1) 否认知情 (2) 拒绝

reprimand (1) n. 训斥，惩戒 (2) vt. 申斥，惩戒，谴责

perceive vt. 感觉，察觉，理解

enlighten vt. 启发，开导，阐明 enlighten sb. on sth. 向某人阐述某物

apprehend vt. (1) 逮捕，拘押 (2) 理解

confirm vt. 证实，证明；肯定，确认

obligate vt. 使（在法律或道义上）负有责任或义务

obligating adj. 有义务的；必要的

she 指代 the principal。set off 这里指"引发"。the suspected students，被怀疑的学生，suspected 为过去分词作定语，修饰 students。

26. Although the late Supreme Court Justice Thurgood Marshall had _____ that his papers be available only to scholars, the Library of Congress _____ his wishes and exhibited them to the general public.

(A) implied…publicized
(B) denied…repealed
(C) stipulated…disregarded
(D) revealed…executed
(E) insisted…honored

【答案】C

【解析】两句话为转折关系。Thurgood 宣称他的论文只能供学者看，但图书馆还是违背了他的意志，将论文向普通公众公开。them 指代 papers。exhibit sth. to sb. 向某人展示某物。

publicize vt. 宣传（某事物）（尤指用广告）

exhibit (1) vt. & vi. 陈列；展览 (2) vt. 显示，显出

general public 公众

repeal vt. 撤销，废除

stipulate vt. 规定，约定，讲明（条件等）

stipulation n. 规定，（条约等的）条款

disregard vt. 不顾，不理会，无视

regard vt. (1) 注视；注意 (2) 认作

assume vt. (1) 假设，臆断（想当然地认为），猜想 (2) 假装 (3) 承担 (4) 呈现，采取
assume a method 采取某种方法

execute vt. (1) 处决 (2) 执行，实现；使生效

honor (1) n. 尊敬 (2) vt. 尊敬，给予荣誉

27. Royal garments found in the tombs of ancient Egyptians reveal no evidence of having been mended; this discovery suggests that the rulers of Egypt opted for ___ rather than ___.

(A) disposal…repair
(B) sacrifice…opulence
(C) wastefulness…comfort
(D) spirituality…worldliness
(E) humiliation…charity

【答案】A

【解析】garment n.（一件）衣服

found in the tombs of ancient Egyptians 为过去分词短语作定语，修饰衣服。谓语为 reveal。衣服没有改动过，表明统治者宁愿处理掉也不愿做修改。

tomb n. 墓穴
amend vt. & vi. 改良；修改，修订
opt for 选择
disposal n. 清除，处理，处置
sacrifice (1) n. 牺牲，舍身 (2) vt. 牺牲
opulence n. 富裕，富饶 opulent adj. 富裕的，充足的
comfort (1) n. 舒适，身心健康 (2) vt. 安慰，使舒适
spirituality n. 精神性，灵性
worldliness n. 俗心，俗气
humiliation n. 丢脸；羞辱；耻辱；蒙羞
charity n. 慈爱，仁慈；救济金；宽厚，宽容，宽大

28. The author used a rhetorical question as a terminal flourish to ___ the section of text.

(A) disclose
(B) rearrange
(C) simplify
(D) conclude
(E) ascertain

【答案】D

【解析】use sth. to do sth. 用某物做什么

conclude sth., 使某物结束，动词短语。to conclude 在这里作目的状语。

作者在结尾使用了反问的修辞方法来给文章结尾。

rhetorical adj. 修辞的，用来产生修辞效果的
terminal adj. 末端的，终点的，极限的
flourish vi. 茂盛，繁荣 n. 繁荣
disclose vt. (1) 说出，表明 (2) 揭露，揭开
rearrange vt. 重新安排，重新布置
simplify vt. 使（某事物）简单/简明；简化

conclude (1) vt. & vi.结束 (2) vt. 得出结论；断定
ascertain vt. 弄清，确定，查明

29. "Foamy" viruses casue cells cultured in laboratories to swell but produce no such ____ in cells of living organisms.

(A) compression
(B) disintegration
(C) distension
(D) deflation
(E) dehydration

【答案】C

【解析】but 表示转折，省略了主语 viruses。
cultured in labs 为过去分词短语作定语，修饰"细胞"。casue sth. to do sth., 引发某物做某事。swelling（动名词）的意思应与填空意思相同。living 为形容词，活着的。

culture vt. 培植，培养
swell vt. & vi. 肿胀，膨胀，鼓起
compression n. 挤压，压缩
disintegrate vt. & vi.（使）破裂/分裂/粉碎；（使）崩溃
distend vt. & vi.（使）膨胀，肿胀
deflate (1) vt. & vi.（使）漏气；（使）……瘪下去 (2) 紧缩（通货）；降低（价格）(3) vt.挫败（某人的）锐气，使……泄气
inflate vt. & vi. 使充气（于轮胎、气球等），（使）膨胀；（使）通货膨胀，物价上涨
dehydrate vt. 使脱水

30. Abida quickly realized that the director was extremely ____: she and the other cast members could never anticipate how he would respond.

(A) negative
(B) boring
(C) unpredictable
(D) humorous
(E) courageous

【解析】C

anticipate vt. (1) 先于……行动 (2) 预感，期望（题干意思）the results anticipated, 名词短语，人们所预期的结果。
predict vt. & vi. 预言；预测；预示 predicable adj. 可推断的, 可肯定的。结果不可预知。The results are unpredictable.
predictive adj. 预言性的

31. Cindy was __ as a writer of __ talent early in her career, receiving high praise for her short stories while she was still a student.

(A) criticized…little

242

(B) challenged…famous
(C) celebrated…shallow
(D) condemned…amazing
(E) recognized…considerable

【解析】E

receiving 是现在分词短语作伴随状语，它的逻辑主语必须和句子主语一致。

challenge (1) n. 挑战 (2) n. 怀疑，质问 pose challenges to sb./sth. 对某人/某事提出质疑 (3) n. 艰巨的任务 (4) vt. 挑战 (5) vt. 质疑

celebrated adj. 有名的，著名的

shallow adj. (1) 浅的 (2) 肤浅的 superficial

condemn vt. (1) 谴责，责备 (2) 宣布……不能使用 Plastic bags are condemned as a threat to human body. 塑料袋被宣布对人体造成威胁不宜使用。

(3) vt. 迫使……陷于不幸的境地 condemn sb. to do sth.

32. The bee hummingbird has an average length of only two inches, making it the most ___ of all hummingbird species.

(A) voracious
(B) diminutive
(C) capricious
(D) superfluous
(E) prodigal

【解析】B

making it 为现在分词短语作结果状语，修饰前面的句子。

【句型】主语+谓语，making sth./sb/+其他成分。前面的事情使得后面怎样。

voracious adj. (1) 贪吃的，狼吞虎咽的 (2) 贪婪的，贪得无厌的 (3) 渴求的；如饥似渴的 a voracious reader 求知欲强的读者

diminutive adj. 小得出奇的，特小的

Despite its diminutive size, the car is quite comfortable. 尽管这辆车很小，但相当舒服。

capricious adj. 无定见的，变幻莫测的

superfluous adj. 过多的；过剩的；多余的

redundant adj. (1) 因人员过剩而被解雇的 The number of redundant workers accounts for 20% of the overall staff. 因为人员过剩而被解雇的员工占总人数的百分之二十。

(2) 不需要的；多余的 redundant information 冗余信息

prodigal adj. (1) 浪费的；铺张的；挥霍的 (2) 慷慨的，不吝啬的

33. Naturally, ___ facilitates friendships: the people we live near or interact with frequently are more likely to become friends.

(A) enmity
(B) proximity
(C) beneficence
(D) partisanship

(E) magnanimity

【解析】B

facilitate vt. 使便利，减轻……的困难
interact vi. 相互作用/影响，互相配合
enmity n. 仇恨，敌意，敌视；敌对的状态
proximity n. 接近，附近 the proximity to sth./sb. 对某人/某物的接近
beneficence n. 善行，仁慈
magnanimous adj. 宽宏大量的，有雅量的

34. Able to survive subzero temperatures, long periods of darkness, and days without food, the Arctic wolf is clearly a very ___ animal.

    (A) greddy
    (B) social
    (C) cunning
    (D) hardy
    (E) aggressive

【解析】D

Able to do 为形容词短语作伴随状语，其逻辑主语与句子主语一致。
survive vi. (1) 幸存，活下来 (2) vt. 经历……之后还存在
hardy adj. (1) 能吃苦耐劳的，坚强的（选项意思）(2)（植物等）耐寒的
cunning adj. 狡猾的，奸诈的

35. Edith's qualities of broad-mindedness and humanism; she cannot, however, ___ them with his ___ support of a political creed that seems to oppose precisely those qualitites.

    (A) repudiate….jingoistic
    (B) undermine…wavering
    (C) assuage…logical
    (D) reconcile… dogmatic
    (E) acknowledge….polemical

【解析】D

dogma n. 教义，教条；信条 dogmatic adj. 教义的，教条的；信条的
reconcile (1) vt. 使和好；和解 be reconciled with sb. 与某人和好 (2) vt. 使一致，使和谐 reconcile A with B (3) vt. 将就；妥协
He could not reconcile himself to the uptight conditions.
He could not concile himself to the prospect of losing the job. 他一想到有可能失去这份工作就觉得难以忍受。
oppose vt. & vi. 反对；使相对
creed n.（尤指宗教）信条，教条
repudiate vt. 拒绝接受，否认，否定
jingoistic adj. 强硬外交政策的，侵略分子的
undermine vt. (1) 在某物下挖洞或挖通道；侵蚀……的基础 (2) 暗中破坏；逐渐削弱

wavering adj. 摇摆的；摇晃的  waver vi. 摇摆；摇晃；动摇
assuage vt. (1) 减轻；缓和；平息 (2) 使安静  assuage the noisy child
acknowledge vt. (1) 承认，供认 (2) 告知已收到 We must acknowledge his money. 我们应当告诉他钱收到了。(3) 鸣谢，感谢
polemical adj. 辩论法的, 辩论术的, 好辩的, 挑起争端的

36. The paucity of autobiographical documents left by the royal attendants has compelled historian Roy to __ the motives of these countiers from their ___ rather than from any diaries or correspondence.

    (A) stipulate…accomplishments
    (B) contemplate…journals
    (C) surmise…deeds
    (D) allege…assertions
    (E) elicit…missives

【解析】C
paucity n. 少量；缺乏；不足
autobiographical adj. 自传的；自传体的
attendant (1) n. 服务人员, 侍者, 随从 (2) adj. 伴随的, 随之而产生的
compel vt. 强迫, 使不得不
compelling adj. (1) 引人入胜的；扣人心弦的 (2) 令人信服的，有说服力的
stipulate vt. （尤指在协议或建议中）规定, 约定, 讲明（条件等）
contemplate vt. & vi. 深思, 细想, 仔细考虑
surmise (1) n. 推测, 猜测 (2) vt. 臆测, 推断
deed n. 行为, 行动
allege vt. 断言, 宣称, 辩解
elicit vt. 引出, 探出 elicit the truth 查明真相
missive n. 信件

37. Excelling in her academic studies, Yuki earned a number of ___ and awards.
    (A) vindications
    (B) proposals
    (C) contingencies
    (D) honors
    (E) reprimands

【解析】D
Excelling in 为现在分词短语作伴随状语，其逻辑主语与句子主语一致。Yuki 在学术研究中表现出色，因此赢得了很多荣誉和奖励。studies 在这里指"研究"。
excel vt. & vi. 优于, 擅长  excel in sth. 擅长某方面  outdo vt. 胜过
earn a good reputation，赢得好的名声，动词短语。
vindicate vt. (1) 澄清受到的责难或嫌疑 (2) 表明或证明（所争辩的事物）属实、正当、有效等

Subsequent events vindicated the policy. 后来的事实证明那条政策是对的。

(3) 维护 vindicate one's reputation

contingency n. 偶然发生的事故，意外事故

reprimand (1) n. 训斥，惩戒 (2) vt. 申斥，惩戒，谴责

38. The newspaper's editorial section regularly publishes the ___ of those readers who are knowledgeable enough about an issue to ___ their points powerfully and articulately.

  (A) suggestions…dismiss
  (B) analyses…subvert
  (C) opinions…argue
  (D) retractions… belabor
  (E) experiments…consider

【解析】C

who are …为定语从句，修饰 readers。

articulate (1) adj. 表达能力强的 (2) vt. & vi. 清楚地表达。points 为名词，观点。

knowledgeable adj. 博学的；有见识的；知识渊博的

subvert vt. 颠覆，破坏（政治制度、宗教信仰等）

retract vt. & vi. (1) 撤回，撤销 (2) 拒绝执行或遵守 retract the law

argue 在这里表示"发表意见"，及物动词。be knowledgeable enough to do sth., 对某方面知识足够渊博，以至于能做某事。

belabour vt. 痛打，责骂

39. Doctors initially feared that antibiotics would have ___ effect, destroying healthy tissue as well as harmful bacteria.

  (A) a deleterious
  (B) a minuscule
  (C) a salutary
  (D) an antiquated
  (E) an immediate

【解析】A

destroying 为现在分词短语作定语，修饰 effect。医生起初担心抗生素会产生有害的效应，这种效应会破坏健康的组织和有害的细菌。as well as 联接了两个名词，前后通常为相通成分，如均为名词或均为形容词。initially 为副词，修饰动词 feared。

antibiotic n. 抗生素，抗菌素

deleterious adj. 有害的 pose deleterious consequence to sb./sth. 对某人/某物有害

minuscule adj. 非常小的，极不重要的

deliberate adj. 深思熟虑的 v. 慎重考虑

initiate vt. (1) 开始，着手 (2) 传授；使初步了解 (3) vt. 接纳新成员，让……加入

initial adj. 最初的，开头的

salutary adj. 有益的，效果好的 antiquated adj. 过时的，陈旧的，老式的

immediate adj. (1) 立即的，即刻的；紧迫的 take immediate actions 采取紧急行动 (2)

目前的，当前的 immediate interests 眼前利益 (3) 直接的 immediate cause of sth. (4) 最接近的 immediate relatives 近亲

40. Native American potters often ___ the shortcuts offered by modern technology (such as the use of commercial clay, pigments, or kiln firing), instead ___ the traditional methods of their ancestors.

  (A) laud…resuscitating
  (B) flout…relinquishing
  (C) circumvent…renouncing
  (D) propound…cleaving to
  (E) eschew…adhering to

【解析】E

potter (1) vi. 懒散地工作，漫无目的地走动 (2) n. 制陶工人
shortcut n. 捷径，近路；快捷办法
eschew vt.（尤指为道德或实际理由而）习惯性避开，回避
adhere to 遵循，依附；坚持
instead 后面加分词，其逻辑主语必须与句子主语一致，为 potters。制陶人拒绝使用现代工艺，而是使用传统工艺。

【举一反三】主语+谓语，instead+分词。主语做了某事，做了分词的事情。分词的逻辑主语与主语一致。

I refused to take his advice, instead adhering to my original plan. 我拒绝了他的建议，而是坚持了我曾经的计划。

laud (1) vt. 称赞，赞美 (2) n. 称赞，赞美
resuscitate vt. 使（某人或某物）恢复知觉，苏醒
flout vt. 藐视，轻视
relinquish (1) vt. 交出 (2) vt. 放弃
circumvent vt. 设法克服或避免（某事物）；回避
renounce vt. 宣布放弃
propound vt. 提出（问题、计划等）供考虑/讨论，提议
cleave to 动词短语，粘着，坚持.

41. Tom leaves an ___ impression on audiences: children especially remember the dazzling costumes and stirring music.

  (A) amorphous
  (B) indelible
  (C) ineffable
  (D) innocuous
  (E) inscrutable

【解析】B

leave an impression on sb., 动词短语，给某人留下某种印象。Tom 经常给观众留下深刻的印象，孩子们尤其记得他那光彩夺目的演出服和激动人心的音乐。

indelible adj. (1) 擦不掉的 (2) 永久的，持久的
amorphous adj. (1) 无固定形状的 (2) 无组织的；难以名状的
ineffable adj. 妙不可言的，不可言喻的
innocuous adj. 无害的，不会招致反对的 nocuous adj. 有害的
inscrutable adj. 不可理解的；谜一样的。还须掌握动词形式：scrutinize vt. 仔细检查，详审

# 第四部分

# 改 错

第四部分

结 语

1. A recent report indicates that sleep-deprived drivers caused more than 10,000 accidents last <u>year, they fall</u> asleep at the wheel.

(A) year, they fall

(B) year, and they fall

(C) year by falling

(D) year and falling

(E) year, they were falling

【答案】C

[考点]句子的连接结构，用分词或连词或状语。

[与阅读的联系]详见讲义句子结构部分。

分析：deprive vt. 剥夺，夺去，使丧失 deprive sb. of sth. 剥夺某人某种权利

构词形式：名词-分词，整体作为形容词。当分词与被修饰的名词呈主动关系时，用现在分词；呈被动关系时，用过去分词。比如：man-dominated society，由男人主宰的社会。society 和主宰呈被动关系，The society is dominated by man.

sleep-deprived: 形容词，sleep 为名词，睡眠。被剥夺睡眠的，缺觉的。

that 到结尾均为宾语从句，而两个宾语从句中用逗号分开，却没有连词，这不符合语言规范。详见句子的几种结构。而且宾语从句前一个为过去时，后一个最好也为过去范围的时态。

fall asleep at the wheel，在方向盘上睡着，即开车时睡觉。与 accidents 有逻辑关系，故改为：Drivers caused accidents by falling asleep at the wheel.

(D) 错在宾语从句两个都需要有谓语，而后者 falling 没有谓语。如果改为 and were falling 就对了。(E) 没有连词。

2. The depths of the Arctic Ocean are hard <u>to study, mainly because the icy surface is being</u> difficult to penetrate using current techniques.

【答案】去掉 being。

[考点] 不定式的用法: be hard to do sth.

[分析] penetrate 表示"穿透"，从语境可以看到这一点：海洋深处难以研究，因为利用现在的技术尚难以穿透冰层。

penetrate (1) vt. & vi. 穿过，渗入（题干意思） (2) vt. 了解

current adj. 现在的，现行的 contemporaneous adj. 同时期的，同时代的

contemporary (1) adj. 当代的 (2) adj. 同时代的，同属一个时期的 (3) n. 同代人，同龄人

using current techniques 为现在分词短语作伴随状语。

3. A thick growth of sunflowers <u>standing ten feet tall, their brown heads drooped</u> over the fence with the weight of their seeds.

(A) standing ten feet tall, their brown heads drooped

(B) standing ten feet tall, their brown heads drooping

(C) standing ten feet tall, and their brown heads droop

(D) stood ten feet tall, their brown heads drooping

(E) stood ten feet tall, and their brown heads drooping

【答案】D

(1) 该题目是每年必考的独立主格与分词作状语的改错题目。

(2) 句子理解：

向日葵高 10 英尺，棕色的花魁由于种子重量的作用垂向了篱笆。两者呈伴随关系。

当前后两个句子主语不一致，而两个句子之间使用逗号，且两者之间没有任何连词时，便采用独立主格。这是学生反复被告知的。但有一点需要学生仔细体会：独立主格中会出现分词，那么究竟用哪个动作作分词呢？在独立主格中分词是表示原因、伴随等的部分，而真正的结果都用动词形式。

High above, comet Hale-Bopp hung like a feathery fishing lure, its tail curving off a bit.

彗星 Hale-Bopp 像有羽毛的鱼饵一般挂在高高的空中，（因为）它的尾巴有些许弯曲。首先确实为独立主格，主语不一致；其次，彗星像鱼饵是结果，是作者要表达的直接信息，用了动词 hung，原因是什么呢？因为尾巴弯弯的，因此用了分词。这里只是附带的原因。

句子的几种结构：

(A) 分词短语，主语+谓语。分词短语的逻辑主语必须与句子主语一致。如果分词表示的动作与主语呈主动关系，用现在分词；反之，用过去分词。

(B) 主语 1+谓语，主语 2+分词。这种结构为独立主格。主语 1 与主语 2 不同。如果主语 2 与分词表达的动作呈主动关系时，用现在分词；反之，用过去分词。本句结构属于此类。

(3) 严格地讲，A 从语法上来讲，不存在任何错误，但是逻辑性差一些，不太符合语言习惯。英语靠的更多的是体会和语感，而非死记硬背。

(4) weight 为"重力"，与地球加速度有关，这里不是"质量"，使某物下垂要靠 g，并非单纯的 m，地球引力是月球的 6 倍，所以向日葵放到月球上不会弯得那么厉害。

(5) a thick growth，浓密地生长，这里已经提示了：浓密，即种子很多很密，导致花魁下垂。

(6) their 为物主代词，独立主格中含有分词的分句才可以用代词，因此 droop 应改为 drooping。

with 在句中表示原因，相当于 because of sth.。比如：

(1) The company was nearly on the verge of bankruptcy with/owing to/because of the unprecedented global economical crisis. 由于前所未有的全球性经济危机，该公司面临破产。

(2) Draft of the work was sharply compromised with excessive consideration of the author for commercial profits. 由于作者过度考虑经济利益，书稿的质量大幅降低。

compromise (1) n. 妥协，折中方法 (2) vi. 折中解决 compromise to sth. (3) vt. 连累，危害（例句意思）

4. The shift from the traditional to cosmetic dentistry <u>is because adults are getting fewer cavities and becoming</u> more vain.

(A) is because adults are getting fewer cavities and becoming

(B) is because of adults getting fewer cavities and their becoming

(C) is caused from adults getting fewer cavities and in addition become

(D) is occurring because adults are getting fewer cavities and becoming

(E) occurs because of adults getting fewer cavities and become

【答案】D

【单词及短语】shift (1) vt. & vi. 改变，变换 (2) vi. 去掉；摆脱掉 The stain shifts. 污点去掉了（用主动形式）。

Sth. has shifted. 某物被去掉了。

(3) n. 转换，转变（题干意思）the shift from A to B，从 A 到 B 的转换

(4) n. 计谋，手段

dentistry n. 牙医业；牙科医术

cavity n. 腔，洞 a cavity in the tooth 牙上的一个洞

vain adj. (1) 自负的；爱慕虚荣的（题干意思）(2) 徒劳的，无用的，无效的 make a vain attempt to do sth. 做某事徒劳

【句式解析】句子主语为：shift。

(A) 原句没有语法问题。原因状语从句可作表语，放在 be 动词后面。但是这种说法太罗嗦。

(B) 错误。because of 后面为名词或动名词。getting 为动名词，修饰动名词要用形容词或形容词性物主代词，因此 adults 应改为 adults'。

(C) 与 B 错误原因一样，改为 adults'。 另外，getting 和 become 不够连贯。

(D) 主语为 shift，谓语为 is occurring，后面跟随原因状语从句。are getting XXX and becoming XXX 连贯，相当于 are getting XXX and are becoming XXX。比(A) 意思明确。

(A) 可以做这样的修改：The shift from the traditional to cosmetic dentistry springs/proceeds from adults' getting fewer cavities and becoming more vain.

spring from sth., 动词短语，源自什么。

(E) 与(B)、(C) 错误一样，adults 应改为 adults'。

5. Mediators were standing by, prepared to intervene in(A) the labor dispute even though(B) both sides had refused(C) earlier offers for(D) assistance. No error.(E)

【答案】D

【单词及短语】mediate (1) vi./vt. 调停，调解，斡旋 (2) vt. 影响……的发生；使……可能发生

mediator n. 调停者；调解人

【句型】某人主动要求当调解人。Somebody offers to act as a mediator of XXX.

intervene vi. 干涉，干预；调解

dispute (1) vt. & vi. 辩论 (2) vt. 怀疑……的真实性或妥当性 dispute the figures，动词短语，怀疑那些数字；dispute+that+宾语从句，怀疑某事。(3) n. 辩论，争执

offer (1) vt. 主动提供；主动提出；出价 offer to do sth. (2) vt. & vi. 表示愿意等

He offered to go where there were difficulties. 他表示愿意到艰苦的地方去。 (3) n. 提议，提供（题干意思）

assist vt. & vi. 帮助，促进

assistance n. 帮助，援助

earlier (1) adj. 早期的；初期的；早先的（题干意思） (2) adv. 早期地

stand by 动词短语 (1) 站在旁边；袖手旁观 (2) 准备行动, 待命（题干意思）

(3) 支持，支援 (4) 信守诺言 stand by one's promises

【句式解析】主句的主语为 Mediators, 主句谓语为 were, "prepared to intervene in the labor dispute" 为分词短语作伴随状语, 其逻辑主语必须与句子主语一致。"even though"引导从句。"earlier" 为形容词, 先前的, 修饰名词 offers。

句意：尽管双方均拒绝了调解人先前的调解帮助，但调解人依然随时待命，准备介入这场劳工争执。

the offers of sth., 对某物的提供, 比如：the offers of finance, 资金提供。the offer of assistance, 援助。of 表示什么样的提供。for 表示为了谁。He had supplied offers of finance for the research group. 他为这个科研小组提供了资金援助。因此, 原句的 for 应该换为 of。

6. According to some theorists, what(A) any(B) particular bird can eat could change with even(C) the slightest(D) variation in the shape of its beak. No error(E)

【答案】E

【单词及短语】variation n. 变化, 变动（的程度）

beak 鸟嘴

slight (1) adj. 微小的, 轻微的, 微不足道的 (2) n. 轻蔑, 忽视；冷落 a slight on sth./sb. 对某事（人）的轻蔑 (3) vt. 轻蔑, 忽视, 怠慢

according to sth.=in terms of sth. 依照什么

【句式解析】change with sth., 随什么而变化。The prices of commodities fluctuate with relation of supply and demand. 价格随供求关系而波动。

even the slightest 甚至最轻微的

【举一反三】He couldn't work out even the easiest problems. 他甚至连最简单的题目都不会做。

主语：what any particular bird can eat. 典型的主语从句, 意为：某种特定的鸟所能吃的东西。what 不能用 that 取代, 因为 what 在从句中作 eat 的宾语。即：只要从句中缺成分, 就要用除 that 以外的引导词来引导。主语从句以 what 开头, 因此"some"要换为疑问句中的"any", 这也是考点之一。谓语为 could change。the variation in sth., 某方面的变化。variation in the shape of its beak, 鸟嘴形状的变化。相应的动词短语：vary in sth. 某方面发生变化。

The variation in scale of the project was surprising. 该工程在规模方面的变化令人惊讶。

主语从句 he failed 不缺任何成分, 故用 that 引导。

句意：一些理论家认为：某些特定的鸟所能够吃的食物甚至会随鸟嘴形状最细微的变化而改变。

7. Several of the forest fires that occurred last summer which were because people are careless.

(A) which were because people are careless

(B) were caused by human carelessness

(C) because people are careless

(D) are because of human carelessness

(E) happened from people being careless

254

【答案】B

【解析】原句错误,因为没有谓语,that occurred last summer 和 which were because people are careless 均为名词性从句,修饰 fires。

"某物由于什么而发生"的表达方式:

主语从句 happened/occurred because+原因状语从句。

(D) 时态不对,last summer 去年发生的火灾,谓语应该用 were。

(E) happen from sth.: 没有这种用法。

8. Dr. Chien-Shiung Wu <u>has disproved</u> a widely accepted theory of physics when she showed that identical nuclear particles do not always act alike.

(A) has disproved

(B) having disproved

(C) disproved

(D) disproves

(E) disproving

【答案】C

【解析】disprove vt. 证明(理论等)错误,反驳

refute vt. 驳斥,驳倒

alike (1) adj. 同样的,相像的 Sth. be alike in sth. 某物在某方面很相似。(2) adv. 同样地 treat sb. alike 同等对待某人(题干意思)。act alike,动词短语,运转方式相同。

从句用过去时,主句应该用过去时态,况且证明该理论错误的事情发生在过去。

widely accepted theory,被人们广泛接受的理论,副词修饰形容词。

9. We generally think of Canada as the northern neighbor of the United <u>States, and more than half of the states extend</u> farther than Canada's southernmost point.

(A) States, and more than half of the states extend

(B) States, and it is the case that more than half of the states extend

(C) States, but more than half of the states extending

(D) States, whereas more than half of the states are extending

(E) States, however, more than half of the states extend

【答案】E

whereas conj. 但是,而

extend (1) vt. & vi. (空间、时间等)延伸(题干意思)(2) vt. 延长;扩展;达到(某一点) extend one's influence 扩大影响 (3) vt. 给予,提供,发出 extend an invitation

southernmost adj. 最南的;极南的

10. The three volumes of memoirs by Wole Soyinka <u>begin with his childhood in a Nigerian village and culminate</u> with his years at the University of Ibadan, one of the best universities in West Africa.

【解析】原句正确。

memoir n. 回忆录,自传

批注 [370]:
university 的同位语,同位语一般为名词短语或名词性从句。

volume  n. 卷，册，书卷
culminate (1) vt. & vi. 达到极点 (2) vt./vi.（以某种结果）告终（题干意思）

11. Dressed in a crisp, clean uniform, it reflected the efficient manner of the tour guide as she distributed maps for a walking tour of central Canberra.
【解析】分词的逻辑主语与句子 it 主语不一致。某人穿什么衣服：Somebody be dressed in sth.

12. A review of the composer's new symphony called it confusing because of its unusual structure, and its melodious final movement makes it elegant.
【解析】划线部分不当。
原句存在语法错误。because of 后面加名词/名词性短语/名词性从句/动名词，而 its melodious final movement makes it elegant 不是名词性从句，所以不能加在 be cause of 后面。
改为 structure but elegant because of melodious final movement。

> 批注 [371]: 指代"交响乐"
> 批注 [372]: 令人迷惑的
> 批注 [373]: 逻辑关系错误，应为转折。新的交响乐因其不同寻常的结构令人迷惑，而它那优美的最终节奏令它优雅。but 表示转折。

13. Since last September Patricia has been working at the convenience store down the road.
(A) 原句不变
(B) works
(C) is working
(D) will be working
(E) worked
【解析】A。自从去年某时起一直在做某事用现在完成时。

14. To help freshmen and sophomores in selecting their courses, candid reviews of courses and instructors compiled by juniors and seniors.
(A) candid reviews of courses and instructors compiled by juniors and seniors
(B) candid reviews of courses and instructors being compiled by juniors and seniors
(C) and to compile candid reviews of courses and instructors by juniors and seniors
(D) juniors and seniors have compiled candid reviews of courses and instructors
(E) with juniors and seniors compiling candid reviews of courses and instructors
【解析】D
candid adj. (1) 耿直的，坦率的 (2) 自然的，非故意摆出姿势的（文中意思） (3) 公正的，不偏不倚的
不定式作目的状语，其逻辑主语须与句子主语一致。

15. In areas where deer roam freely, residents must dress to protect themselves against deer ticks that might transmit diseases.
(A) 原句不变
(B) areas roamed by deer freely
(C) areas, freely roamed by deer
(D) areas, in which there are deer that roam freely
(E) areas which deer roam free

【解析】A

roam　vt. & vi. 随便走, 漫步, 漫游

tick (1) n. 钟的嘀嗒声　(2)（表示正确无误的）记号　(3)（寄生于体大动物的吸血小虫）壁虱

16. A great gray owl <u>flying low</u> across a forest clearing, its <u>wings beating</u> quietly, and its ultrasensitive ears tuned to the <u>faint sounds</u> made by small creature concealed under leaves.

【解析】这个句子没有谓语动词，分词不能作谓语，因此语法错误，须加入一个动词。该句为典型的独立主格。

tune vt. 调节

主语 be tuned to 名词：主语适应名词。本句意思是：猫头鹰在低空飞行，它的耳朵很灵敏，可以听到隐藏在树叶下面的生物所发出的微弱声音。主语不一致，有逻辑关系，即伴随，因此可用独立主格。its 为物主代词，一般有物主代词的部分用分词，其余部分用谓语动词。concealed 为过去分词作定语，修饰 creature。因此，本句改为：

A great gray owl <u>was flying low</u> across a forest clearing, its <u>wings beating</u> quietly, and its ultrasensitive ears tuned to the <u>faint sounds</u> made by small creature concealed under leaves.

tuned 和 beating 分别为过去分词和现在分词，作独立主格的分词部分。

Ears are tuned to faint sounds. Wings beat quietly.

本句还可改为：A great gray owl was <u>flying low</u> across a forest clearing with its <u>wings beating</u> quietly, and its ultrasensitive ears tuned to the <u>faint sounds</u> made by small creature concealed under leaves.

17. Explaining modern art is impossible, partly because of its complexity but largely because <u>of it rapidly changing.</u>

(A) of it rapidly changing

(B) it makes rapid changes

(C) of the rapidity with which it changes

(D) changing it is rapid

(E) it changes so rapid

【解析】C

主语为 Explaining modern art, 动名词作主语，对现代艺术的解释。谓语为 is。partly because 为状语，原因是什么。

because of A and B, 因为 A 也因为 B, A 和 B 都是名词、动名词或名词性从句。but 联接了 partly（一部分地）和 largely（大部分地），两者有转折关系。一部分是因为艺术的复杂性，另一部分是因为艺术很快的变化速度。

largely, adv. 很大程度上

The project, largely dependant of the government for financial support, has to involve a large amount of specialized staff. 该项目极度依靠政府为其提供资金，需要大量的专业人员。largely dependant 为形容词短语作定语，修饰 project。副词 largely 修饰形容词 dependant。谓语为 has。involve 这里为 vt, 需要。

A 和 B 尽量都用名词，或都用动名词，或都用名词性从句，这样的结构较简洁一致。

原句中，it rapidly changing 错在动名词的修饰上。because of 后面的 changing 肯定为动名词，而动名词的修饰一般用形容词性物主代词，即 it 改为 its（the art's）。如：His being rude made me angry. 他很粗鲁这件事让我很生气。being rude 为动名词短语，而修饰动名词的为物主代词 His。所以本句可改为 its rapid changing。

(B) because 后面为从句，而非 because of，与前面不一致，语法上不算错，但不够地道。it 指代 art。

(C) because of 后面跟随的是名词短语，这个用法很地道。

rapidity n. 快，迅速

例 1：The current digitalized commodities manifest the rapidity of changes in IT technology. 这些现代的数字化产品反应了 IT 技术快速的更新速度。

例 2：The current digitalized commodities manifest the rapidity with which IT technology changes.

即：(1) IT technology changes with the rapidity.

(2) The current digitalized commodities manifest the rapidity.

例 3：The achievments manifested the prudence with which he had dedicated himself into the research. 这些成就表明了，他在这项研究中付出了怎样的严谨。

即：He had dedicated himself with prudence in the research. which 指代 prudence。

例 4：The report reflects the intensity with which the public appeal for tax reduction. 这篇报道反应了公众要求降低税收的强烈程度。

以上几个句子都可以改为副词形式，意义没有大的区别，而前者更强调 prudence 和 rapidity 两个名词，严谨性和高速度。

副词形式改为宾语从句，即：

The current digitalized commodities manifest that IT technology changes <u>rapidly</u>.

The achievments manifested that he had dedicated himself to the research <u>prudently</u>.

(C) 中的 which 指代 rapidty。it 指代 modern art。

(D) 语法不对。

(E) 副词修饰动词，应为 rapidly。即使改为 rapidly，语法不错，但是本句就成为了句子，与 because of 结构不一致。

18. Most major air pollutants cannot be seen, although large amounts <u>of them</u>(A) <u>concentrated in</u>(B) cities <u>are visible</u>(C) <u>as</u>(D) smog. <u>No error.</u>(E)

【解析】pollutant 为名词，污染物。尽管空气污染物大量聚集在城市中会以雾气的形式可见，但是大部分污染物无法用肉眼看到。

concentrate (1) vt. & vi. 专心于；注意 (2) vt. 集中，聚集（题干意思）某些事情集中起来用于做什么。Sth. be concentrated to do sth.

(3) vt. 浓缩

concentrated in 为过去分词短语作定语，修饰 them，指代 major pollutants。

be visable as sth., 以某种东西可见

本句没有错误。

19. The time and the place for such a large event is subject to approving from the mayor's

office.

(A) 原句不变

(B) For such a large event, the time and the place are subject to the mayor's office's approving them.

(C) The time and the place for such a large event are subject to approval of the mayor's office.

(D) The time and the place for such a large event are subject to be approved by the mayor's office.

(E) Subject to the approval of the mayor's office are the time and place for such a large event taking place.

【解析】这样一个重要事件的时间和地点听从于市长办公室的许可。即何时何地举行市长说了算。两个名词作主语时，谓语动词用复数形式。

subject (1) n. 主题；题目；问题 (2) adj. 常有/常患/常遭受……的；倾向于……的 be subject to sth.

Japan is subject to earthquakes. 日本常发生地震。

The prices are subject to changes at short notice. 只要一有通知，价格就可能马上改变。

(3) adj. 须服从……的；受……支配的（题干意思）be subject to sth.

(4) vt. 使服从，征服，制伏 subject sb./sth. to sb./sth. 使某人/某物屈从于后面的人或物

approve (1) vt. & vi. 赞成，同意 (2) vt. 批准，通过

approval n. (1) 赞成，同意 (2) 批准，认可（文中意思）某人的批准，the approval of sb.

原句除了谓语复数以外，还存在一个问题：approve 这个动词有特定的名词形式，这种情况下，如果需要该动词的名词形式，**尽量用特定的名词，而不用动名词**。所以(C) 正确。

(B) 太罗嗦，某事的时间地点可以用 time and place for sth.这个名词短语，如果再将 for sth. 作状语提前则罗嗦了；其次，office's approving them 为动名词用物主代词修饰，与(C) 相比罗嗦。

(D) 短语错了：be subject to doing sth. 原句用了 be 动词原型。

(E) 倒装句，表语提前，但是 taking place 多余了，去掉的话是正确的。

20. Only by tapping(A) their last reserves of energy were(B) the team members able to salvage(C) what was beginning(D) to look like a lost cause. No error.(E)

【解析】tap (1) n. 塞子，龙头 (2) n. 电话窃听 (3) n. 轻敲，轻拍 give a tap at sb./sth. (4) vt. 割/打开……取/放液体 (5) vt. 开发；利用（选项意思）

We have enormous reserves of oil still waiting to be tapped. 我们有巨大的石油矿藏在等待开发。

(6) vt. 窃听

eavesdrop vi. 偷听（别人的谈话）eavesdrop on sth. 窃听某物

She knew you were going to have a baby. She must have been eavesdropping on your conversation.

她知道你们想有个孩子。她准是总在偷听你们的谈话。

reserve (1) vt. 保留/储备某物 (2) vt. 具有或保持（某种权利）(3) n. 贮藏；储备（文中意思）(4) n. 保护区

salvage (1) n. 救援 (2) n. 海上营救 (3) vt.（从火灾、海难等中）抢救（某物）（题干意思）

only 放句首，用倒装句。Only by doing sth.+谓语+主语。what was beginning to look like a lost cause 为名词性从句，作 salvage 的宾语，正在开始看起来是注定的败局的事情，what 不能换为 that，因为 what 为从句的主语，有所指代，表示所什么的事情。有所指代或作从句主语时不能用 that。比如：

What made me surprised was the news. What 指代"使我吃惊的事"，作主语从句的主语。

tap one's last energy，利用某人全部的力量

本句意思为：只有利用队员的全部保存的力量，才能拯救已经看起来开始走向败局的局面。

lost cause，名词短语，注定要失败的事业。

本句没错。

只有采用先进的科学技术，我们才能成功地开采出储存在我国西部地下的大量石油资源。Only by sophisticated technology are we able to successfully tap the enormous reserves of oil resources in the westen parts of our nation underground.

我们要采取全力措施来挽救公司正在面临的破产。We must tap our last reserves of energy to salvage what was beginning to wreak havoc on the company.

21. Not many(A) authors have described(B) the effects of environmental pollution as effective as(C) Rachel Carson, whose work is still a model for(D) nature writers. No error.(E)

【解析】as+adj./adv./分词 as sth.，和某物一样怎么样。注意两者比较必须是同一个事物。本句将大多数作者与 Rachel Carson 比较是对的，并且 Carson 后面省略了 has described。但是，应用副词 effectively 修饰 described。

C 改为 as effectively as。

22. Five years in the writing(A), her new book is both a response(B) to her critics' mistrust with(C) her earlier findings and an elaboration(D) of her original thesis. No error(E).

【解析】mistrust (1) vt. 不信任 (2) n. 不信任 the mistrust of sb. 对某人的不信任，名词短语。(C)错误，应改为 of。

23. The owner of stadiums that bear the names of now bankrupt companies have a problem what to do about the names.

(A)原句不变
(B) what they should do about the names
(C) deciding what to do about those names
(D) to decide as to whether the names should stay
(E) should they change those names or not

【解析】C

bear vt. (1) 支持，承受；承担 bear expenses 承担费用 (2) vt. 运送；携带；带走 (3) vt. 忍受；经得起 bear to do sth./bear doing sth. (4) vt. 佩戴；拥有；具有 (5) vt. 写有，印有，带有 bear the name of 持……的名字 bear the signs of sth. 带有某种痕迹（题目意思） (6) vt.

怀有，对……抱有 bear for/against sth./sb.

原句分析：that bear the names of now bankrupt companies 为定语从句，修饰 stadiums。谓语为 have。体育馆的老板有一个问题：应该拿体育馆的名字怎么办？因为体育馆的名字和现在破产了的公司的名字是一样的。bear the name of sth., 带有什么的名字。

比如：The book bears the name of "Theory of communications". 这本书的名字是《通信原理》。

bankrupt (1) adj. 破产的，倒闭的（选项意思）(2) adj. 完全缺乏的 bankrupt of sth. (3) n. 破产者 (4) vt. 使破产，使枯竭，使极端贫困

what to do 为 what+不定式，起名词的作用，注意它不是名词性从句，因为该结构没有谓语。本题涉及**名词后面加什么成分**。

(1) 名词+adj./分词，作后置定语，比如：Is there water available here? available 为形容词，可获得的。即：这有水吗？

This is the book bought yesterday. bought 为过去分词作定语，修饰 book。即：这就是昨天买到的书。是谁买的并没有交待。

(2) 名词+定语从句，其中定语从句由 that/which/who/whom 引导。

This is the book I bought yesterday. 这就是我昨天买到的书。

(3) 名词+同位语从句。同位语从句和定语从句易混淆，可以这样加以辨别：名词后面的从句内容与名词完全等价时，为同位语从句，即同位语从句只是为了解释名词具体的内容。比如：

I am in favor of the idea that immediate measures have to be taken. 我同意这个观点：我们必须采取紧急措施。that immediate measures have to be taken 为同位语从句，内容就是 idea 的内容。同位语从句必须由 that 引导。

名词后**不能**加什么成分？

(1) 不能加"特殊疑问词+不定式"。因为："特殊疑问词+不定式"等价于名词短语，一般情况下，两个名词短语或名词性从句不能罗列在一起使用。比如：apples bananas 不能这样联接使用。一定要放在一起使用时必须加入相应的连词等成分。

(2) 不能加 what 或特殊疑问词引导的名词性从句，道理同(1)。名词性从句起名词作用，两个名词一般不能罗列在一起。换句话说，很多语法书上讲：定语从句不能以 what 引导，其根本道理在于：定语从句或定语的作用等价于形容词！而 what 引导的名词性从句或名词性短语等价于名词！故不能作定语！

综上(A)、(B) 都不对。(A) 为特殊疑问词+不定式；(B) 为 what 引导的名词性从句。

改正：(1) 固定搭配改法：have a problem in doing sth., 做某事有困难。故(C) 正确。

(2) have a problem about/as to/with regards to+名词短语、名词性从句。做某事有困难。

【举一反三】I have some question/problem/suspect as to what to do/what we should do next. 我有一个疑问：接下来咱们做什么？

(D) to decide 不好，最好用 have a problem deciding（固定搭配）。as to 是对的，介词短语，关于什么。即使改过后也比较罗嗦。

(E) 语序错误。任何一种从句都要用陈述句，不论状语从句或名词性从句等（倒装除外）。

问题：what+不定式或 what 引导的名词性从句能做什么成分？

(1) 主语 What he did made me surprised.

(2) 宾语 I was surprised at what he did.

(3) 表语 What surprised me was what he had done.

24. Below the bend, the <u>river, flowing more swiftly, as it cuts</u> through sand hills covered with pine trees.

(A) river, flowing more swiftly, as it cuts

(B) river, flowing more swiftly, cutting

(C) river, flowing more swiftly and it is cutting

(D) river flows more swiftly as it cuts

(E) river, flowing more swiftly, it cuts

【解析】D

原句错误，没有谓语。

bend (1) vt. & vi.（使）弯曲；屈身 (2) n. 弯曲（处）（句中意思）

swiftly adv. (1) 迅速地，速度快地（句中意思） (2) 敏捷地，反应快地

covered with pine trees 为过去分词短语作定语，修饰 trees。

25. Although the Milky is now two and a half million light-years away from the Andromeda Galaxy, <u>but it is predicted by scientists that</u> the two galaxies will merge into one in a few billion year.

(A) 原句不变

(B) but scientists predict

(C) scientists who predict

(D) scientists predicting

(E) scientists predict that

【解析】E

原句语法错误，although 与 but 不能连用。(E) 更简洁。或改用 it is predicted that。

merge vt. & vi.（使）混合，（使）合并

26. After receiving a degree in agriculture from Iowa State Agricultural and Mechanical Collge, <u>a faculty position at the college was accepted by George, and he took</u> charge of the college greenhouses.

(A) 原句不变

(B) a faculty position was accepted by George at the college, he took

(C) George accepted a faculty position at the college and took

(D) George, accepting a position on the faculty at the college, taking

(E) George, who accepted a faculty position at the college and took

【解析】C

After 后面加分词，其逻辑主语必须与句子主语一致，receiving 的逻辑主语是人，因此句子主语必须是人。(D)、(E) 均没有谓语。

After+分词短语，主语+谓语。

faculty n. (1) 能力，才能 (2) 院，系，部 (3) 全体教职员，全体从业人员

27. Although Dick and Roy are generally considered <u>an impressionist composer, their compositional styles are quite distinct</u> from one another.

(A) 原句不变

(B) to be an impressionist composer, their compositional style is

(C) as having been impressionist composers, their compositional style is

(D) impressionist composers, their compositional styles are

(E) impressionist composers, whose compositional styles are

【解析】D

原句单数错误。

distinct adj. (1) 截然不同的，完全分开的 be distinct from sth. (2) 清晰的，明白的，明显的

distinctive adj. 有特色的，与众不同的

这本书与那本书内容上的特色之处在于对这个理论的阐述。

Contents of this book distinctive to those of that one lie in demonstration of a specific theory.

28. The underside of the starfish is covered with hundreds of tube feet, which it uses <u>to walk around, for attaching tightly to rocks, and holding</u> on to prey.

(A) 原句不变

(B) to walk around, for its tight attachment to rocks, and to hold

(C) for walking around, to attach tightly to rocks, and holding

(D) for walking around, attaching tightly to rocks, and holding

(E) for walking around, it can also attach tightly to rocks and hold

【解析】D

原句没有语法错误，但结构太混乱。采用一致的结构最佳。

which 指代 tube feet。

underside n. 下侧；下部表面；底面；底部；阴暗面

starfish n. 海星（一种海洋动物）

attach (1) vt. & vi. 贴上；系；附上（文中意思）(2) vt. 认为有重要性（或意义、价值、分量等）；重视 (3) vt. 把……归因于，把（过错的责任等）归于

我读了一本书，这本书阐述了历史的演进。I read a book, which demonstrates evolvement of history.

我读了一本书，我将这本书引用在我的论文中。 I read a book, which I quoted in my thesis.

29. In 1853 African American residents founded the San Francisco Athenaeum; <u>its library and museum served</u> as the hub of Black intellectual life in the region.

(A) 原句不变

(B) its libray and museum, they served

(C) their library and museum serving

(D) the library and museum will be to serve

(E) the library and the museum of it serving

【解析】A

原句没有错误。its 指代 Athenaeum。两个句子之间如有分号，则不需要连词联接。如果是逗号，必须有连词联接。

hub n. (1) 轮毂 (2) 中心，中心所在（题干意思）

serve as sth., 动词短语，起某种作用；serve to do sth., 用于什么

(C) 欲使用独立主格方式。独立主格的使用详见后文，这里只谈结构错误：独立主格前面要用逗号。

30. Television weather forecasters sometimes overdramatize the severity of an approaching snowstorm, <u>cause</u> segments of their audience unnecessary anxiety.

(A) cause
(B) which cause
(C) causing
(D) they cause
(E) yet caused

【解析】C

句子结构错误：逗号之前为完整句子，逗号后面只有谓语，没有主语。这种情况下，如果两个主语一致，且存在逻辑关系时，其中一个换为分词。因此，本句改为 causing。causing 为现在分词短语作结果状语，逻辑主语为 forecasters。意为：电视气象播报员有时会夸大即将来临的暴风雨的严重程度，从而引发部分观众不必要的焦虑。

overdramatize vt. 过分戏剧性地表达，过分夸大

dramatize vt. (1) 将（小说或事件）改编成剧本 (2) vt. & vi. 使（事情）戏剧化，夸张

Don't dramatize so much, just give us the facts. 不要过于渲染，告诉我们实情就行了。

approaching adj. 侵入的；逼近的；接近的。可作定语，修饰名词。

severity n. 严重 severity of sth. 某物的严重程度

或改为 which causes，which 指代逗号前面的句子，句子是单数。

句子，which+谓语+其他成分。

句子，分词+其他成分。

句子+to do。

她沦落到一贫如洗的境地，引起了她的密友的同情。该句有以下几种表达方式：

She has been reduced to near poverty, which aroused sympathy of her close friends.
She has been reduced to near poverty, arousing sympathy of her close friends.
She has been reduced to near poverty to arouse sympathy of her close friends.
Having been reduced to near poverty, sympathy of her close friends was shown on her.
His outstanding talents in telecommunications industry aroused my sympathy.

31. <u>Were I to be granted</u> a whole month in which to do whatever I wanted, I would travel throughout Africa and see as much of that continent as I could.

【解析】句子无误。

which 指代 month, whatever I wanted 为宾语从句，作 do 的宾语。本句为虚拟语气，

批注 [376]: 志趣相投。我欣赏他的才华。

批注 [377]: 不定式作结果状语，which 指代前面的句子。三者都表达：句子中的事件引发了后面的事情。

如果给我一个月时间，在这一个月时间内我可以做我想做的任何事的话，我将旅游整个非洲并且去看我能够看到的尽可能多的非洲大陆。

I was granted a whole month. 我被给予了一个月时间，即别人给了我一个月时间。

grant vt. (1) 准许；答应给予（文中意思）  (2) vt. 承认

entitle vt. (1) 使有资格；使有权  (2) 给……题名

bestow vt. 赠给；授予

whatever sb. do 为名词性从句，在句子中起名词作用，比如：I am in favor of whatever you do. 你做什么我都支持。

If granted/allowed 10 minutes, I would take a break. 如果给我十分钟，我会休息一下。

as much of that continent: as+名词性从句（much of that continent，尽可能多的大陆）

I will finance the research group as much as I could. 我将尽全力资助科研小组。

本句为对现在的假设，主句用过去将来时，从句用过去时，谓语为 were，不论主语单复数。

If I had not been completely aware of my duty to my family and the country, I would not have come back tonight, or else never shall I.

Had I not been completely aware of my duty to my family and the country, I would not have come back tonight, or else never shall I.

本句为对过去发生事情的假设虚拟，从句用过去完成时，主句用过去将来完成时。

32. Only after reading it carefully several times <u>was the poem beginning to make sense to me</u>.

【解析】did I begin to make sense of the poem

Only after doing sth.为时间状语，其分词的逻辑主语必须与句子主语一致。reading 的逻辑主语是"我"，主句的主语也必须是 I，因此原句错误。且 only 放在句首，要求主谓倒置。I began 变为 did I begin。

intelligible adj. 可理解的，明白易懂的，清楚的  The poem is intelligible to me.

Only the products are applied widely are flaws/defects of the products to be found.

Only approaching his life did I make sense of him.

A make sense of B. A 理解 B。    B makes sense to A. A 理解 B。

33. He presented himself before the judge, knowing full well that he was guilty <u>yet hoping</u> for leniency.

【批注 [378]】：分词短语作让步状语。

【解析】原句无误。

leniency n.（惩罚或执法时）宽大；仁慈

knowing 为现在分词短语作让步状语，其逻辑主语必须与句子主语一致。相当于：

Although he knew full well that he was guilty, he presented himself before the judge yet hoping for leniency.

yet 后面跟分词，分词的逻辑主语必须与句子主语一致。

34. <u>They had never before been</u> in a museum with such an extensive collection, they had a difficult time deciding how to make the most of the limited time they could spend there.

(A) 原句不变
(B) They never before were
(C) Never before had they been
(D) Never before having been
(E) Because of never before being

【解析】D

原句为两个简单句，中间为逗号且没有连词，因此原句错误。

(B) 时态不对，应该用完成时，且即使时态正确了，依然为两个简单句用逗号联接，中间无连词。

(C) never（否定词）放句首须主谓倒装。时态正确，但依然为简单句用逗号联接，且无连词。

(D) never 放句首主谓倒装，且使用了分词结构，作原因状语，分词的逻辑主语与句子主语 they 一致。

(E) 时态不好，应用 Because of having never been。

extensive adj. 广阔的，广泛的；大量的，大规模的

a person with extensive knowledge of arts 一个具有广博艺术的人

extend (1) vt. & vi.（空间、时间等）延伸；延续 (2) vt. 延长；扩展；达到 (3) vt. 给予，提供，发出

It is an extended debate as to whether the abuses of the medicine would wreak havoc on the body's functioning. 这种药物的滥用是否会对人体器官的正常运转构成损害是一场旷日持久的争论。

批注 [379]:
adj. 旷日持久的

批注 [380]:
as to 后面接名词短语或名词性从句，关于。

批注 [381]:
whether 引导名词性从句，是否。

The malfunction of a critical device posed an extremely serious threat to the project. 某台关键设备的故障对该工程构成了极大威胁。

35. Unlike bears and some other carnivorous animals that can survive on plants when meat is scarce, wild cats must capture prey or <u>to go</u> hungry.

【解析】划线部分不当。

Unlike…为介词短语，其逻辑主语必须与句子主语一致。that can survive 为定语从句，修饰 animals。must 联接两个动词 capture 和 go。go hungry，动词短语，挨饿。or 表示"否则"。野猫必须去捕食猎物，否则就会挨饿。改为 go。

36. When a steel mill is shut down because its production methods have become antiquated, what is lost is not only jobs <u>and also</u> a piece of industrial history.

【解析】划线部分不当。

steel mill 钢厂 antiquated adj. 过时的，陈旧的，老式的

When 引导时间状语从句，后面嵌套了原因状语从句，what is lost 是主语，is 是谓语。丢失的不仅是工作，而且是一段工业历史。not only…but also…为固定搭配。

37. At least one course in statistics is recommended for <u>them</u> who plan to become journalists, because they will often need to evaluate whether information based on statistics is dependable.

【解析】划线部分不当。

them 后面用定语从句，这个用法是错误的。能用定语从句修饰的只有 those, the one, ones, the boy。they, them, him 不能用定语或定语从句修饰！them 改为 those 或 ones。

based on statistics 为过去分词短语作定语，修饰 information，以统计学为基础的信息。他们需要评估以统计学为基础的信息是否可靠。

以 A 为基础的 B，名词短语：B based on A。以数学为基础的学科：a maths based subject。

dependable adj. 可信赖的，可靠的  dependable evidence 可靠的证据

38. Coffee tastes <u>bitterly</u> and gives off a burned smell if it is overheated or brewed for too long.

【解析】划线部分不当。

brew (1) vt. & vi. 调制，酿造（文中意思）  (2) vt. 酝酿，图谋

39. The Grenshaw melon, named after the person <u>which</u> developed it, is a cross between a cantaloupe and a honeydew melon.

【解析】The Grenshaw melon 为主语，is 为谓语，named after 为过去分词短语作定语，修饰 melon。which 指代人，应改为 who。cross 为名词，杂交品。

40. Few people could have guessed, as they <u>watch</u> Anna win the tennis match with apparent ease, how pessimistic she had been about her chances of beating her opponent.

【解析】原句时态不对，could have done 表示对过去的推测，当人们观看 Anna 轻而易举地赢得比赛时，很少有人能想象到她曾经对战胜对手持多么悲观的态度。watch 应用过去时态，改为 were watching 或 watched。she had been 为过去完成时，这是在比赛之前发生的事，而比赛在过去，故用过去的过去时态，过去完成时。pessimistic 必须用形容词，因为本句原句为：be pessimistic about sth.，对某事感到悲观。

41. While many people believe that television commercials are quite harmful to children, others contend that such advertising has very little or no negative effect.

【解析】注意 such 的用法：such（如此这样的）+名词。本句没有错误。

42. The European magpie, a bird well known for <u>their</u> tendency to steal shinny objects, is common in European folklore, with many superstitions surrounding it.

【解析】superstition n. 迷信，迷信行为

注意 with+名词+分词结构，使得句子简洁。使用现在分词或过去分词取决于名词和分词的关系为主动还是被动。迷信围绕着 it（指代鸟），主动形式，故用现在分词。这种句式为：

主语+谓语+其他成分, with+名词+分词。名词不要求与主语一致。

I went to a theater, with a substantial number of paintings displayed. painting 和 display 是被动的关系，画作被展览，因此用过去分词。

have the tendency to do sth., 动词短语，to do 为不定式作定语，修饰 tendency，具有做某事的倾向。 a bird well known for 为 magpie 的同位语。同位语一般为名词短语或同位语

从句。

物主代词 their 换为 its。应格外注意代词和物主代词的指代！

43. <u>A stranger, the students were surprised to see him enter the classroom carrying a bowling ball.</u>

(A) 原句不变

(B) A stranger, carrying a bowling ball, the students were surprised to see him entering the classroom.

(C) The students were surprised to see a stranger enter the classroom, and he carried a bowling ball.

(D) The students were surprised to see a stranger carrying a bowling ball enter the classroom.

(E) The students, who were surprised to see a stranger enter the classroom carrying a bowling ball.

【答案】D

44. Several of Frank's <u>paintings were inspired by the shapes of waves and whales, titled</u> after chapter headings from *Moby-Dick*.

(A) 原句不变

(B) paintings had their inspiration from the shapes of waves and whales with titles

(C) paintings, inspired by the shapes of waves and whales, are titled

(D) paintings, which were inspired by the shapes of waves and whales and which were titled

(E) paintings, being inspired by the shapes of waves and whales, titled

【解析】C

chapter headings，回目

Sth. be title after+名词：某物以某事来命名。原句的过去分词短语 titled after 修饰名词 whales，语法没错但句意不同。正确句意为：那些受波浪和鲸鱼启发的画以《白鲸》的回目来命名。

inspire 在这里为 vt，受启发，激发（灵感）。inspired by 为过去分词短语作定语，修饰 paintings。句子的谓语为 are titled。

Fine qualities of our products inspired a sharply-increasing demand for them. inspire 在这里表示引发好的事情发生。

(B) 语序不对，有歧义。with titles 只能修饰"鲸鱼"，句意为：鲸鱼的名字是 XXX。

(D) 没有谓语。

(E) 没有谓语。

<u>用 with 介词短语来改写：</u>

Several of Frank's paintings were inspired by the shapes of waves and whales, with their titles titled after chapter headings from *Moby-Dick*.

<u>用分词作伴随状语来改写：</u>

Inspired by the shapes of waves and whales, several of Frank's paintings are titled after chapter headings from *Moby-Dick*.

45. The mayor claimed that a majority of the property owners <u>would have favored her proposal if put</u> to the vote.

(A) 原句不变

(B) would have favored her proposal if it had been put

(C) favored her proposal if it would have been put

(D) favored her proposal if put

(E) favored her proposal if they were put

【解析】B

句子主语为 mayor，谓语为 claimed，that 至结尾为宾语从句。宾语从句中嵌套了 if+分词的条件状语，此时，要求分词的逻辑主语与宾语从句的主语一致。因此，本句意思为：如果绝大部分财产拥有者去投票的话，他们将支持市长的提议。

原句可改为：if the owners were put to vote。即别人投 owners 的票。意思错误。

真正意思为：如果市长的方案拿去让 owners 投票，绝大部分 owners 会支持她的这个方案。

Sth. be put to the vote. 某个事情进行投票。因此，if 后面的主语不能丢，改为 if the proposal had been put。本句为虚拟语气，即市长的提案并没有要大家去投票。

主语+would have done，if+主语+had done。 对过去事情的假设。如果过去做了某事，就会怎样。言外之意，这件事没有做。

言外之意：市长的建议没有拿去投票。

46. By employing exotic harmonies and making unusual use of instruments, <u>Mary was a pathfinder</u> from romanticism to modern music.

(A) 原句不变

(B) a path was created by Mary

(C) Mary created a path

(D) Mary was the creator of a path

(E) was how Mary created a path

【解析】C

pathfinder 是人，寻路人。寻路人用"浪漫主义到现代音乐"来修饰不恰当。from A to B 最好用来修饰路径或时间，而非人。

By employing 为介词短语作方式状语，要求句子主语与介词短语逻辑主语一致，均为人。因此，改为某人创造了一条路径，该路径从浪漫主义到现代音乐。

Mary created a path from romanticism to modern music.

exotic adj. (1) 由外国引进的，非本地的 (2) 奇异的，醒目的，吸引人的（文中意思）

harmony n. (1) 和睦，融洽，一致；和谐，协调 (2) 和声（文中意思）

本句也可以这样改：Mary was a pathfinder from composer of romanticism to that of modern music. 人和人的比较。从创作浪漫主义音乐的制作人到创造现代派的制作人。that 指代 composer。

(D) 不够简洁。

47. In the past, many famous painters meticulously ground their own colors, an attention to detail that is noteworthy.

【解析】原句正确。

meticulous adj. 极仔细的；一丝不苟的

noteworthy adj. 值得注意的；显著的；重要的

an attention to detail 为名词短语，修饰前面这句话：许多著名的画家小心严谨地做画画用的底色。

that is noteworthy 为定语从句，修饰 detail。

48. Once American films looked slick and commercial compared to European imports; now, almost the reverse is true.

(A) 原句不变

(B) now they are almost the reverse

(C) instead, there is almost a reversal now

(D) now it is almost the reverse that is ture

(E) it has now been almost reversed

【解析】slick adj. (1) 顺利而有效的, 不费力的 (2) 圆滑的, 油滑的（题干意思）

It's precisely that sort of slick sales-talk that I mistrust. 我不相信的正是那种油腔滑调的推销宣传。

分号联接两个完整的句子。

(B) they 指代不明。

(C) instead 不恰当。

(D) 罗嗦。

(E) it 指代不明，显然出题人希望 it 指代分号前面的句子，句子的指代一般用 which，而不用 it。本句可改为：Once American films looked slick and commercial compared to European imports, which has been almost reversed now.

或：Once American films looked slick and commercial compared to European imports, reversed now. reversed 为过去分词作结果状语。

49. What was not achieved in last year's county voter registration drive was more than compensated for by this year, which registered over three thousand new voters.

(A) 原句不变

(B) by this year, having over three thousand new voters registered

(C) by this year's drive, which registered over 3,000 new voters

【解析】C

voter registration drive 选民登记运动

more than (1) 超过, 多于 (2) 很, 非常（选项意思） (3) 不只是

本句意思：去年县选民登记势头不强的遗憾，被今年的势头大大弥补了，新登记的选民超过三千。

compensated for by 被……所弥补

主语为 what 引导的主语从句：What was not achieved in last year's county voter registration drive。

谓语为：was more than compensated for。

弥补某事 compensate for sth.

这里正常语序是 This year's drive compensated for what was not achieved last year，中间必须有介词 for。(C) 中的 which 指代 this year's drive。

50. The construction of a waterway linking the Atlantic and Pacific Oceans <u>was first proposed</u>(A) in 1524, <u>but not until</u>(B) the Panama Canal opened in 1914 did <u>such a project</u>(C) become <u>a reality</u>(D). <u>No error</u>.(E)

【解析】主谓倒装。没有错误。linking 为现在分词短语作定语，修饰 waterway。

51. People were trained to perform one tiny part of one process in one department of one industry and <u>so having</u> no sense of the process as a whole.

【解析】so/because 后面要加完整的句子。本句改为：so they have no sense of the process as a whole。

分词短语作原因状语，因为人们只被培训着执行一个行业中的一个小部分，所以缺乏整体意识。

本句还有以下表达方式：

Trained to perform one tiny part of one process in one department of one industry, people have no sense of the process as a whole.

52. The Stegosaurus, <u>plant-eating dinosaurs</u>(A) with <u>protective</u>(B) bony plate and tail spikes, was <u>once common in</u>(C) <u>what is now</u>(D) Colorado. <u>No error</u>.(E)

【解析】plant-eating，吃植物的，形容词。主语为"剑龙"，plant-eating dinosaurs 为"剑龙"的同位语，主语为单数，因此将 dinosaurs 改为单数。

53. Some plants use chemical signals that repel insects, and <u>also, these</u> signals help to put neiboring plants on alert so they can mount their own defenses.

【解析】去掉 also，因为 and 和 also 重复。

repellent n. 驱虫剂

mount (1) vt. & vi. 登上；骑上 (2) vi. 增加；上升

Social problems in modern society are mounting. 现代社会问题日益增加。

The price has been mounting. 价格正在上涨。

(3) vt. 上演；配有……

It'll cost a great deal of money to mount the play. 要上演这场戏得花很多钱。

(4) vt. 发动攻击；攻击（选项意思） mount attacks 发起攻击

alert (1) adj. 警惕的, 警觉的, 注意的 (2) vt. 使（某人）保持警觉 (3) n. 警戒；警报（选项意思）

54. When one is researching the customs of a community, <u>you</u> must learn about its history and observe its people going about ordinary activities.

【解析】one 只能用 one 重复。将 you 改为 one。

go about (1) 到处走动 (2) 流传 (3) 改变方向=come about (4) 处理，从事，做，忙于（选项意思）

55. Working with(A) consummate skill, Picasso skethed a portrait of(B) the youthful but(C) experienced dancer who was posing for(D) him. No error.(E)

【解析】本句没错。Working with 为现在分词短语作伴随状语，逻辑主语必须与句子主语"毕加索"一致！but 表示"然而"。

consummate (1) vt. 使结束，使完美 (2) adj. 完美的（选项意思）

pose for (1) 为……摆好姿势 (2) 给……带来，向……提出

The high cost of oil poses serious problems for industry. 昂贵的石油价格给工业造成了严重困难。

sketch (1) n. 草图；素描；速写 (2) n. 梗概，大意 a sketch of sth. (3) vt. & vi. 素描；作……的略图

experienced adj. 有经验的，老练的，经验丰富的

Working with 为现在分词短语作伴随状语，逻辑主语为画家毕加索。毕加索以娴熟的技巧来作画，描绘了一位正在为他摆造型的模特，该模特既年轻又经验丰富。

56. Despite(A) the attorney's moving plea, the judge placed(B) the juvenile offender on(C) a probation for an indecisive(D) period. No error.(E)

【解析】本句没有错误。Despite 后面加名词、动名词或名词性从句。

attorney n. 代理人，律师

moving adj. (1) 感动人的，使人同情的（题干意思） (2) 具有推动力的

plea (1) n. 请愿，请求（选项意思） the plea for sth. (2) n. 借口，托辞

juvenile adj. 少年的

offender n. (1) 罪犯 （选项意思）(2) 妨害……的人（或事物）

probation n. (1) 缓刑（期）（选项意思）(2) 试用（期），试读（期）

indefinite adj. (1) 无限期的（选项意思）(2) 不明确的，含糊的

57. Yearning for(A) a truly representative art form of the Americas, the art world of the 1920's looked hopefully(C) to the three popular Mexican mural artists of the day(D). No error.(E)

【解析】本句没有错误。非常容易错选为(C)。

yearn vi. 渴望，切盼，向往

look 在这里表示"看"，不是系动词"看上去怎样"。look hopefully to sb., 满怀希望地看着某人。20 世纪 20 年代的艺术界渴求一种真正的具有代表性的美国艺术形式的出现，因此艺术界满怀希望地看着三位当时流行的墨西哥壁画艺术家。Yearning 的逻辑主语为 the art world of the 1920's，现在分词短语作伴随状语，of the day 为介词短语作定语，修饰 artists。

58. There has always been a great deal of friction between Joan and I because we have opposing political views about which we are very vocal.

【解析】划线部分改为 Joan and me。

vocal adj. (1) 口头的，有声的，发音的 (2) 直言不讳的；畅所欲言的 （选项意思）be vocal about sth.

which 指代 political views。我们经常有摩擦，因为我们所畅谈的政治观点有冲突。

friction (1) n. 摩擦；摩擦力 (2) n. 冲突，不和

Joan and I 应为宾格，所以将 I 改为 me。

59. When Mr. Harrington, an archaeologist from the museum of the American Indian, began to excavate the ruins he name the Pueblo Grande de Nevada, he unearthed artifacts indicating a 500-year occupation by indigenous peoples.

批注 [382]: Harrington 的同位语

【解析】本句没有错误。

excavate vt. 挖掘，开凿

unearth vt. (1) 发掘或挖出某物（选项意思）(2) 搜寻到某事物；发现并披露

indigenous people 原住民

indigenous adj. (1) 土生土长的 (2) 生来的，固有的 indigenous to sth.

60. Freedom of action and expression are(A) at the foundation not only of(B) our system of government but also of our expectations concerning(C) human relations at all(D) levels of society. No error.(E)

【解析】A

主语是 Freedom。Freedom of action and expression，名词短语，行动和言论的自由。

A is the foundation not only of B but also of C. A 不仅是 B 的基础，也是 C 的基础。

A is at the foundation of B. A 在 B 的基础上。

行动和言论不仅是政府系统的基石，也是和人类关系相关的我们的期待的基础。主语是单数，所以谓语动词改为单数动词 is。

61. While both disaster rescue workers and news reporters may face(A) physical danger, the latter(B) can usually control his or her(C) exposure to risk, whereas(D) rescue workers often cannot. No error.(E)

【解析】C

the latter 可以指代单数或复数，这里指代 news reporters，为复数，因此 his or her 应改为 their。

尽管灾难救援人员和记者同样面临身体上的危险，但后者（记者）通常可以控制尽量降低身处的危险，而救援人员则不能。

62. Maxine Hong Kingston's surprisingly unconventional book *The Woman Warrior* blends Chinese myth with American reality, fiction with fact, and memory with imagination to create a fascinating tale.

【解析】本句没有错误。

surprisingly 为副词，修饰 unconventional。省略了：blends fiction with fact, blends memory with imagination。to create 为不定式作目的状语，修饰 blend。融合这些的目的是创造一个神秘的故事。应学会适当的省略。

63. Ancient documents wrote on vellum, a form of fine parchment made of animal hides, must be stored under carefully controlled conditions because changes in humidity can be damaging.

【解析】古代写在由动物皮制成的上等羊皮纸上的文档，必须小心保管，因为湿度上的变化对文档可能是毁灭性的。

主语为 documents，谓语为 must be。written on 为过去分词短语作定语，修饰 documents，a form of fine parchment made of animal hides 为 vellum 的同位语，由名词短语作同位语。made of animal hides 为过去分词短语作定语，修饰 parchment，由动物皮革制成的上等羊皮纸。

controlled 为过去分词作形容词，由副词 carefully 修饰，严格控制的。changes in sth.，某方面的变化。damaging 为现在分词作形容词，意为"具有毁灭性的"。damaging effects，具有毁灭性的效果。

原句应将 wrote 改为 written。本题考查了含有分词作定语的句式构成。
vellum (1) n. 上等犊皮纸，皮纸文书，牛皮纸（文中意思） (2) adj. 犊皮纸的
parchment n. 羊皮纸  hide n. 兽皮 humidity n. 湿度，潮湿，湿气

64. The aquatic weed called "giant salvinia," which grows far more rapidly than do plants native to the lakes it infests, threaten many freshwater ecosystems.

【解析】
aquatic adj. 水生的，水产的，水栖的
native adj. (1) 原产地的（选项意思）(2) 天生的，有天赋的 The ability to swim is native to fish. 鱼生来就会游泳。
infest vt. (1) 害虫、野兽大批出没于 (2) 遍布于（选项意思）Crime infests that poor neighbourhood. 那个贫困街区犯罪猖獗。

本句可拆分为以下几个简单句：
(1) The aquatic weed is called "giant salvinia."
(2) The weed grows far more rapidly than the plants do/grow.
(3) The plants are native to the lakes.
(4) The weed infests the lake.
(5) The weed threatens many freshwater ecosystems.

主语为 aquatic weed，谓语动词为 threatens。threaten 应改为单数动词形式。

65. If it is(A) confirmed experimentally(B), the theories of Lucy and Roy will be among (C) the greatest (D) advances in physics of the past few decades.

【解析】A

如果 Lucy 和 Roy 的理论能够从实验角度得到验证，那么，他们的理论将是过去几十年以来物理界最伟大的进步。

it is 改为 they are。

---

批注 [383]: 过去分词短语作定语，修饰 weed。

批注 [384]: which 指代 weed，定语从句修饰 weed。

批注 [385]: 形容词短语作后置定语，修饰 plants。湖中特产的植物。products native to Tianjin，天津本地的产品。

批注 [386]: 定语从句，该定语从句不缺任何成分，故不须 that/which 引导。修饰 lakes。it 指代 the weed，杂草遍及的湖。

批注 [387]: 句子谓语，主语为单数 weed，因此动词应用 threatens。